FROM EPIC TO CANON

FRANK MOORE CROSS

From Epic to Canon

HISTORY AND LITERATURE IN ANCIENT ISRAEL

THE JOHNS HOPKINS UNIVERSITY PRESS
BALTIMORE AND LONDON

Printed in the United States of America on acid-free paper
9 8 7 6 5 4 3 2 1

The Johns Hopkins University Press
2715 North Charles Street
Baltimore, Maryland 21218-4363
The Johns Hopkins Press Ltd., London
www.press.jhu.edu

Library of Congress Cataloging-in-Publication Data
will be found at the end of this book.

A catalog record for this book is available from the British Library.

ISBN 0-8018-5982-4

To Lawrence E. Stager

Contents

PART VI TYPOLOGY AND HISTORICAL METHOD

Illustrations

Preface and Acknowledgments

THIS VOLUME OF ESSAYS WAS DESIGNED ORIGINALLY TO FILL INTERstices in my earlier study *Canaanite Myth and Hebrew Epic* (Cambridge: Harvard University Press, 1973 [ninth printing, 1997]). The first three essays in particular reflect similar concerns with epic tradition and historical reconstruction. The last essay discusses typological method that may appear alien in this collection. In fact, it makes explicit, for better or for worse, some of the methodological presuppositions that inform much of my work in the history of religion as well as in epigraphy and palaeography.

Several of the essays appear here for the first time, notably "Kinship and Covenant in Ancient Israel." Many of the essays have appeared earlier in print in very different form and are here expanded or developed. Several of the essays are only slightly revised versions of papers which have appeared previously or which are scheduled for publication elsewhere in the future. They are scattered, however, in symposia, Festschriften, and occasional publications; colleagues have suggested to me that it would serve a useful purpose to bring them together in a single volume.

An earlier and shorter version of Chapter 2 was published in *The Poet and the Historian: Essays in Literary and Historical Biblical Criticism, HSM* 26, ed. Richard E. Freedman (Chico, Calif.: Scholars Press, 1983), 13–39.

Chapter 3 is a revised and expanded version of an essay that appeared in the *Zeitschrift für die alttestamentliche Wissenschaft* vol. 100, suppl. (1988): 46–66.

Chapter 4 is a revision of a paper published in *Magnalia Dei: Essays on the Bible and Archaeology in Memory of G. Ernest Wright,* ed. F. M. Cross, Werner E. Lemke, and Patrick D. Miller Jr. (Garden City, N.Y.: Doubleday, 1976), 329–338.

Chapter 5 is an expanded version of a paper published in *Temples and*

High Places in Biblical Times, ed. A. Biran (Jerusalem: Hebrew Union College—Jewish Institute of Religion, 1981), 169–180.

Chapter 6 is a combination and revision of two papers, "Studies in the Structure of Hebrew Verse: The Prosody of Lamentations 1:1–22," in *The Word of the Lord Shall Go Forth: Essays in Honor of David Noel Freedman in Celebration of His Sixtieth Birthday,* ed. Carol L. Myers and M. O'Connor (Winona Lake, Ind.: Eisenbrauns, 1983), 129–155; and "Studies in the Structure of Hebrew Verse: The Prosody of the Psalm of Jonah," in *The Quest for the Kingdom of God: Studies in Honor of George E. Mendenhall* (Winona Lake, Ind.: Eisenbrauns, 1983), 159–167. Republished with permission.

Chapter 7 was published in *Fortunate the Eyes That See: Essays in Honor of David Noel Freedman in Celebration of His Seventieth Birthday,* ed. Astrid B. Beck, Andrew H. Bartelt, Paul R. Raabe, and Chris A. Franke (Grand Rapids, Mich.: Eerdmans, 1995), 298–309. Republished with permission.

Chapter 8 is a revision and expansion of the Presidential Address delivered 25 October 1974 at the annual meeting of the Society of Biblical Literature, republished with revisions in *Interpretation* 29 (1975), 188–201, a volume in honor of John Bright.

Chapter 9 is a revision and greatly expanded version of a chapter published in Hebrew in "Samaria and Jerusalem: The Early History of the Samaritans and Their Relations with the Jews (722–64 B.C.E.)" [šwmrwn wyrwšlym: twldwt hšwmrwnym wyḥsyhm ʿm hyhwdym], in *hhysṭwryh šl ʿm yśrʾl: šybt ṣywn ymy šlṭwn prs* [*The World History of the People of Israel: The Restoration—The Persian Period*], ed. Hayim Tadmor (Jerusalem: Alexander Peli, 1983), 81–94.

Chapter 10 is a revision of the chapter "The Fixation of the Text and Canon of the Hebrew Bible," scheduled to be published in *The Cambridge History of Judaism,* vol. 4, ed. W. D. Davies, by Cambridge University Press. Published here with advanced permission.

Chapter 12 is a slightly revised version of the W. F. Albright Lecture for 1980 at the Johns Hopkins University, published in *Maarav* 3 (1982): 32–41.

I wish to acknowledge indebtedness and express gratitude to many friends, including colleagues and students, who have come to my aid in the preparation of this book, especially to Mrs. Robin DeWitt Knauth and Professor David VanderHooft, who have read the manuscript and saved me from many errors. To Julie McCarthy, a senior production editor at the Johns Hopkins University Press, I owe special thanks. My wife of fifty years has as ever been my right hand, figuratively, and indeed literally since nerves were damaged in my right hand a few years ago.

Abbreviations

AAA	*Annual of Archaeology and Anthropology*
AASOR	*Annual of the American Schools of Oriental Research*
ADAJ	*Annual of the Department of Antiquities of Jordan*
AfO	*Archiv für Orientforschung*
AJA	*American Journal of Archaeology*
AJP	*American Journal of Philology*
ALQ[2]	F. M. Cross, *The Ancient Library of Qumrân and Modern Biblical Studies*, rev. ed. (Garden City, N.Y.: Anchor Books, 1961)
ALQ[3]	F. M. Cross, *The Ancient Library of Qumrân*, 3d ed. (Sheffield: Sheffield Academic Press; Minneapolis: Fortress Press, 1995)
ANET	*Ancient Near Eastern Texts*, ed. James B. Pritchard (Princeton: Princeton University Press, 1950)
AP	A. E. Cowley, *Aramaic Papyri of the Fifth Century* B.C. (Oxford: Clarendon Press, 1923)
AR	*Ancient Records: Egypt*, ed. J. H. Breasted; *Assyria* and *Babylonia*, ed. D. D. Luckenbill
ASOR	American Schools of Oriental Research
AUSS	*Andrews University Seminary Studies*
AYP	F. M. Cross and D. N. Freedman, *Studies in Ancient Yahwistic Poetry*, *SBLDS* 21 (Missoula, Mont.: Scholars Press, 1975)
B	Codex Vaticanus
BA	*Biblical Archaeologist*
BANE	*The Bible and the Ancient Near East: Essays in Honor of William Foxwell Albright*, ed. G. Ernest Wright (Garden City, N.Y.: Doubleday, 1961)
BAR	*Biblical Archaeology Review*
BASOR	*Bulletin of the American Schools of Oriental Research*
BEThL	*Bibliotheca ephemeridum theologicarum lovaniensium*

BJRL	*Bulletin of the John Rylands Library*
BR	*Bible Review*
BZ	*Biblische Zeitschrift*
BZAW	*Beiheft zur Zeitschrift für die alttestamentliche Wissenschaft*
CAD	*Chicago Assyrian Dictionary* (Chicago: Oriental Institute, 1954–)
CBQ	*Catholic Biblical Quarterly*
CBQMS	*Catholic Biblical Quarterly Monograph Series*
CIS	*Corpus inscriptionum semiticarum*
CMHE	F. M. Cross, *Canaanite Myth and Hebrew Epic* (Cambridge: Harvard University Press, 1973)
CRB	*Cahiers de la Revue biblique*
CT	*Cuneiform Texts from Babylonian Tablets*
CTA	A. Herdner, *Corpus des tablettes en cunéiformes alphabétiques* (Paris: Imprimerie Nationale, 1963)
DJD	*Discoveries in the Judaean Desert* (Oxford: Clarendon Press, 1955–)
EI	*Eretz-Israel*
𝔊 or OG	Old Greek
GAG	W. von Soden, *Grundriss der akkadischen Grammatik*
GvG	C. Brockelmann, *Grundriss der vergleichenden Grammatik der semitischen Sprachen* (Berlin, 1908)
HSM	*Harvard Semitic Monographs*
HSS	*Harvard Semitic Studies*
HTR	*Harvard Theological Review*
HTS	*Harvard Theological Studies*
HUCA	*Hebrew Union College Annual*
IEJ	*Israel Exploration Journal*
IES	Israel Exploration Society
INJ	*Israel Numismatic Journal*
JAOS	*Journal of the American Oriental Society*
JBL	*Journal of Biblical Literature*
JBR	*Journal of Bible and Religion*
JCS	*Journal of Cuneiform Studies*
JJS	*Journal of Jewish Studies*
JNES	*Journal of Near Eastern Studies*
JPOS	*Journal of the Palestine Oriental Society*
JQR	*Jewish Quarterly Review*
JSOT	*Journal for the Study of the Old Testament*
JSS	*Journal of Semitic Studies*
JTC	*Journal for Theology and the Church*
JTS	*Journal of Theological Studies*

KAI	H. Donner and W. Röllig, *Kanaanäiche und aramäische Inschriften* (Wiesbaden: Harrassowitz, 1962–1964)
KTU	*Die keilalphabetischen Texte aus Ugarit*, ed. M. Dietrich, O. Loretz, and J. Sanmartin (Neukirchen-Vluyn: Neukirchener Verlag, 1976)
𝔐 or MT	Masoretic text
PJB	*Palästina Jahrbuch*
PRU	*Palais Royal d'Ugarit*, ed. C. F. A. Schaeffer (Paris: Imprimerie Nationale, 1955–)
PTU	*Die Personennamen der Texte aus Ugarit*
4QSam[a]	The great Samuel scroll from Cave 4, Qumrân
RA	*Revue d'Assyriologie*
RB	*Revue biblique*
RÉS	*Répertoire d'épigraphie sémitique*
RLA	*Reallexikon der Assyriologie*
RQ	*Revue de Qumrân*
SBLDS	*Society of Biblical Literature Dissertation Series*
SBLMS	*Society of Biblical Literature Monograph Series*
SBTSS	*Studies in Biblical Theology, Second Series*
SEL	*Studi epigraphici e linguistici*
SVT	*Supplement to Vetus Testamentum*
TA	*Tel Aviv*
ThWAT	*Theologisches Wörterbuch zum Alttestament*
TSK	*Theologische Studien und Kritiken*
UF	*Ugarit Forschungen*
VT	*Vetus Testamentum*
WMANT	*Wissenschaftlichen Monografien zum Alten und Neuen Testament*
WO	*Die Welt des Orients*
YNER	*Yale Near Eastern Researches*
ZAW	*Zeitschrift für die alttestamentliche Wissenschaft*
ZDMG	*Zeitschrift der Deutschen Morgenlandischen Gesellschaft*
ZDPV	*Zeitschrift des Deutschen Palästina Vereins*

PART I

EPIC TRADITIONS OF EARLY ISRAEL

1

Kinship and Covenant in Ancient Israel

THE RELATIONSHIP BETWEEN THE LANGUAGE OF KINSHIP IN WEST SEmitic tribal societies and the language of covenant in such groups has been little studied in recent years and is poorly understood.

West Semitic Tribal Societies and Kinship

The social organization of West Semitic tribal groups was grounded in kinship. Kinship relations defined the rights and obligations, the duties, status, and privileges of tribal members, and kinship terminology provided the only language for expressing legal, political, and religious institutions. Kinship was conceived in terms of one blood flowing through the veins of the kinship group. If the blood of a kinsman was spilled, the blood of the kinship group, of each member, was spilled. Kindred were of one flesh, one bone. "The whole kindred conceives of itself as having a single life."[1] On meeting Jacob, Laban says, "Surely thou art my bone

1. W. Robertson Smith, *Kinship and Marriage in Early Arabia,* new edition, ed. Stanley A. Cook (London: Adam and Charles Black, 1903), 46. Smith's classic work here cited is badly flawed by theories of matrilineal descent among the early Semites and notions of their "totemism," views taken up by Smith from his close friend John F. McLennan and, unfortunately, developed enthusiastically. As E. E. Evans-Pritchard, a great admirer of Smith, has said, "Even so great a scholar as Smith sometimes fell into traps. But if he sometimes misinterpreted the evidence, there is no question about his significance for the history of thought, especially for the history of social anthropological thought." Moreover, his rich insights in social anthropology are presently enjoying a revival of interest among anthropologists; social historians of ancient Israel should not lag behind. See further, T. O. Beidelman, *W. Robertson Smith and the Sociological Study of Religion,* with a foreword by E. E. Evans-Pritchard (Chicago: University of Chicago Press, 1974); and Robert A. Oden Jr., "The Place of Covenant in the Religion of Israel," in *Ancient Israelite Religion: Essays in Honor of Frank Moore Cross,* ed. Patrick D. Miller Jr., Paul D. Hanson, and S. Dean McBride (Philadelphia: Fortress Press, 1987), 437–440. More generally on kinship, see Meyer Fortes, *Kinship and the Social Order* (Chicago: Aldine, 1969).

and flesh [*bāśār*]."[2] Tribesmen of Israel meeting David at Hebron introduce their negotiations with him by saying, "Behold we are thy bone and thy flesh."[3] Another term for flesh, *šĕʾēr,* both in Hebrew and Canaanite means 'blood relation' in many contexts, and in Leviticus 18:6 and 25:41, the two terms for flesh, *šĕʾēr* and *bāśār,* are compounded, to designate the 'near of kin.'

Rooted in the concept of kinship was the obligation to protect one's kindred. It is incumbent on the tribesman to kill the killer of his kinsman, and in time of war, offensive or defensive, to rally to the tribal muster. His kinsman's enemy is his enemy. Of early tribal society in Arabia, Robertson Smith wrote as follows:

> The key to all divisions and aggregations of Arab groups lies in the action and reaction of two principles: that the only effective bond is a bond of blood, and that the purpose of society is to unite men for offense and defense. These two principles meet in the law of blood-feud, the theory of which is that the blood-bond, embracing all men who bear a common *nisba* or group-name, constitutes a standing obligation to take up the quarrel of every tribal brother.[4]

The obligation of the kinsman is also to uphold the welfare of his fellow kinsman. Properly vengeance is proscribed within the kinship group. The law of Leviticus 19:17–18 refracts in a new framework old principles of the kinship ethos: "You shall not hate your brother in your heart. . . . You shall not take vengeance nor bear a grudge against the members of your people [i.e., your kindred], but you shall love your fellow [tribesman] as yourself." One is obliged to love one's kinsman as himself, as his own soul.[5] Joab, with some justification, accused David of reversing the requirements of traditional behavior toward one's own by "loving those who hate you and hating those who love you." Properly the bond of kinship requires that one bless those who bless one's brother, curse those who curse one's brother.

To the kinship group, the family (*mišpāḥāh*), falls the duty of redemption. Redemption, *gĕʾūlāh,* indeed, defines the kinship group,[6] and the verb *gāʾal,* 'to redeem,' is often best translated 'to act as kinsman.' The

2. Gen. 29:14.

3. 2 Sam. 5:1; cf. Judg. 9:1–4; Gen. 37:27 (*ʾḥynw bśrnw*); etc.

4. *Kinship and Marriage,* 69. Compare the "laconic formula" cited by Emanuel Marx, "they pursue and are pursued together (*biṭardu wa-yanṭaridu maʿa baʿaḍ*)," and his quotation from A. Musil of a Rwala saying: "bound to mutual protection, both aggressive and defensive." See Marx, *Bedouin of the Negev* (New York: Praeger, 1967).

5. Cf. 1 Sam. 18:1–3 and 20:17 for the expression "to love as one's own soul"; also the discussion below.

6. Cf. Ezek. 11:1.

duties of the *gō'ēl* are several: to avenge the blood of a kinsman,[7] to redeem property sold by a poor kinsman,[8] to redeem the kinsman sold into debt slavery,[9] to marry the widow of a brother or near kinsman to secure his line.[10] Certain laws, embedded in the Priestly Work and in Deuteronomy, proscribe the taking of interest or rent and require that interest-free loans be given to needy brethren. These laws, which may be regarded as idealistic or unrealistic in their present framework—applied to all Israel—have their origin in the kinship group, the lineage (*bêt 'āb*) or family (*mišpāḥāh*), which held property in common as an inalienable patrimony.[11]

We have noted that the language of love (*'ahăbāh*) is kinship language, the bond that holds together those in intimate relationships, the relationships of family and kindred. *Ḥesed* ('loyalty') too, I should argue, originally was a term designating that loyal and loving behavior appropriate to a kinship relationship. "Kinship," Meyer Fortes has written, "predicates the axiom of amity, the prescriptive . . . altruism exhibited in the ethic of generosity. . . . Kinsfolk are expected to be loving, just and generous to one another and not to demand strictly equivalent returns of one another." *Ḥesed* as used in early Israel, a society structured by kinship bonds, covers precisely this semantic field. On the other hand, when extended in use outside the kinship group, behavior required by or appropriate to a kinship relationship becomes "gracious" or "altruistic" behavior. With the breakdown of kinship structures in society, and

7. See Num. 35:19–27.

8. Lev. 25:25–33.

9. Lev. 25:48–49.

10. Ruth 3:9, 12–13 and 4:1–14. See Baruch A. Levine, "In Praise of the Israelite *mišpāḥâ:* Legal Themes in the Book of Ruth," in *The Quest for the Kingdom of God: Studies in Honor of George E. Mendenhall,* ed. H. B. Huffmon, F. A. Spina, and A. R. W. Green (Winona Lake, Ind.: Eisenbrauns, 1983), 95–106, and Hanan Brichto, "Kin, Cult, Land, and Afterlife—A Biblical Complex," *HUCA* 44 (1973), 1–54 (called to my attention by Lawrence Stager).

11. It is not my purpose here to analyze the several levels in the structure of tribal Israel, from 'lineage,' *bêt 'āb,* to 'tribe,' *šebeṭ*. There is a rich literature relating to this topic including the following useful studies: George E. Mendenhall, "Social Organization in Early Israel," in *Magnalia Dei: Essays on the Bible and Archaeology in Memory of G. Ernest Wright,* ed. F. M. Cross, W. E. Lemke, and Patrick D. Miller Jr. (Garden City, N.Y.: Doubleday, 1976), 132–151, and *The Tenth Generation: The Origins of the Biblical Tradition* (Baltimore: Johns Hopkins University Press, 1973), 174–197; C. H. J. de Geus, *The Tribes of Israel* (Assen, Amsterdam: Van Gorcum, 1976), 120–164; Norman Gottwald, *The Tribes of Yahweh* (Maryknoll, N.Y.: Orbis Books, 1979), 237–376; Robert R. Wilson, "The Mechanisms of Judicial Authority in Early Israel," in *The Quest for the Kingdom of God,* 59–75; and Lawrence E. Stager, "The Archaeology of the Family in Ancient Israel," *BASOR* 260 (1985): 1–35 and bibliography.

in social metaphors in theological language, the extended meaning of *ḥesed* became increasingly prominent. But its rootage in kinship obligations is primary. Strictly speaking, *ḥesed* is a kinship term.[12]

The Divine Kinsman

In the religious sphere, the intimate relationship with the family god, the "God of the Fathers," was expressed in the only language available to members of a tribal society. Their god was the Divine Kinsman. We are dealing here obviously with a sociomorphism.

The notion of the Divine Kinsman is especially vivid in the West Semitic onomasticon, in theophorous names.[13] Especially common in Amorite, Canaanite, and Hebrew names is the element *ʾāb,* 'father.' It is used both as a theophorous element and as a divine epithet: [*ʾabī ʾIl*] 'my father is ʾEl'; [*yadiʿ-ʾabu*] 'may the Divine Father know (us)' or 'The Divine Father has known (us),'[14] that is, 'entered into an intimate relationship.' The element *ʾaḫ,* 'brother,' or better, 'male kinsman,' is used similarly: [*ʾaḫī-ʾIl*], 'my kinsman is ʾEl,' or [*yamaʾ-ʾaḫum*], 'the Kinsman has sworn.' Other kinship terms include *ʾimm* or *ʾumm,* 'mother,' *ʾaḫāt,* 'sister,' used of female deities. Of special interest are the terms *ʿamm* and *ḫal,* usually translated 'paternal uncle' and 'maternal uncle.' They are especially frequent in Amorite names and probably meant 'unspecified paternal kinsman' and 'unspecified maternal kinsman.' In any case, we best translate them by 'kinsman' or 'clansman.' *ʿAmm* names were popular also in Canaan and Israel. *Gaʾyum,* 'clan' or 'clansman,' is also found in Amorite names as a theophorous element or epithet, as is the more bizarre *ḥam,* 'father-in-law,' which survives in Hebrew and Ammonite as an element in feminine names. These terms do not exhaust the list of kinship ap-

12. See the classic study by Nelson Glueck, *Ḥesed in the Bible,* trans. Alfred Gottschalk (Cincinnati: Hebrew Union College Press, 1967), and, more recently, Katharine Doob Sakenfeld, *The Meaning of* Ḥesed *in the Hebrew Bible: A New Inquiry, HSM* 17 (Missoula, Mont.: Scholars Press, 1978). The quotations from Meyer Fortes are from his influential volume *Kinship and the Social Order: The Legacy of Lewis Henry Morgan* (Chicago: Aldine, 1969), 237–241. Fortes (241) discusses the term *nanunanu* used by the Garia of New Guinea, which means 'to have a proper attitude toward a person' and thus 'to fulfill all the obligations due to him': "*Nanunanu,* strictly and ideally speaking refers only to conduct towards members of one's security circle [kinship group]; it may be extended, however, to include associates or farming neighbors to whom one is not by kinship reckoning under any moral obligation." The parallel to the term *ḥesed* is striking.

13. See *CMHE,* 14 and 89; M. Noth, *Die israelitischen Personennamen im Rahmen der gemeinsemitischen Namengebung* (Stuttgart: Kohlhammer, 1928), 66–82.

14. *Yadiʿ* may be taken as a jussive, or more probably as an old preterite.

pellations used of the 'god of the father.' I shall mention only one other pertinent example, *ʾilʾib,* the 'Divine Ancestor,' who takes first position in pantheon lists from Ugarit and who survives into Late Bronze Age Palestine in an inscription from Lachish and on a seal from Philistia.[15]

The Divine Kinsman, it is assumed, fulfills the mutual obligations and receives the privileges of kinship. He leads in battle, redeems from slavery, loves his family, shares the land of his heritage (*naḥălāh*), provides and protects. He blesses those who bless his kindred, curses those who curse his kindred.[16] The family of the deity rallies to his call to holy war, "the wars of Yahweh," keeps his cultus, obeys his patriarchal commands, maintains familial loyalty (*ḥesed*), loves him with all their soul, calls on his name.

Kinship-in-Law

The kinship bonds that give unity and cohesion to the lineage and family in tribal societies become attenuated as tribal societies become more complex, as we move to the level of the tribe or a confederation of tribes. Mendenhall, in an excellent study of the nature of the biblical community, puts it thus: "No one is likely to deny the constant importance of real kinship in ancient Near Eastern cultures. . . . Nevertheless, the function of real kinship ties in society is so limited that something larger is needed, particularly as population density increases and social conflicts become more complex."[17] And again, "As social units become larger, kinship ties become increasingly dysfunctional as the basis for the larger group; but kinship terminology seems to become *more used* [italics added] to express the new bond that ties the larger group together."[18]

In tribal societies there were legal mechanisms or devices—we might even say legal fictions—by which outsiders, non-kin, might be incorporated into the kinship group. Those incorporated, an individual or a group, gained fictive kinship and shared the mutual obligations and privileges of real kinsmen. In the West Semitic tribal societies we know best, such individuals or groups were grafted onto the genealogies and fictive kinship became kinship of the flesh or blood. In a word, kinship-in-law became kinship-in-flesh.

In Israel, contrary to many primitive band or tribal societies, the legal compact of marriage introduced the bride into the kinship group or

15. See my discussion in "An Old Canaanite Inscription Recently Found at Lachish," *Tel Aviv* 11 (1984): 71–75.

16. Cf. Gen. 12:3.

17. Mendenhall, *The Tenth Generation,* 177.

18. Ibid., 176.

family. This is the proper understanding of Genesis 2:24: "Therefore a man will abandon his father and his mother and cleave to his wife, and [the two of them] will become one flesh." Flesh refers not to carnal union but to identity of "flesh," kinship, "bone of my bone, flesh of my flesh." Obviously offspring of the marital union will be of one flesh; what is asserted is that the covenant of marriage establishes kinship bonds of the first rank between spouses.

Adoption of sons or daughters is another means of ingrafting non-kin or distant kin into the lineage. The practice was widespread in the Near East and in Israel. Its formulae survive (often in secondary settings): "I will be to him a father and he will become my son," or "my son art thou, today I have begotten thee," or "a child is born to us, a son is given to us."[19]

Oath and covenant, in which the deity is witness, guarantor, or participant, is also a widespread legal means by which the duties and privileges of kinship may be extended to another individual or group, including aliens. In describing early Arab tribalism, Robertson Smith writes:

> The commingling of blood [in the oath and covenant ritual] by which two men became brothers or two kins allies, and the [legal] fiction of adoption by which a new tribesman was feigned to be the veritable son of a member of the tribe, are both evidences of the highest value, that the Arabs were incapable of conceiving any absolute social obligations of social unity which was not based on kinship; for a legal fiction is always adopted to reconcile an act with a principle too firmly established to be simply ignored.

Again, Smith says that "a covenant of alliance and protection was based on an oath. Such an oath was necessarily a religious act; it is called [*qasāma*] . . . a word which almost certainly implies that there was a reference to the god at the sanctuary before the alliance was sealed, and that he was made a party to the act. . . . We see that two groups might make themselves of one blood by a process of which the essence was that they commingled their blood, at the same time applying the blood to the god or fetish so as to make him a party to the covenant also. Quite similar is the ritual in Exodus 24 where blood is applied to the people of Israel and to the altar."[20]

19. See 1 Sam. 7:14; Ps. 2:7; and Isa. 9:5.

20. Smith, *Kinship and Marriage,* 56–62. See also the neglected but fundamental study of Johs. Pedersen, *Der Eid bei den Semiten: Studien zur Geschichte und Kultur des islamischen Orients,* Drittes Heft, ed. C. H. Becker (Strassburg: Trübner, 1914), 21–51. I quote one excerpt (21):

Covenants bound with covenant oaths may be made with individuals or groups. An example of an individual covenant is that between Jonathan and David. Note the following phrases: "And Jonathan loved him [David] as himself [*kĕ-napšô*]. . . . And Jonathan made a covenant with David in that he loved him as himself."[21] In 1 Samuel 20:14–20, in a partially corrupt text, the covenant is further specified:

> Only this, if I am still alive, may you maintain Yahweh's loyalty [*ḥesed*] to me. But if I die, never break faith [*ḥesed*] with my house [lineage]. And when Yahweh exterminates all the enemies of David from the face of the earth, the name of Jonathan must never be allowed by the family of David to die out from among you, or Yahweh will make you answer for it. And in his love for David, Jonathan renewed his oath to him, because he loved him as his very self.[22]

In 2 Samuel 1:26, in the Lament of David, is a further reference to Jonathan and David's relationship: "I grieve over thee Jonathan my brother. . . . To love thee was for me / Better than the love of women." The language used in these passages is transparently the language of kinship and mutual kinship obligation. Jonathan loves David as himself; David's love for Jonathan exceeds that of sexual love. The oath and covenant is binding on the offspring of David and Jonathan. David is to protect Jonathan's name (lineage) in the event of his death. In life and death, loyalty appropriate to kinsmen (*ḥesed*) is to be kept unbroken. And David addresses Jonathan as "my brother."[23]

> Bei den Arabern beruht jeder Schutz, jedes Recht und jede Pflicht auf Stammesgenossenschaft. Nur innerhalb des Stammes lässt sich ein menschliches, normales Leben führen, denn ausserhalb des Stammes herrscht nur Tod und Flucht, alles böse und unmenschlich ist. Dies Verhält mit den unverbrüchlichen Pflichten und Rechten, die darin einbegriffen sind, wird, wie wir gesehen haben, von den Arabern mit dem Wort *ʿahd* bezeichnet. Wenn zwei Parteien ein *ʿahd* mit einander eingehen bilden sie dadurch eine neue Lebensgemeinshaft von derselben innegen Art wie das Verhältnis zwischen den Stammesverwanten. Das ganze Leben, alle Rechte und Pflichten werden gemeinsam.

21. 1 Sam. 18:1–3.

22. The text is that of the New American Bible, prepared by the late Patrick W. Skehan and the writer. It is based partly on the OG, partly on conjecture. See also Kyle McCarter, *1 Samuel,* in the Anchor Bible (Garden City, N.Y.: Doubleday, 1980), 337. David's endeavor to carry out his obligation to Jonathan is recorded in 2 Sam. 9:1–7 and 21:7.

23. Cf. J. A. Thompson, "The Significance of the Verb *Love* in the David-Jonathan Narratives in 1 Samuel," *VT* 24 (1974): 34–38, and McCarter, *1 Samuel,* 341 f., who stress the political significance of the covenant and its analogy with suzerainty treaties.

The language of kinship used in marriage, adoption, and covenants of individuals and groups is put to use even in parity treaties and vassal treaties negotiated at the international level between independent states. That such language survives in societies evolved far beyond the tribal level is remarkable, and it points to the tenacity of the kinship ethos, especially in peoples of the West Semitic world.

In the treaty between Ḥiram of Tyre and Israel, Ḥiram is called a "lover" of David, and Solomon and Ḥiram entered into a covenant, presumably a renewal of a treaty between Ḥiram and David, a "treaty of brotherhood."[24]

William L. Moran and Hayim Tadmor have investigated the use of the term *love* in treaties of the second and first millennium B.C.E.[25] Especially vivid is the use of the term *ra'amūtu,* 'love,' in the Amarna correspondence between kings in a treaty relationship. This use of *love,* as Tadmor has pointed out, was restricted to the "diplomatic parlance" of the West in the Second International Period. It returns in the *adê* documents of eighth- to seventh-century Assyria, whose form and terminology was borrowed from the West. In Tadmor's words, "Thus by way of the Aramaic intermediaries, the Neo-Assyrian *adê* documents continue the highly developed Syro-Anatolian and possibly also north Mesopotamian second-millennium traditions."[26] Thus in a treaty of Esarhaddon, vassals are to swear concerning Assurbanipal, his heir: "You shall love [him] as yourselves" (*kī napšāt[i]kunu lā tarammāni*).[27]

Similarly, in the language of second-millennium treaties we find such terms as *aḫḫūtum* or *atḫūtum,* 'brotherhood,' usually used by kings of equal rank, and *abbūtum* and *mārūtum,* 'fatherhood' and 'sonship,' usually used of overlord and vassal respectively.[28] Munn-Rankin com-

It must be said, however, that the expression "to love as himself" is a kinship term and need imply nothing as to David's "suzerainty" over Jonathan. The covenant binds David and Jonathan in the bonds of kinship, reflecting their mutual love and more practically binding their offspring in the obligations of kinship, thereby preserving their offspring—ideally—from murder and countermurder of their opposing dynasties.

24. See 1 Kings 5:14–26; cf. Amos 1:9.

25. See William L. Moran, "The Ancient Near Eastern Background of the Love of God in Deuteronomy," *CBQ* 25 (1963): 77–87, and Hayim Tadmor, "Treaty and Oath in the Ancient Near East: A Historian's Approach," in *Humanizing America's Iconic Book,* ed. G. M. Tucker and D. A. Knight (Chico, Calif.: Scholars Press, 1982), 125–152.

26. Tadmor, "Treaty and Oath," 145; cf. 152.

27. See Moran, "Love of God," 80, and references, n. 23.

28. See especially J. M. Munn-Rankin, "Diplomacy in Western Asia in the Early Second Millennium B.C.," *Iraq* 18 (1956): 68–110; Tadmor, "Treaty and Oath," 131 f.; M. Weinfeld, "Covenant Terminology in the Ancient Near East and Its Influence on

ments, "In every case in which one ruler calls another 'brother' in the Mari correspondence there is either direct evidence that they were in treaty relations, or that they were jointly engaged in military operations, which presuppose the existence of a treaty."[29]

Not infrequently the daughter of a king was given to his treaty partner, with the proviso that their offspring mount the throne after the ally's death. Thus kinsman-in-law (the father-in-law) became the kinsman-in-flesh of the ally's heir.[30]

Often it has been asserted that the language of "brotherhood" and "fatherhood," "love," and "loyalty" is "covenant terminology." This is to turn things upside down. The language of covenant, kinship-in-law, is taken from the language of kinship, kinship-in-flesh.

Kinship and Tribal Federation

Early Israel must be designated a tribal league or federation. The tribe has been described as a fragile social entity, dependent on so-called sodalities, that is, kinship, religious, and military associations, to give it stability and unity.[31] If this is so, the tribal federation is even more fragile, coming into being when tribal societies are threatened by external and internal pressures that threaten their security and peace. Not least of the internal pressures is the need to restrain the terror and ravages of the blood feud. External threat in the chaotic age in which the Israelite league came into being included the armies of highly organized city states as well as opposing tribal leagues of the southeast (to which we shall return below).

The federation of Israelite tribes, as we have observed, was united by military, kinship, and religious ties, "sodalities" in anthropological jargon. We may describe the social organization of the league from three standpoints.

The league was a military organization first of all, designed to marshal a militia for offense and defense, especially for *ḥerem*, 'Holy War.' The league militia, ideally, was formed by an alliance of clan musters,

---

the West," *JAOS* 93 (1973): 190–199; and Weinfeld, "The Covenant of Grant in the Old Testament and in the Ancient Near East," *JAOS* 90 (1970): 184–203.

29. Munn-Rankin, "Diplomacy in Western Asia," 84.

30. See, for example, the treaty of Suppiluliuma and Mattiwaza, and the treaty of Hattusili with Pendšenna of Amurru, published by E. F. Weidner, *Politische Documente aus Kleinasien,* Boghazköi-Studien 8. und 9. Heft (Leipzig: Hinrichs, 1923), 1–36 and 129–135.

31. See Elman R. Service, *Primitive Social Organization: An Evolutionary Perspective,* 2nd ed. (New York: Random House, 1971), 103–105.

the *ʾelep.* In the rituals of Holy War, the "militia of Yahweh" was called up by the god of the league, that is, by priestly oracle and/or the *šôpēṭ,* a term we usually translate imprecisely as 'judge', the temporary leader in battle, under the sanctions of covenant oaths or curses. In such rituals we find the social function of the epic of the Divine Warrior recited and reenacted in cult.

The league was also a kinship organization, a covenant of families and tribes organized by the creation or identification of a common ancestor and related by segmented genealogies. Such genealogies are in substantial part constructs, based as much on "kinship-in-law" as real kinship, and the genealogies tend to be fluid, shifting to reflect social and historical changes and developments. The league in ideal form was conceived as twelve tribes, related at once by covenant and kinship.

The Israelite league was also a religious organization or society. Priestly families, linked by genealogy to create a priestly "tribe," were set aside to conduct rituals and sacrifices and to preserve religious lore. The league was called the *ʿam Yahweh,* which we generally translate the 'people of Yahweh.' However, as we have seen, *ʿam(m)* is a kinship term, and for our purposes here is perhaps better translated the 'kindred' of Yahweh. Yahweh is the god of Israel, the Divine Kinsman, the god of the covenant. Religious unity is undergirded by the institution of the pilgrimage feasts, where Israel's epic is sung, and covenant ceremonies or covenant renewal ceremonies reconstitute the league anew.

To be sure, these three aspects of league organization are overlapping. The *ʿam Yahweh,* 'kindred of Yahweh,' in some contexts must be translated the 'militia of Yahweh,' and in other contexts the *ʿam Yahweh* is a community of worshippers, a cultic association.[32]

I have discussed elsewhere the evidence that confederations of tribes flourished in southeastern Palestine and northern Arabia before their evolution into "nation states" headed by kings: Edom, Moab, Ammon, Midian, Ishmael, and Qedar.[33] The Israelite league was called the *ʿam Yahweh;* indeed, this is the old proper name of the league. So too Moab was called the *ʿam Kĕmōš,* 'sacral league' or 'kindred' of Chemosh, and Ammon the *ʿam Milkōm.*[34] In North Arabic is found the *ʾahl ʿAθtar,* 'the

32. Note the language of 2 Kings 11:17 (= 2 Chron. 23:16): "Jehoida made a covenant between Yahweh, the king, and the people that they should become the 'kindred of Yahweh.'" For a recent discussion of *ʿam(m),* and a review of the literature dealing with the term, see Robert M. Good, *The Sheep of His Pasture: A Study of the Hebrew Noun ʿAm(m) and Its Semitic Cognates, HSM* 29 (Chico, Calif.: Scholars Press, 1983).

33. See below, chapter 2.

34. See Jer. 49:1 where Milcom is to be read (with the versions), and the expression *ʿammô,* 'his [Milcom's] people' or 'kindred' is found. For *ʿam Yahweh,* see Judg. 5:11, 1 Sam. 2:24, 2 Sam. 1:12, etc.

family of the god ʿAθtar.' We have noted also that, just as names with the theophorous element Yahweh dominate the Israelite onomasticon, so too in Ammon, Moab, and Edom their onomastica are dominated by the name of their league god.[35]

Israel is the kindred (*ʿam*) of Yahweh; Yahweh is the God of Israel. This is an old formula. But this formula must be understood as legal language, the language of kinship-in-law, or in other words, the language of covenant.

Social Metaphors in Israel's Religious Language

In light of our exposition of the social institutions of tribal Israel, institutions rooted in an ideology of kinship and its legal substitutes that I have dubbed "kinship-in-law," it will be useful, I believe, to reexamine social metaphors, "sociomorphisms," in Israel's religious language.

The God of Israel adopts Israel as a "son" and is called "father," enters a marriage contract with Israel and is designated "husband," swears fealty oaths together with Israel and enters into covenant, assuming the mutual obligations of kinship, taking vengeance on Israel's enemies, going to war at the head of Israel's militia.

In Israel marriage may be described as entry into a mutual covenant of love, loyalty (*ḥesed*), and fidelity (*ʾĕmet*). In Ezekiel 16, Jerusalem is addressed as a beautiful woman of mixed ancestry. Yahweh came upon her and said, "I looked upon thee, and behold thy time was a time of love, and I spread my skirt over thee and covered thy nakedness, and I made oaths to thee and entered into a covenant with thee . . . and thou becamest mine."[36]

In Hosea 2:4–25 there is the song of the divorce of wife Israel by her husband Yahweh, an alloform of the covenant lawsuit (found *inter alia* in Hosea 4), followed by a song of wooing and remarriage as Israel is led by her lover in the wilderness, retracing the way of the Exodus and the entry into the land. The new espousal will be eternal, marked by loyalty (*ḥesed*) and fidelity (*ʾĕmūnāh*), and Israel will "know" Yahweh, and call him "my husband." The child called *lôʾ ʿammî*, 'no kin of mine,' shall be called *ʿammî*, 'my kin.' In this lovely song the terms for kinship, marriage, covenant, and kinship-in-law are interchangeable social metaphors drawn from the traditional ethos of the tribal league. Hosea with

35. See below, chapter 2. On the Israelite onomasticon, see Jeffrey H. Tigay, *You Shall Have No Other Gods: Israelite Religion in the Light of Hebrew Inscriptions, HSS* 31 (Atlanta: Scholars Press, 1986).

36. Ezek. 16:8; cf. Mal. 2:14 ("wife of my covenant"); and Prov. 2:17. Tadmor, "Treaty and Oath," 139, observes that the Akkadian term for marriage is *riksātum*, 'binding agreement,' 'pact,' 'covenant.'

equal case uses the language of "sonship" or adoptive sonship in describing his relation with Israel: "When Israel was a lad then I came to love him, and I called my son out of Egypt."[37]

The interchangeability of the terms of "kinship-in-law" is well illustrated in the ideology of Davidic kingship. I have quoted above from royal liturgies: "I will be to him a father and he will become my son"; "My son art thou, today I have begotten thee"; and "A child is born to us, a son is given to us," all formulas of Yahweh's adoption of David, or the Davidid, as his son. Side by side we find the relation of David to the deity specified in terms of oaths sworn by David and Yahweh, and of Yahweh's covenant (*bĕrît*) and covenant oath(s) (*ʿēdôt*).[38] The royal liturgy preserved in Psalm 89 contains the verses "Forever will I keep loyalty to him [David], and my covenant is secure with him; his seed I make to endure forever, and his throne as the days of heaven."[39]

The ideology of divine sonship was also at home in Canaan; both the language of adoptive sonship and of the Davidic covenant were at home in the Israelite kingdom. We may compare the discrete meanings of Akkadian *mārūtum:* 'sonship,' 'adoption,' 'status of being a natural or adopted son or daughter,' 'status of vassal (under treaty).'[40]

It should be stressed that adoptive sonship places obligations of kinship on the father, as is generally recognized, and also on the son, which is often forgotten. Kinship obligations are necessarily mutual. In the language of kinship-in-law, the so-called Davidic Covenant, the same is true. Whether one chooses a royal ideology in which the language of divine sonship is used or chooses one using the language of covenant, mutual relations are established between king and Deity. There are no "unilateral" covenants in a kinship-based society.[41]

37. Hos. 11:1.

38. Ps. 132:1–2, 11, 12. On *ʿēdōt,* see below, and *CMHE,* 267, and n. 209. *ʿdwtw* 'his covenant oaths' should be read in Ps. 132:1 parallel to *ʿdty* in v. 12.

39. Ps. 89:29–30; cf. 2 Sam. 23:5.

40. See *CAD* vol. 10, pt. 1, pp. 319–321; *RLA* 1:37–38 and references.

41. There are, to be sure, some interesting parallels between two types of "dynastic promise to David" and two types of dynastic clauses of suzerainty treaties of the second millennium. Certain elements are common to both types: the suzerain secures the vassal on the throne, secures the land in his possession, and lists land boundaries. Sometimes "sonship" is granted. But two types of promise are found in regard to the future of the dynasty. The usual is to promise that a king's heirs will remain on the throne under the protection of the suzerain so long as they are obedient to the stipulations of the covenant. The treaty makes the perpetuation of the dynasty conditional. In the second type, the promise of the land and promise of the dynastic succession are unconditional. This type is found in pure form in the treaty of Tudkhaliyas IV and Ulmi-Teshup of Dattassa. It is said that if Ulmi-Teshup is faithful to his covenant with his suzerain, it is the obligation of the suzerain to preserve his heirs on the throne of

Elements of Confusion in the Understanding of Israel's Ancient Covenant

The failure to recognize the rootage of the institution of covenant and covenant obligations in the structures of kinship societies has led to confusion and even gross distortion in the scholarly discussion of the term *bĕrît,* 'covenant,' and in the description of early Israelite religion.

From the time of Wellhausen there has been the tendency to strip the term *bĕrît,* 'covenant,' of any element of mutuality, or of any legal overtones, at least in its use in early contexts. Hence it has been claimed that the term denotes primarily 'obligation,' either an obligation taken on by the deity voluntarily (grace), or obligations imposed by a superior (the deity) upon an inferior. In the latter case the stipulations of covenant can secondarily come to mean 'law.' The covenants of Abraham and David thus are claimed to be covenants of grace, the Sinaitic covenant a covenant of law. For Wellhausen and his modern successors, a mutual covenant with legal stipulations is a construct of the late monarchy, especially of the Deuteronomistic school and the Priestly tradent of the Pentateuch.[42]

For Wellhausen, the relationship between God and Israel in premonarchical times and in early prophecy was "natural," spontaneous, free, interior (individualistic). Such language is his inheritance from a philosophic milieu created by idealism and romanticism, borrowed immediately from Vatke, and congruent with Protestant antinomianism. That

---

Dattassa, and to preserve the land in the heirs' possession. If a future son sins (rebels), he may be punished or removed, but kingship and land must pass to another heir of Ulmi-Teshup, in theory thereby creating an eternal dynasty. Put another way, it can be said that permanence of dynasty and possession of land rests on the "reservoir of grace" filled by the obedience of Ulmi-Teshup alone, and therefore is not dependent on the fidelity of each succeeding heir—presumably intensifying Ulmi-Teshup's motivation to obedience. The analogy with the "high" or unconditional royal ideology of the Davidids is obvious. Thanks to the piety of David, the throne is eternally promised to the house of David; thanks to the fidelity of Abraham, the land is promised perpetually to his seed. One suspects that in this unconditional promise to heirs, archaic kinship ideology is at work: the family of the faithful covenant partner is bound forever in kinship bonds with the suzerain, and his family. For references, see *CMHE,* 268 and notes; and Baruch Halpern, *The Constitution of the Monarchy in Israel, HSM* 25 (Chico, Calif.: Scholars Press, 1981), 45–47.

42. See the useful sketch of the history of the discussion by Oden, "The Place of Covenant," 429–447. Cf. Moshe Weinfeld, "*bĕrît*" in *ThWAT,* cols. 781–808, and the literature cited; L. Perlitt, *Bundestheologie im Alten Testament, WMANT* 36 (Neukirchen-Vluyn: Neukirchener Verlag, 1969); and E. Kutsch, *Verheissung und Gesetz, BZAW* 131 (Berlin: De Gruyter, 1973).

early covenant forms were sociocentric, mutual, and expressed in legal institutions (kinship-in-law) was unthinkable. Law—static, petrified, exterior, abstract—was the creation of the Judaic spirit, hence late and perverse. That such views persist in the face of new knowledge of the ancient Near East, the history of religion and law, and advances in social anthropology is a testimony, not to the soundness of the Wellhausenist synthesis but to the power and perversity of Paulinist and anti-Judaic dogma, or, in other words, to the survival of stubbornly, often unconsciously held traditions of Christian apologetics in biblical scholarship.

Tribal covenants structured by kinship-in-law as well as federations of tribes under a league god were mutual covenants. Even the international treaties of the Hittites and the suzerainty or parity treaties of north Syrian Semites in the second millennium were mutual, at least in form and language, obligations being undertaken by both parties.[43]

Pedersen's classic study of oath and covenant gives the following definition of *ʿahd,* the primary term for covenant among the early Arabs: "*ʿAhd* means generally the relationship between those who belong together with all the rights and obligations which spring from this relationship. It encompasses consequently both the relationship between those related by kinship and those united by covenant."[44] In some contexts 'right' or 'obligation' may be primarily in view; but, says Pedersen, "if we translate the word [*ʿahd*] with 'obligation' [*Pflicht*], yet always underlying this meaning at the same time is the presupposition of the mutual relationship of the parties which is the ground of the obligation." The term *ʿahd* is cognate with Hebrew **ʿâd* < *ʿêdōt* / *ʿêdūt,*[45] Aramaic *ʿdyʾ*, borrowed into the Assyrian dialect in the frozen form *adê.*[46] The plural form in Aramaic and Hebrew, comparable to Homeric *horkia* in the idiom *horkia pista tamnein* and Phoenician *ʾlt* in the idiom *krt ʾlt,* has generally been taken to mean 'covenant oaths' but is better taken to be a *plurale tantum* like Akkadian *rikšātum* since the idiom is 'to cut': *krt, gzr, tamnein* (*sic*). Evidently, *ʿêdōt* / *ʿêdūt* is one of the Priestly tradent's characteristic archaisms.[47] The

43. See Tadmor, "Treaty and Oath," 138–140; William L. Moran, *ANET,* 628, n. 64.

44. Pedersen, *Der Eid bei den Semiten,* 8.

45. *ʿÊdōt* shows the usual dissimilation of (long) u-class vowels in proximity, characteristic of Hebrew (*ʿâdāt* > *ʿôdōt* > *ʿēdōt*); *ʿēdūt* is a secondary form, the feminine plural being normal. See *CMHE,* 267 and references.

46. *CMHE,* 267, n. 209; H. Tadmor, "The Aramaization of Assyria: Aspects of Western Impact," in *Mesopotamien und seine Nachbarn,* ed. Hartmut Kühne, H. S. Nissen, and J. Renger, *XXV Rencontre Assyriologique Internationale* (Berlin: Dietrich Reiner, 1982), 455–458; Tadmor, "Treaty and Oath," 143–152.

47. See *CMHE,* 322 f., and 314; cf. C. L. Seow, "The Designation of the Ark in Priestly Theology," *HTR* 8 (1984): 185–198.

usual term in Hebrew is, of course, *bĕrît*.[48] Its etymology is obscure, but the term is identical in its distribution with Arabic *ʿahd,* Hebrew *ʿêdōt,* Aramaic *ʿâdayyāʾ,* Akkadian *rikšātum,* 'bond, covenant, treaty.'

Religion and religious sodalities in a tribal society were an essential instrument of social bonding.[49] In the Israelite league kinship ties were extended by the bonds of a covenant of which Yahweh was party and guarantor. The league covenant bound the tribes to the deity, and tribe with tribe, with stipulations as to the deity's cult and stipulations governing tribal behavior. These were the basis of solidarity and peace (*šālōm*), mutual responsibilities in time of war, and the duties of conducting a common cult. The whole design and motivation of the covenanted league was the establishment of mutual obligations. The notion of a *bĕrît,* 'covenant,' in the era of early Israel without the mutual bonds of kinship-in-law between Yahweh and Israel, and between the tribes of the league, is not merely unlikely; it runs counter to all we have learned of such societies. Moreover, the survival of the social forms of covenant and law, even in the era of Israel's full-fledged state, is dramatic witness to their liveliness in the era before the rise of the state. States, designed to centralize power, and to impose hierarchical rule, do not generate rules based on kinship. They do not legislate egalitarian laws, nor devise segmentary genealogies. On the contrary, the survival of the league and covenantal institutions in Israel placed limits on the evolution of kingship and the arbitrary powers ordinarily exercised by the monarchical city state. Indeed the perception in Israel that the era of the league was Israel's normative age, and that the law of the league remained a check on kingship—traditions cherished by the prophetic movement—ever remained an obstacle to Israel's development into full-scale Oriental despotism. Attempts were made to suppress these traditions, notably by Solomon and Ahab, and each brought protest and prophetic reaction, and in the north, revolutions and the overthrow of dynasties.

The antiquity of covenant forms, of the language of kinship-in-law, and of religio-military federations of tribes is not in doubt. This has been clear since the discovery of the texts of international treaties of

48. On extrabiblical occurrences of *bĕrît* from the end of the second millennium, see *CMHE,* 267 and notes, and more recently, Tadmor, "Treaty and Oath," 138, n. 61. Tadmor's suggestion that *bĕrît* originally meant 'cutting,' 'slaughter,' in reference to the cutting up of the animal in covenant rites, following M. Held, is not implausible. In this case, however, biblical *brʾ* 'to cut, kill,' *bry* in Jewish Aramaic, is not to be related to *brʾ* 'create,' but to *brw,* in Old South Arabic, 'to cut, kill,' used in parallel with *hrg* and *θbr.*

49. See Mendenhall, *The Tenth Generation,* 179; Oden, "The Place of Covenant," 439 f.

the second millennium. Such forms were constitutive of West Semitic tribal societies including Israel, and persisted after the emergence of the West Semitic states, especially in "nation states" (as opposed to city states), and was peculiarly persistent in Israel in the era of the monarchy. The studies of Bickerman, Mendenhall, Baltzer, and Korošec placed the treaty formulations of the second millennium into particular prominence in the discussions of covenant and law in Israel.[50] The importance of these studies cannot be overstressed, both in providing analogies to the covenant forms in Israel and in pointing to the antiquity of such legal formulations. At the same time the very concentration of scholars on these parallels to Israelite institutions, all drawn from the formularies surviving in state juristic documents, has tended to obscure the actual social matrix of Israel's covenant institutions in the tribal confederacy. Above all, the misuse of the Neo-Assyrian vassal treaties for dating and defining covenant formulations in Israel has led to confusion. The papers of Hayim Tadmor have been decisive in correcting misunderstanding of the Neo-Assyrian vassal treaties.[51] The *adê* documents, which appear first in the mid–eighth century B.C.E., borrow much of their formulary and technical terms from West Semitic, especially Aramaic sources, where they had been at home for a thousand years or more, forms absent from the native culture of Mesopotamia proper. Moreover, in Assyrian hands, the old treaty type was transformed into essentially a fealty oath although it also had wider usage. "Borrowed from lands west of the Euphrates, it became a ruthless tool in the hands of the Neo-Assyrian and Neo-Babylonian emperors and was in fact instrumental in the final destruction of the west itself."[52] While the Neo-Assyrian fealty

50. E. Bickerman, "Couper une alliance," *Archives d'Histoire du Droit Orientale* 5 (1950/1951), 133–156; George E. Mendenhall, *Law and Covenant in Israel and the Ancient Near East* (Pittsburgh: Biblical Colloquium, 1955), reprinted from *BA* 17/2 (1954): 26–46 and 17/3 (1954): 49–76; Klaus Baltzer, *The Covenant Formulary,* trans. D. E. Green (Philadelphia: Fortress, 1971), which appeared in German under the title *Das Bundesformular, WMANT* 4 (Neukirchen-Vluyn: Neukirchener Verlag, 1960; 2nd rev. ed., 1964); and V. Korošec, *Hethitische Staatsverträge, ein Beitrag zu ihren juristischen Wertung,* Leipziger rechtswissenschaftliche Studien 60 (Leipzig: Weicher, 1931).

51. See the studies listed in note 46.

52. Tadmor, "Treaty and Oath," 152; cf. A. Kirk Grayson, "Akkadian Treaties of the Seventh Century B.C.," *JCS* 39 (1987): 127–160, and Simo Parpola, "Neo-Assyrian Treaties from the Royal Archives at Nineveh," *JCS* 39 (1987): 161–189. I am indebted to J. J. M. Roberts for calling my attention to the latter two studies. Parpola gives evidence for qualifying Tadmor's narrow definition of the Assyrian use of the Aramaic loanword *adē,* and questions his contention that the *adē* institution is borrowed from the West. However, he has no adequate explanation for its being borrowed in Neo-Assyrian times and transformed into a plural *tantum.* Nor does he adequately address

oaths are useful in providing parallels, especially to the curse formulae of Deuteronomy and Leviticus, they are as analogies to Israel's early covenant institutions even more remote than Syrian and Hittite international treaties.

It must be emphasized, however, that the formulary of West Semitic international treaties and its kinship language are a survival of prestate tribal societies. In the Israelite state "covenant ideology" also survived, especially, as we shall see, in the nostalgic reconstruction of the institutions of the league in the Deuteronomic and Priestly sources of the Pentateuch. But its origin, and the social context in which the covenant relationship was authentic and fully functional, must be located in the society of the confederation of Yahweh, in the era of the league. Nor are the covenant institutions of the league wholly unique. They appear to share common institutions with the leagues of the south insofar as we can reconstruct these societies. These leagues, named after a deity, possess certain sodalities of complex tribal societies: the construct of a twelve-tribe system, tribal heads called *nāśîʾ* (in Hebrew), segmented genealogies traced back to putative eponymous ancestors, and the institution of *ḥerem*. These sodalities of kinship, the cultic society of a patron god, and religio-military rites are not the creation of a centralized state. They are in some sense antistate, and survive into the era of the state as vestiges of an earlier society. It is remarkable that we can trace the rites of covenant making or covenant renewal—the cutting up of an animal, often the rite of passing between the parts or "touching the throat," and the sanction of mutilation implied or explicit—from the early second millennium to late monarchical times in Israel.[53] The call-up of the militia has an associated rite: the sending to the tribes of a dismembered human being or animal.[54]

A Brief Sketch of the Stages of the Covenant Institutions in Israel

The twelve-tribe league of Yahweh, the *ʿam Yahweh,* whose bonds to each other and bonds to Yahweh were formulated in terms of the covenant of Yahweh, is the primary locus of covenant institutions. In this society the covenanted tribes were a salient sodality. Covenant language was "at home," living and immediate. No doubt older socioreligious lan-

Tadmor's broader thesis in his paper "The Aramaization of Assyria: Aspects of Western Impact." See now also G. N. Knoppers, "Ancient Near Eastern Royal Grants and the Davidic Covenant," *JAOS* 116 (1996): 670–697.

53. See *CMHE,* 265–273.

54. See especially Judg. 19:11–20:48; 1 Sam. 11:1–11.

guage stands behind the institutions of the league (older typologically): the language and legal institutions of the Divine Kinsman, who adopted (or entered into covenant with) the patriarch, the lineage, or tribe, in other words the "god of the father."[55]

In the historical context of the league we find the *Sitz im Leben,* the cultic and social function of old "liturgical law." By "liturgical law," I mean to specify the legal type called by Alt "apodeictic law" (a less than felicitous designation): succinct formulae in origin, "Thou shalts," and series of curses, shaped by oral recitation and preserved in decalogues or dodecalogues. Such covenant law evidently belonged to the rites of covenant or covenant renewal. So too we are inclined to place the cycles of tribal blessings in Genesis 49, Deuteronomy 33, and Judges 5 in the context of the rites of Holy War, or their equivalent, the reenactment of the epic victory of Yahweh which I have labeled the "ritual conquest," celebrated in the pilgrimage festivals.[56]

Again it is in the historical context of league institutions that the law of the *gôʾēl,* the "redeemer," the law proscribing the taking of interest, and the law of the inalienable patrimony have their natural setting. While we find these laws at present in late settings in the Pentateuch, they run counter to the claims and interests of kingship and monarchy and could not have been invented in late monarchical times.[57]

In the early monarchy the covenantal and kinship institutions that flourished in the days of the league were in part displaced by royal institutions and in part transmuted into new forms, maintaining some continuity with league values and social structures but reshaped to conform to a monarchical superstructure. There was, particularly in the Solomonic era, a systematic assault on the structures of the league and its sodalities which shored up tribal loyalties. New instruments were introduced to centralize power: the nation was partitioned into administrative districts which in part cut across traditional tribal boundaries; the militia was subordinated to a standing army and royal guard; *corvée* and taxation were instituted; and family patrimonies were seized by the crown in order to provide royal grants to the king's nobles, especially the military nobility. A royal cultus was instituted centered on Yahweh's choice of Zion and the house of David.[58] Yahweh's covenant with the

55. The term *personal god* is especially unfortunate in describing this type of deity. Alt's term *theoi patrōoi* is much more felicitous.

56. *CMHE,* 99–111.

57. It has sometimes been claimed that rules concerning redemption from debt slavery cannot be native to a tribal society. Such a view is contradicted by anthropological data and is baseless.

58. See especially J. J. M. Roberts, "The Davidic Origin of the Zion Tradition," *JBL* 92 (1973): 329–344, and "Zion in the Theology of the Davidic-Solomonic Empire," in

tribes of Israel was narrowed in focus to Yahweh's covenant with David, or the house of David, as Israel's representative. Yet this reformulated covenant language is relatively rare—despite its frequency in scholarly literature. The language of divine sonship, adoption of the king by the deity, is the preferred "high Judaean" royal ideology, preferred even by the Deuteronomist. A temple in the Canaanite mode was built in Jerusalem, compromised only by the introduction of the league palladium, the ark of the covenant, into its holy of holies, in place of a cult statue.

At the same time the memory of the old constitution of the league remained lively, especially in prophetic circles, the ground of the prophetic critique of crown and temple cult. And if Lawrence Stager is correct, rural Israel maintained certain of its kinship structures and tribal institutions—covenantal traditions—in the face of all attempts to transform Israel into a city state of Canaanite polity.[59]

Late in the monarchy and in the Exile there was a revival of covenantal ideology, law, and cultic practice. Drawing on surviving elements of league and kinship structures, as well as traditional religious and legal lore, the tradents of the school of Deuteronomy and of the Priestly school made a stalwart effort to reconstruct and resurrect the covenantal institutions of the "Mosaic Age," that is, of the era of the league. To be sure, their efforts to recover the past were flawed, and they produced nostalgic constructs of the era conceived as normative. Their efforts were shaped by the special concerns of their own times as they drew up programs of reform or programs for an ideal future. The covenantal law, for example, draws on traditional law of the old time, but it is schematized, idealized, and reformulated with the introduction of late elements alongside the genuinely archaic. In any case I should assert that the Pentateuchal tradents, D and P, were more successful in their reconstructions of the covenantal institutions of early Israel than we critical historians have supposed, and that their traditionalist approaches are often less doctrinaire and closer to historical reality than the unilinear historical schemes imposed by scholars of yesteryear.[60]

Studies in the Period of David and Solomon, ed. T. Ishida (Winona Lake, Ind.: Eisenbrauns, 1982), 93–108.

59. See Stager, "The Archaeology of the Family in Ancient Israel," 24–28; Halpern, *The Constitution of the Monarchy in Israel,* 175–249; H. Tadmor, "Traditional Institutions and the Monarchy: Social and Political Tensions in the Time of David and Solomon," in *Studies in the Period of David and Solomon,* 239–257.

60. I am indebted to Professor Stager for a number of helpful criticisms of this chapter.

2

Traditional Narrative and the Reconstruction of Early Israelite Institutions

I

THE EARLY NARRATIVE TRADITIONS OF ISRAEL PRESERVED IN THE MOST archaic sources of the Tetrateuch in some respects resemble historical narrative, in other respects a mythic cycle. They recount the past of Israel, notably the events that brought Israel into being as a nation. To be sure, the narrative is "fraught with meaning," composed to reveal the meaning of Israel's past, and therewith to define the identity and destiny of the nation. Further, while the actors are human beings for the most part, and the events and settings appear on the surface to be accessible to the historian, the principal hero is a Divine Warrior, Yahweh of Hosts by name, who called the nation into being, led them to victory over their enemies with many marvels, and revealed himself as their ruler. In both the structure of the great complex of tradition and in individual poetic units embedded therein,[1] a familiar mythic pattern may be discerned. The Divine Warrior marched forth in wrath to win a crucial victory—at the sea, or in variant tradition by cleaving through Sea—and then led a triumphal procession to his mountain, where he appeared in glory, constructed his sanctuary, and established his kingdom. A similar if not identical pattern of themes is found in the mythic cycle of Baʿl in Late Bronze Age Canaan (Ugarit) and in the classic Akkadian cosmogony known as *Enūma eliš.* In the former, Baʿl-Haddu, the young storm god, defeats Prince Sea and gains kingship among the gods. He builds his temple on Mount Ṣapōn, his "mount of victory," and displays his glory before the gods in the storm theophany. In the Mesopotamian cosmogony *Enūma eliš,* the young warrior of the gods, Marduk, defeats Tiāmat, whose name means 'the Deep,' and fashions cosmic order from her split carcass. He returns to the assembly of the gods, receives kingship over the gods, and constructs his temple. In both the West and East Semitic myths, the actors are exclusively the gods, the terrain cosmic (or sacral). The Divine Warrior, through his victory over watery chaos, or the sea, creates order, conceived as a divine state.

Yet beneath the surface of these great mythic compositions, one per-

1. Above all in the Song of the Sea, Exod. 15.

ceives a counterpoint: the establishment of earthly kingship, even the empire of Babylon, and the inauguration of earthly temples and cults. A characteristic dualism exists here which fixes or strives to fix human institutions in the created and eternal orders. Thus two levels run through these mythic compositions, though it must be emphasized that in these major Near Eastern myths the focus of the narrative is wholly on cosmic events, and the divine actors in the cosmogonic drama exclusively dominate action. In Israel's early orally composed narratives, these two levels, which we may term "divine-cosmic" and "historic-political," are present also, but in a quite different balance. The narrative action takes place, for the most part, in ordinary space and time; major roles are played by human enemies and human heroes; though shaped by mythic themes, the narrative is presented in the form of remembered events. In view of such traits, despite the role played by Israel's divine hero, the category "myth" ill suits the Israelite narrative complex. Nor does it appear precise or useful simply to describe Israel's early traditions as "historical narrative" in view of its shaping in detail and in structure by mythic elements, notably the *magnalia dei.* Ideally the term *historical narrative* should be reserved for that literary genre, usually composed in writing, in which the events narrated are secular or "ordinary," if memorable, in which the protagonists are palpable, historical men or women, and in which the primary level of meaning is immanent in the sequence of narrated events. In "historical narrative," a relatively late and sophisticated genre in ancient literature, divine activity, if alluded to by the narrator, is not so directly perceived or presented as in myth.

If we eschew the designations *mythic narrative* and *historical narrative* as inappropriate or misleading in describing the constitutive genre of early Israelite oral narrative preserved in the Tetrateuch, we do find a third literary genre that fits snugly, namely *epea,* traditional epic. I propose to call Israel's early narrative traditions which originated in oral composition by the term *epic.* Moreover, I wish to define this term rather narrowly, drawing upon studies of Homeric epic for delineating the traits of epic and for analogies to aid in understanding the nature of Hebrew epic lore.

The Homeric epics were composed by an oral technique that utilized a complex of traditional themes and a common repertoire of poetic formulae. The epic elements were carried by a continuous stream of bards, *aoidoi,* reaching back into Mycenaean times, Greece's heroic age.[2] Canaanite epics of contemporary times, the Late Bronze Age of

2. See Martin P. Nilsson's *The Mycenaean Origin of Greek Mythology,* with a new introduction and bibliography by Emily Vermeule (Berkeley: University of California Press, 1972), the pioneer study of the subject, and more recently Cedric H. Whitman, *Homer and the Heroic Tradition* (Cambridge: Harvard University Press, 1963).

Syria, have survived in dictated copies recorded in alphabetic cuneiform.[3] Canaanite epic verse also reveals characteristic oral formulae and themes. It does not, of course, use epic hexameter verse. Its prosody is characterized by parallelism in bicola and tricola, parallelism on phonetic, morphological, and semantic levels. On the last-mentioned level (the parallelismus membrorum, classically described by Bishop Lowth) are to be found word and phrase pairs, which in light of recent studies are newly recognized as belonging to special categories of oral formulae.[4] Israel's early poetry stands in this Canaanite tradition utilizing substantially the same repertoire of formulae and themes, to be sure modified by time, by dialectal and cultural differentiation.[5]

Homeric epic has the concreteness and concentration on memories of the past that give it the appearance of historical narrative. "Yet, wherever it is possible to compare events in epic with their actual history, one sees that what is preserved in poetry bears only a special, sometimes slight, relation to fact, while it is quite normal for the places, dates, and even the characters of a recorded event to be magniloquently confused and distorted."[6] Further, while epic recounts events in the nation's heroic or normative past, the recollection of these great events nevertheless is reshaped using the structures and patterns of traditional myth;[7] epic action takes place in both the human and divine spheres. "Everything in the *Iliad* takes place twice," notes Cedric Whitman, "once on

3. A colophon records the dictation of a tablet of the Baʿl cycle; see F. M. Cross, "Prose and Poetry in the Mythic and Epic Texts from Ugarit," *HTR* 67 (1974): 1, n. 1.

4. See Roman Jakobson's programmatic essay "Grammatical Parallelism and Its Russian Facet," *Language* 42 (1966): 399–429, reprinted in *Language in Literature,* ed. Krystyna Pomorska and Stephen Rudy (Cambridge: Belknap Press, Harvard University Press, 1987), 145–179. Cf. also William Whallon, *Formula, Character, and Context* (Cambridge: Center for Hellenic Studies and Harvard University Press, 1969), 117–173, and Stephen Geller, *Parallelism in Early Hebrew Poetry, HSM* 20 (Missoula, Mont.: Scholars Press, 1979).

5. See U. Cassuto's remarkable early studies, "Parallel Words in Hebrew and Ugaritic" and "The Israelite Epic," in *Biblical and Oriental Studies,* vol. 2 (Jerusalem: Magnes, 1975), 60–109; and the monumental collection edited by Loren Fisher, *Ras Shamra Parallels,* Analecta Orientalia 49–50 (Rome: Pontifical Biblical Institute, 1972). On the transition from oral to written tradition in Mesopotamia, see Thorkild Jacobsen, "Oral to Written," in *Societies and Languages of the Ancient Near East: Studies in Honor of I. M. Diakonoff,* ed. M. A. Dandamayev et al. (Warminster: Aris and Phillips, 1982), 129–137.

6. Whitman, *Homer and the Heroic Tradition,* 17.

7. See Albert B. Lord, *The Singer of Tales* (Cambridge: Harvard University Press, 1964), 141–197, and his more recent paper "Interlocking Mythic Patterns in Beowulf," in *Old English Literature in Context,* ed. John D. Niles (Suffolk: D. S. Brewer, 1981), 137–178.

earth, and once in the timeless world of deity."[8] Israel's epic traditions and narrative poetry bear these same epic characters. The search for the "historical nucleus" of early Hebrew tradition by historical critics has paralleled the efforts of Homeric critics in seeking actual historical events lurking behind the *Iliad,* with not dissimilar results. The role of the divine in Homer and in Israelite epic is comparable, given the peculiarity of Israel's preoccupation with only one god. Theomachy so structurally essential to the *Iliad* is found in Israelite traditional literature very rarely. Further, Greek epic did not play the central cultic role that we should ascribe to the Israelite epic cycle.

Certain other features of Homeric epic will be useful to mention in anticipation of our turning to an examination of Hebrew epic sources. Martin Nilsson initiated a new phase in Homeric studies in demonstrating that the epic preserved—alongside later accretions—elements of Mycenaean culture, its mythology, including archaic divine epithets, its social and political structures and customs, its military practices and accoutrements, its topography.[9] His conclusion, that the roots of Greek epic tradition and Greek mythology were no younger in origin than Late Bronze Age Greece, has been nuanced and qualified in subsequent research, but it can no longer be questioned.[10] Cedric Whitman, writing from the perspective of the Parry-Lord school, expresses himself as follows: "Bardic memory, embalmed in formulae, could keep the general outlines of a culture clear; and though factual details and history in a modern sense were never its chief concerns, whenever such were relevant to the pattern of spiritual reconstruction, they might survive with surprising accuracy. . . . For all its conflations, confusions, and montages, epic has given us a picture of Mycenaean reality, corroborated and refined, rather than denied, by increasing historical knowledge."[11]

8. Whitman, *Homer and the Heroic Tradition,* 248.

9. Nilsson, *The Mycenaean Origin of Greek Mythology,* and Martin P. Nilsson, *Homer and Mycenae* (London: Methuen, 1933).

10. For contrasting perspectives on the extent of Mycenaean survivals, see Whitman, *Homer and the Heroic Tradition,* 17–45, and M. Finley, *The World of Odysseus,* rev. ed. (New York: Viking, 1978). A more cautious approach is found in G. Kirk, "The Homeric Poems as History," in *Cambridge Ancient History* 2.2 (Cambridge: At the University Press, 1975), 820–850.

11. Whitman, *Homer and the Heroic Tradition,* 44 f. Compare the broader discussion of Jan Vansina, *Oral Tradition as History* (Madison: University of Wisconsin Press, 1985), 120–123, where he refutes the contention of J. Goody that "the corpus of tradition constantly changes and cannot correspond to a past reality." He observes (p. 25) that "some epics can be quite old. Thus the epic of Jaziya known from Jordan to Algeria is still told. It refers to the invasion of the Banū Hilāl in 1049–53 into Tunisia, and is mentioned by the historian Ibn Khaldun."

Homeric epic did not arise as an "original" effort of a single bard. The work of Milman Parry renders both the analyst and unitarian positions obsolete. The epic poet did not create his master work by piecing together disparate lays and traditions—a hero from this city or tribe, an enemy from another people or place, a heroic episode from one time or local tradition, another exploit from another time and place. Major epic cycles shaped in public performances took complex form early in the bardic tradition. The outline or plot of the epic was itself traditional. To be sure, various heroic songs, of which only a few survive, once circulated and were drawn upon, and later treatments of major epics by skillful minstrels added accretions and rich ornamentation to the epic core. One finds it difficult to believe that the *Iliad* was not the fullest and most artful performance of the Trojan epic—even in the absence of records of variant renderings. But Homer (or the Homeric school) did not compose the *Iliad* as one sews together a patchwork quilt. A coherent, complex tale drawn from long-formed epic tradition provided his framework and central plot. In Nilsson's words, "it appears that the background of Greek epos, i.e., the Trojan cycle in its chief features, the power of Mycenae, and the kingship of Mycenae, cannot possibly have come into existence through the joining together of minor chants and myths, but that it existed beforehand, being the cycle from which the minstrels took their subjects. A cycle of events with certain chief personages invariably appears in all the epic poetry of which we have a more definite knowledge than we have of Greek epics as the background from which episodes are taken and to which episodes are joined; it is a premise of epics, not their ultimate result."[12]

The epics of Homer have been called ecumenical or Panhellenic in intent and content.[13] In historical times, we know, they were recited by rhapsodists at the great festivals known as the *panegyreis*, notably the Panathenaea, to which pilgrims gathered from far and wide. There is good reason to believe that the original setting of oral presentation of Greek epic was precisely in such festivals, prehistoric forerunners of the Panathenaea, the Delia, and the Panionia.[14]

12. Nilsson, *The Mycenaean Origin of Greek Mythology*, 24 f.

13. On the element of Panhellenism in the evolution of the Homeric epic, see the paper of Gregory Nagy, "An Evolutionary Model for the Text Fixation of the Homeric Epos," in *Oral Traditional Literature: A Festschrift for Albert Bates Lord*, ed. J. M. Foley (Columbus, Ohio: Slavica, 1981), 390–393.

14. See M. P. Nilsson, *Geschichte der griechischen Religion* 1 (Munich: C. H. Beck, 1941), 778–782. The religious and cultic aspects of the Greek festivals have often been underestimated by classical scholars who have stressed their social, commercial, and entertainment aspects. Nilsson takes pains to correct this "Protestant view" which fails to perceive their easy union of religious service and "secular" activities. The

In recent years objections have been raised to my use of the term *epic* in defining the genre of Israel's earliest traditional literature.[15] Some of these objections have substance and require discussion. My choice of the designation *epic* draws on studies of Homeric epic, as we have seen, for aid in understanding the nature of early Israelite literature. There are, however, evident contrasts between Greek epic and early Israelite traditional literature.

In the comparative study of epic, particularly in the monumental work of the Chadwicks, epic has been defined as "heroic" narrative. That is, epic deals with heroes, princes, and kings and their followers, ordinarily military elite, and is preoccupied with the social conventions of a heroic age: courage, strength, loyalty, and vengeance.[16] It is true that the Homeric epics and, indeed, Western epic literature generally are "heroic," and I should concede immediately that early Israel was not a "heroic society" in the Homeric pattern. There are occasional heroic traits attributed to Abraham or Moses, Samson or David. But Israelite epic had only one hero, Yahweh of Hosts. One sings of his wrath, his mighty arm, his vengeance. He alone is the dragon slayer, the glorious king, the man of war, doer of wondrous deeds. Early Israelite society was egalitarian, and, there is good reason to believe, it developed in conscious opposition to the feudal structures of Canaan. Israel's "olden times" were not an age of human heroes and kings, and her soldiers were militiamen.

At the same time I believe it is permissible to define epic as the traditional narrative cycle of an age conceived as *normative,* the events of which give meaning and self-understanding to a people or nation. The Homeric epics shaped the Greek self-consciousness and gave normative expression to Hellenic mythology.[17] The Hebrew epic recounted crucial

---

reverse is probably true of scholarly reconstructions of the activities of Israel's pilgrimage festivals; probably the feasts in Israel as in Greece also took on many of the activities of fairs.

15. See especially Charles Conroy, "Hebrew Epic: Historical Notes and Critical Reflections," *Biblica* 61 (1980): 1–30. Cf. S. Talmon, "The 'Comparative Method' in Biblical Interpretation—Principles and Problems," in *SVT* 29 (Leiden: Brill, 1978), 352–356, and Robert Alter, "Sacred History and Prose Fiction," in *The Creation of Sacred Literature: Composition and Redaction of the Biblical Text,* ed. Richard E. Friedman (Berkeley: University of California Press, 1981), 7–24.

16. H. M. and N. K. Chadwick, *The Growth of Literature,* 3 vols. (Cambridge: At the University Press, 1932–40). See also C. M. Bowra, *Heroic Poetry* (London: Macmillan, 1961). The notion that epic reflects a "heroic age" is much more questionable, even in the West. Bowra has argued, correctly I think, that Spain had no heroic age, despite its creation of the magnificent *Cantar de mío Cid.*

17. See Finley, *The World of Odysseus,* 15.

events of developing nationhood and gave classical expression to Yahwistic religion.

The use of the term *epic* by biblical scholars and Orientalists has often been loose, making no distinction between a purely mythic cycle (like the Baʿl "epic" or *Enūma eliš*, the "creation epic," actually a narrative cosmogony without a human actor), and epic of the Homeric type, or of the type of Keret, with its preoccupation with traditional events in ordinary time and space. Thus Cassuto reconstructed what I should term a mythic cycle, and termed it the Israelite epic. I agree with those who reject such a conception of the Israelite epic, as will be apparent in the following pages. The alternative, however, is not to term the early traditional cycle of Israel *historical narrative.* Robert Alter has recognized the inadequacy of applying the unqualified term *historical* and, following the lead of Herbert Schneidau, speaks of the (early) biblical narrative as "historical prose fiction" or "fictionalized history." I find such terms both misleading and condescending.

The term *fiction* is chosen to point to the nonhistorical features of the narrative, presumably, but it suggests that the composer of Israelite traditional narrative chose to "write" what would look like historiography, but composed fiction in such a guise. I do not believe his intent was to compose history, or to compose "fiction," or to compose one under the guise of the other. I believe he was seeking to sing of Israel's past using traditional themes, the common stuff of generations of singers and tellers of tales. His story, prose or poetry (see below), dealt with the interactions of Yahweh and Israel in the normative past. The historian, even one given to fictionalizing, does not make a deity his main character. The creator of fiction who wishes "to move away from the world of myth" does not make free use of such mythic themes in shaping his "historicized fiction." The term *fiction,* like *history,* is anachronistic when applied to Israel's national story, and derives—to use Ivan Engnell's strong language—from an arrogant *interpretatio europaeica moderna.* Fiction is invention. Cedric Whitman observed that "there is no evidence at all that the poet of the *Iliad* invented a single character or episode in his whole poem."[18] Gregory Nagy speaks with more nuance: "To my mind there is no question, then, about the poet's freedom to say accurately what he means. What he means, however, is strictly regulated by tradition. The poet has no intention of saying anything untraditional. In fact, the poet's inherited conceit is that he has it in his power to recover the exact words that tell what men did and said in the Heroic Age."[19] A simi-

18. Whitman, *Homer and the Homeric Tradition,* 14.

19. G. Nagy, *The Best of the Achaeans* (Baltimore: Johns Hopkins University Press, 1979), 3. Nagy also comments here (§ 6n) on multiforms in traditions and their legitimacy.

lar assertion could be made of the narrator of Israel's national epic. He received a well-shaped and articulated complex of narrative traditions and recast, elaborated, even transformed it.[20] There was, as in the case of Homer, a powerful creative element in his artistry. However, fictional "invention" is the wrong expression to use in describing the essential activity of the traditional poet or storyteller.

I shall continue to use the term *epic*, defining it to include the following elements, which apply equally to Homeric epic and early Israelite traditional narrative:

1. oral composition in formulae and themes of a traditional literature,
2. narrative in which acts of god(s) and men form a double level of action,
3. a composition describing traditional events of an age conceived as normative,
4. a "national" composition, especially one recited at pilgrimage festivals.

II

The partition of the sources of the Pentateuch according to the Documentary Hypothesis posited four major sources: the Yahwist (J), and the Elohist (E), old traditional documents, Deuteronomic tradition (D) composed largely in the seventh century B.C.E. and re-edited in the Exile, and the Priestly document (P) of Exilic date.[21] Our interest here is pri-

20. Y. H. Yerushalmi makes the point simply: "That biblical historiography is not 'factual' in the modern sense is too self-evident to require extensive comment. By the same token, however, its poetic or legendary elements are not fictions in the modern sense either. For people in ancient times these were legitimate and sometimes inevitable modes of historical perceptions and interpretations" (*Zakhor: Jewish History and Jewish Memory* [Seattle: University of Washington Press, 1982], 13).

21. I do not wish to answer here at length recent assaults on the Documentary Hypothesis as it had developed more or less consensus in scholarly studies from Wellhausen and Gunkel to the Alt school (including Martin Noth and Gerhard von Rad) of the last generation. My own understanding of documents of the Tetrateuch, and their transmission and editorial history, was sketched out in *CMHE* and further elaborated in the first version of the present essay published in 1983. In the same year John van Seters published his *In Search of History: Historiography in the Ancient World and the Origins of Biblical History* (New Haven: Yale University Press, 1983), in which he begins his serious and elaborate attack on the older views of the Pentateuch sources, followed up in two volumes, *Prologue to History: The Yahwist as Historian in Genesis* (Louisville: Westminster–John Knox, 1992) and *The Life of Moses: The Yahwist as Historian in Exodus–Numbers* (Louisville: Westminster-John Knox, 1994). I had not seen the first of these volumes when writing in 1983, nor did van Seters—evidently—know of my essay. His view that analogies between JE (his Yahwist) and Greek epic are less impressive than the analogies with Greek historians, notably Herodotus of the fifth century B.C.E., is unconvincing.

marily with the Tetrateuch (Genesis–Numbers), which seems to have escaped *systematic* editing or expansion by the Deuteronomistic school. I have argued at length that the Priestly materials of the Tetrateuch never existed in the form of an independent narrative source; rather the Priestly Work must be seen as a systematic reworking of the traditional

---

He dates the Yahwist—later than D and the Deuteronomistic History—in the Exilic period. He regards the Yahwist as a writer, composing a history, complete and unseamed, alongside the slightly later Herodotus and Thucydides. He sets aside all evidence of the oral background of much of the Yahwist and the oral origin of the archaic poetry of the Pentateuch. He ignores the evidence of the linguistic typology of grammar and lexicon as developed by David A. Robertson ("Linguistic Evidence in the Dating of Early Hebrew Poetry" [Ph.D. diss., Yale University, 1966]), Robert Polzin (*Late Biblical Hebrew: Toward an Historical Typology of Biblical Hebrew Prose*, HSM 12 [Missoula, Mont.: Scholars Press, 1976]), and especially Avi Hurvitz.

It is too bad that Hurvitz' *byn lšwn llšwn: ltwldwt lšwn hmqr' bymy byt šny* (Jerusalem: Magnes Press, 1972) has not been translated. But his work is available in English in such studies as "The Evidence of Language in Dating the Priestly Code: A Linguistic Study in Technical Idioms and Terminology," *RB* 81 (1974): 24–56; *A Linguistic Study of the Relationship between the Priestly Source and the Book of Ezekiel: A New Approach to an Old Problem, CRB* 20 (Paris: Gabalda, 1982); and recently "Terms and Epithets Relating to the Jerusalem Temple Compound in the Book of Chronicles: The Linguistic Aspect," in *Pomegranates and Golden Bells: Studies in Biblical, Jewish, and Near Eastern Ritual, Law, and Literature in Honor of Jacob Milgrom*, ed. D. P. Wright, D. N. Freedman, and Avi Hurvitz (Winona Lake, Ind.: Eisenbrauns, 1995), 165–183.

Van Seters also refuses to take seriously other results of the typological sciences, which produce far more objective evidence than theorizing on the basis of questionable analogies. There are the typologies of prosodic forms and canons (see chapter 7 below), of orthography, of narrative genres. These must be dealt with. Van Seters continues to date the Yahwist after the fashion of the old literary critics who had not learned to deal with the problems of the transmission of traditional literatures which undergo major editing—by searching for the latest reference or anachronisms, for example, to the expression "Ur of the Chaldees." This may point to nothing more than the late editorial updating, or even an explicating gloss. As I discuss in chapter 8 below, the biblical scrolls from Qumrân have shown the existence not only of textual families but of editorial activity on a scale not imagined before. To repeat, we should avoid the blunder of dating by the latest elements in a traditional literary document which passed at least in part from oral to written form, as well as passed through generations of editors, redactors, and copyists. A document like the Yahwist must be dated by searching out its basic political program and social function of the document, not by the isolation of late accretions. See the review of Van Seters' *Prologue to History* by Richard Elliott Friedman, *BR* 9 (1993): 12–16, and rejoinders in *BR* 10 (1994): 40–44; cf. the review of Thomas L. Thompson, *CBQ* 57 (1995): 579–580.

Reviews of recent literature on the Pentateuch may be found in J. Blenkinsopp, *The Pentateuch: An Introduction to the First Five Books of the Bible* (New York: Doubleday, 1992), 1–30; Anthony F. Campbell and Mark A. O'Brian, *Sources of the Pentateuch: Texts, Introduction, Annotations* (Minneapolis: Fortress Press, 1993); E. Otto, "Kritik der

sources, JE, framed and reconstructed, and, at points of special interest, greatly expanded by Priestly lore of diverse date, completed in the course of the Exile.[22]

The pre-Priestly sources, the Yahwist and Elohist, JE, are the focus of our interest. They recount the events that brought old Israel into being. The outline of this history is roughly the same in each source: the call of the patriarchs, the entry into Egypt, the victory at the sea, the formation of the covenanted league at Sinai-Horeb, and the march to the land promised to the fathers. Close analysis of variant forms of tradition as well as assessment of independent elements in each source make clear that neither source was derived from the other. Rather, one must conclude that the two rest on an older basic traditional cycle. Martin Noth has labeled this basis of the JE sources the *Grundlage;* Otto Procksch early proposed a happier designation, the *Ursage.*[23] I prefer to speak of J and E as variant forms of an older, largely poetic epic cycle, and hence to term JE "epic sources." In their present form, that is, in the form revised and presented in the P Work, they consist of prose narrative, interlarded with poetic fragments and occasionally independent poetic units, especially at crucial points in the narrative. It is not impossible that the epic cycle in Israel was composed in a style in which prose narrative dominated but at climactic moments utilized poetic composition. It is a style widely distributed in oral epic literatures and indeed characterized the

---

Pentateuchkomposition," *Theologische Rundschau* 60 (1995): 163–191. Of special interest also are Richard Elliott Friedman, *Who Wrote the Bible?* (New York: Summit Books, 1987); Robert Coote and David Ord, *The Bible's First History* (Philadelphia: Fortress Press, 1989); Theodore Hiebert, *The Yahwist's Landscape* (New York: Oxford University Press, 1996); and Iain W. Provan, "Ideologies, Literary and Critical: Reflections on Recent Writing on the History of Israel," *JBL* 114 (1995): 585–606; Baruch Halpern, "What They Don't Know Won't Hurt Them: Genesis 6–9," in *Fortunate the Eyes That See: Essays in Honor of David Noel Freedman,* ed. Astrid B. Beck, A. H. Bartelt, P. R. Raabe, and C. A. Franke (Grand Rapids, Mich.: Eerdmans, 1995), 16–34; J. Blenkinsopp, "P and J in Genesis 1:1–15," in *Fortunate the Eyes That See,* 1–15; and R. S. Hendel, "Tangled Plots in Genesis," in *Fortunate the Eyes That See,* 35–51.

22. *CMHE,* 293–325. Cf. J. A. Emerton, "The Priestly Writer in Genesis," *JTS* 39 n.s. (1988): 381–400. See also Hurvitz, "The Evidence of Language in Dating the Priestly Code," 24–56; Hurvitz, *A Linguistic Study of the Relationship between the Priestly Source and the Book of Ezekiel;* Moshe Weinfeld, "Social and Cultic Institutions in the Priestly Source against Their Ancient Near Eastern Background," in *Proceedings of the Eighth World Congress of Jewish Studies,* Panel Sessions, Bible and Hebrew Language (Jerusalem, 1983), 95–129; and Israel Knohl, "The Priestly Torah versus the Holiness School: Sabbath and the Festivals," *HUCA* 58 (1987): 65–117.

23. See M. Noth, *A History of Pentateuchal Traditions,* trans. B. W. Anderson (Englewood Cliffs, N.J.: Prentice-Hall, 1972), 38–41; and for a fuller history of the discussion, see Conroy, "Hebrew Epic."

pre-Islamic epic tales of the *ʾAyyām el-ʿarab.*[24] There are some reasons, however, to postulate that the Hebrew epic continued in the tradition of the older Canaanite epic singers, that is, that much was orally composed in poetry. We have noted above that the oral formulae and themes of Late Bronze Age epics persist in early Hebrew poetry, particularly in the archaic poetry of the Pentateuch. The same prosodic styles, "impressionistic" parallelism, repetitive or climactic parallelism, and fundamental verse types mark old Canaanite and early Hebrew poetry.[25] Further, as has been often observed, the subject matter of the Keret Epic—the securing of an heir, a promise of seed given in a revelation of ʾEl, an older son passed over in favor of a younger son—has vivid parallels in the patriarchal cycle in Genesis.

Further, if, as I shall argue, the epic was a creation of the league and had a special function in the cultus of its pilgrim shrines, we expect its form to have been poetic. There can be no question of early Israel eschewing poetry as somehow inappropriate as a vehicle for recounting the mighty acts of Yahweh or Israel's early times. We possess lyric poems with strong narrative content in the Song of the Sea (Exodus 15) and the Song of Deborah (Judges 5).[26] In both instances we possess side-by-side prose narrative accounts (Exodus 14 and Judges 4), and in both instances the poetry is earlier, the prose secondary and derivative. We see the process of prosaizing poetic composition before our eyes.[27] The language that describes the theophany at Sinai in the prose of JE and P obviously derives from the poetic images of the storm theophany, objectified and concretized (or hypostatized) and in part misunderstood, especially by the P tradent.[28]

Even more instructive perhaps is the parallelistic diction and glimpses of poetry which lie immediately beneath the surface of many passages of prose in the epic sources.[29] Let me illustrate with a single example—

24. See recently, Ilse Lichtenstadter, "History in Poetic Garb in Ancient Arabic Literature," *Harvard Ukrainian Studies* 3–4 (1979–80): 559–568.

25. See F. M. Cross and D. N. Freedman, *Studies in Ancient Yahwistic Poetry,* 2nd ed. (Grand Rapids, Mich.: Eerdmans; Livonia, Mich.: Dove Booksellers, 1997) including bibliography (114–121); and chaps. 6 and 7 below.

26. I am not claiming that these two songs are "epics in miniature." They are lyric pieces.

27. See the paper of Baruch Halpern in *The Poet and the Historian: Essays in Literary and Historical Biblical Criticism,* ed. R. E. Friedman (Chico, Calif.: Scholars Press, 1983), 41–73.

28. See my discussion in *CMHE,* 147–177.

29. U. Cassuto has collected examples of "epic style" in *Biblical and Oriental Studies,* vol. 2. Moshe Weinfeld has called my attention to formulaic poetry which occurs

not ordinarily cited—of prose which, when stripped of a few prose particles, becomes exquisite poetry in epic style: Exodus 19:3–6.

kh tʾmr lbyt yʿqb	Thus you shall say to the house of Jacob,
tgd lbny yśrʾl	Make known to the children of Israel,
rʾytm mʿśy bmṣrym	You have seen my acts against the Egyptians,
wʾśʾkm ʿl knpy nšr	How I lifted you up on eagle's wings,
wʾbʾkm bhr ʾly	And brought you to myself in the mount.
ʾm tšmʿw bqwly	If you hearken to my voice,
wšmrtm bryty	And keep my covenant:
thyw ly sglh	You shall become my special possession;
ʾtm ly gwy qdš	You shall be my holy nation,
wmmlkt khnym	And a kingdom of priests.

Hermann Gunkel, who knew nothing of the Canaanite epics and thought in terms of short traditional units, recognized that the older form of many of these "*Sagen*," as he called them, were composed in poetry, and he commented that "the older and strictly rhythmical form, which we must suppose to have been sung, would differ from the later prose form, which was recited, as does the ancient German epic from the *Volksbuch*."[30]

---

not only in narrative texts in Genesis but also in Ps. 72: 11 and 17 (the latter verse reconstructed in part on the basis of the Old Greek):

wyštḥww lw kl mlkym
kl gwym yʿbdwhw

which may be compared with Gen. 27:29:

yʿbdwk ʿmym
wyštḥw lk lʾmym

and:

wnbrkw bk kl mšpḥt hʾdmh
kl gwym yʾšrhw

which may be compared with Gen. 12:3:

wʾbrkh mbrkyk wmqllk ʾʾr
wytbrkw bw mšpḥwt hʾdmh.

30. H. Gunkel, *The Legends of Genesis,* trans. W. H. Carrutti (New York: Schocken, 1964), 38 ff. These comments are from the introduction to his *Genesis* of 1901. In his third edition (1910), he adds a harsh critique of E. Sievers' *Metrische Studien,* vol. 2, an attempt to scan the whole of Genesis in anapaestic meter. Gunkel correctly rejected Sievers' tour de force and properly insists that the bulk of the narrative is prose. He also adds, in excessive reaction to Sievers, I believe, that those materials first cast into poetry, later given prose form, may have been limited to myths and possibly to

The phenomenon of oral poetic epic being converted to oral prose epic, or to written "historical narrative," is easily illustrated in the history of epic literatures. We shall choose a single instance of each.

There exists in Russian oral literature a type of oral prose narrative called the *pobyvalshchina,* derived from the *byliny* (i.e., Russian epic verse) of the Kiev Cycle. To quote N. K. Chadwick: "Although the metre has disappeared for the most part, the *pobyvalshchiny* frequently falls into a form of rhythmic prose . . . and their poetic origin can even be traced, and occasionally reconstituted where the conservative phraseology has preserved whole lines intact from the poetic original to phrase lengths in the prose version corresponding to the line length of the *byliny.*"[31]

A second example is found in Spanish epic literature. Menéndez Pidal and his followers were successful in reconstituting substantial portions of lost Spanish epics preserved in medieval chronicles. Merle E. Simmons has described the circumstances as follows:

> In some cases a chronicler, using traditional songs as source materials for the writing of serious history, and apparently working in some instances with a manuscript of an epic poem before him (probably like the manuscript we have of the *Cantar de mío Cid*), rendered long poetic passages into prose that not infrequently still has lines that scan like poetry, retains unsuppressed rhymes, and in general preserves a lively and dramatic style that makes such passages stand out from the less sprightly narrative that surrounds them.[32]

My argument is not that there is a natural evolution from poetic epic to prose epic. Rather, I am observing that the recasting of poetic epic in prose narrative and indeed its use as a source for the composition of historical narrative is not an isolated occurrence in Israel; the techniques used here to reconstruct Israel's epic have precise analogies in literary scholarship.

The history of Pentateuchal studies from DeWette to Wellhausen has striking parallels to the history of Homeric studies from Friedrich August Wolf to Wilamowitz. A similar rationalistic, literary-critical set of presuppositions informed analysis and dictated conclusions giving rise to disintegration of the traditional complex into fragments, and the dating of traditional elements by the latest discernible anachronisms in the written sources. I have often wondered if Julius Wellhausen's

---

sanctuary legends. See *Genesis,* 7th ed. (Göttingen: Vandenhoeck and Ruprecht, 1966), xxvii–xxx.

31. *The Growth of Literature,* 2: 165.

32. See his paper, "The Spanish Epic," in *Heroic Epic and Saga,* ed. Felix J. Oinas (Bloomington: Indiana University Press, 1978), esp. 222 and references.

change of title of his great work from *Geschichte Israels* (1878) to *Prolegomena zur Geschichte Israels* (1885) was owing less to a desire for accuracy than a subtle claim to parallel rank with Wolf's *Prolegomena ad Homerum* (1795).[33] Hermann Gunkel was to surpass even Wellhausen in his impact on Pentateuchal studies. Unlike Wellhausen, who judged Pentateuchal traditions to reflect more or less on events and lore contemporary with their final authors J and E, Gunkel recognized that the "*Sage* materials" had a long prehistory in oral transmission. Influenced strongly by the classical labors of Eduard Norden (*Die antike Kunstprosa* I [1889]), he introduced *Gattungsforschung* into the study of Pentateuchal narrative. He regarded the undeveloped field of "literary history," *Literaturgeschichte,* to be above all the history of literary units and genres.[34] His analysis of the oral prehistory of the patriarchal legends led him to conclude that the period of their formation closed by about 1200 B.C.E. On the other hand, Gunkel looked upon J and E as collectors of individual units of tradition, and his vision of the final form of these sources was not different from Wilamowitz's conviction that the *Iliad* in its received form was a "wretched patchwork."[35]

Gunkel in developing his form-critical methods was concerned above all with isolating primitive units of tradition. Owing to the intellectual currents of his time—compounded of Romanticism, evolutionism, and German academic idealism—he assumed that complexes of tradition and complicated individual traditions were late; the simpler the tradition, or *Sage,* the closer it was to the primitive unit. "Das älteste hebräische Volkslied umfasst nur eine oder etwa zwei Langzeilen; mehr vermochten die damaligen Menschen nicht zu übersehen."[36] And he quotes with approval Wellhausen's assertion that "die Überlieferung im Volksmund kennt nur einzelne Geschichten."[37] The absurdity of such methodological assumptions is sufficiently shown simply by counting the lines of the Baʿl cycle, or of the Keret and Aqhat epics of Ugarit, not to mention the 15,000 lines of the *Iliad.* Gunkel speaks of the buildup of cycles of saga, but in his view each move toward complexity is taken in a cultural vacuum, one unit spliced to a second, the two to a third until, *mirabile dictu,* a complex, coherent narrative emerges like a mag-

33. One notes that his *Israelitische und jüdische Geschichte* (1894), the completion of his *Prolegomena,* was dedicated to his colleague Wilamowitz as a *Gegengabe.*

34. See, e.g., his "Die Grundprobleme der israelitische Literaturgeschichte," *Reden und Aufsätze* (Göttingen: Vandenhoeck und Ruprecht, 1913), 29–38.

35. Whitman, *Homer and the Heroic Tradition,* 2.

36. "The oldest Hebrew folk songs were made up of only one or perhaps two lines in length." Gunkel, "Die Grundprobleme der israelitische Literaturgeschichte," 34.

37. "Oral tradition knew only single stories." H. Gunkel, *Genesis,* xxxii, n. 1.

pie's nest built from bits and tatters brought from far and wide. There is in Gunkel's application of his method no reckoning with a long and continuous tradition of epic singers and epic cycles, mythic cycles and hierophants. In fact, epic plots and bundles of themes, mythic patterns, and indeed tales sung based on memorable events, throughout the age of epic composition, existed as a background for each new performance of an epic tale and furnished materials for shaping emerging new cycles of epic tradition. Complex traditions and units of tradition, in my view, always existed side by side. Units of tradition may have existed independently in some instances; equally often they came into being only as an element in a complex, a gestalt; sometimes a "unit" was a loose fragment shifted from one bundle of themes to another, but, like a particle in modern physics, it had no existence except in one complex relationship or another. Moreover, if one finds short and long forms of a given tradition or epic tale, it does not follow necessarily that the short is older, the long secondary. It may be that the epic nucleus has gained secondary accretions. But singers of epic poetry also could expand or contract their songs to fit circumstance and occasion. Brief prose summaries of Israelite epic have sometimes been described as archaic on the grounds that they are short and omit secondary elements. Such (for example, G. von Rad's "short historical credos") are highly suspect; to be preferred, if available, are orally composed poetic materials recounting epic themes (e.g., the Song of the Sea). I should find it surprising indeed if Israel's old epic cycle in its oral presentations did not rival or even exceed in length the preserved Yahwistic source.[38]

The legacy of Gunkel survives in lively form in contemporary tradition-criticism. There has been no revolution in biblical criticism comparable to that in Homeric studies initiated by Milman Parry. A number of scholars have engaged in formula analysis (Robert Culley, William Whallon, Richard Whitaker, William Watters, Stephen Geller, to name a few). But aside from reexamination of some of the early narrative poems, notably the Song of the Sea and the Song of Deborah, little has been done to analyze early epic narrative in the light of the new per-

38. The notion that the court of David and Solomon was incapable of producing a written work like the Yahwist must simply be discarded in the view of epigraphical data. The national Hebrew script diverged from the earlier linear Phoenician precisely in the tenth century B.C.E., and indeed by the ninth century had become a facile cursive, as is evidenced by ninth and early eighth-century scripts from Kuntillet ʿAjrûd, and the recently published ostraca from the court of Yehoash/ʾĀšyāhû of Judah (ca. 835–796). See P. Bordreuil, Felice Israel, and Dennis Pardee, "Deux ostraca paléo-hébreux de la collection Sh. Moussäeff," *Semitica* 46 (1996): 76 and pls. 7–8.

I should not assign the long Joseph story to the Yahwist, and indeed its relation to the epic sources is problematical.

spectives afforded by Homeric studies and comparative studies of orally composed epic.[39]

The new perspectives offer little aid in attacking the problem of the actual historical content of a given epic tradition or complex. The degree of shaping given to historical memories by traditional themes and mythic motifs varies widely in epic material, and the extent of distortion in a given instance is not easy to gauge. On the other hand, the extreme skepticism about the ability of the ancient memory to preserve ancient elements of tradition—a recent scholar still asserts that "folk memory" at most spans two generations—is now shown to be without warrant. Epic tradition in particular is able to preserve the color and the substance of old social and institutional forms as well as early cultic and religious lore. Alt's instinct that certain epithets of deity embedded in Genesis were extremely archaic is now reinforced by an understanding of the mechanism that carries precisely such lore over centuries of time, and it is confirmed in several instances by their appearance in texts of the second millennium. In view of the atlas of Mycenaean Greece preserved in the so-called Catalog of Ships cited in the *Iliad,* it is no longer surprising that the patriarchal traditions of Genesis attach the fathers to authentic Canaanite cities of the Middle and Late Bronze Ages, and not to the newly established Israelite towns founded in the hill country at the beginning of the Iron Age.[40]

An understanding of the mechanisms in the transmission of epic poetry also clarifies and complicates questions of the date of an epic cycle and its accretions. In the Tetrateuch this problem is further complicated by the literary reworking and expansion of epic traditions by the Priestly tradent in the sixth century. Older approaches, dating materials by their latest accretions or by anachronisms, yield monarchic or even Exilic dates for the epic sources, and occasionally a scholar will still solemnly assert an Exilic date for the Yahwist. The Trojan cycle evidently began to assume complex epic form not long after the events of which it sings took place, sufficiently early that some authentic memories of the Mycenaean Age were preserved in bardic tradition. It acquired addi-

39. Since these lines were written, two important studies have attempted to repair this deficiency: Howard Neil Wallace, *The Eden Narrative, HSM* 32 (Atlanta: Scholars Press, 1985), and Ronald Stephen Hendel, *The Epic of the Patriarch: The Jacob Cycle and the Narrative Tradition of Canaan and Israel, HSM* 42 (Atlanta: Scholars Press, 1987). Both monographs originated in dissertations directed by the writer with the advice of the late Albert Lord.

40. The list includes Shechem, Hebron, Jerusalem, Dothan, Gerar (Tell Abu Ḥureirah—to be taken as both a city and country), and Bethel. Special problems exist, which need not occupy us here, with Beersheba, and, of course, with the Cities of the Plain. In certain instances a late name is applied to an old city.

tional shaping and accretions in the course of the so-called Dark Age, and in the Geometric Age in which it reached written form. The problems of dating Israel's epic tradition are no simpler. Our use of Homeric analogies obviously is qualified by the long era of literary recasting of biblical epic traditions which has no real counterpart in later recensional activity in the transmission of the text of Homer. On the other hand, Palestine throughout the Late Bronze and Early Iron Ages was a literate society, with alphabetic writing, and in the Late Bronze Age several systems of writing were in use. Thus one must reckon always with the possibility in Israel, as in Ugarit, of written as well as oral transmission of epic texts. In any case, one must take into account the fact that in the nature of epic composition the archaic and the late are intertwined and that the distance in time between the old and the new may vary from generations to centuries.[41]

Perhaps it will be useful to illustrate old and new approaches to oral narrative by examination of a central, climactic portion of the Israelite epic: the Exodus and the revelation at Sinai—the victory at the sea and the creation of the covenant cult at the mount. The epic sources present these events as sequent; indeed the victory of Israel's divine warrior at the sea is preceded by the revelation of his name at the mount and his call for the deliverance of nascent Israel, and it provides the condition for the formation of the nation and its covenant institution—law and cult—at the mount of revelation. In the Song of the Sea, in my opinion the oldest of Israel's narrative poems, the episode at the sea is recounted: Yahweh defeats the Egyptians by casting them into the sea by stirring up the water with the blast of his nostrils—the storm wind; he leads them to his desert encampment; there follows then allusion to the conquest, the crossing of Jordan, and finally to the establishment of the people in Yahweh's mount, the building of his sanctuary, and his eternal rule over the people he had "created." Here the establishment of the people and the cultus in the land terminates the sequence of events initiated at the sea. In the prose epitome of the epic themes in Joshua 24, these central events receive much the same treatment, victory at the sea, the march through the desert, the conquest of the land, and finally formation of a covenant cultus at Shechem, the occasion for the recitation.

Now how does one analyze these refractions of the epic of Israel? One approach, articulated most effectively by G. von Rad and Martin Noth, seeks out units of tradition. One nucleus is the exodus-conquest (or settlement), a second is the revelation at Sinai. Noth adds a problem-

41. Jeffrey Tigay in his study *The Evolution of the Gilgamesh Epic* (Philadelphia: University of Pennsylvania Press, 1982), furnishes much material illustrating conservatism and innovation in the transmission of epic.

atic "Leading in the Wilderness." Each of these in origin is unrelated to the other and stems from an independent cult. The "historical" theme, exodus-conquest, arises in one festival at one tribal shrine; the revelation theme with its law and theophany arises in another festival and shrine. The "kerygmatic" events are contrasted with law and covenant—Gospel versus Law imported into ancient Israel—and stitched together only by the Yahwist (von Rad) or by G (Noth). One observes that "theophany" must be attached to a single theme; theophanic elements in the battle of the Divine Warrior must be secondary, or the theophanic motif at the mountain holy place must be secondary. Why? Because one is simpler than two, and hence prior.

An alternate, and I believe superior, approach is open, at least, to the possibility that both the battle at the sea and the covenant-making and establishment of divine rule belong to a sequence of events or bundle of themes narrated in the primitive epic cycle. That the pattern existed before the elaboration of units in the Israelite epic—and indeed shaped the selection of events to be narrated—can be argued on the basis of the myth of the Divine Warrior from Ugarit, as well as from Hebrew poetry early and late. There are two, paired movements in the drama: (1) The Divine Warrior goes forth to battle against his enemy (Yamm [Sea], Leviathan, Môt [Death]). At his appearance, brandishing his weapons, nature convulses and the heavens languish. He conquers. (2) The victorious god returns to take up kingship and is enthroned on his holy mountain. He cries aloud (thunders) from his temple, and nature responds to his fructifying appearance in the storm. His guests feast at his sanctuary and kingship is established or confirmed in heaven and earth.

The pattern has integrity. Theophany in "judgment" is paired with theophany in "salvation." The cosmogonic battle is the ground for the establishment of the divine state, and on earth temple and kingship reflect the cosmic establishment. The cultic character of the pattern is manifest in its terminus: the festival. In this pattern is a unity of structure and meaning, grounded in the cult, which is destroyed if severed into units.

Epic also has a concrete social function; its oral performances were public, taking place in cultic or national festivals. As the Baʿl cycle served in some sense as an accompaniment to the New Year's festival, and as the Greek epic has its setting in the *panegyreis* in Greece, so the Israelite epic was a feature of league festivals. Always an aspect of these celebrations was the renewal of the league, the rearticulation of the identity of the community, the reinforcement of the unity of the people. In the Canaanite feudal state there was renewal of kingship—not merely a song of creation recited to inform the young or titillate the aesthetic sensibilities of the audience present. In Israel the covenant was renewed or confirmed—not merely a song of Yahweh's old glories sung to evoke nostalgia. Indeed, there is reason to believe that the epic events were reenacted in ritual procession preliminary to the covenant rites proper. Norman Gottwald, approaching from a very different philosophical framework, comes to similar conclusions: "What I simply cannot imagine," he writes, "is a cult in early Israel in which the people merely recited past actions of deity *without any present cultic-ideological rootage in theophany, covenant, and law* [italics in Gottwald's text]."[42]

III

In order to take first steps in the reconstruction of the Hebrew epic cycle, we must begin with the most palpable transformation of the tradition, the Yahwistic source.

The Yahwistic work is best described, I believe, as a propaganda work of the empire. In Genesis 15:7–12 and 17–18 there is a central Yahwistic passage in which archaic material is reworked in a fashion that reveals the Yahwist's intent and anticipates—in epic fashion—the denouement of the narrative. In the older level of the passage is recorded a covenant ceremony of typical primitive type: animals are cut up and fire passes among them, the Yahwist's version of the covenant with Abraham. The content of this covenant is specified as follows: "In that day Yahweh made a covenant with Abraham, saying, 'To your seed I have given this land from the river of Egypt to the great river, the River Euphrates.'"[43] In a sequence of Yahwistic passages, the promise to the patriarchs of seed and land gives structure to the patriarchal narrative. In Genesis 15, however, there is on the one hand old material presuming covenant forms, ordinarily not an interest of the Yahwist, and, on the other hand, a specification of the promise of the land conforming only to the boundaries of the Davidic and Solomonic empire. The Promised Land in late sources (P, Ezekiel) included only Canaan, that is, Cis-Jordan, and there is some evidence that older sources claimed the Egyptian province of Canaan, which included the Phoenician littoral, but not Transjordan.[44] In other words, in the structure of the Yahwistic epic, the promise to the fathers is fulfilled politically in the empire. The typology is, in effect, Abraham-David, rather than Abraham-Moses (the Priestly Work), or the older fulfillment in the conquest of the land.

42. See *CMHE*, 79–144, and N. K. Gottwald, *The Tribes of Yahweh* (Maryknoll, N.Y.: Orbis, 1979), 99.

43. For my view of the Abrahamic covenant, see *CMHE*, 265–273.

44. Cf. Y. Kaufmann, *The Religion of Israel* (Chicago: University of Chicago Press, 1960): 201 f.; *The Biblical Account of the Conquest of Palestine* (Jerusalem: Magnes Press, 1953), passim.

The typology "Abraham-David" has long been noted in the Yahwistic source. The juxtaposition of the revelation and promise of Genesis 15 with Genesis 14:18–24, the narrative of Abram's dealings with Jerusalem, is significant here. Abram is presented as acknowledging the succor of "'El Creator of Earth,"[45] an archaic epithet of 'El known from Late Bronze Age sources, as well as later, including an ostracon from eighth-century Jerusalem. His priest, Melchizedek, bearing a good Canaanite name, is pictured as king of Salem-Jerusalem. He blessed Abram by "El Creator of Earth" and received Abram's tithe. We need not concern ourselves with the origins of the story concerning the war with the eastern kings, in every way a unique element in patriarchal traditions. Rather, we are interested in the legitimation of a cult in Jerusalem and its evident function in legitimizing the national cult of David and Solomon.[46]

Unlike the Elohistic source, the Yahwist does not read prophecy (*sensu stricto*) back into ancient times. His tradition stems from an age before the height of the prophetic movement in the ninth century. Moreover, the Yahwist does not engage in polemics against Baʿlism, the chief issue in ninth-century prophetic circles.[47] His work is essentially pre-Prophetic in content. The Yahwist's work, unlike much of the lore he draws upon, is somewhat removed from direct cultic interest. He has transformed cultically formed tradition and poetry into "history" and prose—or this was his intent. G. von Rad has remarked perceptively, "The atmosphere which surrounds the Yahwistic declaration of faith is almost wholly devoid of cultic associations, a fact which must cause intense surprise to anyone who has followed our investigation from that extremely close association with the cultus which characterizes most of his materials, to the stage where they are fused together in the literary work of the Yahwist."[48] We must suppose that the Yahwist turns epic materials into his prose work at a time when Israel's cultic institutions, notably the covenant festivals of the league, in which the epic events were recited and enacted, had fallen into desuetude, and epic tradition thus loosened from its primary setting and function. The freeing of the epic from its cultic connection no doubt coincides with the establishment of the royal cultus of Solomon, and it is precisely in the age of Solomonic grandeur, coinciding with far-reaching changes in religious institutions, that

45. On the epithet, see *CMHE,* 15–16, 50–52.

46. Compare G. von Rad, *Genesis,* trans. J. Marks (Philadelphia: Westminster, 1961): 175 f.

47. Note the Elohistic lore in Exod. 32, which presumes a polemic against Bethel and its bull iconography.

48. G. von Rad, *The Problem of the Hexateuch and Other Essays,* trans. E. W. T. Dickens (New York: McGraw-Hill, 1966), 68.

we should expect the transformation of the old epic into a prose propaganda work of empire. Von Rad speaks of the Yahwist as "redolent of the untrammeled days of Solomon." And I agree. Its expansive faith in Yahweh's direction of history, its lack of any sense of crisis or foreboding, its wide-ranging interests, its freedom from polemic, all breathe the spirit of triumphant Israel in the days of empire. There are, obviously, anachronisms arising in days later than the united empire. But in a work transmitted and reworked in subsequent centuries, massively in the Exile, anachronisms and modernization are expected.

In remarking above on the dissolution of covenant forms and festivals and its reflection in the form of the Yahwist's composition, a further word should be said. In the patriarchal materials preserved in the Yahwist, he speaks more of the call or promise to the patriarch than of covenants entered into by the patriarch. In the Sinai narrative, the Yahwist to be sure includes the revelation at Sinai, and a torso of a Yahwistic decalogue survives.[49] The Elohist has been the primary source utilized in the P Work for reconstruction of the covenant ritual. This diminution in the Yahwist of covenant forms and language—if not their suppression—is a reflection of a specific royal ideology characteristic of the Solomonic establishment. I have argued elsewhere on the basis of quite different evidence that, with the transformation of David's kingdom into a full-fledged international power in the days of Solomon, kingship and cultus came under the influence of Canaanite monarchical institutions and ideology. The "Davidic covenant"—a dynastic codicil, so to speak, in Israel's covenant—became an unconditional, eternal decree of deity, the mount of Zion his eternal dwelling place. In Solomonic kingship the language of divine sonship became normative, covenantal language disused or reinterpreted. Covenant language and forms survived in the north, to judge from the Elohistic epic source. It is revived and reformed in the nostalgic Deuteronomistic Work, and in the archaizing Priestly Work.[50]

In sum, I argue that the Yahwistic epic is a prosaizing, propaganda work of the united monarchy, and specifically the program of Solomon to constitute an Oriental monarchy in the Canaanite pattern. The older epic, cut loose from the covenantal cultus of the tribal sanctuaries of the

49. Exod. 34:10, 14, 27 preserve a torso including the earliest form of two of the commandments. Intruded, however, is a ritual calendar (34:18–26), a variant of the prescriptions in 23:14–19, and the remaining portion of the decalogue displaced and lost. Presumably the lost portion showed less variation from later forms of the decalogue than the two commandments preserved in the fragment of the J decalogue, and thus was not repeated.

50. See *CMHE,* 219–265, 295–300; and chapter 1 above.

league, was shaped by the Yahwist for new institutions and new functions.[51]

I have not referred to the primeval history, Genesis 1–11. This cycle of tradition is firmly imprinted by the Yahwist and has no counterpart in extant Elohistic tradition.[52] J's traditions are old, and the Priestly tradent drew on primeval material which, on rare occasions, betrays poetic origins.[53]

I am not inclined, however, to believe that the creation and primeval accounts belonged to the earlier Israelite epic. Its prefixing to the patriarchal cycle is reminiscent of the prefixing of theogonies to the cosmogonic myths in *Enūma eliš,* Hesiod, and the third theogony of Sakkunyaton.[54] In any case, the primeval lore provides a universal setting for the central epic narrative and underscores the theme of Israel's universal destiny in the Yahwist's presentation of Israel's history. While such a theme may have been older, and creation stories obviously circulated in premonarchic Israel, its addition to the epic by the hand of the Yahwist, in imperial times, exquisitely fits the motivation and intent of his work.[55]

IV

The epic cycle of old Israel in its mature form was a creation of the Israelite league. It cannot be later than the epic sources of the early monarchy, notably the Yahwistic work from Solomonic times. At the core of the epic, as we have seen, is the divine victory at the sea and the formation of the league at Sinai: exodus and covenant. In archaic hymns, Yahweh marches from the southern mountains out to do battle and leads his redeemed people back to his mountain sanctuary (e.g., in Habakkuk

51. The P Work ends effectively with the death of Moses. While there are bits of Priestly lore—or temple documents reflecting Priestly language and ideology—in Joshua, Joshua like Judges, Samuel, and Kings was edited by the Deuteronomist, Dtr_1, and in the Exile by Dtr_2. It is part of the Deuteronomistic Work. Thus the Israelite epic is truncated in the P Work, in the Tetrateuch. Presumably some of the material in Joshua stems from epic tradition, but it is a moot question whether or not the epic sources JE can be isolated. On the problem, see the still useful comments of S. Mowinckel, *Tetrateuch—Pentateuch—Hexateuch* (Berlin: Topelmann, 1964).

52. For a contrary position, see S. Mowinckel, *The Two Sources of the Predeuteronomic History (JE) in Gen. 1–11* (Oslo: Norske Videnskaps-Akademi, 1937), and W. F. Albright's review article, *JBL* 53 (1939): 93–103.

53. Notably Gen. 1:27 and 7:11; cf. Cassuto, *Biblical and Oriental Studies,* 2: 79 f. and 103–109 on remains of "creation epic" traditions.

54. See my discussion below, chapter 4.

55. The case is eloquently argued by von Rad, *The Problem of the Hexateuch,* 63–67.

3:3–15; Exodus 15:1–18; Deuteronomy 33:2 and 26–29). The movement is expressed in ultimate brevity in the archaic formula of Holy War: "Arise Yahweh, let thine enemies be scattered, let thine adversaries flee before thee. Return Yahweh [with] the myriads, [ʾEl with] the thousands of Israel" (Numbers 10:35f.).[56] The exodus-Sinai pattern, however, was shaped to conform to the cultic requirements of the festivals in the pilgrimage sanctuaries in the land. The victory at the sea is extended, so to speak, to include the conquest of the land. The crossing of the sea is typologically identified with the crossing of the Jordan, an equation rendered easy by the poetic formula that pairs sea and river (in myth: Prince Sea, Judge River). In Psalm 114 the parallelism of the sea and Jordan is vividly expressed.[57] Cultic materials in Joshua 3–5 stemming from the shrine at Gilgal recapitulate the crossing of the sea, the setting up of twelve *maṣṣebôt* at Sinai, in a spring festival. The "march to the sanctuary" symbolizes both the crossing of the sea and the march to the desert mount, the crossing of Jordan, and the march of the conquest of the land.[58]

The Song of the Sea, our earliest hymn describing the epic battle, had its original setting in this cultic context: the march of Yahweh, leading his people through the desert, bringing them across the river to his "mountain" sanctuary. Exodus and conquest have thus become cultically fused themes. Similarly the mountain of God is identified with the shrines of the land where the covenant cultus was celebrated. This equation of covenant rites at Sinai with covenant rites in the land was recognized by Albrecht Alt and his school in their treatment of lore originating in the Shechem cult, notably Joshua 8:30–34 and 24:2–28 and Deuteronomy 27:(11–)15–16. Indeed, we may suppose that in the great pilgrimage festivals in the land, at Gilgal, Shechem, and—though we have little data—presumably also at other pilgrimage shrines: Shiloh, Bethel, Hebron, the ritual processions reenacting the march of victory and its reenactment and confirmation in covenant rites fused in cult the mount of God and the mount of the shrine in the land. Shrines, of course, were built on mountains, in fact, or in mythic identification of the shrine's platform with the cosmic mountain.[59] Finally, in transformations in later Israel, the "Holy Way" through the desert had as its goal and climax the feast on Zion.

In the epic cycles sung in the shrines of the land, there is thus a displacement, so to speak, of the Sinai tradition. In the JE reformulation

56. On the reconstruction of the verse, see the writer's comments, *CMHE,* 100.

57. See also Ps. 74:12–15.

58. See my detailed discussion, *CMHE,* 103–105.

59. See R. J. Clifford's excellent discussion, *The Cosmic Mountain in Canaan and in the Old Testament, HSM* 4 (Cambridge: Harvard University Press, 1972).

of the old epic, however, the southern mountain of revelation was restored in its primitive place and the covenant at Sinai intervenes between exodus and conquest. This reformulation, which involved combination of variant forms of the epic cycle, left seams in the narrative of the epic sources, exacerbated by the thorough reworking of the Sinai pericope by the Priestly tradent, for whom it was the climax of history.[60]

The survival of variant streams of epic tradition from the major sanctuaries of the era of the league is significant evidence of the character of politics and religion in early Israel. We have noted special traditions traceable to Shechem and Gilgal. Special epic lore also is preserved which can be derived from the cult of Shiloh, Bethel, and the pilgrimage shrine in the southern mountains: Sinai-Teman-Seʿir. In each case the traditions are welded to the themes of exodus and covenant. At Shiloh we hear of the "Ark of the Covenant of Yahweh of Hosts who is enthroned on the cherubim," a cult name of the ark, peculiarly associated with Shiloh, as persuasively argued by Eissfeldt,[61] and its Mushite priesthood bears Egyptian names. At Bethel, Jeroboam restored the bull iconography, by tradition (preserved in polemical attacks on the Bethel cult) created by Aaron himself at Sinai,[62] a tradition sufficiently archaic and established that it survived the handling of later Aaronid priests in the Priestly Work. Archaic poems—or poetic materials of early date reutilized in later hymns—preserve clear traditions of Yahweh of the southern mountains: Sinai/Seʿir/Paran, parallel names in the Blessing of Moses; Teman/Paran in Habakkuk 3; Seʿir/steppes of Edom in the Song of Deborah. In the early sections of Habakkuk 3 the epic theme is sung in highly mythological dress. Yahweh marches forth from the southern mountains to battle, appearing in blazing fire, accompanied by *Deber* and *Rešep.* Earth and nations shake, the ancient mountains shatter. The tents of Cushan and Midian tremble. His wrath is directed against Sea, against River, as he rides his chariots of victory. He smashes the head of his enemy (Sea), laying him bare, tail to neck. His horses tread down Sea, as the mighty waters roil and foam. Thus he goes forth to save his people.[63] The sanctuary in the south persisted as a pilgrimage shrine at

60. These "seams" have provided grounds for separating out the "Sinai theme" as alien to the epic events (*Heilsgeschichte*), thus disintegrating the cultic and social integrity of the epic as well as its structural unity, leaving the *magnalia dei* suspended in air.

61. O. Eissfeldt, "Jahwe Zebaoth," *Miscellanea Academia Berolinensia* (Berlin, 1950), 127–150 [*Kleine Schriften* 3: 103–123].

62. See my analysis of these traditions, *CMHE,* 198–200.

63. See Cassuto, *Biblical and Oriental Studies,* 2: 3–15; W. F. Albright, "The Song of Habakkuk," in *Studies in Old Testament Prophecy,* ed. H. H. Rowley (Edinburgh: Clark,

least into the ninth century, as traditions in the Elijah cycle have long suggested and as archaeological remains from Kuntillet ʿAjrūd in Sinai on the road to Elath now confirm.[64] From the pilgrim station of Ajrūd come references to "Yahweh of Teman" (*yhwh htmn;* cf. Zechariah 6:6), alongside "Yahweh of Samaria," and preserved on plaster in a Phoenicianizing script, written in Hebrew, are fragments of a hymn echoing elements of Habakkuk 3.

The Midianite traditions found in both epic sources have led scholars to suspect that a pre-Israelite sanctuary of Yahweh lay in the mountains of the south in the lands on the east of the Gulf of Elath. The geographical terms *Seʿir, Edom, Teman,* as well as *Cushan* and *Midian,* point east of modern Sinai. Moreover, on the basis of both Egyptian records and surface exploration of such sites as Qurayyeh southeast of Elath in Midian, we know that there was a substantial civilization in this area at the end of the Late Bronze Age and the beginning of the Iron Age.[65] On the other hand, the evidence for extensive occupation in the same period in modern Sinai is virtually nil, despite intensive investigation.

At all events early Israel's epic cycle seems to have been at home in a number of sanctuaries in the land, and in addition in an old sanctuary in the south. The Ark of Yahweh moved from shrine to shrine, especially in times of Holy War. The league that celebrated the epic events and confirmed its bonds in the pilgrim festivals had no single, central sanctuary. This, of course, is the plain testimony of the tradition that informs the first of Nathan's oracles in 2 Samuel 7:5–7: "I [Yahweh] have never dwelt in a temple from the day I brought the children of Israel from Egypt until this day, but I was moving about in a tent and in a tabernacle. Wherever among the children of Israel I moved to and fro, did I ever command any judge of Israel . . . saying why did you not build me a temple of cedar?" The force of this league tradition represented by

---

1950), 1–18; and Theodore Hiebert, *God of My Victory: The Ancient Hymn in Habakkuk 3, HSM* 38 (Atlanta: Scholars Press, 1986).

64. See provisionally, Z. Meshel, *Kuntillet ʿAjrud: A Religious Center from the Time of the Judaean Monarchy on the Border of Sinai* (Jerusalem: Israel Museum, 1978); Moshe Weinfeld, "Kuntillet ʿAjrud Inscriptions and Their Significance," *SEL* 1 (1984): 121–130; and A. Lamaire, "Date et origine des inscriptions hebraïque et phéniciennes de Kuntillet ʿAjrud," *SEL* 1 (1984): 131–143. See also M. Noth, "Der Wallfahrtsweg zum Sinai," *Palästinajahrbuch* 36 (1940): 5–28, on the pilgrimage route to Sinai preserved in Num. 33:2–49.

65. See P. J. Parr et al., "Preliminary Survey in N.W. Arabia, 1968," *Bulletin of the Institute of Archaeology* 8–9 (1968–1969) [1970]: 193–242; 10 (1970) [1972]: 23–61; W. F. Albright, "The Oracles of Balaam," *JBL* 63 (1944): 227–230; and M. Weippert, "Semitische Nomader der zweiten Jahrtausend: über die *š'św* der ägyptischen Quellen," *Biblica* 55 (1974): 265–280 and 427–433; and below, chapter 3.

Nathan effectively prevented David from building a permanent national shrine. Practice in early Israel ran counter to the so-called amphictyonic institutions of Greece with their focus on a central sanctuary. In Israel in the days of the league there was no single, fixed league sanctuary. Looked at from another perspective, many shrines served as league sanctuaries in the time of great pilgrim festivals. It may have been that the Ark of the Covenant moved around in its impermanent tent from season to season and by its presence designated a given cultus as the focus of the league. Certainly this was the case in time of war.

The patriarchal traditions were an integral element in Israel's early epic (although it must be said that the history of the patriarchs has been vastly expanded by later accretions before achieving its present agglutinative mass). Much of the patriarchal lore is very old, some of it reaching back, perhaps, into the Middle Bronze Age. As an epic cycle it evidently existed prior to the epic materials recounting exodus, covenant, and conquest. There is, on the other hand, no reason to believe that the bundle of exodus, Sinai, and conquest themes ever existed detached from or separated from patriarchal epic tradition—save in its purely mythic prototype. The epic tradition was continuous, new elements expanding and replacing old, a dynamic process with changing times and institutions. The patriarchal narratives carry certain elements that perform a crucial function in league epic and cultus. The patriarchs legitimize the league sanctuaries of the land: Bethel, Shechem, Hebron, Beersheba. Cult aetiologies of each are narrated in the patriarchal lore. The archaic epithets of deity often associated with these sanctuaries, *ʾēl ʾĕlōhê yiśrāʾēl* at Shechem, *ʾēl bêt ʾēl* at Bethel, together with *ʾēl qōnê ʾereṣ* and *(ʾēl) šadday* are not randomly preserved. They all appear to be epithets of the god ʾEl. ʾEl, identified with Yahweh in league tradition, dominates the religious lore of the fathers. Evidently the choice of patriarchal stories, shrine aetiologies, and divine epithets was a highly controlled process in the formation of the epic of the league. Canaan in pre-Israelite times was plentifully supplied with gods of a rich pantheon and their temples. Most are passed over in Israelite tradition. Save in the intrusive materials of Genesis 14, one detects little shaping by the interests of the Davidids and the Priestly school to promote the royal cultus and shrine.

One structure of the epic, the journey of the patriarch from land granted his fathers and the return to the ancestral land, of course, legitimizes the land claims of the league and needs no elaboration on our part. Another structure does warrant some development here: the covenant of the fathers and the covenant of the league.

Characteristic of patriarchal religion is the "god of the father" or "personal god," the god who revealed himself to the patriarch, blessed him with seed, led his house in war and in migration, in short became "his god." The patriarch in turn, faithful to his special relationship, kept the god's cult, built his altars, paid his tithes and offerings, followed his directives. This special relationship is vivid in the onomasticon of patriarchal folk, and it warrants comparison with Amorite names, names compounded with kinship terms or extended-kinship terms, in which the theophorous element is the (Divine) father, brother, uncle, or father-in-law, and so on. Society was structured by obligations of kinship and extended kinship, by marriage or by covenant. In the early form of the patriarchal tradition—better reflected in the archaizing lore of P than in the epic sources—the covenant of Abraham, Isaac, and Jacob anticipates the covenant of the league.[66]

Much writing has been done on the analogies of the Israelite covenant with the Hittite suzerainty treaties and the West Semitic, especially Aramaic, treaty forms, refracted in Neo-Assyrian treaties.[67] These analogies are most helpful but have tended to obscure the actual covenantal forms of tribal leagues, which develop out of the social and religious forms of a patriarchal society. The god of the father becomes the god of clans and tribes, and thereby the tribes are linked in obligation to their god and to each other by the "substitute" kinship relation afforded by covenant. Such covenants ordinarily bring with them the reordering of genealogies and the "fiction" of actual kinship relations between the tribes, though the rites of covenant or covenant renewal perennially reaffirm their unity.[68]

Confederations of tribes appear to have flourished in southern Palestine and in northern Arabia before their evolution into "nation states" headed by kings: Edom, Moab, and Ammon on Israel's south and east, Midian, Ishmael, and Qedar farther south.[69] In some cases there is evi-

66. I have discussed this aspect of early Israelite society at greater length in chapter 1.

67. On the West Semitic origins of Neo-Assyrian treaties, see H. Tadmor, "Treaty and Oath in the Ancient Near East," in *Humanizing America's Iconic Book,* ed. G. M. Tucker and Douglas A. Knight (Chico, Calif.: Scholars Press, 1982), 127–152.

68. On the function of genealogies, see R. R. Wilson, *Genealogy and History in the Biblical World* (New Haven: Yale University Press, 1977).

69. The annals of Assurbanipal record confrontations with what appear to be Arab leagues, notably the "league" of Attarsamain (ʿAθtar of the heavens) and Qedar. The text reads LU *aʾ / iʾ-lu ša* ^{d}*Atarsamain* who are listed with the Qedarites, Nabayataeans, and Isammeʾ. Akkadian *aʾlu* or *iʾlu* has been connected with Akkadian *eʾēlu / aʾālu,* 'to bind to an agreement' and derivatives. Certainly it is to be derived from *ʾhl,* Old South Arabic *ʾhl,* Lihyanite *ʾl,* 'people, cultic association,' Hebrew *ʾalâ,* 'oath' (< *ʾhl*), ultimately related to Akkadian *ālu,* 'city,' and Hebrew *ʾōhel,* 'tent.' In any case, the term in the Akkadian annals applies to a large group of Arabs who call themselves after the name of a god. From context, 'league,' 'sacral confederation' fits best. The

dence of groupings of twelve, in the pattern of Israel's twelve tribes, and characteristically there is reference to tribal leaders as *nĕśīʾīm* in Israel and in the southern confederations.

It should be noted in passing that Martin Noth's attempt to find the origin of the number twelve in the rota of the care of the central sanctuary is without solid basis either in Israel or in the Greek sacral leagues.[70] We can say no more than that the number twelve was traditional and held onto both in Israel and in Greece, even when it did not reflect reality. In the instances we can control, these leagues rallied to the cult of a particular god, the god of the confederation. Israel may be called the *ʿam Yahweh,* Moab the *ʿam kĕmōš* (Numbers 21:29), and the Arab league the *ʾahl ʿaθtar.* The national gods of Edom (Qôs), Moab (Kĕmōš), Ammon (Milkōm), and Israel (Yahweh) play a role typologically distinct from the gods of the city states. In the Phoenician and Aramaean city states there are city gods, triads of city gods, patron gods of the king, who often differ from the chief city gods, but in both documentary evidence and in the onomastica we find multiple state deities and personal deities. On the contrary, the onomastica of Israel, Ammon, Moab, and Edom are dominated to a remarkable degree by the name or epithet of the national deity: in Israel, by Yahweh or ʾEl (of which Yahweh is the characteristic league epithet), Moab by Chemosh, an epithet of ʿAθtar, so it appears, Edom by Qôs, probably an epithet of Hadad, and Ammon by ʾEl (almost exclusively, although his epithet Milkom appears twice).[71]

Fundamental to league institutions is Holy War. The *ḥerem* is known outside Israel, notably in Moab, and it probably was a central feature of the southern leagues. The leader in Holy War is the Divine Warrior, and the *ʿam Yahweh* fights the wars of Yahweh.

The central cult object is the battle palladium, the Ark of the Covenant. The epic sings of the victory of the Divine Warrior in exodus and conquest, and the festivals of the league recite and reenact these epic events preparatory to reaffirming covenant bonds. The tribal league functions in the first instance as a mechanism for the creation of a militia. The parts

---

CAD definition, 'amphictyony,' is overly precise. See *CAD* 1.1.374; M. Weippert, "Die Kämpfe des assyrischen Königs Assurbanipal gegen die Araben," *WO* 7 (1973): 39–85, esp. 66–69; and I. Ephʿal, *The Ancient Arabs* (Jerusalem: Magnes Press, 1982).

70. See Fritz R. Wust, "Amphiktyonie, Eidgenossenschaft, Symmachie," *Historia* 3 (1954–55): 129–153, and Gottwald, *The Tribes of Yahweh,* 887–889. For a review of Noth's "amphictyony hypothesis," see C. H. J. DeGeus, *The Tribes of Israel* (Amsterdam: Van Gorcum, 1976); R. Smend, "Zur Frage der altisraelitische Amphiktyonie," *Evangelische Theologie* 31 (1971): 623–630; and Gottwald, *The Tribes of Yahweh,* 345–386.

71. One may compare early Israelite usage in which ʾEl names dominate, later replaced by Yahweh names.

of animals distributed to call up the militia recall the cutting into pieces of the animals in the rite of cutting a covenant, and with it the implied threat that the unfaithful will be dismembered or maimed.[72]

Israel's covenant forms are rooted in the institutions of the sacral leagues of the south. They are not a theological construct or a literary borrowing based on the model of international suzerainty treaties. The suzerainty treaty used in West Semitic societies is not without use in providing analogies to league covenants; both stem from social institutions rooted in a common West Semitic ethos. The covenant forms of the league constitute an extended kinship group, provide the means for group action in war by the creation of a militia in times of crisis, and provide a limited judicial system for mediation of intertribal disputes. Unity and order arise in the cult of the Divine Warrior and Judge, in rituals of Holy War and in the pilgrim festivals, rituals and festivals which are only variants of one another, and in the judicial decisions of the deity and his inspired surrogates.[73] The system is marked by patriarchal and egalitarian features quite distinct from the feudal forms of kingship at home in the city states of Syria-Palestine. However, it does not arise *de novo* in Israel's "revolt" against feudal overlords. Both sets of institutions are found, already mixed, in the myths of Ugarit.

V

Israel's ancient epic is not a historical narrative. On the other hand, it is not a collection of fragments. Its essential shaping came not from the Yahwist but from the singers of the early Israelite league. An understanding of the mode of epic composition, most developed in Homeric studies, gives new perspectives on the mechanics of oral composition and the transmission of epic traditions over long periods of time.[74]

72. See *CMHE*, 266, for references; R. Polzin, "*HWQYʿ* and Covenant Institutions in Israel," *HTR* 62 (1969): 227–240; and F. M. Cross, "The Ammonite Oppression of the Tribes of Gad and Reuben," *History, Historiography, and Interpretation*, ed. H. Tadmor and M. Weinfeld (Jerusalem: Magnes Press, 1983), 148–158.

73. An interesting text recording a divine decision in a lawsuit has been published recently by Pierre Bordreuil and Dennis Pardee, "Le papyrus du marzeaḥ," *Semitica* 38 [Hommages à Maurice Sznycer] (1990): 49–68; pls. 7–10. I prefer to read the beginning of the text, *kh ʾmrw ʾlhn lgrʾ . . . ,* "Thus spoke the Godhead to Geraʾ . . ." The plural form as in Hebrew and Phoenician is used in this Transjordanian (Gileadite?) text for the (single) god who speaks. The "gods" are not speaking in unison. The fact that it is construed with the plural is not unexpected, and occurs in Hebrew. Probably the construction was much more common than the survivals in the Bible suggest.

74. I have not had opportunity to discuss certain problems of detail in the light of the technique of epic composition. Epic formulae cherish multiple names and epithets

There is no reason to doubt that Israelite epic traditions preserve more or less accurate reflections of the social institutions, especially the religious lore of the old time of which they sing. Divine epithets and patriarchal covenants in epic traditions go back to pre-Israelite times. The twelve-tribe league is the presumption of the epic and must have existed from the early days of the Israelite settlement of the land. The institutions of Holy War and covenant law are integral to the functioning of the federation.

Traditions that link epic events to the southland, especially to Sinai, rest ultimately on historical memory. Proto-Israel or the "Mosaic group" came into the land from the south. With them came the social, religious, and military customs and institutions imported, so to speak, into feudal Canaan. They are emphatically not at home in a society constructed of royal city states. The twelve-tribe league took classical form in the land in the twelfth century, but its roots were in the customs and experiences of those elements of Israel who came from the southern mountains. Models of peasant revolt, or of infiltration into the hill country from urban centers in Canaan, currently popular in explaining Israel's settlement in the land and which are not without merit in explaining aspects of the archaeological record, should not be permitted to obscure evidence, preserved in epic, of Israelite connections with the peoples of the south who moved between Seʿir, Midian, and Egypt at the end of the Late Bronze Age and the beginning of the Iron Age. Archaeological lore and anthropological models can only propose general patterns. Literary materials properly analyzed may provide the particulars of which history is properly constructed. There is every reason to contend, on the basis of literary remains, that there was an attack from the south through Transjordan by the *ʿam Yahweh,* and that they formed the nucleus around which the early Israelite league took shape and ex-

—no less in parallelistic formulae than in quantitative Greek formulae. The alternate names Jacob/Israel, Esau/Edom, Sinai/Horeb, and the formulaic pairs Seʿir/Edom, Cushan/Midian, Sinai/Mount Paran, Teman/Mount Paran arise inevitably in epic verse. The Achaeans/Argives/Danaeans in the *Iliad* are merely alternate names used for poetic variation in formulae. The attempt to see Jacob and Israel as unrelated names, linked only in secondary tradition, is to misunderstand the character of these traditions. One cannot apply the scissors-and-paste methods of older literary criticism to orally composed epic or the later epic sources derived therefrom. Care must be taken in partitioning documents according to a choice of one name in a particular name pair. To be sure, in turning poetry into prose, there was a tendency in a source to prefer one name or epithet to another. I do not propose to scrap the partition of the Pentateuchal sources based in part on different preferences in the choice of names or epithets. Neither do I propose to look in one place for Sinai, another for Horeb. There is difficulty enough in locating one "Mount of God."

panded, and from whom "all Israel" took their identity and institutions. This is the testimony of the archaic hymns and the historical basis of the early epic. Traditions of the fathers linked in kinship bonds all elements of Israel. The ʾEl of the cults and sanctuaries of the land was identified with ʾEl of the south, Yahweh the Divine Warrior, Lord of Sinai. Israel's epic drew on older epic cycles in dynamic change, molding an epic that was forged into its main lines shortly after the establishment of the league in Canaan: covenants with the fathers in the land of Canaan, their migration to Egypt, their exodus and creation of the nation at Sinai, and then their return to the land of promise and its conquest.

In its life in the cultus of the league the epic acquired accretions and variants in its recompositions by bards and hierophants, and it developed multiforms in the festivals of the pilgrimage shrines. With the transition to monarchy and the breakdown or transformation of league institutions, the epic went through further transformations to fit new settings and to perform new functions, gaining further accretions and losing its close cultic connections. The final deposit was the great conflate amalgam of many ages we call the Pentateuch.

3

Reuben, the Firstborn of Jacob: Sacral Traditions and Early Israelite History

I

REUBEN WAS THE FIRSTBORN OF JACOB; SO WE ARE TOLD IN THE GENEALOGICAL lists early and late, as well as in the cycles of tribal blessings. I, for one, have always been intrigued by the place held by Reuben in the tribal lists. Why is Reuben of all tribes the firstborn? Anthropologists tell us that genealogies serve social, political, or religious functions, and as institutions or historical circumstances change, genealogies shift to meet new circumstances or changed social realities.[1] Evidently the genealogy of the tribes was frozen—in writing or in epic narrative—when Reuben played a role that warranted his preeminence. The Chronicler reflects, if not bewilderment, the judgment that Reuben was unworthy of the birthright, and that it in fact went to Joseph, though Judah became preeminent (1 Chronicles 5:1–2). He notes, however, that one must write genealogies with Reuben as firstborn. My contention is that Reuben's place in the genealogy presumes that Reuben once played a major role in Israelite society, even a dominant one, whether political or religious.[2] This seems confirmed in the premonarchical Blessing of Jacob (Genesis 49:3):

> Reuben my firstborn
> Thou art my strength,
> The prime of my manhood . . .
> Preeminent in power.[3]

However, immediately we hear of a blot on Reuben's escutcheon, the incestuous episode in which Reuben lay with Bilhah, his father's concu-

1. See the study of R. R. Wilson, *Genealogy and History in the Biblical World, YNER* 7 (New Haven: Yale University Press, 1977), and his extensive bibliography.

2. Cf. Noth's comment, "The traditional precedence of the tribes of Reuben, Simeon (and Levi) can only have originated in a situation in which these tribes played an important part" (*The History of Israel*, trans. S. Godman [Edinburgh: Clark, 1958], 88).

3. Cf. *AYP*, 72 and notes; and Stanley Gevirtz, "The Reprimand of Reuben," *JNES* 30 (1971): 87–98. The blessing of Reuben bristles with problems, but the general sense is clear.

bine (cf. Genesis 35:22). In the Blessing of Moses, another early composition, we read (Deuteronomy 33:6):

Let Reuben live; let him not die,
Although his men be few.

Reuben's very existence was threatened in the eleventh century if not earlier. The Jephthah account refers to pressure of the Ammonites on the Israelites of Gilead (Judges 11). More significant is the account in 1 Samuel 11, particularly a new, authentic paragraph lost in the Massoretic Text but preserved in 4QSam[a] (the great Samuel manuscript from Cave 4, Qumrân) and in the Greek text of Josephus.[4] It records the decimation of the Reubenites and Gadites and the flight of seven thousand, who escaped death or mutilation, to Jabesh-Gilead north of the Jabbok. This takes place at the beginning of the reign of Saul. Even earlier we are told (Judges 3:15–30) that Moab had overrun the old territory of Reuben between the Arnon and Heshbon. In the time of David, in his census, we hear only of Gad north of Arnon (2 Samuel 24:5); the twelfth district of Solomon mentions only Gad,[5] and in the Meša' Inscription of the ninth century B.C.E., the territory between Arnon and Heshbon, the old territory of Reuben, reconquered by Omri, and in turn by Meša', king of Moab, is inhabited by Gadites. Reuben as a tribal entity with a fixed territory has disappeared.[6]

Only in the twelfth-century source, the Song of Deborah, does Reuben appear to be flourishing (Judges 5:15f.):

In the divisions of Reuben
Great are the resolves of heart.
Thou indeed hast dwelt among the hearths
Listening to the pipings of the flocks.[7]

4. See F. M. Cross, "The Ammonite Oppression of the Tribes of Gad and Reuben: Missing Verses from 1 Samuel 11 Found in 4QSamuel[a]," in *History, Historiography, and Interpretation,* ed. H. Tadmor and M. Weinfeld (Jerusalem: Magnes Press, 1983), 148–158; cf. A. Rofe, "The Acts of Nahash According to 4QSam[a]," *IEJ* 32 (1982): 129–133.

5. The Solomonic district listed in 1 Kings 4:19 reads *Gilead* in the Massoretic Text; the OG correctly reads *Gad,* as is evident from the geographical notices.

6. See R. de Vaux, *Histoire ancienne d'Israël* (Paris: Librairie LeCoffre, 1971), 534–536. B. Oded, in his dissertation, "The Political Status of Israelite Transjordan during the Period of the Monarchy" (Hebrew University, 1968), argues for the continued existence of Reuben, relying largely on folkloristic elements in 1 Chron. 5:1–10. Scattered elements tracing their lineage to Reuben may have survived, but a consolidated tribe of Reuben, inhabiting the territory between the Arnon and Heshbon, ceased to exist no later than the eleventh century. Cf. M. Cogan, "The Men of Nebo: Repatriated Reubenites," *IEJ* 29 (1979): 37–39.

7. Verse 16b is probably an ancient variant of 15b. On *lmh* as an emphatic plus enclitic, see *CMHE,* 235, n. 74. To the citations there add *CTA* 4.7.38–39, and *CTA* 10.3.6.

The expression 'divisions,' or 'sections,' *pĕlaggôt,* of Reuben is noteworthy, suggesting the complexity of the Reubenite genealogy, if not the large size of its contingents.[8]

B. Halpern suggests an alternative, taking "the lexeme as negative plus enclitic" ("The Resourceful Israelite Historian in the Song of Deborah and Israelite Historiography," *HTR* 76 [1983]: 384). Generally *lmh* has been interpreted as meaning 'why,' its usual sense in Hebrew, and the saying about the tribe taken as a reproach for not joining the league at war against the kings of Canaan. There are two problems with this interpretation. First, any tribe or clan not answering the summons to holy war, the "call up" of the tribal militia, properly should fall under the curse of the league covenant, one of the chief functions of which is the insuring of common defense. Meroz, v. 23, is explicitly and unambiguously cursed for not coming to "the aid of Yahweh with warriors." If the tribes of Reuben, Gilead, Dan, and Asher failed to appear, why is their rebuke so mild? Second, the tribal sayings (blessings, etc.) in vv. 14–18 are in many cases typical "blessings" of the same type found in the cycle of "blessings" found in Gen. 49 and Deut. 33. In fact the saying on Asher (v. 17) is an oral variant of the saying on Zebulun in Gen. 49:13, just as the blessings of Joseph in Gen. 49:22–26 and Deut. 33:13–17 are oral variants. The *Sitz im Leben* of cycles of tribal "blessings," I have long argued, is to be found in the more lighthearted rituals of the gathered tribes in pilgrimage festivals or in assemblies for holy war, i.e., in ritual enactments of the wars of Yahweh, or actual rituals in battle camps. Certainly the cycle of blessings is the primary *Gattung.* The individual blessing did not develop independently, awaiting a collector, as the older Form Critics, obsessed with simplicity and unity, would have us believe. On the love of lists, see M. D. Coogan, "A Structural and Literary Analysis of the Song of Deborah," *CBQ* 40 (1978): 162–165. Coogan also notes that the rare phrase *bên mišpĕtayim* is applied to Issachar in Gen. 49:14 and to Reuben in Judges 5:16. The question I find difficult to resolve is this: does the list of tribal sayings in the Song of Deborah simply give typical sayings—often with martial flavor—or does the bard borrow and modify such sayings to reprimand those who failed to show up for muster? I am inclined to the former view, and hence suggest an archaic usage of *lm(h).*

8. Judah goes unmentioned in Judges 5, and a number of explanations have been given to account for its absence, among them that Judah had not yet coalesced out of the conglomerate of tribal elements which were to make it up, including Simeonite, Calebite, Kenite, and perhaps Reubenite clans, or that Judah had not yet merged with the league of Israelite tribes. It is not impossible that in this era Judah was a western division of Reuben. One may compare the house of Joseph. It has long been observed that the clans of Reuben and Judah share two names, Ḥeṣron and Karmi, and that place names associated with Reuben are found on the west bank of the Jordan along the northern boundary of Judah. This runs from the southern fords of the Jordan opposite traditional Reubenite territory in Transjordan, "up to the stone of Bohan the son of Reuben . . . to Debir from the Valley of Achor, and so northward looking toward Gilgal, that is, over against the ascent of Adummim" (Josh. 15:5–7). On the identification of these sites, see F. M. Cross and J. T. Milik, "Explorations in the Judaean Buqêʿah," *BASOR* 142 (1956): 5–17 and references; *CMHE,* 109 f., n. 57. To the stone of Bohan, son of Reuben (Josh. 15:6 and 18:17) may be added the cairn of ʿAkan, son of Karmi, in the valley of ʿAkor, if the clan of Karmi is shared by Reuben

Evidently Reuben's era of preeminence was early in the history of the tribes, perhaps in the formative era of Israel's religious and political self-consciousness. In this case Reuben's time of greatness may be hidden from the historian, overlain by a patina of traditions stemming from later centers of power and prestige, in Joseph and in Judah. Perhaps we can approach our problem from another direction. What events, according to biblical tradition, transpired in the territory assigned to Reuben?

In the heart of Reuben's allotted territory lies a well-watered valley, the valley opposite Bêt Peʿor.[9] Bêt Peʿor is also called Baʿl Peʿor,[10] and the full name probably was Bêt Baʿl Peʿor. Peʿor is also the name of the mountain associated with the sanctuary.[11] The valley today is called ʿUyûn Mûsā, the 'springs of Moses.' On the south lies the Pisgah-Nebo mountain ridge.[12] On the north is the ridge of Mount (Baʿl) Peʿor, modern Musaqqar.

The salient events that took place in Reuben, "in the valley opposite Bêt Peʿor" deserve enumeration.

1. According to Deuteronomic tradition, the valley in Reuben is the setting of Moses' "second giving" of the law, the recording of the law, and the covenant rites (or covenant renewal rites) before the crossing of the Jordan. The introduction to the old core of Deuteronomic law (Dtn)[13] states: "This is the law which Moses set before the children of Israel . . . beyond the Jordan, in the valley opposite Bêt Peʿor." The covenant ceremony described in Deuteronomy 28:69, and especially in 29:9–14, also takes place here: "These are the words of the covenant which Yahweh commanded Moses to make with the children of Israel in the land of

---

and Judah (Josh. 7:1, 18, 24, and 26). Gilgal too may originally have been a Reubenite shrine in view of Josh. 22 (see below). It may be noted that all of these sites follow the main ancient road from the ford immediately north of the Dead Sea up the Wâdī Dabr by the stone of Bohan, modern Ḥajar el-ʿAṣbaʿ, through the *ʿēmeq ʿākōr*, the modern el-Buqêʿah, then north to Jerusalem, or south to Hebron. The name *Judah* is probably a place-name, not a tribal name in origin (see M. Noth, *History*, 53–58; R. de Vaux, *Histoire*, 507–510). I do not believe that Reuben moved east from Cis-Jordan (*contra* Noth, among others, *History*, 63–65). Rather, as we shall see, I believe Reuben moved from the southeast north into the unsettled country north of the Arnon, and then, if a western Reuben existed, from "Shittim to Gilgal," and westward through the "Valley of Trouble," later to disappear in Cis-Jordan under the umbrella of the geographical name Judah.

9. Deut. 3:29; 4:46; 34:6; Josh. 13:20.

10. Hos. 9:10; Deut. 4:3.

11. *rʾš pʿr*, Num. 23:28; cf. Eusebius, *oros phogor* (*Onomasticon* 48:3–5).

12. The pair of names applies to the same ridge, as is clear from Deut. 34:1. Such double names probably originate in poetic pairs. See above, chapter 2, n. 72.

13. Deut. 4:44–46.

Moab, beside the covenant which he made with them in Horeb."[14] The written form of the law, inscribed on plastered stones (a procedure now documented in the plaster texts of Deir ʿAllā and Kuntillet ʿAjrūd), is to be taken to (the future shrine at) Shechem (Deuteronomy 27:2–8). That these events took place, according to these traditions, precisely in the heart of Reuben is often forgotten since the geographical terms "land of Moab," "steppes of Moab," or "the valley in the land of Moab opposite Bêt Peʿor"—appropriate after Moab had long moved north and occupied Reuben—are used in Deuteronomy. What is astonishing is that the Levitic priests who cherished these traditions—the priestly house tracing its lineage to Moses in our view[15]—attributed their traditions (by way of the old shrine of Shechem) to the valley of Moses in Reuben.

Why would the Mushites preserve or create the claim that their legal tradition had its origin here?

2. There is every reason to believe that there was a Reubenite shrine beneath Mount Nebo, over against Mount Baʿl Peʿor. In the Mešaʿ Stone (ca. 850 B.C.E.), we read how Mešaʿ was told by Chemosh, "Go take Nebo (*nbh*) against Israel, and I went by night, and fought against it from the breaking of dawn to noon, and I captured it and I killed everyone, seven thousand, men, and male children, women and female children, and maidens—for I had devoted it [*hḥrmth*] to ʿAštar-Chemosh. And I took from there the vessels of Yahweh and dragged them before Chemosh."[16] There has been uncertainty about the site of the town of Nebo. In Byzantine times tradition located it on the high, desolate hill of Muḫayyaṭ, where indeed there are some Iron Age remains and Byzantine churches.[17] Its source of water, ʿEn Judêd, is far below in the wâdī, a journey of an hour and a quarter round trip (without the burden of carrying water jars). It is an unlikely site for a major town, a suitable site for a fortress or Byzantine monastery. Certainly the ruin could not sustain seven thousand people, or even a somewhat lesser number if we assume Mešaʿ's count was generous. A better site is north of the ridge of Nebo (Khirbet Muḫayyaṭ is on the south), in the well-watered valley of ʿUyûn Mûsā, the valley over against Bêt Peʿor. Khirbet ʿUyûn Mûsā has produced a large quantity of Iron I pottery, and the general area is the only place suitable to support a sizeable population.

14. On the history of these traditions, see N. Lohfink, "Der Bundesschluss im Land Moab," *BZ* Neue Folge, 1962, Heft 1:32–56.

15. On the rival priestly houses, one tracing its ancestry to Moses, one to Aaron, see *CMHE*, 195–215.

16. Meshaʿ lines 14–18.

17. See S. J. Saller and B. Bagatti, *The Town of Nebo* (Jerusalem: Franciscan Press, 1949), esp. 1–31. The site is at the 790 meter level, only slightly lower than the peak of Nebo (808 meters).

Confirmation of this identification, we believe, is to be found in the Copper Scroll from Cave 3, Qumrân. A treasure, we are told, is hidden "at the waterfall near Kepar Nebo."[18] This can only be the waterfall of the ʿUyûn Mûsā.[19]

The existence of a sanctuary of Yahweh in the valley beneath Nebo over against Bêt Peʿor in the early days when Reuben was preeminent among the tribes—reestablished in the time of Omri—would provide an explanation of why priests who traced their lineage to the priest Moses attributed the origin of their Mosaic legal traditions to Reuben, and specifically to Moses' giving of the law in this valley. Traditions of covenant rites and lawgiving we expect to stem from the lore and etiologies of a holy place or sanctuary. Evidently the lore of the Reubenite sanctuary survived long enough to be turned into the history of events which took place on the eve of entry into the land in Deuteronomic tradition.

3. Tradition, usually assigned to the Elohist—in any case belonging to epic tradition—states that Moses was buried "in the valley in the land of Moab over against Bêt Peʿor."[20]

4. Another legend of a dramatic, but notorious, event is placed in this same locale: the episode of Baʿl Peʿor. The account in the epic sources (primarily J) stands in sharp tension with the account in the Priestly source.[21] The epic account places the event at Shittim,[22] some eight kilo-

18. Col. 9, lines 1 and 11. For a discussion of the text, and the meaning of *qôl hammayim*, 'water-fall,' literally 'roar of water,' see the discussion of J. T. Milik in the *editio princeps*, *Les "Petites grottes" de Qumrân*, by M. Baillet, J. T. Milik, and R. de Vaux, *DJD* 3 (Oxford: At the Clarendon Press, 1962), 294 f., and especially 242 and 265 f. Milik correctly identifies the waterfall as that of one of the springs of ʿUyûn Mûsā (a fall of some thirty feet). Strangely he retains the identification of Khirbet Muḫayyaṭ with Kepar Nebo, some three kilometers distant as the crow flies, over the top of Mt. Nebo. The text reads *hqrwbyn lkpr nbw.*

19. O. Henke has argued ("Zur Lage von Beth Peor," *ZDPV* 75 [1979]: 155–163) that Khirbet ʿUyûn Mûsā is to be identified with Bêt Peʿor. The usual identification is with Khirbet el-Muḫaṭṭah on the Mušaqqar ridge in accord with Eusebius (see S. D. Waterhouse and R. Ibach Jr., "The Topographical Survey," *AUSS* 13 [1975]: 217–233, for a recent discussion). The site is located on the Livias-Ḥesban road; and the remains of a Roman fortress now dominate the site, and Iron Age sherds are few. The sanctuary should be on or near the peak of Mount Peʿor, the *rôʾš pĕʿōr* where tradition locates Balaam's seven altars (Num. 23:28 f.; cf. 31:16).

20. Deut. 34:6a. The added comment (v. 6b), the source of many a legend—"no one knows his grave until this day"—is probably a polemical comment of the Priestly source which continues in vv. 7–9. The grave of Moses no doubt gave the Reubenite holy place a special importance and distinction.

21. Num. 25:1–5 is assigned to J(E); Num. 25:6–16 is P, as is the follow-up account of the slaughter of the Midianites in Num. 31.

22. *ʾĀbēl haš-šiṭṭîm* was decisively identified with Tell Ḥammâm by Nelson Glueck,

meters northeast of Bêt Peʿor, at the battle camp from which, tradition held, Israel launched the crossing of Jordan to Gilgal. Israel is said to have "yoked" themselves to Baʿl Peʿor, an expression with both sexual and covenantal overtones, we suspect.[23] Israel's partners in fertility rites are said to be the daughters of Moab. And it is Moses who directs the "judges" of Israel to slay those of Israel who participated in the rites.

The Priestly story, in contrast, assumes that Israel's partners in fertility rites and apostasy were the Midianites. A plague struck, and Pinḥas, the Aaronid, saved the day and stayed this plague by thrusting a spear through the two chief celebrants, two at one blow: Kozbi, daughter of a prince of Midian, and Zimri, son of a prince of Simeon. The action took place, according to P, "in the sight of Moses" and the congregation of Israel while they "were weeping at the door of the Tent of Meeting." Moses is not explicitly condemned. Yet it is not Moses but Pinḥas who takes action. This is in plain contradiction to the notices of the epic tradition. In the Priestly narrative Pinḥas is the hero, and on this occasion Pinḥas is rewarded: "Pinḥas son of Elʿazar, son of Aaron the Priest, has turned aside my [Yahweh's] wrath from the children of Israel in that he was very jealous for me among them, so that I did not consume the children of Israel in my jealousy. Wherefore say: behold I give to him my covenant of peace, and it shall be for him and his seed after him an eternal covenant of priesthood, because he was jealous for his God."

The award of the priesthood to the Aaronids in this context is reminiscent of a later episode in the history of the priesthood. Some years ago I wrote on the conflict stories in early Israelite tradition, in which the conflict between Moses and his party and Aaron and his party was a recurring theme.[24] I found in the Baʿl Peʿor account an Aaronid polemic against the Levitic (or Mushite) house, of which Eli of Shiloh was preeminent in the late era of the Judges. In the parallel story the Shilonite house of Eli was rejected from the (high) priesthood because Eli's two sons "lay with the women that did service at the door of the Tent of Meeting" (1 Samuel 2:22), and the priesthood of Eli's house, chosen when Yahweh revealed himself to Eli's ancestor in Egypt in Pharoah's household (1 Samuel 2:27f.), was abrogated, and the covenant of priesthood passed to another, namely Zadok, an Aaronid of the Hebronite clan.[25]

Explorations in Eastern Palestine 4, *AASOR* 25–28 (New Haven, Conn.: ASOR, 1951), 378–382.

23. Hos. 9:10 records that "they entered Baʿl Peʿor, and devoted themselves to Baʿl [*bōšet*]."

24. See above, n. 15.

25. See the critical discussion of Saul Olyan, "Zadok's Origins and the Tribal Politics of David," *JBL* 101 (1982): 177–193.

Even more striking are parallels to events at Sinai. The egregious sin at Sinai was, of course, Aaron's fabrication of the golden bull, and the festal uproar that accompanied it. Moses here vigorously intervenes, destroys the image of the young bull, and calls for aid. The sons of Levi—an interesting designation in this period—volunteer and kill three thousand at the command of Moses. As a result, the Levites are ordained to the priesthood[26] and given the Lord's blessing for extirpating Aaron's sin. The traditions in Exodus 32 (E) are clearly shaped by the polemic of Levitic circles against the bull of the Aaronid priests at Bethel.[27] The blessing of Levi in Deuteronomy 33:8–11 is in conformity; Moses and the Levites are given the full priestly office. In these traditions we note that Moses' allies are the Levitical priests confronting the idolators at whose head stands Aaron!

Note the parallels between the traditions of Sinai and the traditions of Ba'l Pe'or:

a. Lawgiving and covenant ceremony at the foot of Mount Sinai = lawgiving and covenant at the foot of Mount Nebo.
b. Aaron's sin and orgiastic rites = the sin of Pe'or, apostasy and fertility rites.
c. Three thousand celebrants at Sinai die by the sword of the Levites = Zimri and the Midianite princess die by the spear thrust of the Aaronid Pinḥas, and 24,000 die of plague.
d. Levites granted priestly ordination for their part in the slaughter of apostates = Pinhas and the Aaronids granted an eternal priesthood for slaying the pair engaged in fertility rites at the Tent of Meeting and expiating the sin of Pe'or.

We may add what may be called echoes of the events in Israelite tradition:

e. The sin of Jeroboam and the curse on Bethel and its bull = the sin of the Elids at Shiloh, lying with women at the Tent of Meeting, and the curse on the Elid house, the priesthood transferred to a "faithful priest" (Zadok).

The role of the Midianites at Sinai-Horeb and at Nebo (or Bêt Pe'or below Pisgah-Nebo) must also be examined. According to epic tradition (E), Moses, while tending the flocks of the priest of Midian, ventured upon the mountain of God, where God's name Yahweh was revealed

26. Exod. 32:29. The expression *ml'w* (OG, *ml'tm*) *yd(y)km* is, of course, the technical expression for priestly ordination. Cf. 29:9, where the same idiom is used of the ordination of Aaron and his sons in the Priestly source.

27. See *CMHE,* 198–200.

to him (Exodus 3:1, 13–15). This text presumes that the mountain is in Midianite territory. The priest of Midian provided Moses with a wife, apparently a priestess in her own right.[28] At the mountain, the priest of Midian offered sacrifices to Yahweh and instituted a juridical system according to Exodus 18. Relations between Moses and Midian could not be more harmonious, and the house of Moses was of mixed Midianite-Israelite blood. At (Mount) Baʿl Peʿor intercourse between an Israelite and a Midianite was the occasion for sin. In the Priestly sequel in Numbers 31, the Midianite women (plural) were declared responsible for causing Israel to revolt and break faith with Yahweh in the matter of Peʿor, and hence were placed under the ban. Indeed, Yahweh declared holy war on Midian and Midian was "annihilated."

5. In epic tradition three of the oracles of Balaam were given at the top of Peʿor, where Balaam is said to have built seven altars. In these traditions (JE), Balaam is treated in effect as a convert and, while reproached by Balaq who summoned him, was permitted to return home in peace. In Priestly tradition in Numbers 31, Balaam was killed in company with the five kings of Midian, and Israel's apostasy at Baʿl Peʿor is described as having occurred at the "counsel of Balaam."

The Midianites, it is important to note, are not absent in the epic lore about Balaam. In the Yahwistic strand, Moab took counsel with the elders of Midian, and elders of both Moab and Midian are described as having served as messengers to fetch Balaam (Numbers 22:4–7). The same strand of epic tradition mentions Edom fighting against Midian in the field of Moab (Genesis 36:35), associating the two nations in the same territory.

In short, the attitude of the epic sources, and notably E, is favorable to Balaam, and his oracles bless Israel—from the peak of Mount Peʿor. The Elohistic tradition mentions only the daughters of Moab at Bêt Peʿor, and only Moab in the affair of Balaam. Oddly, Yahwistic tradition links up with Priestly tradition in placing the Midianites in this terrain. Again Elohistic tradition is favorable to the Midianites in describing their intimate relationships with Moses and Israel in Sinai and in the wilderness, while preserving polemical traditions about Aaron and about Miriam and Aaron's protest against Moses' marriage. The Aaronid (or Zadokite) circles of P are silent about the Midianite connection in Sinai but lash out in violent polemic against Midian and Balaam at Mount Peʿor.

In some sense, Peʿor and Sinai become reversed images in priestly

28. Cf. *CMHE,* 200 and n. 25. In Num. 12:1 Miriam and Aaron protest Moses' marriage to the Cushite woman. *Kûšît* is to be recognized as a gentilic of *kûšān* with loss of the locative (or dual *-ān* before the suffix *ît*). Cf. *GvG* § 220d. *ʾereṣ midyān* and *kûšān* are a formulaic pair in Hab. 3:7.

polemic, the traditions of the Levitic priests and family of Moses surviving especially in Elohistic tradition, the traditions of the Aaronid house surviving in Priestly tradition.

The traditions preserved in Priestly sections of Numbers 25 and 31 probably rest on old tradition. Unevenness in these two chapters has long been noticed. *Ṣûr* is a Midianite king in chapter 31, a *rô'š 'ummôt bêt 'āb* in chapter 25, and the Bêt Peʿor episode and the episode of the war against the five kings of Midian (and Balaam) are probably stitched together by P on the basis of earlier sources. There are archaic, non-Priestly expressions in the account pointing in this direction.[29] Eissfeldt, Albright, and Mendenhall, each from a different point of view, have argued for the antiquity of material in these two chapters, including the primacy of Midian at Bêt Peʿor.[30] To establish the antiquity of this tradition is one thing. To make use of such legendary materials for historical purposes requires different kinds of controls, a problem we shall turn to later.

One additional source needs to be examined in which Reuben and its role in early Israelite religious tradition may have left a deposit. This is the complex and enigmatic story of the altar of Gad and Reuben in Joshua 22. The introduction, vv. 1–8, and the editing of the whole pericope is, as expected, Deuteronomistic. But the old narrative edited derives from a document that exhibits characteristic Priestly terminology, and it must be a document akin to those used by the Exilic Priestly tradent.[31] Thus the narrative uses *ʿadat (yiśrā'ēl)*[32] repeatedly, *nāśî'* or *nĕśî'îm*,[33] *miškān*,[34] and *tabnît*.[35] Pinḥas, son of Elʿazar the priest, is the central character, as in the Priestly story of Peʿor, and reference is made to the plague, *negep*, associated with the sin of Peʿor,[36] a theme only in P. Finally the Deuteronomistic editor has added the half tribe of Manasseh in the early part of the narrative, using the term *šēbeṭ*; at the end of the

29. For example, *qubbāh*, 'tent shrine.' Cf. *CMHE*, 202, n. 22.

30. O. Eissfeldt, "Protektorat der Midianiter über ihre Nachbarn im letzten Viertel des 2. Jahrtausende v. Chr.," *JBL* 87 (1968): 383–393 (with contributions by Albright); W. F. Albright, "Midianite Donkey Caravans," in *Translating and Understanding the Old Testament*, ed. H. T. Frank and W. L. Reed (Nashville: Abingdon, 1970), 197–205; G. E. Mendenhall, *The Tenth Generation* (Baltimore: Johns Hopkins University Press, 1973), 105–121; cf. E. A. Knauf, "Midianites and Ishmaelites," in *Midian, Moab, and Edom*, ed. J. F. A. Sawyer and D. J. Clines (Sheffield: *JSOT* suppl. ser. 24, 1983); and W. J. Dumbrell, "Midian—A Land or a League?" *VT* 25 (1975): 323–337.

31. On early (pre-Exilic) Priestly documents, see *CMHE*, 321 f.

32. Josh. 22:12, 16, 17, 18, 20.

33. Josh. 22:14 (*tris*), 30, 32.

34. Josh. 22:19, 29. Note the verb *škn* in v. 19.

35. Josh. 22:28.

36. Josh. 22:17.

narrative only the children of Gad and the children of Reuben are mentioned, evidently the Priestly form of the story.[37] There is other Priestly language in the narrative, but these telltale signs will suffice. It is clear that the Deuteronomist has taken an old Priestly story, one sharply supporting his interest in the centralization of worship in Cis-Jordan, and retouched it.

The Priestly account focuses on a great altar built by Reuben and Gad near the Jordan.[38] Pinḥas and the Cis-Jordanian brethren threaten war if their Transjordanian brethren sacrifice on the altar, that is, use it for cultic rites. Reuben and Gad swear great oaths that it is not their intention to use the altar for sacrifices. Rather, the altar is a model of the altar of the Tabernacle (in Canaan), a witness that the tribes beyond the Jordan have the right to sacrifice at Israel's central sanctuary, a witness that "Yahweh is God."

Effectively the account asserts a prohibition against the Transjordanian tribes, concretely Gad and Reuben, from maintaining a cult or a shrine, and records Gad and Reuben's solemn agreement to engage in no independent cult. Underlying is an Aaronid polemic against a Reubenite (and perhaps Gadite) cult and shrine. I should add that this polemic, perversely, testifies to an important and traditional cult and shrine (or shrines) in Reuben.[39]

II

What can these traditions located in Reuben, or in the territory allotted to Reuben, tell of Israel's early history and the place of Reuben in the emergence of early Israelite religion? By a combination of these data with extrabiblical discoveries, I believe some progress can be made by the historian.

In recent years there have been intensive surveys of the archaeological remains of Midian—the northern Ḥijâz—of the territories of Edom-Seʿir, Moab, and Reuben, and of the Sinai Peninsula. Most striking perhaps is the discovery of a developed civilization in Midian at the end of the Late Bronze Age and the beginning of the Iron Age. At Quray-

37. Josh. 22:25, 32, 33, 34. Note the Priestly term *maṭṭôt* for tribes in v. 14.

38. Precisely where the altar is built is not clear in vv. 10 and 11. Vs. 10 places the altar *bʾrṣ knʿn*, v. 11 *ʾl mwl ʾrṣ knʿn . . . ʾl ʿbr bny yśrʾl*, apparently contradictory statements. Probably the altar referred to is in Cis-Jordan, at Gilgal. See, e.g., J. Alberto Soggin, *Joshua* (Philadelphia: Westminster Press, 1972), 212–215; contrast B. Mazar, "Biblical Archaeology Today: The Historical Aspect," in *Biblical Archaeology Today* (Jerusalem: IES, 1985), 17.

39. On the (Reubenite) cult of Gilgal, see *CMHE*, 103–105 and references.

yeh a major fortified citadel has been discovered—a walled village and extensive irrigation systems.[40] Characteristic pottery, called "Midianite" or "Ḥijâz" ware, radiates out from the northern Ḥijâz in this period into southern Transjordan and sites near Elath, notably Timna. Extraordinarily enough, it is wholly absent from the Sinai.[41]

In the same era, the occupation of Edom, Moab, and Reuben was exceedingly sparse—though not absent—and it is evident that organized kingdoms in Edom and Moab had yet to appear.[42] These data suggest,

40. See P. J. Parr et al., "Preliminary Survey in N. W. Arabia, 1968," *Bulletin of the Institute of Archaeology* 8–9, 1968–69 (1970): 193–242; 10 (1972): 23–61; P. J. Parr, "Contacts between Northwest Arabia and Jordan in the Late Bronze and Iron Ages," in *Studies in the History and Archaeology of Jordan,* ed. A. Hadidi (Amman: Department of Antiquities of Jordan, 1982), 127–134; and "Aspects of the Archaeology of North West Arabia in the First Millennium B.C.," in *L'Arabie préislamique et son environnement historique et culturel,* Actes du Colloque de Strasbourg 24–27 June 1987, ed. T. Fahd (Strasbourg: Université des Sciences humaines de Strasbourg, 1987), 39–66. M. L. Ingraham, T. J. Johnson, B. Rihani, and I. Shatla, "Saudi Arabian Comprehensive Survey Program, Preliminary Report on a Reconnaissance Survey of the Northwestern Province," *Atlal* 5 (1981): 59–84, esp. 71–75; J. E. Dayton, "Midianite and Edomite Pottery," *Proceedings of the Seminar for Arabian Studies* 2 (1972): 25–37. The Wâdī al-Jubah project has demonstrated that the high cultures of inland South Arabia commence no later than ca. 1200 B.C.E. and perhaps as early as 1300, roughly coeval with the domestication of the camel. See the comments of James Sauer in J. A. Blakely, J. A. Sauer, and M. R. Toplyn, *The Al-Juban Archeological Project II. Site Reconnaissance in North Yemen, 1983* (Washington: American Foundation for the Study of Man, 1985), 151–154.

41. See the papers listed in note 40, and B. Rothenberg and Jonathan Glass, "The Midianite Pottery," in *Midian, Moab, and Edom,* ed. J. F. A. Sawyer and D. J. Clines (Sheffield: Sheffield Academic Press, 1983), 65–124 [= *Eretz Israel* 15 (1981): 85–114]; Garth Bawden, "Painted Pottery of Tayma and Problems of Cultural Chronology in Northwest Arabia," in *Midian, Moab, and Edom,* 37–52; Garth Bawden and C. Edens, "Tayma Painted Ware and the Hejaz Iron Age Ceramic Tradition," *Levant* 20 (1988): 197–213; G. E. Mendenhall, "Qurayya and the Midianites," in *Studies in the History of Arabia 3,* ed. R. Al-Ansari (Riyadh: King Saud University, 1984), 137–141; Peter J. Parr, "Pottery of the Late Second Millennium B.C. from Northwest Arabia and Its Historical Implications," in *Araby the Blest,* ed. D. T. Potts (Copenhagen: Carsten Niebuhr Institute, University of Copenhagen, 1988), 73–89; and "Further Reflections on Late Second Millennium Settlement in North West Arabia," in *Retrieving the Past: Essays on Archaeological Research and Methodology in Honor of Gus W. Van Beek,* ed. Joe D. Seger (Winona Lake, Ind.: Eisenbrauns, 1996), 213–217.

42. Cf. Manfred Weippert, "Remarks on the History of Settlement in Southern Jordan during the Early Iron Age," in *Studies in the History and Archaeology of Jordan,* 153–162, and references. Weippert argues that there was no organized kingdom of Edom in Iron I or the end of the Late Bronze Age, and that Deut. 2:1–8, asserting that Israel passed through Edom without hindrance, is superior to the contrary tradition in Num. 20:14–21. See also J. Maxwell Miller, "Recent Archaeological Developments

as Eissfeldt and Albright had argued before this new evidence was in hand, that Midian reached the summit of its influence in the thirteenth to twelfth centuries and, gaining control of the incense and spice trades that had begun to flourish in precisely this period, established hegemony, at least commercial hegemony, over the northern Ḥijâz and southern Transjordan, including Edom, Moab, and the Reubenite territories north of the Arnon.[43] Like the Qedarites, Lihyanites, and the later Nabataeans, they controlled the caravan routes north from South Arabia.

Relevant to Ancient Moab," in *Studies in the History and Archaeology of Jordan*, 169–173; J. A. Sauer, "Transjordan in the Bronze and Iron Ages: A Critique of Glueck's Synthesis," *BASOR* 263 (1986): 1–26 (with full bibliography); R. Ibach, "Archaeological Survey of the Hesban Region," *AUSS* 14 (1976): 119–126; "An Intensive Surface Survey at Jalul," *AUSS* 16 (1978): 215–222. Lawrence Stager has called my attention to K. A. Kitchen's arguments for a campaign of Ramses II against Moab, "Some New Light on the Asiatic Wars of Ramesses II," *Journal of Egyptian Archaeology* 50 (1964): 47–70, esp. 62 ff. Kitchen's identification of *ta-bu-nu* with Dibon (< *daybōn*) has been questioned. See S. Aḥituv, "Did Ramesses II Conquer Dibon?" *IEJ* 22 (1972): 141 f., and *Canaanite Toponyms in Ancient Egyptian Documents* (Jerusalem: Magnes Press, 1984), 189; cf. R. A. Kitchen's reply in "Two Notes on Ramesside History," *Oriens Antiquus* 15 (1976): 313–315, and his forthcoming review of Aḥituv's *Canaanite Toponyms* in *Chronique d'Égypte* 63 (1988); cf. also M. Weippert, "The Israelite 'Conquest' and the Evidence from Transjordan," in *Symposia Celebrating the Seventy-fifth Anniversary of the Founding of the American Schools of Oriental Research*, ed. F. M. Cross (Cambridge: ASOR, 1979), 27, n. 44. There remains in the Luxor reliefs of Ramses II the mention of the conquest of *bu-ta-ra-ta* in the land of *mu-ʾa-bu*. *Butarata* has not been identified with certitude. Cf. Kitchen, "New Light," 64 f.; Aḥituv, *Canaanite Toponyms*, 82. Weippert ("The Israelite 'Conquest,' " 27) remarks that "it cannot be established whether Ramesses II conquered a fortress, a fortified city, a village, or only a nomad's camp in Moab." While there is no reason to doubt that it is biblical Moab that is mentioned in the Luxor reliefs and in the topographical lists of Ramses II, we are unable to determine its geographical bounds and its level of political development. There is every reason to believe, however, that Moab, like Ammon and Israel, was a late-developing nation state. Even in the inscriptions of Mešaʿ king of Moab, we hear of his calling up two hundred men of Moab, "even all its chieftains" (l. 20) to engage in holy war (*ḥerem*), and of Mešaʿ's rule "[over] one hundred [chieftains]" which he added to the land (reading *wʾnk mlkt⌜y⌝ [ʿl rš] mʾt bqrn ʾšr yspty ʿl hʾrṣ*, ll. 28–29). The language suggests a recent transition from league or patriarchal institutions to monarchy.

43. See the references in n. 29 above. It should be remembered that the end of the Late Bronze Age is precisely the era when the expansion of trade in myrrh and other aromatics begins to be reflected in our texts. Albright's observation that the memory preserved of enormous herds of donkeys kept by the Midianites, and according to tradition taken as booty by Israel, points to the role of the Midianites as caravaneers. The donkey was a beast of burden, used neither for meat nor milk, from the time of its domestication, and large herds can only mean extensive use in caravans. No other function is plausible, as I am assured by A. M. Khazanov. One notes also that about

The absence of material remains from Sinai in the transition from the Late Bronze Age to the Early Iron Age—save for Egyptian mining establishments at Serâbîṭ el-Khâdem and Timna—comes as a surprise. Even the traditional site of Qadesh has produced no remains.[44] The Israeli surveys of the Sinai have been intense, and the lack of archaeological remains from this crucial period becomes a very strong argument (from silence) against the peninsula of Sinai as the area in which Sinai-Horeb and Qadesh were located.[45]

Israel's early contacts with Midian make sense in light of our present knowledge. Sinai-Horeb must be sought in southern Edom or northern Midian. This view, long held by German scholars but rejected by most American and Israeli scholars, including the writer, now appears to be sound. The archaic hymns of Israel are of one voice: Yahweh came from Teman, Mt. Paran, Midian, and Cushan (the Song of Habakkuk); the Song of Deborah sings of Yahweh going forth from Seʿir, marching forth from Edom; the Blessing of Moses states that Yahweh came from Sinai, beamed forth from Seʿir, shone from Mount Paran. These geographical designations cannot be moved west into the peninsula now called Sinai.

A large company of scholars has sought Sinai-Horeb in the Midianite region because they found in the theophanic language of Sinai the imagery of volcanic eruption.[46] I find this approach misconceived. The theophanic language of Sinai is a concretized, literalized form of the poetic language of Canaanite storm theophany and has nothing to do with volcanoes.[47] But the "Midianite Hypothesis" associated with the

---

the same time (the end of the Late Bronze Age), the unruly camel was beginning to be widely domesticated in Arabia, and that by the end of the twelfth century camel riders on a large scale appear first in Near Eastern texts, to wit, in the raid of camel-riding Midianites into Israel. On incense, see Kjeld Nielsen's collection of material, *Incense in Ancient Israel, SVT* 38 (Leiden: E. J. Brill, 1986). On the domestication of the camel (and Arabian trade in the Negev), see recently, Israel Finkelstein, "Arabian Trade and Socio-Political Conditions in the Negev in the Twelfth–Eleventh Centuries B.C.E.," *JNES* 47 (1988): 241–252, and references.

44. See the plaintive remarks of R. Cohen, "Did I Excavate Kadesh-Barnea?" *BAR* 7 (1981): 20–33; cf. "Excavations at Kadesh-barnea 1976–1978," *BA* 44 (1981): 93–107; and *Biblical Archaeology Today* (Jerusalem: IES, 1985), 78–80.

45. The failure to find LB II–EI I remains in Sinai and the Central Negeb has led to extraordinary proposals by those who assume Sinai—modern Sinai—to be the locus of Exodus and Sinai traditions. See, for example, R. Cohen, "The Mysterious MB I People: Does the Exodus Tradition in the Bible Preserve the Memory of Their Entry into Canaan?" *BAR* 9 (1983): 16–29.

46. See the discussions of Jörg Jeremias, *Theophanie,* 2nd ed. (Neukirchen-Vluyn: Neukirchener Verlag, 1977), 100–111, and R. de Vaux, *Histoire,* 403–410 and references.

47. See *CMHE,* 147–194, "Yahweh and Baal," esp. 167 ff.

names of Gressmann, Eduard Meyer, and Gunkel must be reformulated in a new way.[48] M. Noth made an important contribution in demonstrating that the list of stations in Numbers 33 derives from an itinerary of pilgrimage stations leading to Sinai lying east of Elath.[49] And the recent finds at Kuntillet ʿAjrūd, including references to Yahweh of Teman, tend to confirm his view. ʿAjrūd, apparently a pilgrimage station and shrine, lies on a primary road leading to Elath.[50]

Elements of Proto-Israel, or "Moses group," moved between Egypt and Midian, a major caravan route in the thirteenth and twelfth centuries, as we know from Egyptian sources.[51] Their movement then was northward, again along routes controlled by Midian, through the sparsely settled country of Edom and Moab, to settle for a time in the territory assigned to Reuben and later occupied by Moab. This area, the plateau (*mîšōr*) and steppes (*ʿarbôt môʾāb*), including the valley over against Bêt Peʿor, was almost empty of settled population in this era—like the

48. See J. David Schloen, "Caravans, Kenites, and *Casus belli:* Enmity and Alliance in the Song of Deborah," *CBQ* 55 (1993): 18–38. M. Weippert, *The Settlement of the Israelite Tribes in Palestine, SBTSS* 21 (Naperville, Ill.: Allenson, 1971), 105 f., n. 14, traces the hypothesis back to Richard von der Alm (1862), and C. P. Tiele. Cf. H. H. Rowley's review of the literature, *From Joseph to Joshua* (London: Oxford University Press for the British Academy, 1958), 149–156.

49. "Der Wallfahrtsweg zum Sinai," *PJB* 36 (1940): 5–28.

50. See above, chapter 2.

51. Cf. M. Weippert, "Semitische Nomaden des zweiten Jahrtausends: über die *šȝśw* der ägyptischen Quellen," *Biblica* 55 (1974): 265–280 and 427–433. The *šȝśw* of *ya-h-wa* (or *ya-h-wí*), associated with *śa-ʿ-r-ir* in the ʿAmara-West list, have been located by most scholars in Mount Seʿir, and the toponym *ya-h-wí* is assumed to contain the divine name (for *Bêt Yahwi* or the like). This analysis has been used by the writer and others to bolster the Midianite hypothesis. Recently Michael Astour has endeavored to relocate the *šȝśw* of *Yahwi* and of *śa-ʿ-r-ir* (as well as other *šȝśw* in the ʿAmara and Soleb lists) in Syria. See "Yahweh in Egyptian Topographic Lists," in *Festschrift Elmer Edel: 12 Marz 1979,* ed. M. Gorg and E. Pusch (Bamberg: M. Gorg, 1979), 17–33. His arguments have by no means convinced all, but the location of *Yahwi* must remain *sub judice,* and Weippert's suggestion that *Yahwi* is a hypocoristicon of a personal name (attached to a tribe or locality), *Yahwi-DN,* a type well documented in Amorite personal names, is a plausible alternate to the interpretation of *Yahwi* as a divine name (*apud* in Astour, 30, n. 72). Cf. Aḥituv, *Canaanite Toponyms,* 169 and n. 491, who finds Astour's proposal unconvincing. This issue is, basically, whether the Egyptian writing *śa-ʿ-r-ir* is to be identified with *śʿr* and *śa-ʿ-ir,* or with *š-ʿ-ra-ra* of the Tuthmosis III Syrian list. If one follows the Albright-Lambdin system of analyzing Egyptian syllabic orthography, it seems that the reading *śa-ʿ-r-ir* is more easily explained as a careless writing of *śa-ʿ-ir* than as an alternate writing of *š(!)-ʿ-ra-ra/š-ʿ-la-la.* The latter has been identified with Amarna šeḫlal by Albright (*The Vocalization of Egyptian Syllabic Orthography* [New Haven: American Oriental Society, 1934], 48), followed by many, including Astour.

central hill country of Canaan. The days of Moses and Midian in Reuben were remembered in the sanctuary traditions of Nebo and Gilgal.

Reuben too seems to have been a staging area for entrance into Canaan: "from Shittim to Gilgal." And it may be that standing behind Hosea's language, describing a new exodus and a new entrance into the land, is the same strand of archaic tradition: "Behold I shall allure her [Israel], and bring her through the desert, and speak tenderly to her, and give her vineyards from thence, and make the 'Valley of Achor' into a 'Portal of Hope.'"[52] The league of Israel evidently took classical form in the land in the course of the twelfth century, but there is good reason to believe that the religious traditions and military institutions that inspired and shaped the league stemmed from those elements of Israel who came from the southern mountains and entered Canaan from the lands of Reuben.[53]

Recent research on the era of the settlement of the Israelites in Canaan has demonstrated, if nothing else, that the archaeological and historical data are complex, and that no single model of the mechanisms of settlement comprehend the data.[54] The recent intensive surveys of the hill country of Canaan, notably in Ephraim and Manasseh, furnish strong arguments for identifying many elements of later Israel as seminomadic pastoralists, not refugees from, or rebels against, the feudal Canaanite city states.[55] Further, the institutions of the league, the twelve-tribe pat-

52. Hos. 2:16 f. On the Valley of ʿAchor, its location, and its Reubenite associations, see above, n. 8 and references.

53. Some elements no doubt also moved north in Transjordan to penetrate westward at such fords as Adam. Cf. Mazar, "Biblical Archaeology Today"; cf. Mazar, "The Early Israelite Settlement in the Hill Country," in *The Early Biblical Period*, ed. S. Aḥituv and B. A. Levine (Jerusalem: IES, 1986), 35–48.

54. I am reminded of the comment of A. M. Khazanov in his important study *Nomads and the Outside World*, trans. J. Crookenden (Cambridge: Cambridge University Press, 1983): "In the humanities and in anthropology, the reduction of the complex to the simple and of many factors to one often makes more accessible the thought-process of the scholar and the result of his research, but rarely does it truly bear fruit. That which in the natural sciences is possible, or at least considered to be *bon ton*, is not usually applicable to the humanities" (3).

55. See especially I. Finkelstein, *h'rky'wlwgyh šl tqwpt htnḥlwt whšwpṭym* (Jerusalem: IES, 1986), now in English entitled *The Archaeology of the Israelite Settlement* (Jerusalem: IES, 1988); and the papers on the "Israelite Settlement in Canaan: A Case Study," in *Biblical Archaeology Today*, 31–95, including papers by Gottwald, Herrmann, Kochavi, A. Mazar, and their respondents, Callaway, Cohen, Finkelstein, Stager, and Tsevat. Cf. also L. E. Stager, "The Archaeology of the Family in Ancient Israel," *BASOR* 260 (1985): 1–35; Weippert, "The Israelite 'Conquest' and the Evidence from Transjordan," 15–34; and M. L. Chaney, "Ancient Palestinian Peasant Movements and the Formation of Premonarchic Israel," in *Palestine in Transition: The Emergence of Ancient Israel*, ed. D. N. Freedman and D. F. Graf (Sheffield: Almond Press, 1983), 39–89.

tern, the institution of Holy War, *ḥerem,* the extension of kinship obligations by covenant, and the choice of the single, patron god have their closest analogues in the southeast, in Edom and Qedar and in Moab and Ammon. The league god reflected in the onomastica of Edom, Moab, Ammon, and Israel ("nation states") has no analogy in the onomastica of the city states with their pantheons or triads of city gods.[56] These institutions do not stem from the urban, Canaanite culture. The tribal structure of Israel is a difficulty for the defenders of the model of social revolution. The notion of "retribalization" in the frontier zones is problematic in the absence of "outside" tribal groups and ideology. In short, there appears to be evidence of the importation into the Land of Canaan of social and religious institutions and ideology alien to Canaan—but with ties to the southeast.

On the other hand, there is a strong anti-Canaanite, patriarchal-egalitarian, antifeudal polemic in early Israel, which appears to be authentic, grounded in history. The theses of Mendenhall and Gottwald are not simply false. The *ʿApiru,* the client class,[57] despised or feared by Canaanite nobility before Israel's appearance in Canaan, in Israel become the *ʿibrîm,* a class or group—only later carrying ethnic overtones—with whom Israel identified and who had special status in early Israelite legal lore. Surely in the consolidation of the league, serfs, clients, and slaves were readily absorbed into the nation, imprinting Israel with the consciousness of being of lowly origins, outsiders in Canaanite society.

Nor do I believe that the process of settlement and consolidation was

56. See above, chapters 1 and 2.

57. I have long held that *ʿapiru* means 'client,' or 'member of the client class.' The *ʿapiru* had no status in the feudal order but attached himself to it in a variety of roles, in military service, as an agricultural worker, and the like, or, having no legal status, he could turn to outlawry. The term is to be derived from the Hamito-Semitic root *ʿpr,* Akk. *apārum, epēru,* 'to provide (food, rations),' Egyptian *ʿpr,* 'to provide, equip.' Reference to the problematic Ugaritic *ḥpr* has served merely to confuse the discussion of those unfamiliar with the Egyptian data—a red herring. *ʿApiru* is a *qatil* form, as is evident from transcriptions, a stative pattern, 'one who is provided for, given rations or provisions,' in short a client. A group of West Semitic names, found in the Execration Texts, in the Hayes Papyrus, and in New Kingdom texts, exhibit the element *ʿapir-,* 'client,' in the pattern *ʿpr-DN: ʿpr-ʾl, ʿpr-bʿl, ʿpr-Ršpw,* etc. These names are to be analyzed to mean 'client of ʾEl,' 'client of Baʿl,' 'client of Rašpu,' etc. One may compare Phoenician names compounded with *gēr,* 'client.' W. F. Albright recognized both the pattern and the etymology of these names ("Northwest Semitic Names in a List of Egyptian Slaves," *JAOS* 74 [1954]: 225), but inexplicably rejected an etymological connection with the term *ʿapiru.* The derivation of *ʿibrî,* 'Hebrew,' from *ʿapiru* should, I believe, be affirmed. The development follows known patterns of linguistic change. The case is well analyzed (though leading to different conclusions) by M. Weippert in *The Settlement of the Israelite Tribes,* 74–82. Cf. O. Loretz, *Ḫabiru-Hebräer, BZAW* 160 (Berlin: de Gruyter, 1984), esp. 239 and the literature cited.

wholly peaceful. The notion of conquest, largely discredited these days —and properly so in its monolithic (Deuteronomistic) version—is not without testimony, archaeological and literary. Israel's premonarchical hymns, "songs of the wars of Yahweh," testify to early premonarchic wars and conquests. And it should not be forgotten that nomads are not merely pastoralists but also warriors.[58]

To return to our thesis: there is in the traditions we have been investigating historical evidence of a migration or incursion from Reuben of elements of Israel who came from the south, with ties to Midian, and whose original leader was Moses.

Archaic traditions of events in Reuben survived, as did those of Moses' Midianite connections: traditions too old and too well known to suppress and yet which have become obscure and faded. In the Yahwistic source, Moses stands alone. In the Elohist, Aaron appears, but chiefly as a rival and as the butt of polemic. In Priestly tradition, Aaron becomes Moses' alter ego and usurps all priestly functions. These transformations reflect, first, the early dominance of Moses and Transjordanian, especially Reubenite, sacral lore, and then the strife between rival priestly families, Levites and Aaronids, and finally the triumph of the Aaronids and the Zadokite house in Jerusalem. The Levites were demoted to minor clergy and knowledge of the priestly family of Moses forgotten or suppressed. Moses' failure to enter the land of Canaan, and his burial in the valley over against Bêt Peʿor, was explained as the punishment for grave sin.[59]

Reuben's age of preeminence also faded from memory, save for his place in the genealogy of the sons of Jacob: Reuben, the firstborn.

58. I find it bemusing that given the widespread evidence of destruction in Canaan at the end of the Late Bronze Age and the beginning of the Iron Age, some scholars are inclined to attribute the violence to various peoples, to almost anyone—except Israel. A. M. Khazanov, *Nomads and the Outside World,* 152, asserts that "confederations" among nomads "in all circumstances . . . emerge for military-political reasons." The anthropological data stand in odd contrast to the thesis of R. Smend, *Yahweh War and Tribal Confederation,* trans. M. G. Rogers (Nashville: Abingdon, 1970).

59. Moses' (and Aaron's) egregious sin, referred to in Num. 20:12f. (P) but unmentioned in the parallel passage in epic tradition (Exod. 17:1b–7), is never explicitly described. Various attempts to discern it in the present biblical text, in my opinion, fail to convince. I suspect the attack in older Priestly tradition was frontal and harsh, and in the final editing of the Pentateuch was omitted, save for the comment that Moses failed to "uphold the sanctity" of Yahweh (cf. Deut. 32:51).

PART II

PRIESTLY LORE AND ITS NEAR EASTERN BACKGROUND

4

The "Olden Gods" in Ancient Near Eastern Creation Myths and in Israel

IN A PAPER PUBLISHED SOME YEARS AGO, I FOUND IT USEFUL TO DISTINguish two genres or ideal types of creation myth in Canaanite and related ancient Near Eastern cycles.[1] One type is the *theogony,* the birth and succession of the gods, especially the old gods. Only at the end of the theogony proper do we reach the active or young deities, the great gods of the cult. The second type is the *cosmogony,* characterized by a conflict between the old and the young gods out of which order, especially kingship, is established in the cosmos. The theogonic myth normally uses the language of time; its events were of old, at the beginning. Yet the time language points beyond itself to "eternal" structures, which embrace even the gods and which constitute reality at all times. The cosmogony is often used in the rites of the cult.[2] It may or may not use time language. Yet the myth always delineates primordial events, that is, events that constitute cosmos, and hence are properly timeless or cyclical or eschatological in character.

To both the theogony and the cosmogony belong a special class of deities, the so-called olden gods. This class had a precise designation in Hittite, *šiuneš karuileš,* 'the olden gods' and in Akkadian translation *ilānū ša darūti* or *ilānū ša dārātim,* 'primeval gods' (*Urgötter*).[3] In Egypt the Ogdoad of Hermopolis had a similar title, *nčr.w pȝw.ty.w,* 'primeval gods.'[4] In the theogony, the olden gods are the focus of attention; in

1. See F. M. Cross, "The Song of the Sea and Canaanite Myth," *JTS* 5 (1968): 9 and n. 26.

2. I do not mean to suggest a general theory of the relation of myth to cultic rites, much less the priority of one over the other.

3. See especially O. R. Gurney, "Hittite Prayers of Mursili II," *AAA* 27 (1940): 81 f., and his references, especially E. Forrer, "Eine Geschichte des Götterkönigtums aus dem Hatti Reiche," *Annuaire de l'Institut de Phil. et d'Hist. Orientale (Mélanges Franz Cumont)* 4 (1963): 687–713.

4. For this and other designations including 'the old(est) gods,' see K. Sethe, *Amun und die acht Urgötter von Hermopolis* (Berlin: Abh. der preuss. Akad. der Wissenschaft, 1929), 45–48.

the cosmogony, the olden gods are pitted against the young god(s) in a titanic struggle. *Titanic* here is used in its original sense; the Titans were among the olden gods of Greece.

I

In the theogony, creation is described utilizing the language of sexual procreation. Characteristically, we find a series of pairs of gods, most pairs made up of a male and a female, frequently with rhyming or etymologically related names. For example, the primordial gods of Egypt, the Ogdoad of Hermopolis, consisted of four symmetrical, theogonic pairs: Nūn and Nawnet, Ḥūḥ and Ḥawḥet, Kūk and Kawket, Amūn and Amawnet.[5] An old Babylonian list begins with the names of fifteen matched pairs, which constitute the genealogy of Enlil: Enki and Ninki, Enmul and Ninmul, Enul and Ninul, Ennun and Ninnun, Enkur and Ninkur, and on to Enmešarra and Ninmešarra.[6]

The theogonic divine pairs are often binary opposites: Heaven and Earth (*Šamêm* and *ʾArṣ*) in the Phoenician theogony of Sakkunyaton; *Ouranos* and *Gē* in Hesiod, etc.; in the theogony introducing the Babylonian creation epic *Enūma eliš* we find *Apsu* and *Tiamāt,* perhaps 'the sweet waters' (male) and 'the salty abyss' (female); *Anšar* and *Kišar,* the opposing horizons of heaven and earth. Included are the oppositions male/female, heaven/earth, sweet/salt, day/night (light and darkness); less transparent is the opposition in the Hittite natural pairs: mountain and rivers, springs and the Great Sea, heaven and earth, winds and clouds. The olden gods may bear highly abstract names. Striking are the Egyptian pairs: 'Inertness' (*Nūn,* a name of the primordial waters),

5. For the last-named pair often a substitution is made of the names *Ny3.w/Ny3.t.* The vocalization of the series is ascertained by the series in Greek transcription: *Noun, Nouni,* etc.

6. This series comes from the Genouillac List, published in *Textes cunéiformes du Louvre (=Textes religieux sumériens du Louvre 10),* and discussed by H. de Genouillac in his paper "Grande liste de noms divins sumériens," *RA* 20 (1923): 89–106; 25 (1928): 133–319. For this and other lists see provisionally W. G. Lambert, "Götterlisten" and "Göttergenealogie" in *RLA,* and Lambert and S. Parker, *Enūma Eliš, the Babylonian Epic of Creation: The Cuneiform Text* (Oxford: Clarendon Press, 1966). Sanford Goldfess has investigated the character of Mesopotamian "ancestor gods," notably those in the list of forebears of Anu and Enlil ("Babylonian Theogony: Divine Origins in Ancient Mesopotamian Religion and Literature," Ph.D. diss., Harvard University, 1980). His results bring into question the legitimacy of my use of the ancestor gods of the Sumerian list in a comparative discussion of the "olden gods" in ancient Near Eastern mythology, and it may be that they should be relegated to a related, but distinct, genre.

'Unbounded' (*Ḥuḥ,* infinite in space, presumably used of the primordial space), 'Primeval Darkness' (*Kūk,* the darkness before the rising of the stars), 'Invisibility' (*Amūn,* evidently the air or wind originally), 'Nothingness' (*Ny3.w,* an alias of *Amūn*). Here belong also Greek *chaos* and perhaps Sumerian Enmešarra and Ninmešarra, 'Lord world order' and 'Lady world order.'[7] The olden gods may be described in some sense as "dead" gods. To be sure, a dead god does not cease to exist or to function. The old gods, at any rate, are placed in the netherworld. The Hittite *šiuneš karuileš* dwelt in the underworld and were also called "lords of earth."[8] The Hermopolite Ogdoad were dead and had their necropolis (*t3-dśr*) in Medinet Habu.[9] Zeus cast Cronos and the Titans into deep Tartaros, bound in chains. The gods that make up the genealogies of Anu and Enlil also appear to be "dead" gods or, in any case, gods confined to the underworld.[10] A newly published theogony from Babylon gives us new insights into this aspect of the old gods.[11] Seven generations are listed before one comes to the great gods, the living gods of the cult. For six generations there is repeated an oedipal pattern of patricide and incest. The first pair, of which only one name, Erṣitu (Earth), is certain, gives birth to Sumuqan (^{d}AMA.GAN.DU) and Tāmtu (Sea). Sumuqan killed his father and took to wife his mother Earth and his sister Sea. Sea kills her mother for good measure. Incest and patricide persist generation after generation, until the seventh, when the old god is merely chained by his son in taking power.

Incest marks the uncivilized, disordered behavior of the old gods. Of course incest was as inevitable at the beginnings of the family of the gods as among the children of Adam. Reflections of the pattern of patricide occur also in the theogonies of the Hittites (Hurrians), the Greeks,

7. T. Jacobsen translates the name, 'Lord *modus operandi* of the universe' and 'Lady *modus operandi* of the universe,' *Toward the Image of Tammuz, HSS* 21 (Cambridge: Harvard University Press, 1970), 116.

8. See the remarks of Gurney, "Hittite Prayers," 81, and n. 4, where he refers to the phrase *kat-te-ir-ri-eš ka-ru-u-e-li-e-eš* DINGIR.MEŠ, 'infernal and ancient gods.'

9. See Sethe, *Amun und die acht Urgötter,* 53 ff.

10. Cf. S. N. Kramer, "The Death of Gilgamesh," *BASOR* 94 (1944): 12 and n. 30. Jacobsen in *Image of Tammuz,* 115, writes of the old god En-uru-ulla, 'The Lord of the primeval city' as follows: "Since this deity is known . . . to be located in the nether world, we may assume that 'the primeval city' is the city of the dead. . . . Death, it would appear, was and ruled before life and all that came into being."

11. W. G. Lambert and A. R. Millard, *CT,* 46, 43. See also W. G. Lambert and P. Walcot, "A New Babylonian Theogony and Hesiod," *Kadmos* 4 (1965): 64–72; A. K. Grayson in *ANET,* 517. I have also had access to an unpublished paper of Thorkild Jacobsen, who has been able to reconstruct much more of this text than his predecessors. I owe much to his interpretation.

and the Canaanites, especially at the transitional generation or generations between the olden gods and the young cult gods. In the *Theogony* of Hesiod, Cronos emasculated his father Heaven (*Ouranos*), with the connivance of his mother Earth (*Gē*), and Zeus in turn defeated Cronos. In a Hurrian theogony[12] Alalu was defeated in battle by his son Anu and fled into the underworld; Anu was emasculated by his son Kumarbi, who in turn appears to have been overthrown by the storm-god Tešup. Under the label "olden gods," the Hittites regularly listed two series of foreign deities: Naraš, Napšaraš, Minki, Tuḫuši, Ammunki, Ammizzadu (of uncertain origin), Alalu, Anu, Antu, Apantu, Enlil, and Ninlil, all Mesopotamian gods. Appended was a third group: mountains and rivers, springs and Great Sea, Heaven and Earth, winds and clouds.

In one of the theogonies of the Phoenician hierophant Sakkunyaton (Sanchuniathon),[13] the god ʾEl, son of Šamêm, Heaven, avenged his mother Earth by castrating Heaven, leaving him to die. Here the oedipal pattern stops. In Canaanite lore ʾEl remained head of the pantheon, judge over the council of the gods, and was not ousted by the young storm-god Baʿl (alias Haddu). Rather, Sakkunyaton relates that ʾEl associated Astarte and Adod (that is, Baʿl-Haddu) in his rule.[14]

12. The basic treatments are those of Forrer, "Götterkönigtums," and H. G. Güterbock, *Kumarbi, Mythen vom hurritischen Kronos* (New York: Europaverlag, 1946).

13. See the edition of K. Mras, *Eusebius Werke,* vol. 8, part 1, *Praeparatio evangelica* (Berlin, 1954), 10.1–44; C. Clemen, *Die phönikische Religion nach Philo von Byblos* (Leipzig, 1939); and H. W. Attridge and R. A. Oden, *Philo of Byblos: The Phoenician History, CBQMS* 9 (Washington, D.C.: Catholic Biblical Association of America, 1981).

14. A text from Ugarit may confirm this (*KTU* 1.108, lines 2–4):

ʾilu yaθibu bi-ʿaθtarti	*ʾEl sits enthroned with Astarte*
ʾilu θapaṭa bi-haddi rāʿiyu	*ʾEl sits as judge with Haddu his shepherd*
dī yašīru wa-yaðammiru bi-kinnāri	*Who sings and plays on the lyre . . .*

See *CMHE,* 20 ff. To recent bibliography can be added Saul M. Olyan, *Asherah and the Cult of Yahweh in Israel, SBLMS* 34 (Atlanta: Scholars Press, 1988), 48 f. and references. Scholars are sharply divided on the interpretation of this text. Many, following Margalit ("A Ugaritic Psalm [RS 24.252]," *JBL* 89 [1970]: 292–304), have taken *bʿθtrt* and *bhdrʿy* to mean 'in Ashtaroth' and 'in Edrei,' place names in Bashan. There are many problems with such an interpretation. The god whose principal cult is in *ʿθtrt* is named *mlk,* Mulk, elsewhere at Ugarit (*KTU* 1.100.41 *mlk ʿθtrth,* 'Mulk at ʿAštarot,' and *KTU* 1.107.17 *mlk bʿθtrt).* This can be accommodated by translating as 'the god who dwells in Ashtarot, the god who judges in Edrei, who sings and plays on the lyre.' Or indeed *mlk* can be taken as an epithet (along with *rpiʾ*) of the cult of ʾEl in Bashan. I am somewhat dubious about discovering that ʾEl or Mulk at Ashtaroth in Transjordan is of major interest at Ugarit and indeed is the subject of the blessing of Ugarit in the final lines of the text. One is reminded of the notorious Negebite hypothesis, motivated by an excessively enthusiastic search for biblical references and parallels at Ugarit. Further, *hdrʿy* is a most peculiar transcription in Ugaritic of *ʾdrʿy*

The oedipal pattern also is largely absent from the theogony that introduced the late Mesopotamian creation myth Enūma eliš. Old gods Apsu and Tiāmat are killed by young gods Ea and Marduk, the first pair separated by a number of generations from the young gods who dispatch them.

The lists of the olden gods exhibit great variation in the number of generations and in the names of the theogonic pairs. Five generations separate Enlil from the first generation in *Enūma eliš,* at least seven in the Lambert theogony. Sakkunyaton gives three theogonies. The first, however, called the theogony of Taauth (Ṫhoth), is directly borrowed from the Hermopolite theogony of the Ogdoad, as shown persuasively by Albright.[15] The latter two, however, are fragments to be pieced together making six or seven generations to ʾEl, the head of the pantheon of the active deities of the cosmic state.

Some confusion has resulted in the failure of scholars in the past to recognize the two classes of deities, the old gods and the young gods. Names of old gods may overlap with those of young gods. For example, Enki in the pair Enki and Ninki bears the same name as the cult god Enki, but the two gods are not identical. The same is probably to be said of the god of the Ogdoad, Amūn, who in origin was unrelated to Amūn of Heliopolis, the king of the gods.[16] *ʿÔlām* (*Oulomos* of Mochus) is the name of a Phoenician old god, 'the ancient one' literally. The epithet *ʿÔlām,* and its equivalent *Saeculum, Senex,* or *Gerōn,* in the Punic world,[17] also was used of ʾEl, but the two must not be confused. Similarly, there is

---

with prothetic *ʾalep.* I know of no parallels. Margalit's suggestion that it is a scribal error is, of course, a *pis aller.* One notes also the parallel passage in *KTU* 1.101.1–3:

bʿl.yθb.kθbt.ġr	Baʿl sits enthroned, [his] mountain like a dais,
hd.r[ʿy?]kmdb	Haddu the shepherd—like the Flood Dragon
btk.ġrh.ʾil.ṣpn	In the midst of his mount, Divine Ṣapān,
b[m]ġr.tlʾiyt	On the mount of [his] victory.

The argument which has swayed many, that the expression *yθb b-* must indicate the place where one sits, is disingenuous. To be sure, this is the regular idiom for 'dwelling in a (place).' But the preposition *b-* may mark a variety of circumstances, including the so-called *bet comitantiae* (see B. Waltke and M. O'Connor, *Biblical Hebrew Syntax* [Winona Lake, Ind.: Eisenbrauns, 1990], § 11.2.5d).

15. See Albright's paper (published posthumously), "Neglected Factors in the Greek Intellectual Revolution," *Proceedings of the American Philosophical Society* 116 (1972): 225–242.

16. It is clear that in this case the Egyptians confused them, and indeed the confusion produced finally four Amūns. See Sethe, *Amun und die acht Urgötter,* 60, and especially W. Helck, *Wörterbuch der Mythologie,* ed. H. W. Haussig (Stuttgart: Ernst Klett Verlag), 3:331 f.

17. See my discussion in *CMHE,* 24–35.

an old god name *'Elyon* 'Most High,' to be distinguished carefully from the god of the Jerusalem cult called *'Elyon.*[18] One should not mix dead gods with living gods, even those with identical epithets or names.

We may conclude our remarks on this divine type by observing that the olden gods ordinarily had no temples or cults.[19] They rarely received sacrifices, to judge from extant texts, and were not the objects of hymns or praise. In the pantheon lists of Ugarit they go unrecorded thus far. 'El heads the pantheon and his genealogy is ignored. Nor do the olden gods appear normally as theophorous elements in personal names.[20] This is as it should be. Who desires an inert or dead god as his patron?

II

The olden gods also play a role in the second type of creation myth, the type we have called the cosmogony. The great cosmogonic myths of Mesopotamia and Canaan were associated with the central rites of the cult and as such are of much greater importance than the theogonic myths for our understanding of ancient, mythopoeic religion. The cosmogonies recount the warfare between the olden god or gods and the young god, or gods, a conflict out of which emerges victory for the young god and the establishment of kingship among the gods, and an orderly, cosmic government. Kingship and its hierarchical institutions are thus fixed in the orders of creation, and human kingship, patterned after the cosmic government, gains religious sanction.

In the Babylonian creation epic *Enūma eliš,* the conflict emerges from a clash between the primordial gods and the young gods.[21] The old, inert gods are disturbed by the activity of the youngsters. They want sleep and silence. The struggle reflects the duality of reality: stagnation, sterility, death, chaos are ranged against life, violence, fertility in the cosmos. Tiāmat, the sleepy dragon, and Apsū, her watery spouse, are goaded to fury and determine to destroy their offspring. Apsū is finished off early by wise Ea, and the ultimate struggle is between Sea and the young

18. Gen. 14:19, 20, 22.

19. The funerary cult of the Egyptian Ogdoad is in point of fact the exception that proves the rule. For other possible exceptions, see W. J. Moran, "Some Remarks on the Song of Moses," *Biblica* 43 (1962): 319 and n. 2.

20. The names *'Abd-Ṣapōn* and *'Abd-Ḥamon* are apparently exceptions, mountains (Cassius and Amanus) being reckoned as old gods. However, the names may be hypocoristica for *'Abd-ba'l-Ṣapōn* and *'Abd-ba'l-Ḥamōn.*

21. See Lambert and Parker, *Enūma Eliš.* Citations from Tablet V are after B. Landsberger and J. V. Kinnier Wilson, "The Fifth Tablet of Enūma Eliš," *JNES* 20 (1961): 154–179.

champion of the gods, Marduk. Tiāmat meanwhile has exalted her son Kingu in her assembly and he becomes her new spouse after the incestuous pattern of the old gods.

Marduk, invested with provisional kingship, is armed with weapons appropriate to the storm-god: the cloud chariot, lightning bolts, a bow, and a magical club. With his irresistible weapons he slays the ancient dragon. He splits her carcass to form the heavenly ocean and the nether sea, and the bubble of order in between becomes the ordered universe. The climax of the cosmogony comes with the return of the divine warrior in triumph and his enthronement as king. The gods greet him on his return to the assembly. "Assembled were the Igigi, they prostrated themselves before him altogether; as many as they were, the Anunnaki kissed his feet. Their assembly [came] to pay him reverence, and stood before him, did obeisance [saying]: 'He is king indeed.' "[22] Marduk then took up his royal insignia and was invested as king. He also announced his building project: the construction of his temple and residence in Babylon in the pattern of his cosmic temple. The foundation of the temple is equated in mythic dualism with creation. The establishment of Babylonian rule becomes identical with the establishment of cosmic order. Kingship, divine and human, is fixed in the orders of creation, properly eternal. Finally, the gods feast in the royal temple, celebrating the banquet of the divine king, the archetype of the royal enthronement festival on earth. In these lines the myth and the cultic drama become plain, and the political and propagandistic features of the cosmogonic myth emerge clearly. The cosmic state of the gods and the political community of Babylon are institutions fixed in eternity. The myth records primordial events; the drama also actualizes the creation ever anew. It is not astonishing, if the myth is properly understood, that at the end of *Enūma eliš* we find the petition: "May [Marduk] shepherd all the gods like sheep. May he subdue Tiāmat." The primeval event, celebrated in the cultus, now is also the new creation. Sacred time is fluid. Unhappily, there is no space here to deal with the several creation stories in the cosmogonic form. However, the form and function of these cosmogonies of Mesopotamia and Canaan (the Ugaritic cycle), are well known, and we are more interested here to examine the function and history of the theogonic form in Near Eastern mythology.[23]

22. Tablet V, 85–88.
23. On the Ugaritic cycle, see *CMHE,* 112–144.

III

Commonly the theogony may serve as a prologue to the cosmogony, pointing to the primeval nature of the mythic events by using the language of time. The dualism of the binary oppositions, male and female, heaven and earth, and so on, supports and turns into the dualism of the cosmogony which opposes the old gods and the new, the dead or inert and the living or active, the gods of chaos and the gods of order. This is not the only context in which we find the listing of the theogonic pairs, and both the theogony and the cosmogony may stand alone. As a matter of fact, the cosmogonies introduced by theogonies are mostly late, sophisticated texts: *Enūma eliš*, the *Theogony* of Hesiod, and the third theogony of Sakkunyaton all reflect impulses to systematize the divine powers. The Ugaritic cosmogonic cycle (in which Baʿl battles with Sea and Death to secure kingship) is not prefaced by a theogony. Indeed, no theogonic myth is extant in the Canaanite cuneiform texts. This circumstance has led certain scholars to claim that there is no creation myth at Ugarit. Such a view is wholly wrongheaded in my judgment. The absence of a theogonic prologue is merely a primitive feature of the Ugaritic cosmogonic cycle. Otherwise, it bears all the traits of the cosmogony. The conflict between Baʿl and Yamm-Nahar (Sea and River), Môt (Death), and Lôtān are alloforms reflecting the usual conflict between the old gods and the young gods of the cult. The primary focus of the cycle is the emergence of kingship among the gods. Baʿl the divine warrior returns victorious to the divine assembly, receives kingship, builds his royal temple on Mount Ṣapôn, and invites the gods to the royal banquet. The pattern of the cosmogonic myth could not be more evident. Moreover, one remembers that in biblical lore the defeat of the sea or the dragon is properly placed in time, at creation, or, to say the same thing, in the new creation. In the banquet of the end-time, the faithful feast on the flesh of Leviathan.

The theogony may also stand alone in Phoenician mythopoeic lore, as is the case with the first theogony of Sakkunyaton or the Hermopolite theogony.

Interesting also is the use of the theogonic pairs in lists of witnesses in Hittite and West Semitic treaty texts. In the treaties they are named following the patron gods of the parties to the treaty and after the great gods and the gods of the cult places. They are often designated by the rubric "olden gods" in Hittite texts, distinguishing them from the principal, active gods. Heaven and Earth form the pivotal pair, often, between the executive gods and the old gods, followed by mountains, rivers, sea, and so on. It is not surprising to find that the order of the theogonic pairs is reversed in many treaty texts, as is natural since the "living" deities are named first: thus the eighth-century treaty of Sefire lists: "ʾEl and ʿElyôn, Heaven and Earth, Abyss and Sources, Night and Day."[24] Evidently there is revealed here the desire for completeness in listing witnesses to the treaty. Also even the young gods are bound by or contained in the prototypic structures of the universe represented by the primeval powers.

This function of the theogonic pairs survives in attenuated form in Israel in the context of the "covenant lawsuit." Witnesses to Israel's covenant or treaty with Yahweh are called upon to attend the cosmic legal proceedings in which Israel is prosecuted for breach of treaty. The classical formulae of the prophetic process include the address to the olden gods: "Hear O Mountains the lawsuit of Yahweh, and ⌜give ear⌝ O Foundations of the Earth" (Micah 6:2a); "Listen O Heavens, give ear O Earth" (Isaiah 1:2a); "Be astonished, O Heavens, on this account, be greatly appalled ⌜O Mountains⌝" (Jeremiah 2:12; cf. Jeremiah 2:9f.).[25] The speculative and classificatory function of the theogonic pairs alluded to earlier needs to be further underlined. The theogony was created by a mythopoeic mind enchanted by binary opposites that seemed fixed in the structure of reality.

It is not by chance that in the proto-philosophic speculations of the pre-Socratics of the Milesian school, lists of opposites played a fundamental role.[26] One thinks particularly of the pairs cold (wind/air) and hot (fire), wet (water) and dry (earth), which separate out of the substratum 'the Unbounded' (*apeiron*) in the thought of Anaximander. The abstraction vividly reflected in the theogonic genre of gods no doubt gave impetus to philosophical abstraction and classification. In any case, the linkage and continuity between theogonic speculation and cosmological speculation of the Milesian school is difficult to deny. As for the substratum of Thales (primordial water), of Anaximander (the Unbounded), and of Anaximenes (air-wind-vapor), all are found in the theogonies of Phoenicia and Egypt.[27]

24. *KAI*, 222, A.11 f.; cf. J. A. Fitzmyer, *The Aramaic Inscriptions of Sefire* (Rome: Pontifical Biblical Institute, 1967), 37–39. On the pairs Heaven and Earth and Day and Night, see Moran, *Biblica* 43 (1962): 317 ff., and references.

25. See also Deut. 32:1 and Ps. 50:4, hymns that echo the covenant-lawsuit formula.

26. See Albright, "Neglected Factors in the Greek Intellectual Revolution," 236–238.

27. O. Eissfeldt in his paper "Phönikische und griechische Kosmogonie," in *Kleine Schriften* 3 (Tübingen: J. C. B. Mohr [Paul Siebeck], 1966), 501–512, has argued for direct influence of the Phoenician theogony of Taaut (Thoth) found in Sakkunyaton (*Praeparatio evangelica* 1.10.1), noting among many resemblances the key term *apeiron* used in Anaximander of the substrate, and Sakkunyaton's characteristic description of elements of primordial chaos as *apeira* and *mē echein peras.* Albright (in "Neglected Factors in the Greek Intellectual Revolution") has demonstrated further that the first

IV

I wish to turn finally to a discussion of the Phoenician theogony and its transformation in the biblical account of creation. As noted above, Sakkunyaton's lore as preserved by Philo Byblius contains three theogonic cycles, the first the theology of Thoth, which need not detain us, the second and third, fragments of a single theogony transformed under Euhemeristic influence into a history of culture. Together the fragments permit us to piece together a substantial part of a canonical Phoenician theogony.

The first pair are the wind *Qodm* and his spouse *Baau* (biblical *bōhû*).[28] 'Qodm the Wind' may mean either the east wind or the primordial wind, or still more likely, both. The second pair is *ʿÔlām* (later Phoenician *ûlōm*) and his female counterpart, perhaps *ʿÔlamt*.[29] In early Phoenician, *ʿÔlām* means only 'the ancient one' or the 'eternal one.' The Greek term is *Aiōn,* the Mandaic *ʿalma* in later Gnostic systems. *ʿÔlām,* the child of *Baau,* is identical with the Gnostic *yaldabaōt,* that is, 'the child of Chaos.' The third pair is listed in Greek as *Genos* and *Genea* and imitates the Phoenician by being derived from the same stem. *Yald* and *Yaldat* are possible names suggesting that this pair is a doublet of the second pair. From them stem Light, Fire, Flame, and the giants, Mount Casius, Lebanon, Hermon, and Amanus (the cedar mountain, *barathu,* Hebrew *bĕrōš*). Here the series breaks off to be taken up again in the third fragment[30] with the pair Elyūn (Hebrew ʿElyôn) and Bērūt (Hebrew *bĕʾērôt*). The pair is not symmetrical: 'The Most High' and 'Springs.' There may be confusion or an omission in the transmitted lore. The final pair is Heaven and Earth (*Šamêm* and *ʾArṣ*) before the appearance of the great gods, ʾEl, Dagon, ʿAštart, and so on, the children of Heaven and Earth. To this theogony is attached only a brief reference to the establishment of kingship among the gods—enough, however, to recognize the linkage between the two types of creation myth in Phoenicia.

The biblical account of creation in the first chapter of Genesis belongs clearly to the theogonic genre, not to the cosmogonic form. It begins with the theogonic formula, "When God began to create heaven and earth . . .

---

theogony of Sakkunyaton is taken over as a whole from the Hermopolite theology. We note the pair Ḥūḥ and Ḥawḥet 'Lord Unlimited-in-Space' and 'Lady Unlimited-in-Space.'

28. The emendation of KOLPI to KODM, graphically nearly identical, is that of Albright, *JBL* 43 (1923): 66 f. Cf. L. Clapham, "Sanchuniathon: The First Two Cycles" (Ph.D. diss., Harvard University, 1969), 83.

29. Compare the Mesopotamian theogonic pair Duri and Dari, whose names have the same meaning.

30. *Praep. evang.* 1.10.14–15.

then he said, 'Let light come into existence.'" In a parenthesis we are told that the earth was chaos and disorder: *tōhû wa-bōhû,* Sakkunyaton's *Baau,* Hesiod's *Chaos.* Darkness was on the face of the Deep, *tĕhōm,* Babylonian *Tiāmat,* Egyptian *Nūn,* and the divine wind (*rûaḥ 'ĕlōhîm*) soared over the surface of the waters of the deep, the primordial wind of Sakkunyaton and Anaximenes. Thus allusion is made to several of the theogonic pairs: wind and watery chaos, heaven and earth, darkness and light. To be sure, the olden gods are here natural pairs, abstracted like the elements of the Ionian cosmologists. More important, there is in the Genesis creation story no element of cosmogonic conflict, no linkage to a cosmogony. God creates by fiat. On the other hand, the creation account is a prologue attached to an epic account of the call of the fathers, the victory of the Divine Warrior in the exodus and conquest, and the creation of the covenantal political order at Sinai. The creation story provides a universal context and a temporal setting to the Israelite epic. We have argued that the theogonic myth used the language of time to point to the primordial or eternal dimension of the cosmogonic myth. That is, the time language refers to fluid, not to ordinary linear, time in the creation cycles of Mesopotamia and Canaan. In Israel time is linear or a forward-moving spiral (Vico), a radical transformation of the older Near Eastern tradition. Creation is merely a first event—without exclusive significance—in a series of epic events.

The history of the theogony comes to an end, so to speak, in two transformations, in the monotheistic creation story of Genesis 1 and in the cosmology of the Ionian philosophers. It is of considerable interest that the composition of the Hebrew creation story and the activity of the Greek philosophers coincided in time, in the course of the sixth century B.C.E. when the ancient Semitic empires were brought to an end and the age of Persia and Greece was dawning.

5

The Priestly Tabernacle and the Temple of Solomon

IN 1947 I UNDERTOOK TO REVISE THE STANDARD VIEW OF THE PRIESTLY Tabernacle (described in Exodus 25–31 and 35–40) as it had developed in nineteenth- and early-twentieth-century scholarship.[1] This view, which still represents the consensus of European scholars, holds that the Priestly account of the Tabernacle was the creation of the Priestly school, which flourished after the fall of the First Temple, and that it was a fanciful vision designed for the future, projected back on Mosaic times—a "pious fraud." In 1947 there seemed to be new ground upon which to reconsider the historicity of the Tabernacle traditions. Advances in tradition-critical analysis and in the history of West Semitic religion have provided data that have shown repeatedly that the Priestly tradent drew on older documents in his edition of the Tetrateuch.[2] Such

1. F. M. Cross, "The Tabernacle: A Study from an Archaeological and Historical Approach," *BA* 10 (1947): 45–68; reprinted in a slightly revised form as "The Priestly Tabernacle," in *The Biblical Archaeologist Reader*, ed. G. Ernest Wright and D. N. Freedman (New York: Anchor Books, 1961), 201–228. Earlier versions of the present study of the Priestly Tabernacle have appeared in *Temples and High Places in Biblical Times*, ed. A. Biran (Jerusalem: Hebrew Union College–Jewish Institute of Religion, 1981), 169–180; and *The Temple in Antiquity*, ed. Truman G. Madsen (Provo, Utah: Religious Studies Center, 1984), 91–105. An extended discussion and literature may be found in M. Haran, *Temples and Temple Service in Ancient Israel* (Oxford: Clarendon Press, 1978), 189–204. A recent study, citing especially Mesopotamian parallels to the account of the building of the Tabernacle is that of Victor [Avigdor] Hurowitz, "The Priestly Account of Building the Tabernacle," *JAOS* 105 (1985): 21–30.

2. For a more general discussion of the composition of the Priestly work, see *CMHE*, 293–325; R. E. Friedman, *The Exile and Biblical Narrative, HSM* 22 (Chico, Calif.: Scholars Press, 1981), 44–147 and bibliography; Sven Tengstrom's useful monograph, *Die Toledotformel. Coniectanea Biblica, Old Testament Series* 17 (Uppsala: Gleerup, 1981); A. Hurvitz, *A Linguistic Study of the Relationship between the Priestly Source and the Book of Ezekiel* (Paris: Gabalda, 1982) and "The Evidence of Language in Dating the Priestly Code," *RB* 81 (1974): 24–56. B. A. Levine's paper "The Descriptive Tabernacle Texts of the Pentateuch," *JAOS* 85 (1965): 307–318, is also of importance in the history of the

documents are of various date, and, from the point of view of modern scholarship, they were often used improperly to re-create patriarchal or Mosaic times. Their misuse, however, was naive or unknowing, not the product of intentional fraud, pious or impious. The description of the Tabernacle indeed is derived, in my view, from an older document belonging to the Temple archives, utilized by P (= the Priestly tradent) and turned to narrative use, first to reconstruct the demands of the deity as to the nature of the sanctuary to be built, and then to recount the carrying out of these directives in the construction and establishment of the Israelite cultus.[3] While the Tabernacle as described in the document incorporated in the Priestly strata is perhaps too complex and richly ornamented to reflect a tent shrine of early Israel, the description does appear to reflect an actual tent shrine at some stage in the evolution of the tent sanctuaries used in pre-Solomonic Israel.

I have argued that the most likely candidate was the Tent of Yahweh erected by David in conscious imitation of Israel's earlier shrines of the Ark and its cherubim throne. Further, it seemed clear already fifty years ago that the Tabernacle as described in P features many Canaanite, or old West Semitic, elements not found in the Temple of Solomon, elements most unlikely to be introduced in a fantasy of late, orthodox priests.

In the last years new data have accumulated which in my view tend to confirm that historical elements are found in the traditions of the Priestly Tabernacle, at least as a shrine that existed at some stage in Israel's early cultus. Perhaps more important, they give insight into its origin and the meaning of its symbols and design.

I

The design of the Tabernacle in Exodus is richer and more elaborate than a simple nomad's tent or a booth housing a portable palladium of battle. Here the scholars of a past generation were correct even if the conclusions they drew were wrong. Four sets of curtains were spread over

---

discussion, as is M. Weinfeld's study "Social and Cultic Institutions in the Priestly Source against Their Ancient Near Eastern Background," *Proceedings of the Eighth World Congress of Jewish Studies* (Jerusalem, 1983): 95–129.

3. Among the signs that P has incorporated an older document is the contrasting usage of the terms *miškān* and *ʾōhel môʿēd* in chapters 26 and 36 of Exodus (where *miškān* is used to the exclusion of *ʾōhel môʿēd*) and elsewhere (where *ʾôhel môʿēd* is the dominant term used). These data conform with other evidence to suggest that the old document used *miškān* as its primary name for the Tabernacle (as well as the inner shrine—see Exod. 26:7; 36:14) while P used both designations but much more frequently *ʾōhel môʿēd*.

a wooden skeleton of *qĕrāšîm,* latticework frames,[4] constituting a rectangular enclosure of two rooms. The structure has the proportions of three cubes, a double-cube for the holy place, a single, perfect cube for the most holy place, ten cubits to each dimension.[5] The floor plan (but not other dimensions) has the same proportions as the Temple of Solomon, if we ignore the Temple's porch, *'ûlām.* The floor plan of the Temple's holy place and most holy place consisted of three squares, twenty cubits to a side, two squares constituting the holy place, one square the holy of holies. The parallel proportions of the inner rooms of the Temple and Tabernacle cannot be explained as chance. Evidently one has influenced the other or both derive from an older model. In the understanding of the Priestly tradent the proportions are derived from a *tabnît,* a model of the cosmic Tabernacle of Yahweh. This dualism of earthly/cosmic is characteristically Canaanite. The Canaanite temple was founded on New Year's Day, identified with the foundation of the cosmic temple at creation, confirming the victory of the Divine Warrior over his enemies, who represent chaos and death. Reflecting the same dualism, each mountain on which a sanctuary was built was identified with the cosmic 'mount of possession,' *hr/ġr nḥlt,* upon which the deity established his royal shrine or cosmic government.[6] For example, Zion is once given the epithet *yarkĕtê ṣāpôn,* literally, 'Far North,' comparable to the Sidonian sacred precinct called *šamêm rōmīm,* 'High Heaven.'[7] The epithet has generally been taken as an identification of Zion with Mount *Ṣāpôn,* the cosmic/earthly mountain of Ba'l-Haddu. However, it can apply equally to Mount Amanus, truly the "Far North," the traditional mountain of 'El, also referred to straightforwardly in Isaiah 14:13: "I shall be enthroned in the mount of the council [of 'El] in the distant north [*yarkĕtê ṣāpôn*]."[8]

4. A. R. S. Kennedy's reconstruction has been reinforced by the use of *qrš* of 'El's tent (see below).

5. A rather different reconstruction of the proportions of the Tabernacle is suggested in the study of Friedman, *The Exile and Biblical Narrative,* 47–60 and figures, pp. 137–140.

6. See at length the monograph of Richard Clifford, *The Cosmic Mountain in Canaan and in the Old Testament, HSM* 4 (Cambridge: Harvard University Press, 1972).

7. See most recently, Clifford, *The Cosmic Mountain,* 133, n. 40. The biblical reference is Ps. 48:3.

8. See *CMHE,* 26–28 and esp. 37 f. It needs hardly be said that *ṣāpôn* in Hebrew comes to mean simply 'north,' and that the idiom means 'the distant north.' It is by no means an equivalent of Ugaritic *mrym ṣpn,* the formulaic expression for the 'pinnacles of the Cassius,' Ba'l's abode. In the Ugaritic texts, at least, the mount of assembly is never placed on Mount Ṣāpôn; it convenes in the mount of 'El. In view of the conflation of elements of Ba'l myths as well as 'El myths in early Israelite religion, one might argue for the confusion of Ṣāpôn and the mount of 'El in later transformations

I am inclined therefore to understand the proportions of both the Tent and the Temple as derived from an older mythic convention, the earthly shrine as a microcosm of the cosmic shrine. This need not mean that the precise measurements of the Tabernacle and Temple stem from a common source. The Priestly tradent may have calculated, so to speak, the measurements of the Tabernacle by reducing the measurements of the Temple, reckoning on the assumption—or knowledge—that both followed traditional proportions. Equally plausibly we could argue that the Temple in its basic floor plan preserved the proportions of the Davidic sanctuary, the first shrine of the empire, as it preserved much of the iconography of the older shrine. In any case, the earthly shrine was conceived as preserving the proportions of the cosmic abode of deity in reduced measure.

II

In pursuing the question of Canaanite elements in the Priestly Tabernacle I wish to examine the term *qereš,* used of the rigid structure of the tent. Some have seized on this feature to insist that the Tabernacle is a "portable temple," an anachronistic conception which could have come into existence only after the building of the Temple of Solomon. The term *qereš/qaršu* is used of the divine abode only in one other context: it is used, probably in the plural, in the description of the tent of ʾEl, the father and judge of the gods in the Canaanite pantheon. Here there can be no doubt. The term *qereš* in particular points to the authenticity of the Priestly Tabernacle as an old tent shrine, not a temple in sheep's clothing. Frequently, the tent of ʾEl appears in stereotyped language in scenes of the meeting of the council of the gods. Here we find the formulaic pair: *ðd/θd* and *qrš.* The former term clearly means tent, as shown by Richard Clifford, referring in particular to its use in the ʾAqhat epic in parallel to *ʾuhalīma.*[9]

---

of Canaanite elements in Israel's cultic ideology when the Temple replaced the Tabernacle. I am disposed to doubt such a conflation in this instance. Jerusalem in Israelite tradition is associated with "ʾEl, creator of earth,' a tradition remembered still in pure form about 700 B.C.E. on a Hebrew ostracon from Jerusalem (N. Avigad, *IEJ* 22 [1972]: 195; pl. 42B: [[*ʾl*]*qn ʾrṣ*]), as well as in expanded form in Gen. 14:19. Further, the tent tradition associated with ʾEl remained a powerful one among the priests and singers of the Jerusalem temple.

9. *CTA* 19:211–214. See Richard J. Clifford, "The Tent of El and the Israelite Tent of Meeting," *CBQ* 33 (1971): 221–227. In the Hittite version of an ʾEl myth (*Ilkunirsa*) the translation of his abode's designation is GIŠ.ZA.LAM.GAR = Akk. *kuštāru,* 'tent'; cf. *CMHE,* 72, n. 112.

The abode of the god ʾEl warrants further description. ʾEl's tent is pitched in the far north, in Mount Ḫamōn, whence ʾEl's epithet Baʿl Ḫamōn. At the same time he dwells "in the midst of the sea," that is, on the mount out of which springs the sources of the cosmic rivers (*mabbīkê naharêmi*), in the midst of the fountains of the double-deep (*ʾapiqê tihāmatêmi*). Several mythological themes come together here. The mount is the mountain of the assembly of ʾEl, biblical *har môʿēd.* Here also is the garden of God where grew the cedars of ʾEl, biblical ʾarzê ʾEl.[10] The cosmic river springing up from the underworld is also 'Judge River,' *θāpiṭu nahari,* as in Mesopotamia the place of the river ordeal, the place of questioning or judgment, as one enters the underworld, whence the term *šĕʾōl.*[11]

The curtains of the Tabernacle were fourfold. The innermost curtain of linen decorated with cherubim, traditional guardians of ʾEl's throne, is called *miškān,* 'tabernacle' *par excellence* as opposed to the outer three, properly the tent. This usage may be compared with the Aramaic term *mškn*ʾ used in an inscription from Hatra applied to the forbidden, innermost part of a sanctuary (as shown by Delbert Hillers).[12] Above a set of curtains of goats' hair, the usual stuff of tents, there is a set of curtains of sheepskin dyed red, a motif that survives in Arab portable shrines of red leather.[13] The outermost curtain is made of *taḥaš* skins. The term *taḥaš* has been a source of great puzzlement. It has a perfectly simple etymology being cognate with Arabic *tuḫas,* a word applied to small cetaceans, notably the dolphin.[14] An enormous amount of effort and ingenuity has been expended by Semitists in searching for an alternate etymology. In 1947 I favored an Egyptian derivation—a *pis aller.*[15] For a time there was an Akkadian etymology—until Assyriologists discovered the putative etymon did not exist, its origin stemming from the misreading of a syllabic value. We are left with dolphin skins. One may easily see why dolphins' hide appeared undesirable or unavailable for the manufacture of a desert tent. So far as I am aware, the first English version to give up the

10. Ezek. 31:8 f; cf. Ps. 80:11. Cf. F. M. Cross, "ʾĒl," *ThWAT* 1, col. 272.

11. I have long held to this etymology in view of Akkadian use of the same root, *šālu,* of judicial inquiry, haling to judgment, and most significant, precisely in connection with the river ordeal.

12. "Mškn' 'Temple' in Inscriptions from Hatra," *BASOR* 207 (1972): 54–56.

13. See Cross, "The Priestly Tabernacle," 218 f. Of particular interest is the portrayal of a tent shrine in bas relief from Palmyra (third to first centuries B.C.E.) with traces of red paint still adhering to it.

14. Of course, *tuḫas* is the precise etymological reflex of Hebrew *taḥaš* in its consonantal structure. In Arabic a byform *duḫas* also is found, presumably created by attraction to the root *dḫs,* 'fat,' 'fleshy,' 'having much vigor.'

15. "The Priestly Tabernacle," 220, n. 21.

struggle and translate 'dolphin' was the new Jewish Publication Society translation. I must say that I find it hard to believe that priests bent on producing a fraudulent description of Moses' Tabernacle would have chosen dolphin skin for outer curtains. However, once the connection between the Tent of ʾEl and Israel's tent shrine is recognized, the difficulties dissolve. ʾEl's abode "in the midst of the sea" at the "fountain of the double-deep" provides the proper setting for a tent of dolphin skins. The dolphin is, of course, a favorite motif in Phoenician art, both on the mainland and in the Punic colonies, where it is associated with ʾEl and Tannit.

The ties between the iconography of Canaanite ʾEl and the iconography of the Tabernacle are striking. Representations of the god ʾEl both at Ugarit and in the Punic West portray him as an old man with a long beard, wearing a high conical hat, ordinarily horned. While ancient and benign in physiognomy, he also appears powerful and vigorous. Characteristically this bearded god sits on a cherubim throne, his right hand lifted in blessing.[16] I believe that the cherubim throne, which if Eissfeldt is right had its origin in the Shiloh cultus, is ultimately derived from the typical iconography of ʾEl.[17] This is wholly fitting if I am correct in identifying most if not all of the patriarchal epithets of deity as epithets of ʾEl: (*ʾēl*) *ʿôlām,* 'the ancient god,' an epithet used in Canaanite, Phoenician, and in the Punic West, as well as in Genesis; biblical *melek ʿôlām,* 'ancient king,' now appears in a Ugaritic text applied, in my opinion, to ʾEl. A similar liturgical name of ʾEl is *malk ʾabū šanīma,* 'king, father of years.'[18] This in turn is reminiscent of biblical *ʾēl gibbôr ʾabī ʿad,* 'El the warrior, eternal father,' and of the white-haired 'Ancient of Days' of Daniel 7. A number of other titles can be listed: (*ʾēl*) *šadday,* 'the one of the mountain'; *ʾēl qônê ʾarṣ,* 'ʾEl creator of earth,'[19] and *ʾēl ʾĕlôhê yiśrāʾēl,* 'ʾEl god of (the patriarch) Israel.' Indeed the epithet of the cult of the Ark, *yahweh ṣĕbāʾôt,* may originate in an ʾEl epithet (*ʾēl zū*) *yahweh ṣĕbāʾôt,* '(ʾEl who) creates the (heavenly) armies.'[20] Continuities between the abode of ʾEl and the tent shrine of Yahweh therefore occasion no surprise.

I am disposed to argue in short that the *tabnît* or model of the Tabernacle is derived ultimately from mythological conceptions of the Tent of ʾEl. Further, the designation *ʾōhel môʿēd,* the Priestly tradent's favorite name of the Tabernacle, is to be translated 'tent of assembly.' In Phoe-

16. For references, see *CMHE,* 35 f.

17. O. Eissfeldt, "Jahwe Zebaoth," *Kleine Schriften* 3 (Tübingen: Mohr, 1966), 103–123. I should add that the typical iconography of Baʿl-Haddu portrays the divine figure standing in battle dress, thunderbolt held in his hand poised to be hurled.

18. Isa. 9:5.

19. See above n. 8 for references including reference to the Jerusalem ostracon.

20. See *CMHE,* 60–71.

nicia in the early time *môʿēd* is used of a political assembly;[21] at Ugarit *môʿidu* (along with *puḫru*) is also used of the council or assembly of the gods in the mountain of ʾEl. Thus *ʾōhel môʿēd,* 'tent of assembly,' is the appropriate designation of ʾEl's tent, and at the same time of its earthly counterpart, the shrine of the Israelite federation where the league council met "before Yahweh."[22]

III

A few words must be said about the history of Israel's tent traditions. A most extraordinary statement is found embedded in Nathan's oracle in 2 Samuel 7. Yahweh speaks in slightly prosaized poetry: "Indeed I have never dwelt in a temple [*bêt*] . . . but I have moved about in a tent or in a tabernacle." The assertion is that Yahweh's shrine has always been a tent, and hence the king is not to build a temple.[23] The statement raises two questions. First of all, is it true that Yahweh's legitimate shrine[24] was always a tent? One prose source in the Deuteronomistic history in fact refers to a *hêkāl,* 'temple' or *bêt Yahweh* at Shiloh, the shrine of Eli and Samuel, and no doubt a league sanctuary of old Israel. Other sources, prose and poetic, refer to the shrine at Shiloh as a tent or tabernacle. In such case credence should be given to the poetic sources, especially if they are old. Psalm 78:60 speaks of the sanctuary of Shiloh as a 'tent' and 'tabernacle,' and in view of its early date, confirms the assertion of Nathan's oracle. One may compare the early hymn of the Davidic cult that refers to the shrine of the Ark at Kiryat-Yĕʿārîm as Yahweh's *miškĕnôt,* 'encampment.'[25] The second question is more important: what is the basis of the opposition by the prophet, and presumably other traditionalists in Israel, to the building of a temple or *bêt Yahweh* to replace the old tent shrine? Clear expression of this opposition is lost in the overwriting of later generations after Solomon's temple came into being and the traditionalists' case became moot. The opposition was strong enough in any event for David to give up his early intention and to construct a tent shrine as the successor to Shiloh's sanctuary.

An explanation of the conflict can be found in part in the mythic background of two types of shrine. Baʿl founded his temple on Mount Ṣāpôn in order to make manifest his establishment of order, especially king-

21. The term *môʿēd* appears as a loanword in the Tale of Wenamun, as first observed by John Wilson.

22. See in detail, Clifford, "The Tent of El and the Israelite Tent of Meeting."

23. A full analysis of the oracle is found in *CMHE,* 241–257.

24. That is, a shrine of the Ark.

25. Ps. 132:7.

ship among the gods. The earthly temple of Baʿl not only manifested Baʿl's creation of order but at the same time established the rule of the earthly king. There is thus a tie between the temple as the abode of the king of the gods and the temple as a dynastic shrine of the earthly king, the adopted son of the god. The temple and kingship are thus part of the "orders of creation," properly the eternal kingship of the god of order, the eternal dynasty of his earthly counterpart. The tent of ʾEl reflects a different political ideology. ʾEl was the divine patriarch, god of the father, of the league, of covenant. ʾEl sits as judge in the assembly of the gods. In Israel the political counterpart was the tent of assembly, the shrine of the federated tribes bound together in a conditional covenant.

The "temple of Baʿl" and the "tent of ʾEl" thus symbolize alternate political ideologies. In the rise of kingship in Israel there were those who wished Israel's old constitution to limit kingship and its cultic trappings, others ready to embrace Canaanite ideology of the divine king and his dynastic shrine. It is not by chance that the old royal hymn Psalm 132 speaks of David's shrine as the *miškĕnôt*, 'tabernacle' (or 'tent-complex') of Yahweh, and stresses the conditional nature of Yahweh's covenant with the Davidic dynasty. On the contrary the ideology of the later Davidic dynasty speaks of the eternal choice of Zion and David's seed, and the adoption of the king as son. In Psalm 89 (from an early Temple liturgy) this absolutist ideology reaches its highest pitch. After a description of the Divine Warrior slaying the dragon and establishing the created order, we read of Yahweh's eternal choice of David (i.e., David's dynasty), which is unconditional, and most striking: "I [the deity is speaking] will establish his hand over Sea, his right hand over Rivers; he will proclaim, 'my father art thou, my God and the Rock of my salvation'; Yea, I will make him my first born, the most high of the kings of earth."

In fact Israel's temple incorporated compromises between the older traditions of the league tent-shrine and the dynastic temple of Canaanite kingship. The portable Ark with its cherubim became the "centerpiece" usurping the place of the divine image of Canaanite temples. According to one tradition, the Tent of Meeting was taken up and placed in the Temple.[26] The language of tent and temple continues to be mixed in psalms of the First Temple. The conditionality of temple and dynasty—

26. 1 Kings 8:4 = 2 Chron. 5:5. Verse 4b is suspect—with its specifically Priestly distinction between the priests and Levites in a Deuteronomistic work—and is established as an explicating gloss by its absence in 𝔊^{BL}. There is no reason, however, to delete the entire verse as spurious. Richard Friedman in *The Exile and Biblical Narrative* attempts to deal with the conflicting traditions concerning the Tent of Meeting in materials of Kings and Chronicles and argues that the notice in 1 Kings 8:4 is historical.

bêt Yahweh and *bêt* David—persisted, albeit intermittently, until the end, thanks to the prophetic and traditional insistence that kingship was forfeited when the ancient covenant was violated, and that the temple in which Israel trusted could be destroyed as was the shrine at Shiloh.

IV

The highest development of Israel's tradition of tent shrines of Yahweh was reached no doubt in the Davidic tent. The Tent of David was the centerpiece of an imperial cultus. It was designed as the successor of the Tabernacle of the Ark at Shiloh, the sanctuary of old Israel's most prestigious priestly dynasty.[27] It was built at the height of David's power and glory, when his empire was fully established. Unhappily we have no detailed description of this tent in the Deuteronomistic sources; however, all we can learn from brief references conforms to the Priestly descriptions of the tabernacle. It was of sufficient size to house the Ark of the Covenant and an altar, presumably in separated rooms.[28] In the Tent also was kept the sacred oil used for Solomon's anointing. Two high priests, Zadok, scion of the family of Aaron and the Hebronite priesthood, and Abiathar, descendant of Moses and the priests of Shiloh, headed its cultic personnel, a grandiose scheme of David's to legitimize and magnify the importance of the national shrine.

I have long favored the identification of the description of the Tabernacle in Priestly sources with the tent designed and established by David, believing it most likely that the old document utilized by P pictured the Israelite tent shrine in its ultimate development. The richness and sophistication of the Priestly tabernacle which make it conform ill with our notions of a desert tent shrine fit ideally into the context of Davidic Jerusalem. While it is not impossible that such a grand shrine stood at Shiloh, Jerusalem is the better candidate. A long gap in time, and probably in records, separates the shrines of Shiloh and Jerusalem, and the source of the Priestly document—if it is not P's creation—is surely the temple of Jerusalem. To be sure, the tent shrine of David is called the *ʾōhel Yahweh* in Deuteronomistic sources, rather than *ʾōhel môʿēd,* the term used chiefly by the Priestly tradent of the Mosaic shrine. In this case the Priestly language is archaizing (as often), I believe, drawing from

27. On the early priestly houses of Israel, see *CMHE,* 195–215.

28. The language in 1 Kings 2:30 (*wybʾ bnyhw ʾl ʾhl yhwh . . . kh ʾmr hmlk ṣʾ . . .*) is most naturally taken to mean that the altar was in the sanctuary, and Benaiah killed therein. Cf. 2 Kings 11:13–16. In this case it is the golden altar on which Adonijah and Benaiah lay hold; the horns of the altar of burnt offering, it may be judged, would be, for much of the time, too hot to handle.

the politico-religious terminology of the tribal federation and its "Tent of Assembly." The *ʾōhel* Yahweh stands, so to speak, between *ʾōhel môʿēd*, 'the tent of the council,' and *bêt* Yahweh, the 'house of Yahweh,' even as the Davidic tent was transitional between the tribal shrine of Shiloh and the dynastic chapel of Solomon.[29]

In some circles the Tent of David has been regarded as insignificant—a provisional housing for the Ark until the planned, permanent temple could be built. Late tradition attributes the plan and designs to build the temple to David, the founder of the Jerusalem cultus. These traditions need critical investigation. In the early sources, David's obedience to Nathan's proscription appears unqualified. Further, there are grounds to believe that he made no move to build a temple, not as a penance for bloodshed but because he respected the old traditions enunciated by Nathan and chose to keep them for both pious and political reasons.

Early in Solomon's reign, indeed already in his consolidation of his realm by murder and mayhem, we note an emerging new policy and a characteristic political technique in establishing innovation. Solomon proposed to break free of all vestiges of older political forms and to establish an absolute kingship and a cultus more in keeping with his imperial and cosmopolitan tastes. Solomon early arranged the death of Adonijah, Joab, and Shimei, the latter two on David's deathbed instructions. Deathbed words, whispered in secret, or last instructions, have many times over in history been fabricated or "doctored" to legitimize successors and their policies, especially policies at odds with those of their predecessors. Most recently we have witnessed Mao's last messages used to legitimate Hua and to extirpate the Chinese radicals including Mao's widow! Inasmuch as David until his death spared Joab and Shimei, and both were threats to Solomon, Solomon's attribution of such instructions to David arouses suspicion.

Certainly the official propaganda reported in Kings concerning the occasion for Adonijah's execution rings false. According to the account in 1 Kings, Adonijah, David's eldest surviving son and rightful heir to the throne, failed in his attempt to mount David's throne. With the support of Zadok, Nathan, Benaiah, and Solomon's mother Bathsheba, and, we are told, of David on his deathbed, Solomon consolidated power and mounted the throne in his stead.

We are told further that Adonijah then asked for the hand of Abishag,

29. The Chronicler's notion that the Tent of Meeting was at the great high place at Gibeon (1 Chron. 16:39; 2 Chron. 1:3,6,13) is, of course, confused and without counterpart in Kings. It may stem from his interpretation of 2 Sam. 21:9 and the assumption that Solomon would sacrifice only at a legitimate sanctuary in the period before the construction of the Temple.

David's last consort. Moreover, he sought out Bathsheba, of all people, to intercede with Solomon for permission for the marriage. Solomon replied that such a request was equivalent to asking for the kingdom. It was well understood in Israel that taking a king's harem was a formal sign, asserting the transfer of kingship. Absalom during his revolt "went in unto his father's concubines in the sight of all Israel." Now if Adonijah did seek Abishag's hand in marriage, and if he did approach Bathsheba to entreat Solomon on his behalf, he deserved his speedy execution—for stupidity.

Abiathar was deposed, and with his fall we suspect a chief advocate for older Shilonite traditions was removed, as well as a supporter of Adonijah. Nathan the prophet disappears after the anointing of Solomon, and, hardly by chance, no effective prophetic voice was heard again in Judah during the empire. Moves were made by Solomon to centralize authority and minimize the independence and power of lingering tribal institutions.

The building of the Temple of Solomon must be viewed against this background. The replacement of David's Tent of Yahweh with Solomon's temple is best viewed, I believe, as an innovation conceived by Solomon alongside his other reversals of Davidic policy and practice. Evidently he attributed the design of the new departure to David, disarming or muting opposition, as was his frequent tactic in other political moves. Actually the account in Kings makes no mention of David instructing

30. There is a curious conflict between the Deuteronomistic account of Solomon's speech to Hiram explaining that David was too busy with wars to build the temple (1 Kings 5:17), and the Deuteronomistic source in 2 Sam. 7:1 f. where David, having been given rest from his enemies, proposed to build a house for Yahweh. This is not to mention the tension between the two sections of Nathan's oracle. The Chronicler, of course, harmonizes the passages by asserting that David cannot build the house because he has "shed much blood upon the earth in [Yahweh's] sight" (1 Chron. 22:8).

31. Moshe Weinfeld in the discussion following the presentation of this paper suggested that Amos 9:11 and Isa. 16:5 preserve memories of the Davidic Tent of Yahweh. The expression "*sukkat* David" in Amos 9:11 refers on the surface, of course, to the restoration of the Davidic dynasty. This 'rebuilding' may refer either to rule again over the north (and the old empire), if the oracle is early, or, if the oracle is late, to restoration after the Exile. The choice of the term *sukkāh*, 'tabernacle,' also recalls—drawing on the typology between dynasty and dynastic shrine—the Tent of Yahweh. Isa. 16:5 with its reference to the "*ʾōhel* David" is most obscure in its context in an oracle concerning Moab, but it may preserve a like reminiscence. Ezekiel's name for Jerusalem under the figure of a woman, Oholibah, may belong to the same constellation of motifs. For a different view of David's policy, see Carol Meyers, "David as Temple Builder," in *Ancient Israelite Religion: Essays in Honor of Frank Moore Cross*, ed. Patrick D. Miller Jr., Paul D. Hanson, and S. Dean McBride (Philadelphia: Fortress Press, 1987), 357–376.

Solomon to build a temple, nor is there an account of his supplying blueprints and materials; it is the Chronicler who enlarges David's role in preparing for the building of the Temple. The Deuteronomist reports the prophecy that Solomon will build Yahweh's house as Yahweh will build David's house, but his presumption is that Solomon is carrying out the desires of David's heart and he puts those words in Solomon's mouth.[30] If our reconstruction is correct, Solomon's propaganda was marvelously successful, and the historical opposition between Tent and Temple was largely dissolved in Judaean tradition with the passage of time.[31]

PART III

STUDIES IN THE STRUCTURE OF HEBREW VERSE

6

The Prosody of Lamentations 1 and the Psalm of Jonah

I

SINCE THE EIGHTEENTH CENTURY THE STUDY OF HEBREW POETRY HAS tended to focus on the semantic symmetries of Hebrew verse: binary structures conventionally termed *parallelismus membrorum.* Fault has been found with the term *parallelism,* which indeed fails to comprehend the full binarism of Hebrew poetry, even at the lexical and semantic level. However, alternate terms are unlikely to replace the traditional term, which has been taken up enthusiastically in the comparative study of a wide range of orally composed literatures that exhibit similar features. Intense scholarly energy has also been directed toward the analysis of auditory features of Hebrew poetry in inconclusive searches for the structure of Hebrew meter. A variety of systems have been proposed. The dominant system, usually called after the names of Ley and Sievers, postulates an accentual rhythm, in which the basic units are cola of three stressed syllables or alternately cola of two stressed syllables, given the notation 3 + 3 or 2 + 2. More loosely Hebrew meter has been described as "word" meter, basic units of three words or two words that may be given the same notation. Much poetry of the early period (i.e., the era when oral composition was lively and flourishing) can be fitted into these systems, presuming some minor use of poetic license. The real difficulty with these systems of metrical analysis is that they fail to reflect the full or precise symmetries of early Hebrew verse and wholly break down when applied to late Hebrew verse, in which new prosodic canons rooted in written composition evolved and became dominant.[1]

The papers of the late Roman Jakobson dealing with grammatical parallelism in traditional (oral) poetry have greatly deepened our insight into "the refinement in 'verbal polyphony' and its semantic tension." Jakobson showed how "pervasive parallelism inevitably activates all the

1. See the important but unpublished study of Arlis J. Ehlen, "The Poetic Structure of a Hodayah from Qumran: An Analysis of Grammatical, Semantic, and Auditory Correspondence in 1QH 3:19–36" (Ph.D. diss., Harvard University, 1970).

levels of language—the distinctive features, inherent and prosodic, the morphologic and syntactic categories and forms, the lexical units and their semantic classes in both their convergences and divergences acquire an autonomous poetic value."[2] His illustrations come from Finnish, Chinese, and especially Russian and Hebrew traditional poetry. His work has stimulated a number of recent studies of Canaanite (Ugaritic) and Hebrew poetry which have tightened our controls upon the prosodic canons of Hebrew poetry as well as extended our understanding of its complexity.[3]

In this chapter I present two studies of a complex verse form first isolated in Budde's study of the meter of laments, and since commonly called Qinah meter.[4] In the first study, I take up the acrostic lament found in the first chapter of Lamentations, making use of new textual resources found in 4QLam^a.[5] In the second, I turn to a more traditional and superior exemplar of the verse form preserved in the Psalm of Jonah.

In our early study of ancient Yahwistic poetry, Noel Freedman and I recognized two basic building blocks of Hebrew and Ugaritic poetry, the so-called three-stress colon and the so-called two-stress colon, structured to form balanced or symmetrical bicola and tricola.[6] At the same time, we observed that apparent violations of the balance of stress often occurred without violating the canons of symmetry. "It may be very difficult or impossible to assign the same number of stresses to parallel cola; at the same time they may have an equal number of syllables and balance perfectly. Thus it appears that a deep sense of symmetry is the guiding

2. "Grammatical Parallelism and Its Russian Facet," *Language* 42 (1966): 399–429, esp. 423.

3. See especially the important if difficult monograph of Stephen A. Geller, *Parallelism in Early Hebrew Poetry, HSM* 20 (Missoula, Mont.: Scholars Press, 1979); and his more transparent discussion, "The Dynamics of Parallel Verse: A Poetic Analysis of Deuteronomy 32:6–12," *HTR* 75 (1982): 35–56. Ehlen's "The Poetic Structure of a Hodayah from Qumran" also builds heavily on Jakobson's insights, as does my own paper "Prose and Poetry in the Mythic and Epic Texts from Ugaritic," *HTR* 67 (1974): 1–15. Remarkably, certain other recent studies appear innocent of the implications of Jakobson's work, including that of my colleague James L. Kugel, *The Idea of Biblical Poetry: Parallelism and Its History* (New Haven: Yale University Press, 1981).

4. The term is not a happy one since, as is well known, this verse form has far wider distribution among the genres of Hebrew poetry.

5. My study of Lam. 1 was first prepared as an act of homage to David Noel Freedman, a respected colleague of more than forty years, whose contributions to the study of Qinah meter have broken important new ground. See especially his "Acrostics and Metrics in Hebrew Poetry," *HTR* 65 (1972): 367–392, reprinted in *Pottery, Poetry, and Prophecy: Studies in Early Hebrew Poetry* (Winona Lake, Ind.: Eisenbrauns, 1980), 51–76.

6. *AYP*, 8–12.

principle of metrical structure, and that the stress pattern (3:3, 2:2) is only the most convenient . . . method of expressing this symmetry."[7]

As an alternate to accentual balance, we have searched for syllabic symmetry of one kind or another. Here the difficulties are different, but no less formidable. Syllabic symmetry obtains, with extraordinary frequency, between the cola in a single bicolon or single tricolon, but rarely persists throughout a sequence of bicola or tricola. An example may be taken from a Ugaritic text (*CTA* 23.49–51; cf. 55–56).

yáhburu šapatêhúma yíšša[qu]	11	He bowed, he kissed their lips;
hin šapatāhúma matuqatāmi	11	Behold their lips were sweet,
matuqatāmi kalarammānīma	11	Sweet like pomegranates.
bímā nášaqi wa-hárī	8	In kissing there was conceiving,
bi-ḥúbuqi ḥimḥámatu	8	In embracing, heat of conception.

The symmetry of the first tricolon is clear, eleven syllables to the colon (though the stress pattern is asymmetrical); the following bicolon is symmetrical, but with eight syllables to the colon. Another example is found in *CTA* 2.4.23–27 (cf. 13–18).

wa-yírtaqiṣ ṣámdu badê báʿli	10	The mace swooped in the hand of Baʿl,
[*kámā*] *nášri bi-ʾuṣbaʿātihu*	10	Like a vulture in his fingers.
yálimu qúdquda zubūli [*yámmi*]	11	He smote the back of Prince Sea,
bêna ʿênêmi θāpiṭi náhari	11	Between the eyes of Judge River.
yapársihu yámmu	6	Sea fell,
yaqíllu la-ʾárṣi	6	Sank to earth.
tinnaǵíṣna pinnātihu	8	His joints trembled,
wa-yádlupu tamūnihu	8	His frame collapsed.
yaqúθθu báʿlu wa-yášti yámma	10	Baʿl crushed and drank Sea,
yakálliyu θāpiṭa náhara	10	He annihilated Judge River.

The first and second bicola have long cola; each is symmetrical; and the fifth bicolon, with long cola, is symmetrical. The third bicolon with short cola is balanced, as is the fourth, again with short cola, but the balance is limited to the bicolon. In the same general context (*CTA* 2.4.10) is this marvelously assonant bicolon.

tíqqaḥa mulka ʿālámika	9	May you take thy eternal kingship,
dárkata dāta dārdārika	9	Thy rule which will be forever

7. Ibid., 9.

Thus we have discovered sequences of individually symmetrical bicola, but having syllable counts 6:6, 8:8, 9:9, 10:10, and 11:11.[8]

My conclusion has been that the ancient Canaanite and Hebrew poets were not counting syllables, at least in the pattern familiar in other oral, syllabic verse. It must be emphasized, moreover, that the oral formulae of Ugaritic and early Hebrew meter are binary, not chronemic as in Greek epic verse. These are constructed in pairs: word, phrase, and colon pairs, including paired epithets and proper names, complementing grammatical parallelism at every level.

It has been my practice for many years, therefore, to use a notation, *l(ongum)* and *b(reve)*, to label respectively the long colon and the short colon fundamental to Hebrew verse, a notation which leaves open the question of auditory (stress or quantitative) rhythm.[9] Often it is useful to note the syllable count in verse as an indication of its levels of balance in a bicolon or tricolon, or in a couplet or triplet of more complex structure, but such counts in my analysis imply no theory of chronemic meter.

In archaic poetry the standard verse forms are the *l:l* and *l:l:l*. In lyric poetry one often finds *b:b::b:b*, or better 2 (*b:b*), and *b:b::b:b::b:b*, that is, 3 (*b:b*). The simple verse *b:b* exists but is rare. In verse composed of *b* units, parallelism is found ordinarily between two bicola forming a couplet (*b:b* || *b:b*), but parallelism also appears not infrequently between the cola (*b* || *b*), which, along with the regularity of the caesural pause, confirms the analysis that the unit is a short colon.

In such early poems as the Song of the Sea and the Lament of David, one finds the combination of these verse forms, often referred to as "mixed meter," usually in sequences of couplets and triplets (e.g., 2(*b:b*)–*l:l*–3(*b:b*)–*l:l:l*, etc.).[10]

The complex verse form found *inter alia* in Lamentations 1 and the Psalm of Jonah—Budde's Qinah meter—was first analyzed in stress notation as 3:2; alternately it has been described as 5:5. Each description has merit, each defects. The dominant structure, I shall argue, is *l:b::l:b* (using our notation) in which grammatical and semantic binarism is chiefly between corresponding bicola. However, "internal" parallelism between the "mixed" (long and short) cola of the individual bicolons is not infrequent, especially in older, orally composed verse of this type. While

8. It may be noted that if we scan in stress meter, the bicola cited give the following: 4:3, 4:4, 2:2, 2:2, 4:3, and 3:3. Such an analysis veils even the binary symmetry of the verses.

9. See, for example, my treatments of Hebrew poetry in *CMHE*, 115 f.; 122; 126–131; 152–155; 170–173, and passim; and "The Song of the Sea and Canaanite Myth," *JTC* 5 (1968): 4, n. 12, and passim.

10. Cf. *CMHE*, 126.

l:b::l:b is the most frequent verse pattern, there are also variant patterns: *l:b:b:l* and *b:l::l:b*. In the older examples of this complex verse the variant patterns are used more widely than in later verse, and with great effect.

The analysis of the prosody of Hebrew verse has always been complicated by two difficult, but necessary tasks: the establishment of a sound text and the reconstruction of the early Hebrew language in which the poetry was composed. In fact, progress in the study of Hebrew prosody has been slow in direct relation to the data available for textual and historico-linguistic research. To be sure, there are scholars—frequently those with a traditional approach to the received text—who choose to ignore these tasks in their analysis and then issue pronouncements, usually asserting the "irregularity" of Hebrew prosody. Such analyses, unless designed for an apologetic end, serve little purpose. No one seriously doubts that verse preserved in a corrupt text in "modernized" Hebrew is irregular. At the same time the interdependence of the tasks of analysis and reconstruction, prosodic, textual, and historico-linguistic, involves the student of Hebrew poetry in the circular reasoning inevitable in all complex inductive research. Accordingly, premature or forced theories proliferate, and progress toward sound results is halting. Fortunately, epigraphic research is producing rich new data for the reconstruction of the history of the Hebrew dialects, and new textual resources are greatly facilitating our understanding of the textual history of biblical works. More rapid progress in the study of Hebrew prosody may thus be anticipated.

II

The Lamentations manuscript published here, 4QLam[a], is inscribed in a Herodian script belonging to the tradition I have termed "vulgar semi-formal."[11] Its leather is tan or beige and rough in texture. Portions of three columns of Chapter 1 of Lamentations are preserved: Column I (of the material extant), containing eleven lines of script (1:1ab–6); Column II, containing also eleven lines of script (1:6–10); and Column III, containing ten lines of writing (1:10–16). A small fragment from later in the scroll (2:5) also is extant. We do not possess the first column(s) of the scroll. Column III is substantially preserved, albeit in shrunken and wrinkled condition and with lacework produced by worms. It measures about 10 cm high (the width of the scroll), the lined portion forming a column of writing about 15 cm broad, 7 cm high. Column II was about 8 cm broad, as was Column I, to judge in the latter case from its reconstruction. In antiquity these measurements undoubtedly would have

11. F. M. Cross, "The Development of the Jewish Scripts," in *BANE*, 173–181.

been larger; they have been reduced by the shrinkage of the leather. Irregular shrinkage, it should be noted, has produced vertical splitting of the leather. The orthographic style of the manuscript is the late, full Palestinian type which developed in Maccabean times.[12] There follows a reconstruction of its text.

FIGURE 1

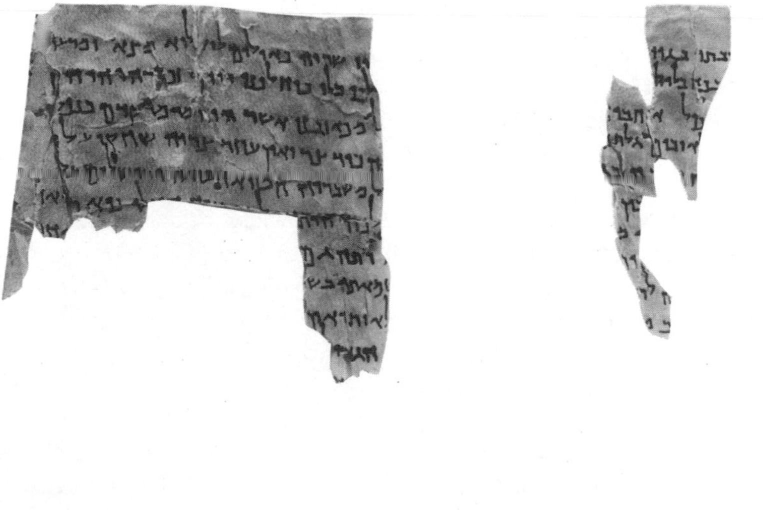

A Lamentations Scroll from Cave 4, Qumrân

12. See F. M. Cross, "The Contribution of the Qumran Discoveries to the Study of the Biblical Text," *IEJ* 16 (1966): 286.

COLUMN I (LAMENTATIONS 1:1ab–6)

1] היתה כאלמנה[רׄבתי בגויםׄ]שרתי במדינות [
2] היתה למס בכה ת[בכה בלילהׄ]ודמעתה על [
3] לחיה אין לה מנחם [מׄכול אוׄהביהׄ] כול רעיה [
4] בגדו בה היו לה [לאיבים גלתהׄ]יהודה מעני [
5] ומרוב עבודה היא[ה יׄ]שׄ[בׄה בג]וים לוא מצאה [
6] מנוח כול רדפיה השיגוה[בין]המצרים דרכי [
7] ציון אבלות מבלי בא[י מ]ועד כול שעריה [
8] שוממים כוהניה נאנ[חׄים]בתולותיה נוגות [
9] והיאה מר לה היו צר[יה לראושׁ]איביה שלו [
10] כיא יהוה הוגה על רו[ב פשעׄ]יה עולליה הלכו [
11] שבי לפני צריה ויצ[א מבת]ציון כול הדרה [

COLUMN II (LAMENTATIONS 1:6–10)

1] ה[יו שריה כאילים לואׄ לוא מצא ומרעה
2] ו[ילכו בלי כוח לפני רודף זכוׄרה יהוה
3] כו[מכאובנו אשר היו מימי קדם בנפל
4] עמ[ה ביד צר ואין עוזר צריה שחקו על
5] כו[ל משבריה חטוא חטאה ירושלים על
6] כן [לנוד היתהׄ]כו[ל]מכב[דׄיׄהׄ הׄזׄילו כיא ראו
7] ע[רׄותה גם]היאה נאנחה ותשב[אׄחורׄ
8 טׄמאתה בש]וליה לוא זכרה אחריתה ותרד [
9] פ[לאות ואין]מנחם לה ראה יהוה את עניי [
10] כי[הגדול]אויב ידו פרש צד על כול [
11] מחמ[דׄ]יה כיא ראתה גוים באו מקדשה [

COLUMN III (LAMENTATIONS 11:10–16)

1 אשר צויתה לוא יבואו מחמדיה באוׄכׄל להׄשיב נפשה ראה יהוה והׄ'בטה
2 כיא הייתי זולל לוא אליכ]   [הכול עברי דׄ]רך הביטו ור[אוׄ אם יש מכאוב
3 כמכאבי אשר עוללו לי אשר הגירני י]הוה ביו[ם]חרו[נו ממרום שלח אׄ]ש[
4 בעצמותי ויורידנו פרש רשׁת לרגלי הׄשיבנׄי]אחו[רׄ נתנני שומם כול
5 הׄיום וד]ו[י נקשרה על פשעי בידו וישתרג עולו על צׄ]וארי[הׄכשיל כוחׄי נתנני
6 יהוה ביד לוא אוכל לקוׄם סלה כול אבידי אדוׄנׄיׄ בׄקרבי קרא עלי מׄוׄ]עד [
7 לשבור בחורי גת דרך יהׄוׄה לבתוׄלת בת יהודה פרשה ///* ציון בׄי]דיה אין [
8 מנחם לה מכול אוהביה צדיק אתה יהוה צפה אדוני ליעקוב סביב]יו צריו [
9 היתה ציוׄן לנדוח בינהמהׄ על אלה בכוׄ עיני ירדו דמעתי כיא רחקׄ]ממני [
10 מׄ]נחם משיב[נפש היו בניׄ שוממים]כיא[גׄבר אויב צדיק הוא אדוני כיא [

*erasure

III

In the following notes I take up the verses of the acrostic *seriatim,* giving special attention to (1) textual problems and (2) problems of poetic artifice.

VERSE 1 [*ʾAlep*]

1. *l* [7]	*ʾykh yšbh bdd*	How alone does she sit,
2. *b* [6]	*hʿyr rbty ʿm*	The city [which was] mistress of people.
3. *l* [7]	*hyth kʾlmnh*	She has become as a widow,
4. *b* [6]	*rbty bgwym*	[One who was] mistress among the nations.
5. *l* [7]	*śrty bmdynwt*	[One who was] princess among the provinces,
6. *b* [5]	*hyth lms*	She has become a serf.

The structure of the triplet is *l:b::l:b::l:b.* The syllable count reveals the symmetry of the verse. If one attempts to scan either in stress or "word" meter he must resort to license in each of the three bicola. Parallelism is elaborately structured. Correspondence is between the first, third, and sixth cola, and between the second, fourth, and fifth cola:

1. ʾykh yšbh bdd	*2. hʿyr rbty ʿm*
3. hyth kʾlmnh	*4. rbty bgwym*
6. hyth lms	*5. śrty bmdynwt*

Cola 1, 3, and 6 possess the parallel verbal elements and metaphors of the sad end of the personified city. Cola 2, 4, and 5 list epithets of the city reflecting her former estate. The correspondence of colon 1 and 6 is chiastic, colon 1 an *l* in first position in the bicolon, colon 6 a *b* in second position in its bicolon; at the same time, first and last, the cola yield cyclic structure, an *inclusio.* Colon 3 (*l*) and colon 6 (*b*) beginning with the repetition of *hyth* form a similar chiasm in position; colon 4 (*b*) and colon 5 (*l*) are positionally chiastic. Repetition of *rbty* is to be noted, tying together structurally cola 2 and 4, as does the repetition of *b* in *rbty bgwym* and *śrty bmdynwt;* the repetition of the archaizing forms *rbty-rbty-śrty* further links cola 2, 4, and 5. These repetitions, including that of *hyth* initially in colon 3 and colon 6, create auditory as well as semantic and grammatical correspondence. The first two words of colon 1 and colon 3 end in the syllable -â, as does the first word of colon 6. While this may not be conscious artifice, it should be noted since in Israel's early poetry studied sequences of phonemic and syllabic assonance (parallelism) abound. Finally we should not forget the commonly recognized formulaic pair *ʿm/gwym* extended here in the triplet with *mdynwt* (cola 2, 4, 5).

These observations make clear that the parallelistic structure is far more intricate than the simple semantic correspondence of the three bicola (1-2 // 3-4 // 5-6). The poet consciously manipulates both the short (*b*) cola and the long (*l*) cola for "dense" poetic structure.

The expression *rbty ʿm* has traditionally been taken to mean 'full of people' and been compared to *rbt bnym ʾmllh* (1 Samuel 2:5). Recently it has been argued that *rbty* must be taken as the familiar epithet *rbt* 'lady', 'mistress.'[13] The correspondence with *rbt bgwym* and especially *śrty bmdynwt* requires this understanding of *rbty* in my opinion, but I see no reason to exclude a play on alternate idiomatic meanings of *rbt* in the second colon.[14]

VERSE 2 [*Bet*]

1. *l* [7]	*bkh tbkh blylh*	She weeps bitterly in the night;
2. *b* [5]	*dmʿh ʿl lḥyh*	Tears are on her cheek.
3. *b* [5]	*ʾyn lh mnḥm*	There is none to comfort her
4. *l* [6]	*mkl ʾhbyh*	Among all her lovers.
5. *l* [8]	*kl rʿyh bgdw bh*	All her friends have deceived her;
6. *b* [7]	*hyw lh lʾybym*	They have become her enemies.

In colon 1 I have restored the earlier orthographic form of *bkh* (MT *bkw*); in colon 2 I prefer *dmʿh* to *wdmʿth*.[15] The repetition of the pronoun is tautological and awkward. Moreover, the colon appears to have been influenced by a text like that of 4QLam in v. 16, where *bkw* and *dmʿty* stand in parallelism (see below). There is no direct textual support for my preferred reading. 4QLam has been reconstructed to conform to MT, but this is arbitrary. We cannot distinguish between readings differing only by a letter in length. The Greek text of Lamentations is of relatively little use; it belongs to the *kaige* (Proto-Theodotionic) school which corrected according to a Hebrew text of Proto-Rabbinic type.[16] The secondary introduction of the conjunction *w-* at the beginning of cola is, of course, extremely frequent, as has been shown in the study of texts in parallel transmission.[17]

The structure of the triplet is *l:b::b:l::l:b.* There is internal parallelism between colon 1 and colon 2 as well as between colon 5 and colon 6. In the first instance the formulaic pair *bky / / dmʿ*, well known in both Ugaritic and Hebrew poetry, is noteworthy. The second and third bicola of the triplet are intricately linked by parallelism and chiasm. Colon 3 and colon 6, positionally chiastic, are bound by the opposition *ʾyn lh–hyw lh.* Colon 4 and colon 5, positionally chiastic, begin with *(m)kl ʾhbyh* and *kl rʿyh.* The roots *ʾhb* and *rʿ* form a formulaic pair in Hebrew poetry, and in the present instance *ʾhbyh* is juxtaposed to *ʾybym* in colon 6, an extension of the formulaic pair with an antonym which at the same time produces assonance between the final members of each bicolon (*ʾhb/ʾyb*). The repe-

13. T. F. McDaniel, "Philological Studies in Lamentations I," *Biblica* 49 (1968): 29–31.

14. Contrast D. Hillers, *Lamentations,* Anchor Bible Series, vol. 7A (Garden City, N.Y.: Doubleday, 1972), 5 f.

15. This suggestion is not new but goes back at least as far as Budde.

16. Cf. D. Barthélemy, *Les Devanciers d'Aquila* (Leiden: Brill, 1963), 33, 47.

17. *AYP,* 126–128, and especially the table, pp. 161–168.

tition of the syllable/word *-lâ/lāh* is hardly fortuitous in colon 1 (*blylh*), colon 3 (*lh*), and colon 6 (*lh*), with its cyclic distribution. The colon *ʾyn lh mnḥm* is repeated in variant forms at intervals throughout the lament: v. 9 (*ʾyn mnḥm lh*), v. 17 (*ʾyn mnḥm lh*), and v. 21 (*ʾyn mnḥm ly*). The distribution of this colon in its variations is interesting: twice in vv. 1–11 (Part I, prevailingly third person), and twice in vv. 12–22 (Part II, prevailingly first person). Further, it appears first in the second triplet from the beginning of the poem (v. 2 *ʾyn lh mnḥm*), last in the second but final triplet (v. 21 *ʾyn mnḥm ly*). Such long-range repetition suggests that the lament was composed in writing, as does the use of certain prosaic elements necessary to the structure of the poem, elements absent or excessively rare in older, orally composed verse. This is not surprising. In the sixth century we find evidence broadly of major transformations and new configurations of poetic genres and styles—imitative of old oral forms in part, and still using language originating in oral formulae, but anticipating many elements of later poetry certainly composed in writing—which mark a watershed in the evolution of biblical poetry.

VERSE 3 [*Gimel*]

1. *l* [9]	*glth yhwdh mʿny*	Judah is gone into exile out of [great] affliction,
2. *b* [6]	*wmrb ʿbdh*	And out of abundance of servitude.
3. *l* [8]	*hyʾh yšbh bgwym*	She herself sits among the nations;
4. *b* [6]	*lʾ mṣʾh mnwḥ*	She has found no rest.
5. *l* [9]	*kl rdpyh hśygwh*	All who pursued her have overtaken her,
6. *b* [5]	*byn hmṣrym*	Within the straits.

I have chosen the archaic, long form of the pronoun *hyʾh* in colon 3 with 4QLam. To be sure, at Qumrân there is a secondary multiplication of such forms; on the other hand, MT has tended to level through the short forms even in poetic contexts where the form properly survived. The bicola in this triplet tend to be long; thus the longer pronoun heightens the symmetry.

The structure of the triplet is *l:b::l:b::l:b*.

There is internal parallelism between the elements in the first bicolon, an "echo" parallelism, as well as the expected correspondence of the first and second bicola. On the other hand, the correspondence between colon 3 and colon 4 is vague; colon 4 (*b*) is more closely linked semantically with colon 5 (*l*), with which it is in chiastic tension.

Elements of auditory correspondence are not dramatic, but note *-â/-â* ending the first two words of colon 1 and colon 3, echoed in -â in colon 2 (*ʿbdh*) and colon 4 (*mṣʾh*). The repetition of the nasal *m* may be observed: *mʿny, mrb, mṣʾh, mnwḥ,* and the (unusual) *hmṣrym.*

Long-range structure appears in the sequence "The city, the mistress" v. 1, "Judah" (as a maiden) v. 3 (cf. *bt yhwdh,* 'Maiden Judah,' v. 15), "Zion" or "Maiden Zion" (*bt ṣywn*) vv. 4, 6, and "Jerusalem" (as a maiden) vv. 7, 8. Compare v. 17 where "Zion" and "Jerusalem" stand in the same triplet in parallelism.

VERSE 4 [*Dalet*]

1. *l* [8]	*drky ṣywn ʾblwt*	The ways of Zion mourn
2. *b* [7]	*mbly bʾy mwʿd*	Because none comes to the sacral assembly.
3. *l* [8]	*kl šʿryh šmmym*	All her gates are desolate;
4. *b* [7]	*khnyh nʾnḥym*	Her priests sigh.
5. *l* [8]	*btwltyh nhwgwt*	Her virgins are led away,
6. *b* [5]	*whyʾh mr lh*	And she is bitter.

This triplet, like the last, is composed of long bicola.[18] Its structure is *l:b::l:b::l:b.* Binary parallels and contrasts are complex in the verse, and generally misunderstood. Colon 1 (Zion's streets mourn), colon 4 (her priests sigh), and colon 6 (she [Zion] is bitter) are strictly parallel, colon 6 returning to colon 1 as an *inclusio.* Colon 2 (none enters the assembly [in the sanctuary]) and colon 5 (her virgins are led out) correspond (no men enter—virgins go out—*bʾy nhwgwt*)[19] in a second cyclic device. At another level there is parallelism between elements in colon 1 (Zion's streets), colon 3 ([Zion's] gates), and less strictly *ʾblwt* (colon 1) and *šmmym* (colon 3), which belong in the same semantic field and contrast in gender. Grammatical parallelism also obtains between *nʾnḥym* and *nhwgwt,* passive participles, beginning with *nun,* contrasting in gender.

The reading *nhwgwt,* MT *nwgwt* requires discussion. Generally *nwgwt* has been taken as an anomalous *nipʿal* participle of a root *ygy,* 'to suffer' (cf. *hwgh* v. 5), appearing only here and in Zephaniah 3:18, in the expression *nwgy mmwʿd.* The latter is most difficult and has also been analyzed as from *ygy* II 'to thrust away,' 'exclude.' The Greek here translated *agomenai,* obviously for *n(h)wgwt,* Aquila *diōkomenai,* probably on the basis of *nwgy* in Zephaniah 3:18 (*ygy* II); Symmachus has (inexactly) *aichmalōtoi,* 'prisoners.' To complicate matters, Hebrew furnishes a *nhg* II 'to mourn'; cf. Syriac *yhg.* There is no problem in taking the reading of MT, *nwgwt,* as standing for *nhwgwt.* The syncope of intervocalic *he* in speech and writing is evidenced already in pre-Exilic Hebrew inscriptions, and is frequent, not to say ubiquitous, in the manuscripts of

18. Note that the syllable count of *drky* is three, *darakê,* of which a trace is found in the spirant *kap,* assimilated to the second *a,* later lost.

19. Cf. Isa. 60:11, where *lhbyʾ* and *nh(w)gym* are parallel.

Qumrân and contemporary material (e.g., the Nash Papyrus). The structures of the poem must be determinative. Our analysis above suggests strongly that *nhwgwt,* 'led out,' rather than a meaning 'mourn' from *ygy* (I), is to be preferred. I should add, negatively, that reading 'mourn' makes for a mechanical, unvaried, even wearisome parallelism.

In the case of *šwmmyn* of the Massoretic Text, I have corrected to *šwmmym* on the assumption that this is simply one of many instances, well documented at Qumrân, of a scribal slip with later (or dialectal) ending, *-în* replacing classical *-îm.* Cf. *šwmmym* (v. 16) and *šmmh* (v. 13).

The expression *b'y mwʿd* is to be compared with *b'w mqdšh* and *lw' ybw'w [mwʿdyh]* (4QLam, see below), said of the nations in v. 10. This is another instance of "long-range structure," the extension of the parallelistic principle beyond the units of verse or triplet. And again, in v. 18 the theme of virgins (and striplings) going captive, and in v. 19 priests (and elders) expiring, recall the themes here in v. 4.

VERSE 5 [*He*]

1. *l* [7]	*hyw ṣryh lr'š*	Her adversaries have become head;
2. *b* [6]	*'ybyh šlw*	Her enemies are at ease.
3. *b* [5]	*ky yhwh hwgh*	But Yahweh had made her suffer
4. *l* [6]	*ʿl rb pšʿyh*	For the multitude of her transgressions.
5. *l* [7]	*ʿllyh hlkw*	Her children have gone—
6. *b* [6]	*šby lpny ṣr*	Captives before the adversary.

The structure of the triplet is *l:b::b:l::l:b.* The first bicolon has internal parallelism, the formulaic pair *ṣr/'yb* in evidence. At the same time colon 2 (enemies at ease) corresponds by contrast with colon 3 (Zion made to suffer). Colon 1 *ṣryh lr'š* also stands in contrast with colon 6 *lpny ṣr,* the elements *r'š* and *pny* consciously chosen, *ṣr* in each forming an *inclusio,* victors and vanquished, juxtaposed in position.

At longer range, colon 2, "her enemies are at ease," recalls v. 3, colon 4, "she finds no rest," and *mrb pšʿym* colon 4 echoes *mrb ʿbdh,* v. 3, colon 2. The final bicolon also has parallelistic links with v. 6, the final bicolon:

ʿllyh hlkw	*šby lpny ṣr*
wylkw bly kḥ	*lpny rwdp*

VERSE 6 [*Waw*]

1. *l* [7]	*wyṣ' mbt ṣywn*	And there went forth from Daughter Zion
2. *b* [4]	*kl hdrh*	All her splendor.
3. *l* [9]	*hyw šryh k'ylym*	Her princes became like stags
4. *b* [6]	*l' mṣ'w mrʿh*	That find no pasturage.

5. *l* [7]	*wylkw bly kḥ*	And they went on without strength,
6. *b* [5]	*lpny rwdp*	Before the chaser.

The Hebrew *ʾylym* was read *ʾēlîm* by the Greek translator and by Jerome. Ehrlich is probably correct, however, in arguing that *ʾayyālîm* of MT is better. The figure seems to be that of the chase in the final bicolon, and *rdp* is used of hunting (1 Samuel 26:20).

In colon 4, the text of 4QLam is corrupt. The sequence *lwʾ lwʾ* is an obvious dittography, and the sequence *mṣʾ wmrʿh* is wrongly divided—a sleepy scribe. On the other hand, 4QLam *bly kwḥ* is perhaps to be preferred over MT *blʾ kwḥ*. The form *blʾ* arises easily from misreading *bly* as *blw*, corrected orthographically to *blʾ*. It is not easy to see how an original *blʾ* would have been corrupted to *bly*.

The structure of the triplet is *l:b::l:b::l:b*. The cola of the second bicolon are both long, in contrast to the first and third bicola, which are comparatively short. The triplet is rather devoid of artifice. The unusual *waw*-consecutive *wyṣʾ* beginning colon 1 is decreed by the acrostic form but is inelegant judged by older poetic norms.[20] The repetition of the grammatical form beginning colon 5, *wylkw*, accents a faint parallelism. Strong synonymous parallelism is found actually between the third bicolon of the verse and the final bicolon of verse 5 (see above).

VERSE 7 [*Zayin*]

1. *l* [8]	*zkrh yhwh mrdyh*	Remember Yahweh, her troubles,
2. *b* [6]	*ʾšr mymy qdm*	Which are from the days of old.
3. *l* [8]	*bnpl ʿmh byd ṣr*	When her people fell into the adversary's hand,
4. *b* [5]	*wʾyn ʿwzr lh*	And she had no helper,
5. *b* [5]	*rʾwh ṣrym*	The adversaries looked on her, gloating,
6. *l* [8]	*šḥqw ʿl mšbryh*	They mocked at her ruins.

As long recognized, the Massoretic Text of v. 7 is corrupt, and, as often is the case when corruption has occurred, it has spread like a cancer. 4QLam presents us with a badly corrupt text also, but the corruptions in the two are not identical. By tracing the history of the readings, I believe, progress can be made toward establishing a text that gave rise to the variant corrupt forms of the text.

There appear to be two primary sources of corruption. Most serious is the development by misreading of an original *mrwdyh* (variant *kl mrwdyh*) as *kl mḥm(w)dyh . . . mḥmdyh* (v. 11 4QLam) and *kl mḥmdyh* (v. 10) are presumably the cause of the "assimilation" or anticipation triggering the error. MT in its present form preserves a doublet: *wmrwdyh kl*

20. See the discussion of Hillers, *Lamentations*, 7 f.

mḥmdyh. The inappropriateness of *mḥmdyh* 'her delights' in this context is evident. MT has suffered yet another expansion, by conflation with the parallel readings: *zkr ʿnyy wmrwdy* from Lamentations 3:19.

4QLam for original *mrwdyh* reads *mk'wbnw* (for *mk'wbyh*), either as a revision of the rare word under the influence of *mk'wb/mk'by* later in the lament (vv. 12, 18), or much more likely as a correction, conscious or unconscious, of the impossible *mḥm(w)dyh* in its manuscript tradition: *kl mḥmwdyh* > *kl mk'wbyh*.

The second part of the infection is the form *zkrh;* MT reads the 3.f.s. perfect, 4QLam the emphatic imperative, *zkwrh* (equivalent to Tiberian *zokrā*). The alternate readings *yrwšlm* MT, *yhwh* 4Q, are triggered by the interpretation of the verb. To be preferred is *yhwh*. The reading *yrwšlm* is easily explained as an assimilation to *yrwšlm* (4QLam *yrwšlym*), the subject of the first colon of the next verse. Further the imperative *zkrh yhwh* begins a long-range sequence of addresses to the deity: *r'h yhwh 't ʿnyh* (v. 9c) and *r'h yhwh whbyṭh* (v. 11c), in the structure of Part I (vv. 1–11) of the lament. Finally, the reading with *yhwh* produces a colon of normal length, *yrwšlm* a colon of abnormal length.

Once corrupt, the corruption spread in such a fashion as to produce what appears to be a four-line verse in the otherwise invariable sequence of triplets.

Other readings require comment. In MT (v. 7a) *ymy* is a secondary intrusion under the influence of *mymy* in colon 2; it perhaps arose from a text with the sequence: ירושלממרודיה in a script in which *y, w,* and *r* were easily confused (for example, in third century B.C.E. scripts of the type of 4QSam^b) and in which medial and final mem were not distinguished. In any case, there is no trace of it in 4QLam, or in the reconstructed early stages of the corruption of the verse. In colon 5, there is a haplography in 4QLam, caused no doubt by homoioteleuton: *ʿwzr ‹ lh r'wh › ṣryh*. And finally, 4QLam reads *šbryh* for *mšbth*. One might be tempted to choose *mšbth* as *lectio difficilior,* were not the graphic confusion of *t* and *ry* simple in the Jewish script (before the reduction of the size of *yod*), and *mšbt* a *hapax legomenon* of dubious meaning in this context.

The structure of the reconstructed triplet is *l:b::l:b::b:l*. There is internal parallelism between colon 5 (*b*) and colon 6 (*l*). The expression *r'wh* carries the connotation of 'gloat over,' 'look with pleasure on,' as often in biblical Hebrew and in the Mešaʿ Inscription.[21] Indeed *r'y* and *śhq* are strictly parallel grammatically and semantically. The second and third bicola are bound together syntactically, and together recount the troubles mentioned in the first bicolon. This is an unusual structure in early poetry. Minor correspondences may be noted: the repetition of

21. See, e.g., Ps. 54:9; 112:8; 118:7; Mešaʿ 1:4, 7; in Judg. 16: 27 there is the combination *hr'ym bśḥwq šmšwn*.

the element *ṣr* (s./pl.) in the final element of colon 3 and colon 5, and the formal and semantic parallelism of *mrwdyh* and *mšbryh,* the final elements in colon 1 and colon 6, a cyclic feature.

I have referred above to the correspondence of *zkrh yhwh* to other addresses to deity in alternating triples: v. 7, v. 9, and v. 11. Mention should be made also of *ʾyn ʿwzr lh,* echoing in variant form the sequence *ʾyn lh mnḥm* (v. 2), *ʾyn mnḥm lh* (v. 9), *ʾyn mnḥm lh* (v. 17), and *ʾyn mnḥm ly* (v. 21).

VERSE 8 [*Ḥet*]

1. *l* [9]	*ḥṭʾ ḥṭʾh yrwšlm*	Jerusalem has sinned grievously;
2. *b* [7]	*ʿl kn lnwd hyth*	Thus she has become an object of derision.
3. *l* [10]	*kl mkbdyh hzylwh*	All who honored her now despise her,
4. *b* [6]	*ky rʾw ʿrwth*	For they have seen her nakedness.
5. *l* [6]	*gm hyʾh nʾnḥh*	Also she herself groans,
6. *b* [5]	*wtšb ʾḥwr*	And turns back [defeated].

4QLam takes *ḥṭʾ* to be an infinitive absolute (*ḥṭwʾ*), adding weight to Ehrlich's argument for reading the infinitive rather than a noun.[22] More dramatic is the reading *lnwd* in 4QLam. The material reading is certain in the manuscript, and is reflected in 𝔊 *eis salon. lnydh* of MT (read also by Aquila *eis kechōrismenēn* and Syr *ndtʾ*) arose in assimilation to *lndh* v. 17 (cf. Zechariah 13:1 *lḥṭʾt wlndh*). The *he* of *lnydh* is a dittograph of the following *he* of *hyth,* and *waw* is confused with *yod,* as persistently in Late Hasmonaean and Herodian Jewish scripts. That the meaning 'object of (head-) wagging' was required in the context was recognized as early as Ibn Ezra.

The structure of the triplet is *l:b::l:b::l:b.* There is parallelism between cola 2 and 3, and internal parallelism of sorts in cola 5 and 6. The concentration (repetition) of the phonemes ʾ and *ḥ* in colon 1 and again in cola 5 and 6 may be observed. The triplet in v. 7 and the triplet in v. 8 are bound together by corresponding themes: *rʾwh, śḥqw* (v. 7), and *hzylwh, rʾw* (v. 8).

VERSE 9 [*Ṭet*]

1. *b* [6]	*ṭmʾh bšwlyh*	Filthiness is in her skirts,
2. *l* [7]	*lʾ zkrh ʾḥryth*	She is not mindful of her fate.
3. *l* [6]	*wtrd plʾym*	And she has fallen wonderfully,
4. *b* [5]	*ʾyn mnḥm lh*	There is none to comfort her.
5. *l* [7]	*rʾh yhwh ʾt ʿnyy*	Look Yahweh, on my affliction,
6. *b* [5]	*ky hgdyl ʾwyb*	For the enemy has magnified himself.

22. *Randglossen zur hebräischen Bibel* (Leipzig: 1914), 7:31.

I have emended the text at one point: *ṭm'h* for *ṭm'th*. The repetition of the pronoun offends, or at least is unnecessary, and colon 1 appears to be the *'b'*-colon. For *pl'ym* (colon 3), 4QLam reads *pl'wt*.

Colon 5, a cry to the deity in the first person, is surprising. Part I (vv. 1–11) of the poem thus far has maintained a consistent point of view: observing Zion in the third person. In Part II (vv. 12–22) the point of view is that of Zion, speaking in the first person. However, the third-person stance reappears twice in Part II, in v. 15c and v. 17. It appears then that the present shift in v. 9c and the shift to first person in v. 11c point ahead, structurally, to the stance of Part II in conscious artifice. It may also be observed that both the exceptional bicola in Part I (v. 9c and v. 11c) are parallel, the first colon of each beginning *r'h yhwh*, a cry to the deity, the second colon of each commencing with *ky*.

The structure of the triplet is *b:l::l:b::l:b*. It is not particularly rich in binary parallels and contrasts—unlike the better triplets in the lament, and quite unlike the classical verse form.

VERSE 10 [*Yod*]

1. *b* [5]	*ydw prś ṣr*	The adversary has grasped
2. *l* [6]	*'l kl mḥmdyh*	After all her treasures.
3. *l* [6]	*ky r'th gwym*	Indeed she looked on the heathen:
4. *b* [5]	*b'w mqdšh*	They entered her sanctuary,
5. *b* [5]	*'šr ṣwyth*	Concerning whom you commanded:
6. *l* [6]	*l' yb'w mw'dyh*	"They shall not enter her assemblies."

I have reconstructed *mw'dyh* in colon 6 on the basis of the indirect evidence of 4QLam. 4QLam has suffered haplography as follows: *lw' ybw'w* [*mmw'dy* . . .] *mḥmdyh*. The text of MT gives no basis for the haplography. The reconstructed *mw'dyh* provides this basis. The reading *bqhl lk* conforms to the usual form of the commandment in Deuteronomy 23:2ff. (*bqhl yhwh*) and Nehemiah 13:1 (*bqhl h'lhym*). The variant expression may be compared with *bbw'* . . . *lpny yhwh bmw'dym* (Ezekiel 46:9), and indeed, *b'y mw'd* in Lamentations 1:4. While my reconstruction entails speculation, it has the advantage of providing an explanation of the haplography in the text of 4QLam, and it binds the text in thematic and verbal correspondence (both likeness and contrast) to colon 2 in Lamentations 1:4. I prefer also reading *yb'w mw'dyh* to a more usual (*yb'w*) *bmw'dyh* to parallel *b'w mqdšh*.

The structure of the triplet is *b:l::l:b::b:l*, a chiastic pattern of long and short cola, or it may be described as a cyclic pattern of bicola, the reverse of the pattern *l:b::b:l::l:b* found in triplets in v. 2 and v. 5. Each of the bicola in this triplet is quite short—but of the same length.

The parallelism between *b'w* in colon 5 and *l' yb'w* is rather flat; more interesting is the set *mʿmdyh* (colon 2), *mqdšh* (colon 4), and *mwʿdyh* (colon 6) with their phonetic (*m . . . d . . . h*) and morphological correspondences.

VERSE 11 [*Kap*]

1. *l* [6]	*kl ʿmh n'nḥym*	All her people sigh;
2. *b* [5]	*mbqšym lḥm*	They seek bread.
3. *l* [8]	*ntnw mḥmdyh b'kl*	They have given her treasures for food
4. *b* [4]	*lhšyb npš*	To keep alive.
5. *l* [8]	*r'h yhwh whbyṭh*	Look, Yahweh, and behold,
6. *b* [7]	*ky hyyty zwllh*	Yea, I have become of no account.

4QLam and the Greek read *mḥmdyh,* with the f.s. suffix, probably correctly. There is no reason, I believe, to repoint *mē-ḥămūdêhem* (Ehrlich), which may or may not be the *kĕtîb,* and interpret the expression to mean 'some of their darling (children).' Rather, Zion's treasures are meant, and *mḥmdyh* (or *mḥmdyhm*) is meant to recall the treasures after which the enemy grasped in v. 10a. Such repetition is characteristic of the poetic structure of the lament.

4QLam has the variant *npšh* for *npš* in MT, 'her (i.e., Zion's) life.' This strikes me as an "explicating plus." The picture of the people selling Zion's treasure to revivify Zion is, however, an appealing one, and not to be dismissed automatically, at least in the interpretation of the poet's meaning. In this case the children feed the mother rather than mother eating the children, the more usual image in famine or siege.

In the final colon, 4QLam provides the reading *zwll.* In v. 13c similarly 4QLam has the variant *šwmm* (for *šmmh*). Evidently in the textual tradition it represents, the "I" of personified Zion has been incorrectly taken as the "I" of the poet in these passages.

The structure of the triplet is *l:b::l:b::l:b.* The first and second bicola are in parallelistic correspondence, with the formulaic pair *lḥm* (colon 2[*b*]) and *'kl* (colon 3[*l*]) in chiastic order. In colon 6 *zwllh* 'worthless' stands in subtle contrast to *mḥmdyh* 'treasures' in colon 3.

In colon 1 *n'nḥym* links with *n'nḥym* in v. 4b (priests sigh), *n'nḥh* in v. 8c (she [Jerusalem] sighs), *n'nḥh* in v. 21a (I [Zion] sigh).[23] To be sure, "sighing" in a lament is not unexpected. It must be observed, however, that *n'nḥ* is a relatively rare word, found nowhere else in the poems of the Book of Lamentations, and not once in the laments of the Psalter.

The final colon *ky hyyty zwllh,* which brings to a close Part I of the lament, at the half point in the acrostic, is strongly reminiscent of the

23. Cf. *'nḥty* in v. 22c.

paired cola of v. 1 beginning the section: *hyth k'lmnh* and *hyth lms.* There is thus a return to the beginning, and with the shift of person, at the same time, an anticipation of the second part of the lament.

VERSE 12 [*Lamed*]

1. *l* [8]	*lw' 'ly kl ʿbry drk*	Would that on me all who pass by the way
2. *b* [6]	*hbyṭw wr'w.*	Gaze and see:
3. *l* [8]	*'m yš mk'b kmk'by.*	If there has been any pain like my pain
4. *b* [5]	*'šr ʿwll ly.*	Which He has dealt out to me—
5. *l* [8]	*'šr hwgyrny yhwh.*	Wherewith Yahweh has terrified me
6. *b* [5]	*bywm ḥrwnw.*	In the day of his wrath.

The text of colon 1 is corrupted both in the received text and in 4QLam. The reading of the latter is uncertain in part, a break in the leather and surface damage obscuring the letter following *k* and before *h.* Little space is found in the break (note the stretching apart of the split above the first line of the column). I do not believe that there is room for the letter *mem; yod* (for archaizing *ʿlyky*) conforms best, perhaps, to the traces of ink on the leather.

I am inclined to read *lû' 'ēlay . . . hbyṭw,* "Would that they look closely at me."

As has been observed (Budde), *lw'* in MT is easily pointed *lû'* and *hbyṭ* regularly takes *'l* with its object.[24] The placement of *'ly* may arise from poetic artifice—in a chiastic structure with *ly* at the end of colon 4. The reading *'lykm kl* may have arisen in an initial dittography, later wrongly corrected: *'ly kl > 'lyk kl > 'lykm kl;* the reading of 4QLam may be explained similarly: *'ly kl > 'lyk kwl > 'lyk hkwl > 'lyky hkwl.*

4QLam has the variant reading *hwgyrny* for *hwgh* in colon 5. It is a unique form, an otherwise unattested *hipʿil* of *ygr.* The root itself (in *qal*) occurs in similar contexts in Deuteronomy 9:19 (where the divine wrath is the source of terror), and in Deuteronomy 28:60 (where disease is the cause of fear). The reading in MT, *hwgh yhwh,* immediately recalls *yhwh hwgh* in v. 5. One must ask, is the repetition of *hwgh* an artifice of the poet or a corruption of an original *hwg(y)rny* by reminiscence of *hwgh* in v. 5? I am inclined to choose *hwgyrny* provisionally on the basis of the principle of *lectio difficilior praeferenda est.* This choice is reinforced by the reading of the pronominal suffix in the Greek and in the *Pešiṭta.*

In colon 4 we find in 4QLam the variant *ʿwllw ly* corresponding to

24. On *lw'* with the imperative, see Gen. 23:13 (where *'m* also appears in the context), and F. M. Cross, "David, Orpheus, and Psalm 151," *BASOR* 231 (1978): 69, n. 1.

ʿwll ly in MT. The former reflects late usage, the indefinite 3.m.pl. passive with *l-*, a slight modernizing of the passive indefinite construction marked by the Massoretic pointing. The text I believe should be read *ʿōlēl lî* 'which He [Yahweh], dealt out to me,' the active form with *l-* found twice in v. 22. Both the Syriac and Vulgate versions so read, and parallelism with *hwgyrny* (or *hwgh*) *yhwh* demands it.

I have chosen the variant *bywm ḥrwnw* (4QLam) in colon 6, preferring the shorter reading. The longer reading *bywm ḥrwn ʾpw* is easily explained as an expansion to a familiar cliché.

The structure of the triplet is *l:b::l:b::l:b.* We noted above the parallelism between *ʾšr ʿwll ly* (colon 4) and *ʾšr hwgyrny yhwh* (colon 5). The cola, one *b,* one *l,* are in chiastic order. The theme of "harsh treatment dealt out by Yahweh" begins Part II of the lament here in v. 12, and in v. 22, ending the lament, we find the *inclusio: wʿwll lmw / kʾšr ʿwllt ly* (cola 2 and 3).

VERSE 13 [*Mem*]

1. *b* [6]	*mmrwm šlḥ ʾš.*	From on high he sent fire,
2. *l* [8]	*bʿṣmty ywrydnh.*	Into my bones he made it sink.
3. *l* [6]	*prś ršt lrgly.*	He spread a snare for my feet,
4. *b* [6]	*hšybny ʾḥwr.*	He turned me back.
5. *l* [7]	*ntnny šmmh.*	He made me desolate,
6. *b* [5]	*kl hywm dwh.*	Ill all the day long.

In colon 2 MT reads *wyrdnh,* 4QLam *wywrydnw* or *wywrydny.* The Greek translates *wywrydnh* or *ywrydnw* (*katēgage auto*). These variants provide a basis of reconstructing an original *ywrdnh* (*ʾš* taken as feminine). The variant *ywrydnw* is possible, especially later with *ʾēš* often treated as masculine; presumably this is the reading of 4QLam (or stands behind a corruption to *wywrydny*).[25]

In cola 5 and 6 4QLam has the variants *šwmm* and *dwy,* masculines, according to its tendency, recognized above, to take the first person on occasion as the poet.

The structure of the triplet is *b:l::l:b::l:b.*[26] Binary correspondence in chiastic patterns is frequent in the triplet: *mmrwm* (first element of colon 1) contrasts with *lrgly* (last element in colon 3), *šlḥ ʾš* (last elements of colon 1) correspond to *prś ršt* (first elements of colon 3), reinforced

25. The last letter in 4QLam is more easily read *yod,* perhaps, but in ligatured forms *yod* and *waw* are all but interchangeable.

26. In fact cola 3 and 4 are balanced in syllable count, the single instance in this poem. Such license seems to have been allowed even in older, more traditional exemplars of this verse form, to judge from its rare appearance elsewhere, for example, in the Song of Jonah (see below).

with the repetition of sibilants. In cola 4 and 5, chiastically positioned, *hšybny* corresponds to *ntnny* grammatically and semantically, each initiating its colon. At the same time, there is some internal parallelism within the first bicolon: *šlḥ ʾš* stands parallel to *ywrdnh* as well as to *prś ršt.* Also *lrgly* is parallel to *bʿṣmty* as well as contrasting with *mmrwm.* At longer range, *hšybny ʾḥwr* echoes *wtšb ʾḥwr* (v. 8c), and *ntnny šmmh* faintly recalls *šʿryh šwmmym* (v. 4b).

VERSE 14 [*Nun*]

1. *b* [5]	*nqšr ʿl pšʿy.*	The yoke of my rebellion is bound on,
2. *l* [6]	*bydw yśtrg.*	By his hand it is tied together.
3. *l* [6]	*ʿlw ʿl ṣwʾry.*	His yoke is on my neck.
4. *b* [4]	*hkšyl kwḥy.*	He has made my strength ebb.
5. *b* [6]	*ntty yhwh.*	Yahweh has delivered me
6. *l* [7]	*bydy lʾ ʾwkl qwm.*	Into the hand of those I am unable to resist.

In colon 1, 4QLam reads *nqšrh* for the *hapax legomenon nśqd.* Evidently this tradition takes the subject to be the speaker: "Bound (am I [f.])."[27]

The subject, however, is "the yoke of my rebellion," i.e., the yoke due a captured rebel, and the better reading is *niqšar,* which also stands behind MT, *nśqd* arising from metathesis and the confusion of *reš* and *dalet.* The evidence of 4QLam justifies the emendations of Oettli (*nqšr*) and (in part) Ehrlich (*nqšrw*). For *yśtrgw,* 4QLam reads *wyśtrg;* the structure of the bicolon requires that we read *yśtrg* as original, partly with MT, partly with 4QLam. The plural form arose out of attraction to *pšʿy* taken as a plural, the reading *wyśtrg* out of wrong division of the colon. In colon 3, 4QLam reads *ʿwlw* (for MT *ʿlw*), certainly reflecting the original reading *ʿullô.* Symmachus interestingly has *ho zygos autou,* reflecting the same text. In colon 5, 4QLam has the reading *yhwh,* to be preferred over *ʾdny* of the received text. The final colon is read in 4QLam *byd lwʾ ʾwkl lqwm,* which has nothing to recommend it over the text of MT. The construction *byd / bydy lʾ ʾwkl qwm* is, of course, unusual in its elliptical use of a bound construction as a surrogate for a relative clause but is not without parallel, at least in Massoretic Hebrew.

The reconstructed text of the triplet gives a coherent picture of Zion, punished for her rebellion by being bound by Yahweh's own hand in the yoke symbolic of captivity and delivered by Yahweh into the hands of her adversaries. Bowed under the yoke, she is spent in strength and unable to resist her foes.

The structure of the triplet as reconstructed is *b:l::l:b::b:l.* There is in-

27. Cf. *nqšrh,* 'bound' in 1 Sam. 18:1.

ternal parallelism in the first bicolon, *nqšr,* the first word, corresponding to *yśtrg,* the last word. At the same time there is linkage between colon 1 and colon 3 with the repetition of the element *ʿōl.* Cola 3 and 4 also correspond and link with the final bicolon, as they recount parallel actions of Yahweh bringing low captive Zion. Worthy of note also is the juxtaposition of *bydw* in the first bicolon, and *bydy* in the last colon: the hand of God and the hands of the enemy.

VERSE 15 [*Samek*]

1. *l* [6]	*slh kl ʿbyry.*	He has offered as tribute all my mighty ones,
2. *b* [5]	*yhwh bqrby.*	Yahweh in my midst.
3. *l* [6]	*qrʾ ʿly mwʿd.*	He has called up against me an assembly,
4. *b* [5]	*lšbr bḥwry.*	To break [the bones of] my warriors.
5. *b* [5]	*gt drk yhwh.*	Yahweh has trodden the winepress,
6. *l* [8]	*lbtwlt bt yhwdh.*	Of the maiden Judah.

The triplet is made up of images taken from the language of holy war. The last bicolon, Yahweh treading out the vintage, recalls Isaiah 63:1–6, with its combination of vintage festival, slaughter, and the celebration of the rites of holy war. The first two cola recall Isaiah 34:1–8, also a song of holy war, with its combination of the images of animal sacrifice and of the *ḥerem.* Especially important is the play on animal names which are at the same time titles of military leaders. In colon 1 of Lamentations 1:15 we find a similar play: *ʿbyry,* lit., 'my bulls,' parallel to *bḥwry,* 'my young warriors.'[28] The first word, *slh,* must be taken as the *piʿel* of the root *sly/slʾ* 'to weight,' 'pay,' and in Old South Arabic 'to pay tribute,' 'dedicate as an offering,' 'devote to a deity.' Thus we find in the triplet the images of animals/warriors set aside as an offering or booty (the first bicolon), the festival of victory with its slaughter (the second bicolon), and the treading out of the vintage/blood of warriors (the third bicolon).

In colon 1 4QLam appears to read *ʿbydy;* if so, it is a simple lapse for *ʿbyry.* In colon 5 4QLam reads *yhwh* correctly for the *ʾdny* of MT, and *yhwh* is evidently to be restored in colon 2, where both 4QLam and MT have *ʾădōnay.*

The structure of the triplet is *l:b::l:b::b:l.* The general semantic parallelism between the three bicola has been described above, as well as the correspondence of *ʿbyry* (colon 1) and *bḥwry* (colon 4). One notes also the sequence of *bqrby* (colon 2), *ʿly* (colon 3), and *lbtwlt* (colon 6), which are positioned chiastically, as are *yhwh* (colon 2, first element) and *yhwh*

28. See esp. P. W. Miller, "Animal Names as Designations in Ugaritic and Hebrew," *UF* 2 (1970): 177–186 (on *ʿbyr,* pp. 180 ff.).

(colon 5, last element). The shift to the third person in colon 5 has been discussed above in v. 9 and v. 11. The following triplet, v. 17 MT, continues that reprise of the point of view of Part I, before reverting to the first person for the remainder of the poem. The calling of a *mwʿd* by Yahweh in this triplet, a *mwʿd* to which the enemy is invited, stands in interesting tension with v. 10 (as reconstructed) with its allusion to Yahweh's command that the nations shall not enter *mwʿdyh,* as well as with *mbly bʾy mwʿd* in v. 4.

VERSE 17 [MT *Pe*]

1. *l* [9]	*prśh ṣywn bydyh.*	Zion reaches out with her hands,
2. *b* [5]	*ʾyn mnḥm lh.*	There was none to comfort her.
3. *l* [7]	*ṣph yhwh lyʿqb.*	Yahweh kept watch on Jacob:
4. *b* [5]	*sbybyw ṣryw.*	His enemies have surrounded him;
5. *l* [7]	*hyth yrwšlm.*	Jerusalem has become
6. *b* [6]	*lndh bynyhm.*	As an unclean thing among them.

In colon 3, 4QLam has the reading *ṣph* for *ṣwh* of MT. The reading of MT is extremely awkward, if not impossible: "Yahweh commanded as to Jacob those around him [to be] his adversaries." On the contrary, *ṣph,* 'to keep watch,' makes admirable sense. The root may be used of the judge or witness who keeps watch to see that justice is done, a covenant kept, wrongdoers punished, etc. (cf. Genesis 31:49; Psalm 66:7; Proverbs 15:3), as well as one who keeps military watch. The form *ṣph* with *l* appears in one context where evil intent is meant: *ṣwph ršʿ lṣdyq* (Psalm 37:32). The ease with which *ṣph* could be misread as *ṣwh* can be seen by glancing at the reading in 4QLam, and *ṣwyth* in v. 10 may have triggered the error (reminiscence).

Elsewhere in the verse the text of 4QLam is conflate: after *ʾyn mnḥm lh,* 4Q adds *mkwl ʾwhbyh,* expanded from v. 2, *ʾyn lh mnḥm mkwl ʾwhbyh,* and a variant of colon 1 of v. 18 has intruded, presumably the insertion in the text of a marginal reading: *ṣdyq ʾth yhwh.* In colon 3, 4QLam reads *ʾdwny* for the superior reading *yhwh* in MT. In colon 6 4QLam preserves a reading, *lndwḥ bnyhmh,* obviously inferior, arising initially in a graphic confusion of *he* and *ḥet* and confounded by orthographic revision.

In 4QLam, the verse beginning with *pe* precedes the verse beginning *ʿayin* in the acrostic sequence. Thus it conforms to the rare alphabetic order found in Lamentations chapters 2, 3, and 4.[29] One finds a parallel

29. This order of the alphabet is now known outside biblical acrostics in the texts from Kuntillet ʿAjrûd, and in the abecedary from ʿIzbet Ṣarṭah. See F. M. Cross, "Newly Found Inscriptions in Old Canaanite and Early Phoenician Scripts," *BASOR* 238 (1980): 8–30, and the literature cited.

textual variation in Proverbs 31:25–26, where MT has the order *ʿayin–pe,* the Greek text of Proverbs the order *pe–ʿayin.*

The existence of two alphabetic orders in the textual transmission of Lamentations 1 raises the question of the original order. I do not believe the question can be answered. If one posits a single anonymous author for the book, he could well argue that the order of chapters 2–4 reflects the author's preference, and that Lamentations 1 has been secondarily conformed to the standard order. However, we are not sure that the laments come from a single hand. Again, if we assume that Lamentations is the collection of a systematic editor, we might argue that the *pe–ʿayin* order is original at least in the principal edition of the book. But we do not know that the putative editor was systematic; he may have included Lamentations 1 in his collection in the form it came to him, in which case it has been secondarily conformed to the order of Lamentations 2–4 in the textual tradition preserved in 4QLam (and so on).

The structure of the triplet is *l:b::l:b::l:b.* The verse is rich with long-range parallelism. In colon 1 *prśh ṣywn bydyh* corresponds to *ydw prś ṣr* in the first colon of v. 10. Colon 2, *ʾyn mnḥm lh,* repeats a theme which persists throughout the lament in delicate variations: v. 2 *ʾyn lh mnḥm,* v. 7 *ʾyn ʿwzr lh,* v. 9 *ʾyn mnḥm lh,* v. 17 *ʾyn mnḥm lh,* v. 21 *ʾyn mnḥm ly.* In the final bicolon there is a similar repetition of a theme in a grammatically fixed pattern: *hyth . . . ndh,* which is to be compared to *hyth kʾlmnh* and *hyth lms* (v. 1), *lnwd hyth* (v. 9), and *hyyty zwllh* (v. 11).

VERSE 16 [MT *ʿAyin*]

1. *b* [5]	*ʿyny bkyh.*	My eye weeps,
2. *l* [6]	*ʿyny yrdh mym.*	My eye runs with tears.
3. *l* [8]	*rḥq mmny mnḥm.*	A comforter is far from me,
4. *b* [4]	*mšyb npšy.*	One who would restore my soul.
5. *l* [7]	*hyw bny šmmym.*	My children are desolate,
6. *b* [5]	*ky gbr ʾwyb.*	But the enemy is mighty.

The text of MT in the first bicolon is corrupt, as is generally recognized. Behind the received text are probably two variants in colon 1: *ʿyny bkyh* and *bkyh ʿyny,* and 4QLam adds a third variant, *bkw ʿyny.* The word *ʾny* is not found in 4QLam, and its absence in a conflate text like 4QLam requires an explanation. We should argue, therefore, that *ʾny* in the textual tradition behind MT is a simple misreading of *ʿyny.* The combination of two variants has produced the conflate reading *ʾny bkyh ʿny* in MT. The reading of 4QLam (*bkw ʿyny*) is a revision of *bkyh ʿyny,* which takes *ʿyny* as a plural. The second colon also probably existed at one time in two variants: *ʿyny yrdh mym* (MT) and *ʿyny yrdh dmʿty.* Compare Lamentations 3:48, *plgy mym trd ʿyny,* and Jeremiah 13:17, *wtrd ʿyny dmʿh.*

Since both variants are formulaic, it is difficult to choose between them. The versions omit one of the occurrences of *ʿyny* following *bkyh,* further suggesting that the first colon read *ʾny/ʿyny bkyh.* In the second colon the versions read *mym* with the possible exception of Symmachus, who has *dakrua,* the usual translation of *dmʿh,* but this may be interpretive.

The first colon may be reconstructed as a whole either to read *ʿl ʾlh ʿyny bkyh,* which would make a suitable long colon, or to read *ʿyny bkyh,* a short colon. The phrase *ʿl ʾlh* is suspect in good poetry and may be secondary, introduced to head the *ʿayin* triplet when initial *ʿyny* has been corrupted to *ʾny.*[30]

The structure of the triplet as reconstructed is *b:l::l:b::l:b.* The first bicolon exhibits internal parallelism between its members, with the repetition of *ʿyny* beginning each colon reminiscent of archaic repetitive parallelism, and the participles *bkyh* and *yrdh* parallel grammatically and semantically. Zion's weeping and the absence of a comforter in the first and second bicola correspond to the themes of the first and second bicola of v. 2. The phrase *mšyb npšy* (colon 4) echoes *lhšyb npš* of v. 11 (colon 4), and *šmmym* (colon 5) continues a sequence in v. 4 (*šmmym*) and v. 13 (*šmmh*). Finally *ky gbr ʾwyb* repeats with minor variation *ky hgdyl ʾwyb.*

In the second bicolon *mšyb npšy* may be described fairly as a "ballast variant" of *mnḥm,* lending an element of internal parallelism. In the third bicolon there is strong antithetic parallelism between the members.

VERSE 18 [*Ṣade*]

1. *b* [5]	*ṣdyq hwʾ yhwh.*	Yahweh is just,
2. *l* [6]	*ky pyhw mryty.*	For I defied his command.
3. *l* [6]	*šmʿw nʾ kl ʿmym.*	Hear, pray, all you peoples,
4. *b* [5]	*wrʾw mkʾby.*	And behold my pain.
5. *l* [8]	*btwlwty wbḥwry.*	My maidens and young men
6. *b* [6]	*hlkw bšby.*	Have gone into captivity.

The variant misplaced in line 8 of Column III of 4QLam, *ṣdyq ʾth yhwh,* can be filled out to read, presumably, *ky pyk mryty.* However, at the proper place (III, line 10) the manuscript stands with MT save for the substitution of ʾ[*dwny*] for *yhwh.* Unfortunately, 4QLam breaks off here.

The structure of the triplet is *b:l::l:b::l:b.* It is poor in internal parallelistic devices, but brings new variations on persistent themes. In the second bicolon, there is the call on the nations to observe the pain of

30. In colon 3 we have omitted *ky* (found both in MT and 4QLam [*kyʾ*]). This line is rather long, and the tendency of this particle to multiply at the beginning of cola in textual transmission, especially in proximity to other occurrences of *ky* (cf. colon 6), is well documented.

Zion, a theme we have heard in v. 12, where wayfarers are asked to observe her pain. The third bicolon recalls v. 4 (colon 5) *btwltyh nhwgwt.* In colon 2 *mryty* anticipates *mrh mryty* in v. 20b.

VERSE 19 [*Qop*]

1. *l* [8]	*qr'ty lm'hby.*	I appealed to my lovers;
2. *b* [5]	*hmh rmwny.*	They betrayed me.
3. *l* [7]	*khny wzqny.*	My priests and my elders
4. *b* [5]	*bʿyr gwʿw.*	Expire in the city.
5. *l* [7]	*ky bqšw 'kl lmw.*	For they sought food for themselves,
6. *b* [5]	*wl' mṣ'w.*	And found none.

For colon 6 the Greek and Syriac preserve two variants (conflated): *wyšbw 't npšm* (with MT) and *wl' mṣ'w* (*kai ouk euron / wl' 'škḥw*). I am inclined to take *wl' mṣ'w* as original. The reading of MT is long, prosaic (using both the *waw*-consecutive and the particle *'t*), and appears to be an expanded parallel reading introduced from v. 11: (*b'kl*) *lhšyb npš.* Such expansion is well attested in the transmission of Lamentations by the 4QLam manuscript.

The structure of the triplet as reconstructed is *l:b::l:b::l:b.* Antithetical parallelism between cola is found in the first and last bicolon. The words *bqš* and *mṣ'* are a formulaic pair. Zion's faithless lovers, first mentioned in v. 2, return in this verse.[31] The priests who sighed in v. 4 reappear to expire. The theme of famine—the search for food—struck first in the figure of v. 6, more explicitly in parallel language in v. 11 (giving rise to the parallel reading discussed above), returns powerfully in this verse.

VERSE 20 [*Reš*]

1. *l* [7]	*r'h yhwh ky ṣr ly.*	Behold, Yahweh, for I am in anguish
2. *b* [6]	*mʿy ḥmrmrw.*	My bowels churn.
3. *l* [7]	*nhpk lby bqrby.*	My heart is turned over within me,
4. *b* [6]	*ky mrh mryty.*	For I have grievously rebelled.
5. *l* [6]	*mḥwṣ šklh ḥrb.*	Outside the sword has bereaved,
6. *b* [5]	*bbyt 'ymwt.*	Inside there was terror.

There is a textual difficulty in colon 6. The bicolon is a traditional one. Often *ḥrb* and *rʿb* are the formulaic pair. Cf. Ezekiel 7:15 and Jeremiah 14:18. Hillers for this reason suggested the rare term *kāpān,* 'hunger,' 'famine' as an emendation for *kmwt.* An emendation is desiderated, but I much prefer to turn to the closest alloform of this traditional bicolon for

31. On the meaning of the figure, see the excellent discussion of Hillers, *Lamentations,* p. 19.

help: *mḥwṣ tškl ḥrb / wmḥdrym ʾymh* (Deuteronomy 32:25). This verse suggests that an alternate pair is available in old poetic tradition: *ḥrb/ʾymh.* I propose, therefore, to read *ʾymwt* for *kmwt.* It may be observed further that, in another close parallel to cola 3 and 6 in Psalm 55:5, *mwt* occurs as a dittograph of *ʾymwt: lby yḥyl bqrby / wʾymwt mwt nplw ʿly.*

The structure of the triplet is *l:b::l:b::l:b.* In the first bicolon there is internal parallelism, *mʿy ḥmrmrw* acting as a ballast variant of *ṣr ly.* However, the strongest set of correspondence is between colon 2 and colon 3, cola (*b/l*) positioned chiastically with chiastic patterning also in the cola *–ḥmrmrw/nhpk–, mʿy–/–bqrby.*[32] The final bicolon also reveals internal parallelism: *mḥwṣ–/bbyt–* and *–ḥrb/–ʾymwt.*

VERSE 21 [*Šin*]

1. *l* [9]	*šmʿw ky nʾnḥh ʾny.*	They heard that I sigh,
2. *b* [5]	*ʾyn mnḥm ly.*	(That) there was none to comfort me.
3. *l* [8]	*šmʿw rʿty śśw.*	They heard of my evil; they rejoice
4. *b* [6]	*ky ʾth ʿśyt.*	That you have done it.
5. *l* [7]	*hbʾt ywm qrʾt.*	May you bring the day that you proclaimed
6. *b* [6]	*wyhyw kmwny.*	When they will become as I.

In colon 1 we prefer to read with MT *šmʿw,* with the subject (enemies) understood, in view of the structure of the triplet. Colon 2, however, has been expanded by a parallel reading and is impossibly long. We have noted above that the bicolon in v. 2, *ʾyn lh mnḥm mkl ʾhbyh,* has triggered in v. 17 an expansion in 4QLam: *ʾyn mnḥm lh mkwl ʾwhbyh;* we believe that the same expansion by insertion of the parallel reading occurred here: *ʾyn mnḥm ly mkl ʾwhby.* This expanded reading then was further altered to provide a subject for *šmʿw,* producing the variant in MT (*ʾyn mnḥm ly*) *kl ʾ(w)yby šmʿw rʿty śśw.*

The structure of the triplet as reconstructed is *l:b::l:b::l:b.* The repetition of *šmʿw* in colon 1 and colon 2, beginning each colon, is studied. So also is the frequency of sibilants in cola 1, 3, and 4. The themes of "sighing" and "failure of a comforter" have been discussed above; they find their final expression here.

VERSE 22 [*Taw*]

1. *l* [10]	*tbʾ kl rʿtm lpnyk.*	Let all their wickedness come before you,
2. *b* [5]	*wʿwll lmw.*	And deal with them

32. Dashes are used here to indicate the position of an element in a colon.

3. *l* [7]	*k'šr ʿllt ly.*	As you have dealt with me,
4. *b* [5]	*ʿl kl pšʿy.*	For all my acts of rebellion.
5. *l* [6]	*ky rbwt ʾnḥty.*	For many are my sighs,
6. *b* [5]	*wlby dwy.*	And my heart is sick.

This triplet has some striking parallels with the preceding triplet, notably the last two bicola of v. 21 and the first two bicola of v. 22. Note the correspondence of *rʿty* in colon 3 of v. 21 and *rʿtm* in colon 1 of v. 22 and the general semantic correspondence between *ʿśyt* (colon 4, v. 21) and *ʿll/ʿllt* (cola 2 and 3, v. 22). Both verses appeal to Yahweh to reverse the roles of Zion and the enemy, the enemy punished by Yahweh for his sins, as Zion has been punished for her sins. One perceives also an envelope construction in the correspondence of *nʾnḥh ʾny* (colon 1, v. 21) and *ʾnḥty* (colon 5, v. 22).

In the final triplet colon 2 is bound to colon 3 by enjambment and repetition (*ʿwll lmw / ʿllt ly*), an unexpected structure. The phrase *ʿl kl pšʿy* (colon 4) recalls *ʿl rb pšʿyh* (colon 4, v. 5).

IV

The structures of the acrostic poem as a whole may be summarized as follows:

PART I

1.	א	*l:b::l:b::l:b*
2.	ב	*l:b::b:l::l:b*
3.	ג	*l:b::l:b::l:b*
4.	ד	*l:b::l:b::l:b*
5.	ה	*l:b::b:l::l:b*
6.	ו	*l:b::l:b::l:b*
7.	ז	*l:b::l:b::b:l*
8.	ח	*l:b::l:b::l:b*
9.	ט	*b:l::l:b::l:b*
10.	י	*b:l::l:b::b:l*
11.	כ	*l:b::l:b::l:b*

PART II

12.	ל	*l:b::l:b::l:b*
13.	מ	*b:l::l:b::l:b*
14.	נ	*b:l::l:b::b:l*
15.	ס	*l:b::l:b::b:l*
16.	פ	*b:l::l:b::l:b*

17. ע *l:b::l:b::l:b*
18. צ *b:l::l:b::l:b*
19. ק *l:b::l:b::l:b*
20. ר *l:b::l:b::l:b*
21. ש *l:b::l:b::l:b*
22. ת *l:b::l:b::l:b*

The compound verse form found in this lament is built up fundamentally of cola of traditional length, as we have seen, the long colon we have labeled *'l'* and the short colon we have labeled *'b,'* which are the stuff of the traditional oral poetry represented in Ugaritic poetry and especially in the corpus of Israel's most ancient poetry. This is evident from the regularity of the caesural pause and especially in the frequent occurrence of "internal" parallelism, i.e., correspondence at multiple levels between the cola of a bicolon. The long colon is most often seven syllables, but also counts of eight and six are quite common. Nine-syllable cola are rare.[33] A short colon of five syllables is much the most common, but six is frequent, seven or four, rare. Since syllable counts overlap, it seems doubtful that the poet was counting syllables. Cola are long or short within a range, but most important is the relative length of each in a bicolon *l:b* or *b:l*, the contrast between unbalanced units.

The dominant parallel structures are found in corresponding couplets and triplets of bicola. The verse form is thus best described as *l:b::l:b(::l:b)*, with variants *b:l::l:b(::b:l)*, and so on. There is here a powerful cyclic or chiastic impulse, and this impulse is reflected as well in chiastic and cyclic positioning of parallel grammatical and semantic units at every level of the verse. This lament from Lamentations is not the best example of the full potentiality of the verse form. The lament in Jonah, especially in its archaic section, shows a much higher density (*Dichtung*) of such artifice, as will be seen below.

The origin of the verse form *l:b::l:b* (to use its dominant pattern) must be looked for in archaic "mixed meters" of the type *l:l(:l)* alternating with series of verses *b:b::b:b* (see above). Such mixed verse was chosen for the earliest Hebrew lament extant, the Lament of David. In fact, the verse *l:b::l:b* is legitimately described as a variety of "mixed meter" of even more complex structure.

The recurrence of corresponding words, phrases, cola, and themes at "long range," throughout the poem, often in significant cyclic structures, has occupied my attention in analyzing the lament. I may ap-

33. Twice we find long cola of ten syllables, in v. 8, colon 3, and in v. 22, colon 1. Both cola contain a suspicious occurrence of *kl*. I have left them in the text above, but in view of the rarity of cola of such length, it may be better to excise them. The tendency of *kl* to multiply in the process of textual transmission is notorious.

propriately quote again from Roman Jakobson: "We have learned the suggestive etymology of the terms *prose* and *verse*—the former, oratio prosa < prorsa < proversa 'speech turned straightforward,' and the latter, versus 'return.' Hence we must consistently draw all inferences from the obvious fact that on every level of language, the essence of poetic artifice consists in recurrent returns."

V

The Psalm of Jonah, Jonah 2:3–10, is, in its present form, a typical example of the genre labeled "the individual thanksgiving." Vv. 3–7 contain archaic material. The imagery of these verses pictures death, or the approach of death, alternately as entrance into the underworld or as engulfment in cosmic waters. In the Semitic mythological lore that underlies this language—much of it perhaps vague or forgotten in later Israel—are conceptions of an entry into the underworld at the "sources of the two rivers, the fountains of the double deep," at the foot of the cosmic mountain(s). This appears to have been the place of the river ordeal, where one enters *ʾereṣ* 'the underworld,' or Sheol, etymologically '(the place of) questioning (or judgment).' One may speak of entering into the mouth or maw of Môt (Death) on one's way to becoming a denizen of Môt's city ("Ooze, Decay the seat of his enthronement, Slime the land of his heritage").[34] The mingling of images of the realm of the dead seems confused and illogical. The underworld in one image is a monstrous power with gaping jaws and insatiable belly, in another a realm of chaotic waters, in a third a swampy city presided over by Death himself. These images are now better understood, thanks to rich parallels in Babylonian hymns and Ugaritic mythology. These have been collected most recently by Ruth Rosenberg and need not be recited here.[35] The imagery of the Psalm of Jonah is also paralleled in biblical poetry: Psalm 40:3; 42:8; 69:2, 3, 15, 16; 88:5–8; Job 38:16–17, and most closely in 2 Samuel 22:5–7 (= Psalm 18:5–7).[36]

Canaanite myths known from the texts of Ugarit and from their residue in the Bible provide us with complementary accounts of the basic conflict between order and chaos, life and death. These alloforms of cosmogonic conflict include the battle of Baʿl, lord of fertility (life), with Prince Sea / Judge River (the latter title presumably reflecting his role

34. *CTA* 5.2.2–4, 15–16; cf. 4.8.13–14.

35. "The Concept of Biblical Sheol within the Context of Ancient Near Eastern Beliefs" (Ph.D. diss., Harvard University, 1980).

36. On the reconstruction of the text underlying 2 Sam. 22 and Ps. 18, see *AYP,* 125–158; and F. M. Cross and D. N. Freedman, "A Royal Song of Thanksgiving: II Samuel 22 = Psalm 18," *JBL* 72 (1953): 15–34.

in the ordeal); the conflict with Môt, lord of death, Baʿl's defeat and descent into the underworld, and return to life; and variously the defeat of Lôtān/Leviathan or Tĕhōm/Tiāmat, the primordial sea, or her monstrous alter ego. The mythic approach to reality is thus expressed in multiple or complementary models whose logical relationship is left unresolved. The manifestation of the power of death, sterility, or chaos may be described as the attack of Sea or River, or as the attack of Death, or as the attack of their agents, including the rivers and breakers of Sheol. Thus the rich poetic language used in speaking of life and death, or of the manifestation of death or danger in life, may draw on images that stem from mythic geography, and, in some instances, democratized versions of Semitic cosmogonic myths.[37]

The prosodic structure of Jonah 2:3–7 reflects an oral-formulaic style. There is an extraordinarily low density of prosaic particles. The article is absent.[38] The prefix conjugation (without *waw*), used in the past narrative sense, is found in v. 4 (*ysbbny* parallel to *ʿbrw*), and v. 6 (*ysbbny* parallel to *ʾppwny*). The form *wtšlykny* introducing v. 4 is read *tšlykny,* that is, without the conjunction, in the Old Greek, no doubt correctly, giving a third instance.[39] Thus in vv. 3–7 the conjunctive *waw* is not used to introduce a bicolon save in the instance of *wtʿl,* v. 7b, and the originality of this form may be questioned.[40] In contrast vv. 8–10 show few traits of early style either in poetic structure or in syntax, and prosaic particles intrude.

37. See, for example, *CTA* 6.5.1–5, where Baʿl's return from the underworld is described:

yʾiḫd.bʿl.bn.ʾaθrt
rbm. ymḫṣ. bktp
dkym. ymḫṣ. bṣmd
ṣḥr mt. ymṣḫ. lʾarṣ
[yʿl.]b[ʿ]l. lksʾi. mlkh . . .

Baʿl seized the sons of Asherah:
Depths he smashed in the shoulder;
Breakers he smashed with a club;
The Sallow One, Death, he smote to earth;
Baʿl [mounted] to his royal throne. . . .

38. In v. 7, *hʾrṣ* appears without the article in the OG, a reading we take to be original.

39. See the discussion of David A. Robertson, *Linguistic Evidence in Dating Early Hebrew Poetry, SBLDS* 3 (Missoula, Mont.: Scholars Press, 1972), 7–55.

40. See *AYP,* 127–28, and table, pp. 161–168. The *waw* of *wʾny* (vv. 5 and 10) is a special usage. It introduces a *casus pendens,* a construction already found in Ugaritic poetry.

VI

In the following analysis of the structure of the Psalm of Jonah, it will be useful to indicate the position of elements in a colon by dashes; for example *qr'ty*–(first element)–*mṣrh*–(middle element)–*ly* (final element). I have numbered the cola in the right column according to the larger units of the poem, followed by our notation of colon type (*l*/*b*), and in parentheses I have then supplied syllable counts in (reconstructed) early pronunciation.

1. *b* [7]	*qr'ty mṣrh ly.*	[v 3]	I have called out my distress
2. *l* [7]	*'l yhwh wy'nny.*		To Yahweh and he answered me.
3. *l* [7]	*mbṭn š'wl šw'ty.*		Out of the belly of Sheol I cried;
4. *b* [5]	*šm't qwly.*		You heard my voice.
5. *l* [9]	*tšlykny bmṣwlt ym.*	[v 4]	You cast me in the depth of the Sea;
6. *b* [7]	*nhr ysbbny.*		River encircled me.
7. *b* [5]	*kl mšbryk.*		All your breakers
8. *l* [9]	*wglyk 'ly 'brw.*		And all your waves engulfed me.

Poetic license has been taken in the first bicolon for structural reasons described below. The caesural pause is placed unnaturally. Further, the colon length (seven syllables) is borderline, capable of being read *l:b* or *b:l*. One suspects that the original reading of the first colon was *'qr' mṣrh ly*, giving the contrast *b:l*. Compare *bṣr ly 'qr' yhwh* in 2 Samuel 22:7 (= Psalm 18:7). In this case the use of the prefix tense for narrative past (used freely in vv. 4 [bis] and 5) has been suppressed in favor of the standard perfect.

In colon 5 we are inclined to see a conflation of ancient variants, both stock phrases: *mṣwlt ym* and *blbb ymym*. In colon 6 similarly there is evidence of variants: *nhr* and *nhrym* (or *nhrwt*). The Old Greek reads *ym* in colon 5 (*thalassēs*), *nhrym* in colon 6 (*potomoi*).[41] I prefer the singular with its mythological redolence in each colon. The conjunction beginning colon 6 is to be suppressed in view of its rarity elsewhere in the poem in this position, and the notorious tendency for its introduction in the course of textual transmission.

The four bicola form a quatrain of interlocking structure: *b:l::l:b–l:b::b:l*. As reconstructed, the sequence of bicola is both cyclic and chiastic. Primary parallelism is between the bicola 1–2 and 3–4, a couplet within the quatrain, and 5–6 and 7–8, the second couplet of the quatrain.

41. The *kaige* text from Naḥal Ḥever reads [*pota*]*mos*, correcting to the Hebrew. See *DJD* 8, col. 2, 36 (Jonah 2:4).

But there is also internal parallelism between cola in these bicola, and long-range correspondences which bind the whole into a quatrain.

In the first bicolon note the following structures: *qr'ty–/–wy'nny* in chiastic correspondence, as well as *–ly/'l–*. On the other hand there is grammatical parallelism between *–ly* and *–ny*. In the second bicolon we find chiastic order again, *–šw'ty/šm't–*, an assonant pair. The binary correspondences between the two bicola are more dramatic:

qr'ty– (1)
–šw'ty (3)
–y'nny (2)
šm't– (4)

Here there is synonymous parallelism in chiastic order. The elements *–mṣrh ly* and *mbṭn š'wl–* are also parallel and in chiastic order, both introduced by the preposition *m–*. The elements *–ny* and *–qwly* complete the parallelistic structures linking the bicola.

In the third bicolon, the formulaic pair *–ym/nhr–* is arranged chiastically as are the verbs

tšlykny–
–ysbbny

giving the bicolon internally structured parallelism.

In the fourth bicolon the caesural pause must be placed after *mšbryk,* separating it from *glyk,* the second member of the formulaic pair, in *b:l* structure, lending the bicolon internal parallelism and chiasm:

–mšbryk
wglyk–

The second couplet exhibits complex parallelism. Note the following:

tšlykny–
–ysbbny
–'ly 'brw

The chiastic placement of the first two verbal elements is complemented by *'ly 'brw,* parallel semantically to *ysbbny,* but contrasting grammatically (*yqṭl/qṭl*); *'ly 'brw* also is in chiastic relation to *tšlykny.* The reverse relationship exists with the elements

–ny
–ny
–'ly–

The formulaic pairs also bind the second couplet in extended parallelism and studied chiasm:

-ym
nhr-
-mšbryk
wglyk-

The two couplets present two images, one of death reflected in the parallel elements *mṣrh ly* and *mbṭn š'wl,* the other in the expressions *mṣwlt ym* (or *lbb ym*) and its complements *nhr, mšbryk,* and *glyk.* In the traditional pairing of the images of Death and Sea, the maw of Death, and the watery or mucky abyss, the sequence of images in the two couplets resonates semantic parallelism. It is hardly chance that there is the assonant series beginning with *mṣ-, mb-, bmṣ-:*

-mṣrh ly
mbṭn š'wl-
-bmṣwlt ym

The four bicola are then suitably described as a quatrain or a pair of couplets in interlocking structure: *b:l::l:b–l:b::b:l.*

1. *b* [6]	*w'ny 'mrty.*	[v 5]	As for me, I said
2. *l* [8]	*ngršty mngd ʿynyk.*		"I am driven from your sight."
3. *l* [7]	*'ykh 'wsyp lhbyṭ*		"How shall I look again
4. *b* [6]	*'l hykl qdšk.*		Upon your holy temple?"

The couplet is to be understood as part of the description of the poet's plight, not, at this point in the thanksgiving song, an expression of hope or trust. Thus we are not to read *'ak,* but *'êk(ā),* with most commentators. Theodotion reads *pōs, 'yk* or *'ykh.* The frequent use of *'ak* in laments, to introduce an affirmation of confidence, may have triggered the misreading.

The couplet stands alone, preceded and followed by a quatrain. Its structure is *b:l::l:b.* The caesural pause in colon 1 naturally follows *'mrty.* There is little strict parallelism between the bicola. There is polar correspondence between *mngd ʿynyk* and *lhbyṭ 'l.* However, note the phonetic parallelism (assonance) in the repetition of 'alep:

'ny 'mrty (colon 1)
'ykh 'wsyp (colon 3).

There is also the sequence: *-êkā* (colon 2), *'êkā.* (colon 3), and *-ekā* (colon 4). The expression *'l hykl qdšk* also echoes *'l yhwh.*

1. *l* [7]	*'ppwny mym ʿd npš*	[v 6]	The waters surrounded me, up to my throat;
2. *b* [7]	*thwm ysbbny.*		The deep encompassed me.

3. *l* [6]	*swp ḥbwš lr'šy.*		Seaweed enwrapped my head
4. *b* [6]	*lqṣby hrym.*	[v 7]	At the roots of the mountains.
5. *b* [4]	*yrdty 'rṣ*[42]		I went down into the netherworld;
6. *l* [9]	*brḥyh b'dy l'wlm.*		Its bars [locked] behind me forever.
7. *l* [6]	*wt'l mšḥt ḥyy.*		But you brought my life up from the pit,
8. *b* [5]	*yhwh 'lhy.*		O Yahweh my god.

The structure of the quatrain is *l:b::l:b–b:l::l:b.* In the first bicolon there is internal parallelism, semantic and grammatical. The formulaic pair *-mym-/thwm-* is used, and the verbal elements, one suffixal, one prefixal, are arranged chiastically:

'ppwny-
-ysbbny

The first two bicola also reveal parallelistic structures. The phrase *'d npš* corresponds to *lr'šy,* and *ḥbwš,* 'enwrapped,' echoes *'ppwny* and *ysbbny.* The series:

-mym-
thwm-
swp-
-hrym

is subtly related in semantic field. The terms *mym* (sea-)water and *swp* weed in cola 1 and 3 evoke complementary images, and both are monosyllabic; *thwm* and *hrym* form an alternate formulaic pair to *mym* and *thwm* in their polar correspondence. The couplet abounds in the repetition of *m, n, b,* and *p,* nasals and bilabials. One may also raise the question as to whether the poet is playing on the elements

-lr'šy
lqṣby-

literally, 'to my top' and 'to the feet.' If so, the chiastic arrangement is to be noted.

The second couplet exhibits strong parallelism between the two bicola. The polar pair *yrdty-/wt'l-* introduce the bicola. Note also the formulaic pair *-'rṣ,* 'underworld,' and *-šḥt-,* 'pit (of the underworld).' The theme of encompassing, surrounding, binding (*'ppwny, ysbbny, ḥbwš*) is continued in the expression *brḥyh b'dy* alluding to imprisonment, linking the bicola into a quatrain.

In the first quatrain (vv. 3–4), the couplets were linked by the image

42. On this reading, see Robertson, *Linguistic Evidence in Dating Early Hebrew Poetry.*

"the belly of Sheol" (first couplet) over against images of water: Sea/ River (second couplet). In this quatrain (vv. 6–7), the couplets are linked by images of water (*mym, thwm*) in the first couplet over against images of the netherworld (*ʾrṣ, šḥt*) in the second couplet. This may be visualized as follows:

Quatrain 1: underworld :: cosmic waters;
Quatrain 2: cosmic waters :: underworld.

This is an exquisite example of cyclic construction. The cyclic construction and combination of images of cosmic waters and the underworld is closely paralleled in 2 Samuel 22:5–6 (= Psalm 18:5–6):

1. *ʾppwny mšbry mwt*
2. *nḥly blyʿl ybʿtwny*

3. *ḥbly šʾwl sbbwny*
4. *qdmwny mwqšy mwt*

In this quatrain (*l:l::l:l*) one notes chiastic structure:

ʾppwny–
–ybʿtwny
–sbbwny
qdmwny–

While each couplet places its parallel elements in chiastic order, cola 1 and 4 and cola 2 and 3 are linked with parallel elements forming a quatrain in cyclic structure:

–mšbry mwt (colon 1)
–mwqšy mwt (colon 4)

nḥly blyʿ– (colon 2)
ḥbly šʾwl– (colon 3)

Vv. 3–7 of the Psalm of Jonah form an intricately structured complex of traditional poetry. Oral formulae abound. Chiastic and cyclic figures ornament bicola and quatrains and the whole. The overall structure can be pictured as follows:

QUATRAIN	COUPLET	QUATRAIN
b:l::l:b	*b:l::l:b*	*l:b::l:b*
l:b::b:l		*b:l::l:b*

VII

The final section of the Psalm of Jonah yields on analysis far less sophisticated and intricate verse. The verse form is the same, but it monotonously repeats without variation: *l:b::l:b.*

l [8]	*bhtʿṭp ʿly npšy.*	[v 8]	When my soul fainted within me
b [6]	*ʾt yhwh zkrty.*		I remembered Yahweh.
l [10]	*wtbwʾ ʿlyk tplty.*		And my prayer came unto you,
b [6]	*ʾl hykl qdšk.*		To your holy temple.
l [8]	*mšmrym ḥbly šwʾ.*	[v 9]	Those who care for vain things (gods),
b [5]	*ḥsdm yʿzbw.*		Forsake their (source of) mercy.
l [7]	*wʾny bqwl twdh.*	[v 10]	As for me, with a voice of thanksgiving
b [5]	*ʾzbḥh lk.*		I will sacrifice unto you.
l [9]	*ʾšr ndrty ʾšlmh.*		That which I vowed I will pay.
b [7]	*yšwʿth lyhwh.*		Salvation is of Yahweh.

Study quickly reveals that these last verses yield little internal or long-range structure. Oral formulae do not appear. Only in v. 9 do we find a faintly chiastic figure in contrast to its extensive use in vv. 3–7. Grammatical parallelism including assonance is rare. Prosaic elements, wholly missing in vv. 3–7, appear and are difficult to expunge (*ʾt* in v. 8, *ʾšr* in v. 10). The language gives no appearance of early features; indeed the use of pseudo-cohortatives (v. 10) is late, as is the language of v. 9.

The contrast in the language and prosody of vv. 3–7 and vv. 8–10 requires explanation. I do not believe that the sections can stem from the same poet or from the same time. Rather, it appears that vv. 3–7 derive from an old thanksgiving song (or lament) when traditional oral skills were flourishing. Vv. 8–10 appear to be a stock cultic ending of later date welded on to the older traditional verses. I am not suggesting that the author of Jonah has spliced together a thanksgiving hymn to fit his purposes. The standard cultic ending of the psalm of thanksgiving fits no better—and no worse—than vv. 3–7 into the narrative concerning the prophet.

7

Toward a History of Hebrew Prosody

A HISTORY OF HEBREW PROSODY HAS NOT BEEN WRITTEN. YET I BELIEVE that there is no greater need in the study of Hebrew poetry: a systematic, diachronic investigation of one thousand years of poetic composition.[1] All artifacts, in style and form, evolve in the course of time. Like pots or scripts, or more closely allied, musical styles and forms, poetic devices, genres, and canons undergo change. Their evolution may be marked by rapid or slow development, abrupt, "revolutionary" emergence of new types or artifice, or slow, even archaizing periods in which change is little perceptible or obscure.[2] Typologies of various significant features of Hebrew poetry need to be traced and verified, and from the series of typologies, a reconstruction made of the history of Hebrew verse.

Such a task is not simple. Interference with the straightforward pursuit of such a program comes from several sources, some trivial if difficult to surmount, others serious and which will remain formidable obstacles. A trivial source of interference comes from the heritage of past ahistorical approaches to the analysis of biblical poetry, study based on the uncritical presumption that Hebrew poetry can be studied as though it were a homogeneous, written corpus, composed in Massoretic Hebrew.[3] A serious source of interference stems from the effects of the long history of the transmission of our texts. Hebrew poetry—and prose for that matter—has been revised repeatedly in orthography, in grammar, and occasionally in lexicon by generations of scribes.[4] External con-

1. See already James L. Kugel, "Some Thoughts on Future Research into Biblical Style: Addenda to *The Idea of Biblical Poetry*," *JSOT* 28 (1984): 108.

2. See my comments in chapter 12 below.

3. Such ahistorical presuppositions mar the study of Robert Alter, *The Art of Biblical Poetry* (New York: Basic Books, 1985).

4. The manuscript 4QSam[b], dating to the mid-third century B.C.E., can be drawn on for a number of examples illustrating such revision. Take, for example, a reading in 1 Sam. 20:34: *wypḥz ywntn mʿl hšlḥn*. The Massoretic Text reads: *wyqm yhwntn mʿm hšlḥn*. 4QSam[b] is to be translated "And Jonathan sprang up excitedly from the

trols, resisting such change, fixing the text, were applied beginning only in the first century C.E. with the promulgation of the Rabbinic Text.[5] Most of such revision was the result of unconscious, or minor "modernizing," to be sure, but it distances us from the original poetic text. No less serious are textual corruptions which inevitably entered the text, and the establishment of the text by the arts of textual recension and emendation are thus preliminary to any analysis of poetry. The subjective elements introduced by text-critical reconstruction are an impediment to "assured" results. But the toleration of corruption is to insure fallacious analysis. Happily new textual resources, not least those illuminating the character and history of the Old Greek translation, greatly facilitate the text-critical task today. And then there is the graver problem of reconstructing the pronunciation of Hebrew over a thousand years of development. Advances can be made in this endeavor, thanks to epigraphic Hebrew texts as well as to transcriptions of Canaanite and Hebrew in other languages with full notation, notably Akkadian. But the description of the development of the Hebrew language and its pronunciation in the epochs of its evolution proceeds slowly. A newly published ostracon from Khirbet ʿUzza inscribed with a literary text now reveals the distance between formal or poetic Hebrew and the vernacular reflected in most of the pre-Exilic corpus of Hebrew inscriptions.[6]

To put it sharply, I suspect that the Hebrew spoken by Hillel is as distant from the language of the Davidic court as is the language of General Haig from the English of Chaucer.

I

David Noel Freedman and I in our early studies of Ugaritic and ancient Hebrew poetry recognized two types of colon: a long colon, in the

table." The MT for 4Q *wypḥz* substituted *wyqm*, "and he rose up." 4Q is original, a textbook case of *lectio difficilior*. The text of MT has been modernized, the difficult, rare word replaced by the bland, innocuous *wyqm*. The OG reads here *kai anepēdēsen*, 'and he started up,' obviously reflecting *wypḥz*. Modernization is, perhaps, too neutral a term to apply. In Late Hebrew, Middle Hebrew, and Aramaic, the root *pḥz* developed the primary meaning 'to be concupiscent,' 'lewd,' 'lascivious.' The early meaning, 'to be excited,' or 'to act in excitement,' was forgotten or obsolescent. Hence the older reading was more than obscure. It was grotesque, and perhaps suppressed. Cf. Jonas C. Greenfield, "The Meaning of *pḥz*," in *Studies in Bible and the Ancient Near East* (Jerusalem, 1978), 35–40.

5. See below, chapters 10 and 11.

6. I. Beit-Arieh, "A Literary Ostracon from Ḥorvat ʿUza," *TA* 20 (1993): 55–65 (with an appendix, "A Suggested Reading of the Ḥorvat ʿUza Ostracon," by F. M. Cross, pp. 64–65).

Ley-Sievers system "3," and a short colon, in Ley-Sievers notation "2."[7] In terms of syllables, the long colon in Ugaritic is longer than the Hebrew long colon and the short colon in Ugaritic is longer than the Hebrew short colon, but precisely corresponding to the addition or omission of inflectional endings, the final short vowels lost in South Canaanite toward 1200 B.C.E. In other words, the long and short cola reflected a continuity of verse form given the evolution of the Canaanite-Hebrew tongue.

I have never been convinced that early Canaanite meter can be defined as either quantitative or accentual. It is highly symmetrical at the level of the single bicolon or single tricolon, but the symmetry is not necessarily sustained over long intervals of verse. My conclusion has been that the ancient Canaanite and Hebrew poets were not counting syllables, at least in the fashion found in other oral, syllabic verse. It must be emphasized, moreover, that the oral formulae of Ugaritic and early Hebrew verse are binary, not chronemic as in Greek epic verse. They are constructed in pairs: word, phrase, and colon pairs including paired epithets and proper nouns, complementing grammatical parallelism at every level.

It has been my practice for many years, therefore, to use a notation *l* (*longum*) and *b* (*breve*) to label respectively the long colon and the short colon, the building blocks fundamental to early Hebrew verse, a notation that leaves open the question of auditory subrhythms.[8]

In archaic verse, the standard verse forms were *l:l* and *l:l:l,* i.e., a bicolon of two symmetrical long cola, and a tricolon of three symmetrical long cola. The verse patterns formed with the short colon, *b,* were different. The standard verse was *b:b::b:b* in which a bicolon, itself marked by an internal caesura, is parallel to a second bicolon also marked by an internal caesura. However, in addition to the correspondence between the two bicola, parallelism between single cola, a *b* and a *b* in the *b:b* bicolon is not infrequent. Thus the older notation 2:2 is misleading, and the alternate notation 4:4 is misleading, although both describe an aspect of the verse form. The verse structure is in fact more complex. Also frequent is the triplet *b:b::b:b::b:b,* corresponding to the tricolon *l:l:l.* Thus the Lament of David:

l:l:l
2 (*b:b::b:b*)
2 (*b:b::b:b*)
3 (*b:b::b:b::b:b*)
l:l:l

7. See *AYP,* 8–9, and esp. 181–187.
8. See the discussion in the preceding chapter.

b:b::b:b::b:b
l:l.

Exodus 15, The Song of the Sea, also consists of a sequence of couplets and triplets of short cola marked off by tricola and bicola of long cola (*l*).[9]

This "mixed meter" as we called it, or alternation of two verse types, one simple with long bicola, one complex with short bicola pairs, is characteristic of archaic lyric poetry in the Hebrew Bible, but disappears early, the latest specimen apparently the Lament of David.

Poetry of the ninth through the seventh centuries is dominantly of two verse types: *l:l(:l)*, familiar from Ugaritic epic meter as well as early Hebrew poetry, and a new verse type generally designated Qinah meter, although it is by no means restricted to the lament. In early analyses it was described as 3:2 meter or as 5:5 meter. In fact it is built of the fundamental building blocks, the long colon and the short colon in complex patterns. The dominant form in my notation is *l:b::l:b* in which the grammatical and semantic parallelism is chiefly between corresponding bicola. However, internal parallelism between the mixed, long and short cola is not infrequent. While *l:b::l:b* is the most frequent verse pattern, there are also variant patterns: *l:b::b:l, b:l::l:b,* and *b:l::b:l,* especially in earlier poetry of this type.[10]

A sounding in Hellenistic Hebrew poetry by Arlis Ehlen, in the *hôdāyôt* of Qumrân, has shown that the old "building blocks" of early Hebrew poetry have utterly disappeared.[11] While grammatical parallelism of a sort persists, symmetry of colon length does not exist, and in Ehlen's words, "'subrhythms' do not exist, neither quantitative nor stress meters."

Much more needs to be done in tracing the development step by step from archaic Canaanite and Hebrew poetry to Late, Hellenistic, and Persian Hebrew poetry. When and why did symmetry break down, and the basic building blocks, the long and the short colon, disappear?

9. See *CMHE,* 122, n. 34 (on the Lament of David and its reconstruction), and 126–144 (on the Song of the Sea).

10. See chapter 6; and D. N. Freedman, "Acrostics and Metrics in Hebrew Poetry," in *Pottery, Poetry, and Prophecy: Studies in Early Hebrew Poetry* (Winona Lake, Ind.: Eisenbrauns, 1980), 51–76.

11. Arlis John Ehlen, "The Poetic Structure of a Hodayah from Qumran: An Analysis of Grammatical, Semantic, and Auditory Correspondence in 1QH 3:19–36" (Ph.D. diss., Harvard University, 1970).

II

One aspect of the task is to observe movement from orally composed poetry in the early period to poetry composed in writing in the late period. There can be no doubt, in my opinion, that Ugaritic epic verse was composed orally to music. It should be said that parallelism has its origins in oral composition. Parallelism is a technique of the traditional poet, the bard. To be sure, grammatical parallelism can survive in written imitation of traditional poetry, and obviously did in late Hebrew poetry.

In any case, I think it can be shown clearly that Ugaritic epic poetry was composed orally. Its formulae, binary pairs including epithets, and its themes, type scenes, and narrative patterns have been studied by a number of scholars including Whitaker, Hendel, Culley, Gevirtz, and the present writer.[12] The typical repetition of themes and type scenes using identical or near-identical formulae, a sure tell-tale of oral composition, is more frequent and impressive in Ugaritic epics than in classic Greek epic. Furthermore, the repertoire of formulae—and even complete verse forms—is continuous from Old Canaanite to archaic Hebrew verse, a phenomenon best explained by transmission in bardic tradition, not in writing.

I have called attention elsewhere to the tell-tale colophon of *CTA* 6.6 53ff.[13] In the colophon three principal persons are named: *sāpiru ʾilimilku,* 'Elimelek the scribe,' *θāʿiyu niqmadda malku ʾugarīti,* 'Niqmadda, king of Ugarit, the donor,' and between the two names a third: *lamīdu ʾattanu . . . rabbu kāhinīma,* 'ʾAttanu . . . chief priest, the adept.' The term *lamīd,* which I have translated 'the adept,' certainly applies to his function in the preparation of the tablet, and he is neither donor nor scribe. The term *lamīd* immediately reminds us of *mĕlummad šīr* of 1 Chronicles

12. See R. E. Whitaker, "A Formulaic Analysis of Ugaritic Poetry" (Ph.D. diss., Harvard University, 1970); R. S. Hendel, *The Epic of the Patriarch: The Jacob Cycle and the Narrative Tradition of Canaan and Israel, HSM* 39 (Atlanta: Scholars Press, 1988); F. M. Cross, "Prose and Poetry in the Mythic and Epic Texts from Ugarit," *HTR* 67 (1974): 1–15; Robert C. Culley, *Oral Formulaic Language in the Biblical Psalms* (Toronto: University of Toronto Press, 1967); Stanley Gevirtz, *Patterns in the Early Poetry of Israel* (Chicago: University of Chicago Press, 1963). See also the massive volumes *Ras Shamra Parallels,* ed. Loren R. Fisher and S. Rummel (Rome: Pontifical Biblical Institute, vol. 1, 1972; vol. 2, 1975; vol. 3, 1981), esp. vol. 3.

13. See Cross, "Prose and Poetry," 1. See also the paper of Sam Meier, "Baal's Fight with Yam as Known in *KTU* 1.1. 3–6?," *UF* 18 (1986): 241–254, which demonstrates that *CTA* 2 (at least 2.1 and 2.4) in the Baʿl cycle was composed by a bard different from the bard of the remainder of the cycle. His formulae, especially epithets, often vary from those of the other tablets, and the variance where it occurs is systematic.

25:7, 'trained in song.' Certainly the high priest was no student, but evidently the master singer who dictated to the scribe. Another passage of interest is found in *CTA* 3.1.19.

Rising he composed and sang,
With cymbals the bard improvised,
The sweet-voiced hero sang.[14]

The term *naʿīm* (the vocalization is uncertain) cited above, and translated 'bard,' one who composed or improvised (*bdy*), is of some interest. In Arabic the root is *nǵm*, 'to sing,' *naǵmat*, 'melody,' an unusual but by no means rare equation with Ugaritic *nʿm*.[15] It reappears in 2 Samuel 23:1, *nĕʾīm zĕmīrôt yiśrāʾēl* 'bard of Israel's songs.' The term *nāʾīm*, perhaps to be revocalized *nôʿēm*, corresponds to Greek *aoidos*, 'oral poet,' 'bard,' 'composer-singer.'

In the Hebrew Bible all of the hallmarks of oral composition adhere to the corpus of premonarchical poetry. As Freedman and I argued many years ago, there is a common set of formulae including entire cola distinctive of this archaic verse. In some cases obvious oral variants exist, e.g., the blessing of Joseph in Genesis 49:24–26 and the blessing of Joseph in Deuteronomy 33:13–16; or the blessing of Zebulun in Genesis 49:13, and Asher in Judges 5:17. One may compare the bicolon *kāraʿ šākab ka-ʾărî / ū-kĕ-lābîʾ mî yĕqīmennu* in Numbers 24:9 with Genesis 49:9b *kāraʿ rābaṣ kĕ-ʾaryēh / ū-kĕlābîʾ mî yĕqīmennu*. These slightly variant bicola, used in very different contexts in the Blessing of Jacob and the Oracles of Balaam, are best explained as drawn from stock oral formulae, rather than as written borrowing. Again, both oral and written (textual) variants abound in the parallel texts, 2 Samuel 22 = Psalm 18.[16]

It should be remembered that while alphabetic writing rapidly increased literacy in the Early Iron Age, oral forms still dominated in the transmission of literature and culture. This oral character of communication is reflected vividly even in written documents. Letters in Hebrew from the end of the ninth century from Kuntillet ʿAjrûd, and from as late as the seventh to the sixth century from Transjordan and Egypt in Ammonite and Phoenician respectively, preserve similar introductory formulae: "Utterance of So-and-So. Say to So-and-So" (*ʾmr* PN *ʾmr l-*

14. The Ugaritic text in provisional vocalization reads: *qamu yabdī wa-yašīru / maṣil-latêmi badā naʿīmu / yašīrŭ ǵazru ṭābu qôli.*

15. On Ugaritic *ʿayn* = Arabic *ǵayn*, see J. A. Emerton, "Some Notes on the Ugaritic Counterpart of the Arabic *ghain*," in *Studies in Philology in Honour of Ronald James Williams*, ed. G. E. Kadish and G. E. Freeman (Toronto: Benben Publishers, 1982), 31–50.

16. See *AYP*, 125–168, esp. 163–168.

PN).[17] The presupposition of such a formula is that the letter is dictated by the sender, and that the letter is to be read aloud to the recipient.

Perhaps it is also useful to remark that in 2 Kings 3:15 a prophet, asked for an oracle, requested a minstrel in order to prophesy, and Jeremiah, surely literate, still dictated his verse to Baruch.

The transition from oral to written poetry is difficult to fix. A priori, one would expect to perceive in this interval the breakdown of symmetry, of ancient repetitive patterns, and an increase in prose particles. One also would look for the increase in long-range artifice as opposed to couplets and triplets, and for the confusion of fixed, formulaic pairs. In fact all these developments are apparent in psalms of the Persian and Hellenistic periods. I am inclined to believe that in the archaizing, but not archaic, poetry of Second Isaiah one can discern clearly traits of written composition, and the moribund state of older styles of orally composed poetry. I have described the acrostic laments of the Book of Lamentations as written poetry.[18] But late pre-Exilic prophecy needs thorough analysis before we can answer the question as to whether it is written or oral in origin. Much late prophetic material, above all much of Ezekiel, has been preserved in prose or decayed poetry by circles that transmitted the oracles. One could argue that owing to the breakdown of the chain of oral poets, disciples of the prophets who transmitted their lore preserved general memories of oracles but were unable to re-create their poetic-oral form. Of course, prophets may have on occasion used prose utterance in prophesying. But this also would point to the beginnings, at least, of the dissolution of older, rigid musical and oral-poetic canons which earlier constrained oracular utterance.

III

I am convinced also that one can trace typological changes in the formulation of parallelistic verse patterns and in the meaning of parallel-

17. The formula appears at Kuntillet ʿAjrûd, in the Phoenician Letter from Saqqara (*KAI* 50), and on an ostracon from Tell Mazar. See J. C. Greenfield, "Note on the Phoenician Letter from Saqqara," *Orientalia* 53 (1984): 242–244; Khair Yassine and J. Teixidor, "Ammonite and Aramaic Inscriptions from Tell el-Mazar in Jordan," *BASOR* 264 (1986): 45–50, esp. 47. The introductory address should be translated "Utterance of Peleṭ: Say to his brother, to ʿAbdʾel . . . ." In the Saqqara letter we should read similarly, "Say to my sister *ʾršt,* utterance of your sister *bšʾ*." At Kuntillet ʿAjrûd I read *ʾmr ʾšyw hmlk ʾmr lyhl*[ ] *wlywʿšh,* "Utterance of ʾAšyaw, the king: say to *Yhl*[ ] and to Yawʿaśāh . . . ." Cf. M. Weinfeld, "Kuntillet ʿAjrud Inscriptions and Their Significance," *SEL* 1 (1984): 122–130; and Mark Smith, "God Male and Female in the Old Testament: Yahweh and His 'ʾasherah'," *Theological Studies* 48 (1987): 333–340.

18. See above, chapter 6.

istic style in the history of Canaanite and Hebrew poetry. Particularly evident is the popularity at Ugarit and in archaic Hebrew poetry of so-called repetitive parallelism described by H. L. Ginsberg and W. F. Albright. This patterned verse, in ideal form a tricolon *ABC:ABD:EFG,* disintegrated into imitative but inexact forms very early in Israel, by the ninth century.[19]

One of the conventions or styles of early verse I have labeled "impressionistic," lacking a more precise designation, after the analogy of the literary style in which the use of details, visual glimpses, so to speak, attempted to evoke subjective and sensory impressions rather than to re-create objective reality. For example:

Take a lamb in your hand
A sacrifice in your right hand
A kid in your two hands.[20]
(See *CTA* 14.2.65–68; 14.3.159–161)

A literal-minded soul will conceive here a juggling act. In fact the poet uses a set of conventions, including numerical parallelism, to create three pictures, flashes, of sacrificial rite, technically irrational or overlapping, but poetically rich and evocative.

Again:

My temple I have built of silver
My palace I have built of gold.[21]
(*CTA* 4.6.36–38)

The poet obviously is not singing of two buildings, one constructed of silver, one of gold. Rather he pictures a house ornamented with features of precious metal. But so to describe it is to surrender the impressionistic effect of the bicolon.

A third example:

Pour wine in a silver bowl
In a bowl of gold mead.[22]
(*CTA* 14.2.71–72f)

How should we read these lines? Are there two bowls, two alcoholic beverages, the second a grander bowl, the second beverage the more precious liquor? I think not. We are presented rather with two pictures of the rite of libation, two evocative, overlapping impressions.

19. See W. F. Albright, "The Psalm of Habakkuk," in *Studies in Old Testament Prophecy,* ed. H. H. Rowley (Edinburgh: T. and T. Clark, 1950), 1–18.

20. On the reconstruction, see Cross, "Prose and Poetry," 7.

21. See "Prose and Poetry," 8, for variants of this bicolon.

22. Cf. *CTA* 15.2.11–16.

I should argue that the same "impressionism" persists in early Hebrew verse. In the Song of Deborah are these two verses:

Her hand reached for a tent peg,
Her right hand for a workman's hammer.

She struck Sisera; she smashed his head;
She struck Sisera; she pierced his temple.[23]
(Judges 5:26)

The prosaic, later historian gives us an interpretation of the two verses in Judges 4. Jael took a tent peg, presumably in her left hand, a hammer in her right hand, and nailed the peg through Sisera's temple—adding in the interests of realism that Sisera was in a deep sleep at the time. Had the prose historian been even more literalistic, he would have had Jael (1) smash his head and (2) pierce his temple, but even he resolves a portion of the overlapping pictures. In fact the poet in his impressionistic style says only that she grasped a weapon appropriate to the tent dweller, and dispatched Sisera with a blow to the head. There are neither two weapons nor two blows. The poet is interested in two brush-strokes of color to fashion a picture, not in a photographic image of reality.

Later in Hebrew verse, this impressionistic style, as we have called it, gives way to a more realistic style. Overlapping pictures and overlapping time sequences[24] are to some degree resolved. We can illustrate this from the use of so-called numerical parallelism.

At Ugarit we find this extraordinary couplet:

They march, two by two they walk,
They march [three] by three, all of them.[25]

Mathematicians need not apply. This is an impressionistic picture of a massed march.

23. See *AYP* 15 for reconstruction; "Prose and Poetry," 7; and B. Halpern, "Doctrine by Misadventure: Between the Israelite Source and the Biblical Historian," in *The Poet and the Historian: Essays in Literary and Historical Biblical Criticism, HSS* 26 (Chico, Calif.: Scholars Press, 1983), 46–49.

24. *CTA* 23 shows a number of cases of overlapping time sequences. The most dramatic is the sequence: kissing and conception, labor and birth (ll. 49–54), kissing and conception, labor and birth (ll. 55–61). Another example is found in *CTA* 2.4. Kôθar fashions two clubs, names them with magic names (2.3.11–13), Baʿl bludgeons Yamm (2.4.13–17). Kôθar fashions two clubs and names them with names (2.4.18–20), Baʿl bludgeons Yamm (2.4.20–25), and finally Yamm is finished off. Still another curious sequence is found in *CTA* 6.2.30–35 (cf. 6.5.11–19) in which Môt is chopped with a sword, winnowed with a sieve, burnt with fire, ground in mills, sowed in fields. Each of the actions is appropriate to the agricultural cycle with grain, but the order is not sequential. It is impressionistic.

25. *CTA* 14.2.94–95; 14.4.182–183: *ʾaθarū θinê θinê halakū / ʾaθarū θalāta kulluhumu.*

In Amos we find a familiar formula, the first occurrence of which reads:

ʿal šĕlōšāh pišʿê dammeśeq
wĕ-ʿal ʾarbāʿāh lōʾ ʾăšībennū

But in the cycle of nations, neither three nor four sins of the condemned nations are listed. In the case of Israel seven sins are listed (by most counts), but this is neither three nor four. But compare this impressionistic disregard for mathematics with late Wisdom's use of numerical parallelism.[26] Proverbs 6:16–19 sings of six, yea seven things that the Lord hates. Then seven items are carefully listed. Or, read Proverbs 30:18. Here three things, yea four, are too wonderful and then the four are enumerated carefully, the fourth the climax of the series, "the way of a man with a maid."

Evidently in the course of time the impressionistic use of numerical parallelism gave way to a more realistic or rational correspondence between cola in a verse unit, with, at least according to my taste, a loss of poetic power.

There are at the moment two major competing views, two hermeneutics, of Hebrew parallelism. One may be described as a unitary analysis of the meaning of parallelism, the other a climactic analysis. Steven Geller has written, "Nothing can be more misleading than to view the B Line [i.e., the second line of a couplet] as a mere echo or simple variation or even reinforcement of its A Line. In the couplet both lines form a unity of which each is less than half. . . . It is only at the perceived conclusion of the statement that the constraints of potential reanalysis are removed and the final meaning released."[27] Geller's is a useful instrument with which to lay bare the meaning of Ugaritic and early Hebrew poetry. The alternate hermeneutic is that of James Kugel, seconded by others, summarized in the catch phrase "A is so, and what's more B."[28] In this mode of interpretation, the second line of a couplet is taken as

26. The numerical parallelism in Amos has been taken to point to the influence of "Wisdom circles" on Amos. But numerical parallelism is used in mythic cycles, epic poetry, and prophecy. As a matter of fact, the use of numerical parallelism in Wisdom texts contrasts with the impressionistic usage in Amos, and it could be used better as an argument against Wisdom influence on Amos.

27. Steven A. Geller, "The Dynamic of Parallel Verse: A Poetic Analysis of Deuteronomy 32:6–12," *HTR* 75 (1982): 35–56. See also Geller's "Theory and Method in the Study of Biblical Poetry," *JQR* 73 (1982): 65–77. Geller's standard study, *Parallelism in Early Biblical Poetry, HSM* 20 (Missoula, Mont.: Scholars Press, 1979), has not received the attention it deserves.

28. James L. Kugel, *The Idea of Biblical Poetry: Parallelism and Its History* (New Haven: Yale University Press, 1981).

having emphatic character, and all parallelism described as climactic parallelism, the second (and third) line building, emphasizing, "going one better."

These two views of parallelism, both presented as applying to the entire corpus of Hebrew poetry, need to be tested in diachronic study. I am not sure that a typology will emerge—for example, Geller's unitary approach proving valid in the early period, Kugel's climactic theory proving a better instrument in late poetry. I do find Geller's hermeneutic the better key to early poetry. Let us take as an example the refrain in the Lament of David.

Ah, prince [literally gazelle] of Israel [Saul][29]
On thy heights slain,
How the warriors have fallen.

How the warriors have fallen,
In the midst of battle, Jonathan
On thy heights slain.

How the warriors have fallen,
Perished the weapons of war.

In these variations of the refrain, the order of A lines, B lines, and C lines is consciously and skillfully altered to provide variety and chiasm. Identical or similar cola may be in the A position, the B position, or the C position. Geller's system illuminates our understanding of such poetry. Kugel's system is not helpful.

On the other hand, there are couplets and triplets in Hebrew poetry that I am inclined to describe as climactic, and which appear to fit Kugel's analysis. This is especially so in late, more realistic Hebrew poetry. More study is required before these issues can be resolved.

IV

The history of the Hebrew language must also play a decisive role in the sequence dating of Hebrew poetry and in the reconstruction of its stages of development. Avi Hurvitz in his study *Language of the Psalms*[30] has attempted to isolate lexical and syntactic elements which mark the language of post-Exilic psalmody. Moreover, by comparison of the latest psalms of the canonical psalter with the sectarian psalms of Qumrân and other contemporary poetry, we can, I think, distinguish typologically

29. See *CMHE*, 122, n. 34, for a defense of this reconstruction of the text.

30. Avi Hurvitz, *Byn lšwn llšwn* (Jerusalem: Bialik, 1972), to appear soon in English under the title (tentative) *Language of the Psalms*.

psalmody of the Hellenistic age from psalmody of the Persian period. My initial impressions, garnered from such comparison, are that the canonical psalter was closed at the end of the Persian period.[31]

The language utilized in Hebrew poetry can also be used to isolate stages in pre-Exilic poetic composition—despite the interference of leveling by generations of scribes. The oldest poetry eschews the use of "prosaic particles," *ʾašer, ʾet, ha-* (the article). As well, the conjunction *wa-* introducing bicola or tricola is excessively rare. Freedman and Andersen have pursued computer-assisted analyses revealing the relative scarcity of prose particles in poetry, most dramatically in early poetry.[32] More delicate, I believe, than these statistical studies are analyses using humanistic methods, including textual criticism, but the computer studies are confirmatory and evidently more objective. In any case, the historian of the Canaanite dialects can affirm that prose particles were developed in Canaanite only after the loss of inflectional endings, toward 1200 B.C.E. The prose particles did not belong to the bardic tradition of early poetic language. Little wonder therefore that Israel's earliest poems are virtually free of such, despite later modernizing, and, remarkable to say, the Song of the Sea is totally free of such elements. In fact we can postulate that premonarchical poetry in its original form was free of prose particles. The use of the conjunction *wa-* to introduce bicola or tricola was sparing in early poetry, ubiquitous in late poetry. As Freedman and I showed in our early study of the parallel texts of 2 Samuel 22 = Psalm 18, many if not most conjunctions appearing in this early poetry were arbitrarily or unconsciously introduced in the history of scribal transmission.[33] Again it is noteworthy that the conjunction is wholly absent in the Song of the Sea as a particle introducing cola.[34]

The survival of archaic grammar in early Hebrew poetry is remarkable given the long history of textual transmission and scribal revision.

31. See F. M. Cross, *Die Antikebibliothek von Qumran,* trans. K. Bannach and C. Burchard (Neukirchen-Vluyn: Neukirchener Verlag, 1967), 226 f. and n. 23.

32. See D. N. Freedman, "Prose Particles in the Poetry of the Primary History," in *Biblical and Related Studies Presented to Samuel Iwry,* ed. Ann Kort and Scott Morschhauser (Winona Lake, Ind.: Eisenbrauns, 1985), 49–63; and F. Andersen, "'Prose Particle' Counts of the Hebrew Bible," in *The Word of the Lord Shall Go Forth: Essays in Honor of David Noel Freedman,* ed. C. L. Meyers and M. O'Connor (Winona Lake, Ind.: Eisenbrauns, 1983), 165–183, and the literature cited.

33. *AYP,* 125–168, esp. 162–168. An exception to our generalization is the use of *wa-* to introduce a *casus pendens.*

34. I hasten to add that I have not overlooked the conjunction in Exodus 15:2. The second bicolon of v. 2, a bicolon found elsewhere (in Isa. 12:2b and Ps. 18:14) is evidently intrusive on several grounds. See *CMHE,* 127 and n. 49, and F. M. Cross and David Noel Freedman, "The Song of Miriam," *JNES* 14 (1955): 243 and nn. a–d.

Yet the use of the *yaqtul* preterite did in fact survive in ancient Hebrew verse. Robertson has analyzed the data.[35] Again Exodus 15, the Song of the Sea, presents verbal usage of the olden time, identical with Ugaritic and (Canaanite) Amarna usage. Other archaic elements survive sporadically in early poetry. For example, archaic pronominal suffixes are found to be used flawlessly and systematically in the Song of the Sea, still another testimony to its early date and excellent state of preservation.[36]

To summarize: the forms and canons of Hebrew prosody must be studied diachronically if we are to solve many difficult problems in its analysis and interpretation. There is ample evidence of an evolution from highly formal, symmetrical patterns of orally composed verse, to written, parallelistic verse with little symmetry or density (*Dichtung*). Whether meter marks early verse we cannot yet demonstrate with certitude. We can isolate regular building blocks in early verse, long and short cola, and their intricate combinations in several genres of verse. Finally we can assert that in the late period, poetry was composed in writing, and that knowledge of the rigidly controlled symmetrical verse forms of the archaic era was effectively lost and forgotten.

35. David A. Robertson, *Linguistic Evidence in Dating Early Hebrew Poetry, SBLDS* 3 (Missoula, Mont.: SBL, 1972). The language of Job, which in many ways resembles archaic poetry, is evidently written in a learned "hymnal-epic" dialect.

36. See, Robertson, *Linguistic Evidence;* and *AYP.*

PART IV

RETURN TO ZION

8

A Reconstruction of the Judaean Restoration

THE LITERATURE DEALING WITH THE FIFTH AND FOURTH CENTURIES B.C.E. in ancient Palestine appears to expand by geometric progression. Writing in 1975,[1] I observed that little progress had been made in solving the hard problems in the history of the Restoration since the assimilation of new evidence from the Elephantine Papyri published in 1911.[2] If one compares the review of literature on the date of Ezra's mission by H. H. Rowley in 1948[3] and the review by Ulrich Kellermann in 1968,[4] he comes away disappointed; a generation of research had added at best a few plausible speculations but little if any hard, new evidence.[5]

The scholarly procedure had been to review the same body of evidence and arguments and to come boldly down on one of three dates for

1. See my Presidential Address delivered on October 25, 1974, to the Society of Biblical Literature in Washington, D.C., published under the title "A Reconstruction of the Judean Restoration," *JBL* 94 (1975): 4–18. A slightly revised version of the paper was published in the volume honoring John Bright, *The History of Israel and Biblical Faith,* appearing in *Interpretation* 29 (1975): 187–203. See also my chapter, "Samaria and Jerusalem: The Early History of the Samaritans and Their Relations with the Jews," in the *History of the Jewish People: The Restoration, Days of Persian Rule* [Hebrew], ed. H. Tadmor et al. (Jerusalem: Alexander Peli, 1982), 81–94.

2. See *AP,* papyri 21, 30, 31, 32.

3. "The Chronological Order of Ezra and Nehemiah," republished in *The Servant of the Lord* (Oxford: Blackwell, 1965), 137–168; cf. H. H. Rowley, "Nehemiah's Mission and Its Background," *BJRL* 37 (1955): 528–561.

4. "Erwägungen zum Problem der Esradatierung," *ZAW* 80 (1968): 55–87, and "Erwägungen zum Esragesetz," *ZAW* 80 (1968): 373–385.

5. We should place Julian Morgenstern's proposals in "The Dates of Ezra and Nehemiah," *JSS* 7 (1962): 1–11, and Morton Smith's assertions in *Palestinian Parties and Politics That Shaped the Old Testament* (New York: Columbia University Press, 1971), esp. 99–147, in the category of less than plausible speculations. Smith is certainly correct, however, in recognizing that "arguments from personal names (of which Rowley makes much) are generally worthless because of the frequency of papponymy at this period, and the frequency of most names concerned" (253, n. 109).

Ezra's mission in relation to Nehemiah's mission to Jerusalem: (1) Ezra came before Nehemiah, a view we may label the "traditional view," (2) Ezra came after Nehemiah, which for convenience we may call the "Van Hoonacker position," (3) Ezra came during or between Nehemiah's visits to Jerusalem, the "Kosters-Bertholet position." To those we should add the position of C. C. Torrey that Ezra was a fiction of the Chronicler's imagination and consequently had no date.

The voluminous literature of the past thirty years has been built on the steady accumulation of new evidence, some spectacular in import, which when brought together has provided new contexts and perspectives with which to approach old problems. The discovery in 1962 of fourth-century legal papyri executed in "the citadel of Samaria which is in the province of Samaria"[6] is perhaps the most important source of new data.[7] From the papyri we can reconstruct the sequence of the governors of Samaria by virtue of the practice of papponymy, the naming of a child after his grandfather (see the genealogical chart below).

The Samaritan genealogy overlaps with the genealogies of the Judaean Restoration from the sixth to the tenth generation after the return. Sanballaṭ I, the Ḥoronite, is the founder of the dynasty, as his gentilic suggests; the contemporary of Nehemiah and ʾElyāšîb, as biblical references

6. This phrase, *bšmrwn byrtʾ zy bšmrwn mdyntʾ*, is the standard way of recording the place of execution in the papyri.

7. See my several reports, "Samaria Papyrus 1: An Aramaic Slave Conveyance of 335 B.C. Found in The Wâdī ed-Dâliyeh," *EI* 18 [the Avigad volume] (1985): 7*–17* and pl. 2; "The Discovery of the Samaria Papyri," *BA* (1963): 110–121, reprinted in *The Biblical Archaeologist Reader* 3, ed. E. F. Campbell and D. N. Freedman (Garden City, N.Y.: Doubleday Anchor, 1970), 227–239; "A Report on the Samaria Papyri," *SVT* 40 [Jerusalem Congress Volume, 1986] (1988): 17–26; "Samaritans [Hebrew]," in *Encyclopaedia Biblica*, ed. B. Mazar and H. Tadmor (Jerusalem: Bialik, 1982), vol. 8, cols. 164–173; "Aspects of Samaritan and Jewish History in Late Persian and Hellenistic Times, *HTR* 59 (1966): 201–211, reprinted under the same title in *Emerging Judaism: Studies in the Fourth and Third Centuries B.C.E.*, ed. Michael E. Stone and D. Satran (Minneapolis: Fortress Press, 1989), 49–59, and in *Die Samaritaner*, ed. F. Dexinger and R. Pummer (Darmstadt: Wissenschaftliche Buchgesellschaft, 1991), 199–206; "Papyri of the Fourth Century B.C.E. from Dâliyeh," in *New Directions in Biblical Archaeology*, ed. David Noel Freedman and Jonas C. Greenfield (Garden City, N.Y.: Doubleday Anchor, 1971), 45–69; "Samaria and Jerusalem: The Early History of the Samaritans and Their Relations with the Jews (722–64 B.C.E.)" [šwmrwn wyrwšlym: twldwt hšwmrwnym wyḥsyhm ʿm hyhwdym], in *The World History of the People of Israel: The Restoration—The Persian Period* [*hhysṭwryh šl ʿm yśrʾl: šybt ṣywn ymy šlṭwn prs*], ed. Hayim Tadmor (Jerusalem: Alexander Peli, 1983), 81–94. A revised version of this paper is found in chapter 9; and "The Papyri and Their Historical Implications," *Discoveries in the Wâdī ed-Dâliyeh*, ed. Paul W. Lapp and Nancy L. Lapp, *AASOR* 41 (Cambridge: ASOR, 1974): 17–29 and pls. 59–63 (hereafter Cross, *Dâliyeh*).

make clear; and also the contemporary of the high priests Yôyādāʿ and Yôḥānān, as we can deduce from biblical and Elephantine references.[8] The Sanballaṭ of Josephus proves to be Sanballaṭ III, the builder of the temple on Mt. Gerizim, the contemporary of Darius II and of Alexander.[9] Sanballaṭ II, father of the governor Yēšûaʿ / Yĕšaʿyāhû appears in Samaria Papyrus 11:13, a papyrus dated to the reign of Artaxerxes III (359–358 B.C.E.), and on a seal attached to SP 16, a conveyance of a vineyard.[10] Equally important, the sequence of Sanballaṭids makes certain what has long been suspected, that two generations are missing in the biblical genealogy of the Jewish high priests.[11] This lacuna in the fourth century is supplied by Josephus, who is correct in his record that a certain Yôḥānān killed his brother Yēšûaʿ in the temple in the time of the infamous Bagoas, the commander in chief of Artaxerxes III (Ochus, 358–338) in his expeditions to Phoenicia, Palestine, and Egypt during the western insurrections,[12] and that Yôḥānān's successor was Yaddûaʿ, high priest in the days of Darius III (335–330) and Alexander.[13] The appearance of a late-fourth-century silver coin bearing the legends *ywḥnn hkwhn*, 'Yôḥānān the (high) priest' inscribed in Palaeo-Hebrew documented Yôḥānān (III) and the accuracy of Josephus's sources for the late

8. *AP* 30:29 and *AP* 30:18.

9. *Antiquities of the Jews*, 11:302–303, 11:306–312, 11:325, and 11:340–347. Sanballaṭ, according to Josephus (*Antiq.* 11:325), died in the seventh month of Alexander's siege of Tyre, 332 B.C.E.

10. See my discussion in *Dâliyeh*, 18 and esp. n. 10. Joseph Blenkinsopp is simply wrong when he states that "the Sanballaṭ intermediate between the contemporary of Nehemiah and the governor in the Daliyeh papyri exists only by courtesy of the [Cross] hypothesis." The Sanballaṭ of the papyri is, of course, Sanballaṭ II. There is no "intermediate" Sanballaṭ by any hypothesis.

11. 1 Chron. 5:41; Neh. 3:1, 21; 12:10, 22–23; 13:4; Ezra 10:6.

12. This interpretation of the new data was first recognized in my "A Reconstruction of the Judaean Restoration," *Interpretation* 29 (1975): 188 f. The same or similar views arrived at independently appear in the papers of H. G. M. Williamson, "The Historical Value of Josephus' *Jewish Antiquities* XI. 297–301," *JTS* 28 (1977): 49–66, and R. J. Saley, "The Date of Nehemiah Reconsidered," in *Biblical and Near Eastern Studies*, ed. G. A. Tuttle (Grand Rapids, Mich.: Eerdmans, 1978), 156–158. Most scholars in the past have assumed that Josephus confused Bagoas the general with Bagoas (*bgwhy*) of *AP* 30–32, a successor of Nehemiah as governor of Judah; it proves to be an instance of hypercriticism. Still some are dubious about the new identification, e.g., L. L. Grabbe, "Josephus and the Reconstruction of the Judean Restoration," *JBL* 106 (1987): 236. However, see D. Barag, "Bagoas and the Coinage of Judea," in *Proceedings of the XIth International Numismatic Congress*, vol. 1 (Louvain-la Neuve: Séminair de Numismatique Marcel Hoc, 1993), 261–265, who attributes a Yehud coin to Bagoas, the general of Artaxerxes III, who invaded Egypt in 343.

13. *Antiq.* 11:302–303, 11:306–312, 11:347. Yaddûaʿ died, we are told (11:347), ca. 323 B.C.E. (the time of Alexander's death).

fourth century.[14] Hence in my new chart of the genealogy of the high priests, the brackets around the listing of Yôḥānān III (indicating that I had reconstructed the name) can be removed (see below). Again, in 1987 Arnold Spaer published a small silver coin with the legend *ydwʿ*, Yaddûaʿ, in cursive Aramaic characters.[15] The coin is of the same type as the Yôḥānān coin, with the head of Athena on the obverse and the Athenian owl on the reverse, and must be assigned to the end of the Achaemenid times or the beginning of the Ptolemaic period. It belongs to Yaddûaʿ II (Yôyādāʿ III).[16] Hence this name too may now be removed from brackets.[17] In short, we can now reconstitute the end of the list of

14. This coin was published by Leo Mildenberg, "Yehud: A Preliminary Study of the Provincial Coinage of Judaea," in *Greek Numismatics and Archaeology: Essays in Honor of Margaret Thompson*, ed. Otto Mørkholm and N. M. Waggoner (Wetteren, 1979), 194:17, and pl. 22:17. Mildenberg correctly recognized it as late Achaemenid, but failed to read the legend. Y. Meshorer correctly read it *ywḥnn hkwhn* and asked my opinion of his reading (personal letter of April 22, 1980), and I replied agreeing with his reading and observing that this was "my" Yôḥānān III. However, he did not publish his reading and grew skeptical of it. See my report in "Samaria and Jerusalem," esp. n. 50. Independently Dan Barag came to the same reading and to the same conclusion concerning the identity of this Yôḥānān. However, he did not accept my full reconstruction of the list of high priests. See Barag, "A Silver Coin of Yoḥanan the High Priest [Hebrew]," *Qadmoniot* 17 (1984): 59–61; "A Silver Coin of Yoḥanan the High Priest and the Coinage of Judea in the Fourth Century B.C.," *INJ* 9 (1986–87): 4–21 and pl. 1.

15. A. Spaer, "Jaddua the High Priest," *INJ* 9 (1986–87): 1–3 and pl. 2; see also Peter Machinist, "The First Coins of Judah and Samaria: Numismatics and History in the Achaemenid and Early Hellenistic Periods," in *Achaemenid History* VIII: *Continuity and Change,* Proceedings of the Last Achaemenid History Workshop, April 6–8, 1990, ed. H. Sancisi-Weerdenburg, Amélie Kuhrt, and Margaret Cool Root (Leiden: Nederlands Institut voor het Nabije Oosten, 1994), 365–380.

16. Spaer wishes to assign the coin to Yaddûaʿ I (Yôyādāʿ II), noting a difference in fabric and especially noting that the legend is in Aramaic script. The latter is not a compelling reason. Hasmonaean coins also show a fluctuation between Palaeo-Hebrew and cursive Aramaic. The cursive scripts we can date precisely thanks to the Samaria papyri and the earliest of the Dead Sea Scrolls. See Cross, *Dâliyeh,* 25–27 and pl. 59. Furthermore, the earlier *yhd* stamps are inscribed in the old *lapidary* Aramaic script, greatly differing from the *cursive* Aramaic of the *ydwʿ* coin. The broadly open *ʿayin* and the highly cursive *yod* are, in my opinion, clear evidence that this coin does not date earlier than the last quarter of the fourth century. As I argued as early as 1969, the autonomous coinage of Judah dates from after the Tennes Rebellion in which Judah took part, hence after the mid fourth century, long after Yaddûaʿ I flourished. On the dates of the Yehud types of coins, see recently John Wilson Betlyon, "The Provincial Government of Persian Period Judea and the Yehud Coins," *JBL* 105 (1986): 633–642.

17. Grabbe in his discussion of my 1975 paper remarks, "Yet Cross who agrees

high priests as follows: Yôḥānān father of Yaddûaʿ, the father of Onias I.[18] Or in other words, in the sequence Yôḥānān-Yaddûaʿ-Yôḥānān-Yaddûaʿ there has been a parablepsis or haplography with the loss of two names, an extremely easy consequence of the device of papponymy. Whether Josephus's list of high priests was defective or he merely telescoped the genealogy in writing the history of the fifth to fourth centuries, it is clear that he confused Yaddûaʿ I and Yaddûaʿ II as well as Sanballaṭ I and Sanballaṭ III, with diabolical results for his history of the Restoration. Thus Yaddûaʿ of Nehemiah 12:10, 22 (Yaddûaʿ I [Yôyādāʿ II] of our chart) is correctly attributed to the time of Darius II (Nothus 423–404)

---

with the consensus [in treating the Alexander account as legendary], still accepts Jaddua as the name of the high priest at the time of Alexander. This seems completely arbitrary" (Grabbe, 242). Grabbe in general treats Josephus with hypercritical disdain, but he fails to look critically at the biblical sources in Chronicles, Ezra, and Nehemiah. Neither the biblical nor Josephus's sources are free of confusion. And both retain material useful for the historian. Josephus's assertion that the temple was built by Yaddûaʿ in the time of Alexander now proves to be the fact (see below in chapter 9). Josephus's assertions about Alexander's role in sanctioning the building of the Samaritan temple, on the other hand, are dubious—as is his description of Alexander prostrating himself before the Jewish high priest.

18. As we shall see, Onias I is in fact Yôḥānān IV. The name Onias is the Greek form of Hebrew Ḥōnay (biform Ḥōnî), a typical hypocoristicon of the pattern *qutay*. Both the name Ḥōnay and the pattern *qutay* are well known Elephantine names as well as later. See M. H. Silverman, *Jewish Personal Names in the Elephantine Documents* (Ann Arbor: University Microfilms, 1967), 95–96 and references. The name Ḥōnay is, in fact, merely the caritative or diminutive (hypocoristica may be either or both) of Yôḥānān. "Similarly *yaddûaʿ* is the *qattūl* hypocoristic pattern, a caritative of Yôyādāʿ" (Cross, "A Reconstruction of the Judaean Restoration," 6, n. 12). Widengren in his critique of my reconstruction makes comments on my treatment of names which are puzzling if not confused. He remarks that "Joiada and Jaddua are *not* identical names, for Jaddua is a hypocoristicon of the qaṭṭul-type (Noth) [actually a *qaṭṭūl*] whereas Joiada is a complete theophoric name." Widengren seems bent on misunderstanding me and shows little knowledge of the dynamic relationship between full, especially theophoric, names and their hypocoristica. Joseph Blenkinsopp echoes this misunderstanding in *Ezra-Nehemiah: A Commentary* (Philadelphia: Westminster, 1988), 339. At no point do I speak of full, theophoric names and their hypocoristic derivatives as "identical." I say only that Onias I is at the same time Yôḥānān IV; he may be called by his formal name or by his caritative. The American president can be called either Bill or William. Apparently, Widengren doubts that a man *could* be called by either a caritative or a full name in such cases. We need only to quote examples of the practice in this general period. In Brooklyn Papyrus 2, a marriage document, the male principal is named in line 2, *ʿnnyh br ʿzryh*, "ʿĂnanyāh son of ʿĂzaryāh,' his full formal name. In lines 7, 9, 10, 11, 13, 14, and 16, he is called *ʿnny*, the hypocoristicon of ʿĂnanyāh. Another example is the seal impression of *brkyhw bn nryhw*, 'Berekyāhû son of Nērî-

in the Bible, and the Yaddûaʿ of the *Antiquities* is correctly attributed to the time of Alexander.

The High Priests of the Restoration and Their Contemporaries

GENERATION OF HIGH PRIESTS	GENERATION OF DAVIDIDS	GENERATION OF SANBALLAṬIDS
1. Yôṣādāq, b. before 587 B.C.E. father of:	1. Sin-ab-uṣur (Šešbaṣṣar), b. before 592 B.C.E. uncle of:	
2. Yēšûaʿ, b. ca. 570 father of:	2. Zerubbabel, b. ca. 570 father of:	
3. Yôyāqîm, b. ca. 545 brother of (?):	3. Hănanyāh, b. ca. 545 father of:	
3. [ʾElyāšîb I, b. ca. 545] (father of):		
4. [Yôḥānān I, b. ca. 520] (father of):	4. Šĕkanyāh, b. ca. 520 father of:	
5. ʾElyāšîb II, b. ca. 495 father of:	5. Ḥaṭṭûš, b. ca. 495 uncle of:	
6. Yôyādāʿ I, b. ca. 470 father of:	6. ʾElyôʿēnay, b. ca. 470 uncle of:	6. Sanballaṭ I, b. ca. 485 B.C.E. father of:
7. Yôḥānān II, b. ca. 445 (AP 30:18) father of:	7. ʿAnānî, b. ca. 445 (cf. AP 30:19)	7. Dĕlāyāh, b. ca. 460 (cf. AP 30:19) father of:
8. Yaddûaʿ (Yôyādāʿ II), b. ca. 420 father of:		8. Sanballaṭ II, b. 435 (cf. SP 12:13 et al.) father of:
9. Yôḥānān III, b. ca. 395 (cf. silver coin) father of:		9. Yēšûaʿ (?), b. ca. 410 (cf. SP 12, 13) brother of:
		9. Ḥănanyāh, b. ca. 410 (cf. SP 7:17, 9:14) father of:
10. Yaddûaʿ (Yôyādāʿ III), b. ca. 370 (cf. silver coin) father of:		10. Sanballaṭ III, b. ca. 385, d. 332 (cf. Josephus, *Antiq.* 11:339–383)
11. Onias I (= Yôḥānān IV), b. ca. 345		

Similarly, we can observe that Josephus is probably correct in his remark that "Israelites" (that is, Yahwists of Samaria) frequently intermarried with the high-priestly family in Jerusalem.[19] At least two instances must be admitted: the son of Yôyādāʿ I, who married the daughter of Sanballaṭ I,[20] and Manasseh, the brother of Yaddûaʿ II, who married Nikasō, the daughter of Sanballaṭ III.[21] The narratives of these two marriages can no longer be regarded as the reflexes of a single instance of intermarriage. This circumstance is not unimportant in assessing the Zadokite character of the Samaritan religion, or in reconstructing the relations between Samaria and Jerusalem in the era of the Restoration. It should be noted that the Tobiads of Ammon appear to have enjoyed similar relations with the ruling priestly family of Jerusalem despite Nehemiah's polemics.[22]

The practice of papponymy in the ruling houses of the Persian period has long been recognized. Still, new evidence for its practice has drawn our attention more sharply to its importance as a control in reconstructing genealogies. If Benjamin Mazar's reconstruction is correct, the name Tobiah alternates over nine generations of Tobiads.[23] In a bottle inscription from Tell Sîrân in Ammon, the name ʿAmmînadab alternates over six generations.[24]

The dating of Nehemiah's mission to 445, the twentieth year of Artaxerxes I, has not been in serious dispute since the appearance of Sanbal-

yāhû,' published by N. Avigad (*IEJ* 28 [1978]: 52–56), correctly identified by Avigad with Baruch son of Neriah, the amanuensis of Jeremiah. *Bārûk* is, of course, the hypocoristic derivative of Berekyāhû. Other instances are readily available in the Persian and Hellenistic periods. Well-known examples in the Hasmonaean dynasty include Yannay/Jannaeus/Yĕhônātān (on his coins *yhwntn*), and Salome/Šĕlōmṣîyōn. In a culture where papponymy was popular, hypocoristic names, especially for younger members of a dynasty, served to distinguish persons with identical formal names. I should add a caveat; a child might be given only a caritative name or an animal name, or the like, not a formal name, as also happens in English name giving. But in an era in which the onomasticon consisted for a considerable part in pious, theophoric names, consisting of sentences with transparent meanings, bearers of such names were far more conscious of their names' meanings and the relation between theophoric names and hypocoristica.

19. *Antiq.* 11:312.

20. Neh. 13:28.

21. *Antiq.* 11:306–312. See the discussion in "Papyri of the Fourth Century B.C. from Daliyeh," 54–55.

22. Neh. 13:4–9.

23. B. Mazar, "The Tobiads," *IEJ* 7 (1957): 137–145, 229–238.

24. See provisionally, F. M. Cross, "Notes on the Ammonite Inscription from Tell Sīrān," *BASOR* 212 (1973): 12–15. A revised version of this paper will appear in my collected papers in epigraphy and palaeography.

laṭ in an Elephantine letter of 407 B.C.E. The new list of Sanballaṭids further confirms the fifth-century date, and the discovery of a silver bowl inscribed by "Qaynu son of Gašm[u]" (biblical Gĕsem, Gašmu),[25] king of Qedar,[26] would appear to settle the matter.[27]

Another series of advances has been made in the developing study of the several textual families and literary editions of biblical works. This bears on the Greek versions of Ezra, notably in the recognition of the importance of the text of 1 Esdras for historical reconstruction. H. H. Howorth, C. C. Torrey, Sigmund Mowinckel, and K.-F. Pohlman have pioneered in these studies.[28] With the discovery of variant textual traditions and of literary editions,[29] earlier views of the importance and priority of the Hebrew recension of Ezra underlying the Greek of 1 Esdras have been vindicated.[30]

25. Neh. 2:19; 6:1–2, 6.

26. The find was published with other finds in the Wâdī Ṭumeilât by Isaac Rabinowitz, "Aramaic Inscriptions of the Fifth Century B.C.E. from a North-Arab Shrine in Egypt," *JNES* 15 (1956): 1–9. He dates the script of the bowl to ca. 400 B.C.E., a date I should term minimal. See also W. J. Dumbrell, "The Tell el-Maskhuṭa Bowls and the 'Kingdom' of Qedar in the Persian Period," *BASOR* 203 (1971): 33–44. The discovery of the bowl supports the fifth-century dating of an early Liḥyanite inscription from ʾEl-ʿUlā (Dedan), which mentions Gašm bin Šaḥr and ʿAbd, governor (*paḥat*) of Dedan, a dating held by Winnett and Albright not without opposition. See W. F. Albright, "Dedan," in *Geschichte und Altes Testament,* Beiträge zur historischen Theologie 16 [Alt *Festschrift*] (Tübingen: Mohr, 1953), 1–12. Albright's conjecture that the biblical formula *ṭwbyh hʿbd hʿmny* (Neh. 2:10, 19) should be read *ṭwbyh wʿbd hʿmny* is most tempting. It would not be strange at all if ʿAbd, a Persian governor of Dedan, were an Ammonite and associated with Tobiah of Ammon (a Jew), and Geshem, king of Qedar.

27. It must be observed, however, that papponymy was practiced in the Qedarite house. See F. M. Cross, "A New Aramaic Stele from Taymāʾ," *CBQ* 48 (1986): 387–394.

28. See especially, Torrey's *Ezra Studies* (Chicago: University of Chicago Press, 1910); S. Mowinckel, *Studien zu dem Buche Ezra-Nehemiah,* 3 vols. (Oslo: Universitetsforlaget, 1964–65). Our citation of 1 Esdras is from the excellent critical edition of R. Hanhart, *Esdrae liber 1,* Septuaginta: Vetus Testamentum graecum 8/1 (Göttingen: Vandenhoeck and Ruprecht, 1974).

29. See my comments in Cross, "Some Notes on a Generation of Qumran Studies," 6–11, and the studies of Eugene Ulrich, "Pluriformity in the Biblical Text, Text Groups, and Questions of Canon," both in *The Madrid Qumran Congress: Proceedings of the International Congress on the Dead Sea Scrolls, Madrid, 18–21 March 1991,* vol. 1, ed. Julio Trebolle Barrera and Luis Vegas Montaner (Leiden and Madrid: Brill and Editorial Complutense, 1992), 23–41; "Multiple Literary Editions: Reflections toward a Theory of the History of the Biblical Text," in *Current Research and Technological Developments on the Dead Sea Scrolls,* ed. Donald W. Parry and Stephen D. Ricks (Leiden: Brill, 1996), 78–105.

30. Conservative opposition to this view has been eloquently argued by H. G. M. Williamson and Sara Japhet, who follow the canonical division of Chronicles and

Textual families or traditions are not identical with literary editions. The textual families and traditions evolve through the accumulation of scribal errors, corrections, harmonizing, parallel readings, etc. They are the result of the frailty of families of scribes copying texts over centuries. Literary editions reflect more substantial variation, arising in variant editions, oral and written. However, these two categories cannot be neatly separated. For example, two editions of Jeremiah are found at Qumrân, two manuscripts standing close to the *Vorlage* of the Old Greek, 4QJer[b] and 4QJer[d], and three manuscripts standing close to the Rabbinic (Proto-Massoretic) Recension, notably the early 4QJer[a].[31] The edition found in the Old Greek and in the two related 4Q manuscripts is a much shorter recension, less expansionistic, and exhibits different order, probably an earlier order, from that of the Masoretic Text. It witnesses to another stream of tradition best called an edition. On the other hand, where the two texts precisely parallel each other scores of differences have arisen transparently from scribal error or changes, textual variation owing to copying errors, not editorial activity.[32]

The relation of the two editions, one preserved in the Palestinian text known from Qumrân Cave 4 and the Masoretic Text of Ezra, the other preserved in the Alexandrine translation of an Egyptian textual tradition (1 Esdras), has an almost precise analogy in the two editions of Jeremiah. There are major differences in order, and there are portions of the texts that show variations of an editorial sort, and at the same time, in precisely parallel passages, changes owing to copyist's error but based on the same underlying text. Ralph Klein has brought together the evidence for the two editions.[33] The Palestinian (Proto-Rabbinic) edition is conflate

---

Ezra-Nehemiah as original, and treat 1 Esdras as an independent work without bearing on the original order of material in Ezra-Nehemiah. See especially S. Japhet, "The Supposed Common Authorship of Chronicles and Ezra-Nehemiah Investigated Anew," *VT* 18 (1968): 330–371; and Williamson, *Israel,* 5–70.

31. See the editions of Emanuel Tov in *Qumran Cave 4 • X The Prophets, DJD* 15 (Oxford: Clarendon Press, 1997), 145–207 and pls. 24–37.

32. See especially J. G. Janzen, *Studies in the Text of Jeremiah, HSM* 6 (Cambridge: Harvard University Press, 1973). Cf. E. Tov, "Some Aspects of the Textual and Literary History of the Book of Jeremiah," in *Le livre de Jérémie,* ed. P.-M. Bogaert, *BEThL* 54 (1981): 145–176; "The Literary History of the Book of Jeremiah in Light of Its Textual History," in *Empirical Models for Biblical Criticism,* ed. J. Tigay (Philadelphia: University of Pennsylvania Press, 1985), 211–237; and his discussion and references in the *editio princeps* of the 4Q Jeremiah manuscripts (see n. 31).

33. "Studies in the Greek Texts of the Chronicler" (Ph.D. diss., Harvard University, 1966). A summary may be found in *HTR* 59 (1966): 449; see also his paper "Old Readings in 1 Esdras: The List of Returnees from Babylon (Ezra 2 = Nehemiah 7)," *HTR* 62 (1969): 99–107.

and expansionistic and follows a late secondary ordering of pericopes. It is reflected in 4QEzra, in Esdras B, a forerunner of the school of Theodotion,[34] and in the Rabbinic Recension which developed into the Masoretic Text. The Egyptian textual family is reflected in 1 Esdras, translated in Egypt in the mid second century B.C.E.[35] In parallel passages, 1 Esdras proves on the whole to have a shorter, better text, as is widely recognized. Its order of pericopes reflects an older, historically superior edition of the Chronicler's Work (Chronicles-Ezra). Most important, 7:72b through 8:12 of Nehemiah (1 Esdras 9:37–55) is placed immediately after Ezra 10 (1 Esdras 8:88–9:36). That is to say, the entire Ezra Narrative is separated from the Memoirs of Nehemiah. Thus it must be said that in an earlier recension of the Chronicler's Work, the missions of Ezra and Nehemiah did not overlap. Moreover, in 1 Esdras 9:49 (= Nehemiah 8:9), the name Nehemiah is missing in the description of the reading of the law; there is only reference to the *Tiršātā*. That the name of Nehemiah does not belong here is also evidenced by the chronological problem developed thereby: thirteen years would have passed between Ezra's return and his reading of the law that he brought with him—presuming the chronology of the final edition of the Chronicler's Work (Chronicles, Ezra-Nehemiah). In short, we must consider it a fixed point in the discussion that the Ezra Narrative had no mention of Nehemiah in its original form, and that the Nehemiah Memoirs contained no reference to Ezra.[36]

1 Esdras completes the Ezra Narrative (save for a fragment lost at its close) now found in Nehemiah 8:13–18, the account of the preparations for and the celebration of the Feast of Tabernacles. Evidently, the end of the scroll of the Hebrew *Vorlage* of 1 Esdras, which was the basis of the Greek translation, was defective; or, alternately, a defective Greek manuscript of 1 Esdras became by chance the archetype of the surviving text of 1 Esdras. The reading of the Law and the celebration of the high holidays[37] were the appropriate climax and conclusion. That one edition of the Chronicler's Work ended at the close of chapter 8 of Nehemiah (i.e., at the end of the *original* chapter 9 of 1 Esdras) is confirmed by the text of 1 Esdras used by Josephus, who carries the story of Ezra, following precisely the order of 1 Esdras through chapter 8 of Nehemiah, including

34. The translator of 2 Esdras is not Theodotion (*contra* Torrey), nor is he identical with the so-called *καίγε* Recension, though he shares some of the latter's traits.

35. See the arguments of Klein in "Studies in the Greek Texts of the Chronicler."

36. The appearance of the name Nehemiah in Neh. 10:1, of Ezra in Neh. 12:36, and the mention of both in Neh. 12:25 all stem from the editorial hand of the final editor of the Chronicler's Work (Chr_3, see below).

37. Apropos of the high holidays, there is no reason to suppose that Ezra followed a pre-Pentateuchal calendar, moving up *Sukkôt* and ignoring *Yôm Kippûr* (*pace* Morton Smith). Preparations for *Sukkôt* took more than one day.

the celebration of the Feast of Tabernacles.[38] As we shall see, the Chronicler's Work once circulated with only the Ezra Narrative appended. The Nehemiah Memoirs were not part of the work but were circulated separately. Josephus knew a Greek translation (probably Alexandrine in origin) of the Nehemiah Memoirs quite different from the received text of Nehemiah. However, the integration of the Nehemiah Memoirs into the Chronicler's history belongs to the latest stage of revisions of the Chronicler's Work. This edition did not finally oust the earlier edition until the time that the Rabbinic Recension (of the first century of the Christian era) became authoritative following the fall of Jerusalem in 70 C.E.

Reconstruction of the List of High Priests in the Fifth Century B.C.E.

We have discussed the problems of the fourth-century sequence of high priests, restoring names Yôḥānān and Yaddûaʿ on the basis of data from the new list of Sanballaṭids, from the *Antiquities* of Josephus, and—discovered since my reconstruction of 1975—the silver coins of Yôḥānān (III) and Yaddûaʿ (II) confirming the reconstruction. The genealogy of the priests from the sixth to the fourth centuries, without the addition of Yôḥānān III and Yaddûaʿ II, records eight generations for a period of 275 years. This yields the figure of 34.3 years per generation, an incredibly high figure. In Near Eastern antiquity, the generation (i.e., the years between a man's birth and the begetting of his firstborn son) is ordinarily 25 years or less. The inclusion of the priests Yôḥānān III and Yaddûaʿ II reduces the average generation to about 27.5, still suspiciously high.

The genealogy of the Davidids gives a measure of control for the first seven generations of the Restoration, and happily, does not follow the fashion of papponymy, so the risk of names lost by homoteleuton is slight. In any case, it appears to be complete if slightly confused textually. The list names seven Davidids, six generations of the Restoration. These occupy a period of years from before 592 (the thirteenth year of Nebuchadnezzar), to ca. 445 B.C.E., the birth date roughly of ʿAnānî, a total of 147 years. This gives a figure of 24.5 years per generation, which is close to what we should expect. Synchronisms exist for two or three of the

38. There is no allusion in Josephus to the covenant-document preserved in Neh. 9 (historical prologue in the form of a confession) and 10 (witnesses and stipulations). The chapters belong to the latest stratum of the Chronicler's history (Chr_3); it is not clear whether it is an expanded doublet of Ezra's covenant (Ezra 10:3–5), or represents a parallel covenant enacted by Nehemiah. The stipulations conform closely to Nehemiah's reforms. Greek Nehemiah (Esdras B) attributes the confession to Ezra (at 19.6 = Hebrew 9:6).

generations of the Davidids. Zerubbabel and Yēšûaʿ the high priest are linked. Ḥaṭṭûš returned with Ezra.[39] ʿAnānî, the last of the line recorded in 1 Chronicles 3:17–24 *may* be the ʿAnānî named in *AP* 30:19 (410 B.C.E.); on the other hand, his brother *ʾwštn* mentioned in the papyrus is not listed among his six brothers in 1 Chronicles 3 by his Persian name.

The list of high priests in the sixth to fifth centuries, from Yôṣādāq to Yôḥānān, extends over a period of 150 years.[40] Six priests are named in the five generations, giving the figure of thirty years per generation, some five years or more per generation too high. We suspect that at least one generation—two high priests' names—have dropped out of the list owing to the repetition produced by papponymy.

Turning to the list, we note that the first three names appear to be in order. Yôṣādāq went captive.[41] Yēšûaʿ and his son Yôyāqîm returned with Zerubbabel.[42] Similarly the last three names—Yôyādāʿ, Yôḥānān, Yaddûaʿ—seem to be correct.[43] The center of difficulties, however, is the high priest ʾElyāšîb. In Ezra 10:1–6 Ezra commands the priestly and lay officials to make a covenant rejecting foreign wives. He then goes to the room of Yôḥānān the son of ʾElyāšîb, where he lodged.[44] The context suggests that this was the high priest or son of the high priest. In 1 Esdras 9:1, Hebrew *liškā* is correctly translated by *παστοφόριον*, a priestly chamber connected with the temple.[45] In Nehemiah 12:22 we find the series of priests named ʾElyāšîb-Yôyādāʿ-Yôḥānān-Yaddûaʿ, and in the following verse, "until the days of Yôḥānān son of ʾElyāšîb." Prima facie, we must reckon with a high priest ʾElyāšîb father of Yôḥānān and a high priest ʾElyāšîb father of Yôyādāʿ. If so, the high priestly

39. Ezra 8:2.

40. We reckon from 595 B.C.E., a minimal birth date of Yôṣādāq, who went into captivity (1 Chron. 5:41; cf. *Antiq.* 20:231, 234, and 1 Esdras 5:5), to the birth of Yôḥānān ca. 445. In Neh. 12:22 Yôḥānān (along with Yaddûaʿ) is said to have flourished in the reign of Darius (II Nothus, 423–404 B.C.E.), and he (Yôḥānān) is high priest in 410 B.C.E., according to *AP* 330:18.

41. 1 Chron. 5:41.

42. The key passage to which we shall return is 1 Esdras 5:5 f., which dates Zerubbabel's return in "the second year," that is, the second year of Darius I, 520 B.C.E. The text is slightly in disorder. It should read, "Yēšûaʿ the son of Yôṣādāq the son of Sārāyāh, and Yôyāqîm his son and Zerubbabel." Cf. *Antiq.* 11:121, 158.

43. Neh. 12:10, 22.

44. Ezra 10:6; 1 Esdras 9:1.

45. It is difficult to argue that this ʾElyāšîb is not the high priest of that name (*pace* Blenkinsopp), and that Ezra was not the guest of the high priest. He came to Jerusalem with the Persian king's commission to inform the people of the "law of Moses" and to establish it in Judea. Ezra is given a lineage (Ezra 7:1–5) which traces his ancestry through all of the pre-Exilic high priests. The genealogy may be a secondary insertion, but there can be no doubt that Ezra ranked with the chief priests.

genealogy is defective, and we must insert an ʾElyāšîb I, whose son is Yôḥānān I, into the list of high priests. This presumes a haplography in the priestly genealogy, precisely comparable to the documented haplography in the late list and for the same reason: papponymy.[46] Such a reconstruction will solve a number of the notorious historical problems of Ezra-Nehemiah. Thus we have the following sequence (1) ʾElyāšîb I father of (2) Yôḥānān I, the contemporary of Ezra, followed by (3) ʾElyāšîb II, contemporary of Nehemiah and grandfather of (4) Yôḥānān II. Evidently two names fell out of the list of high priests by the skipping of the scribe's eye from "ʾElyāšîb' to "ʾElyāšîb,' a scribal error most common in the copying of ancient texts—or for that matter modern texts. The list of high priests from Yôṣādāq to Yôḥānān spans 150 years, a generation averaging 25 years (see chart).

We have assumed in our reconstruction that, given the change of names from the pattern of papponymy, ʾElyāšîb I was in the same generation as his predecessor Yôyāqîm, perhaps the brother of Yôyāqîm. My reasons for placing ʾElyāšîb in the third generation are ignored by Widengren, who supposes that I have made a mistake, since Nehemiah 12:10 says "Joiakim begat Eliashib." He ignores my explanatory footnotes. The primary reason for placing ʾElyāšîb in the third generation is, of course, the control of the Davidic list in 1 Chronicles 3. It provides five names, four generations between Šenʾaṣṣar (Šešbaṣṣar, Sanabassar, Sin-ab-uṣur) and Ḥaṭṭûš, the contemporary of Ezra and ʾElyāšîb (II). Inasmuch as I wish to reconstruct six names and four generations, I suggested the succession of brother to brother (or the like) in the sequence to ʾElyāšîb I. I should say that if Widengren wishes to follow uncritically the genealogy in Nehemiah 12:10, he should also reckon with two ʾElyāšîbs in view of the text's clear readings "Yôḥānān the son of ʾElyāšîb" (Ezra 10:6; Nehemiah 12:23), and "Yôyādāʿ son of ʾElyāšîb" (Nehemiah 12:10, 22).

Widengren might also have found fault with my critical treatment of the genealogy of the Davidic line in 1 Chronicles 3:22. The Masoretic Text reads *wbny šknyh šmʿyh wbny šmʿyh ḥṭwš wygʾl wbryḥ wnʿryh wšpṭ ššh.* I have taken *wbny šmʿyh* as secondary, in view of the number "six," and the probable reading of Ezra 8:2–3, *mbny dwyd ḥṭwš bn šknyh.* It should be noted, however, that many scholars reconstruct the Davidic genealogy

46. One may compare the list of high priests in the pre-Exilic era, which we know has lost a number of names frequently because of their repetition in the lists—although papponymy was not a regular practice. For example, note the lacuna in the list of Ezra 7:1–5 (cf. 1 Chron. 5:27–41 MT). See Blenkinsopp, *Ezra-Nehemiah,* 136, against Japhet, *I & II Chronicles,* Old Testament Library (Louisville: Westminster–John Knox, 1993), 151–153.

with the sequence Šĕkanyāh–Šĕmaʿyāh–Ḥaṭṭûš. Using the extra Davidid, I could have matched up each generation of Davidids with high priests and kept the text of Nehemiah 12:10 unaltered: seven generations of Davidids, seven generations of high priests. By this reckoning, we arrive at an average of twenty years per generation, preferred by chronologists of the ancient world. As a matter of fact, Widengren does not understand the character of my reconstruction at all. The suggested dates of birth of the high priests and Davidids are schematic and may be moved about in any given instance. We have only a few synchronisms. I could have chosen twenty-year generations as easily as twenty-five. In a given case, one could have a much longer generation—but not repeatedly over a long sequence of generations where the law of averages operates. We have a list of high priests from Yôṣādāq, who went into Exile and thus was born well before 587 (which minimal figure is used in our calculations), to Yaddûaʿ, still in power in 323 B.C.E. We are furnished in the Bible and Josephus with eight names, including Onias I, seven generations. Reckoning twenty years to a generation, we expect 13.2 generations; reckoning twenty-five years to a generation, we expect 10.5 generations. Thus the high priestly genealogy which has come down to us is improbably short. A minimum of three generations must be missing; as many as six generations may be missing. My reconstruction supplies four names, three generations. It may be that both the original ordering of high priests and Sanballaṭids were in reality more complex than I have constructed them. My scheme merely observes the principle of parsimony.

More important, this reconstruction places the mission of Ezra in the seventh year of Artaxerxes I, 458 B.C.E.,[47] and the mission of Nehemiah in 445 B.C.E.,[48] the twentieth year of Artaxerxes I, confirming the traditional order of Ezra and Nehemiah and settling the issues and solving the problems addressed in both the Van Hoonaker and Kosters-Bertholet reconstructions.

Editions of the Chronicler's Work

We have noted above the evidence from First Esdras and from Josephus's *Antiquities* that in an earlier edition of the Chronicler's Work the Narrative of Ezra and the Memoirs of Nehemiah were separate and that in all likelihood Nehemiah's Memoirs were only attached to the Chronicler's Work in its final edition. Confirmation of this view may be found

47. The seventh year is given in Ezra 7:7 and 7:8.

48. Or more precisely, December, 445 B.C.E. Cf. Neh. 1:1 and Neh. 13:6 (the thirty-second year of Artaxerxes I, 433/432).

in Nehemiah 12:23. We read: "The sons of Levi, heads of father's houses, were written in the Book of the Chronicles [*sēper dibrê hay-yāmîm*] even until the days of Yôḥānān the son of ʾElyāšîb." In this text there is evidently a reference to an edition of the Chronicler's Work, which ended in the days of Yôḥānān son of ʾElyāšîb, the contemporary of Ezra in the fourth generation of the Restoration, according to my reconstruction. Thus this earlier edition reached only the era of Ezra and Yôḥānān I, and not to the time of ʾElyāšîb II, the son of Yôḥānān I, who was high priest in the days of Nehemiah's governorship. Our conclusion that Nehemiah's Memoirs were composed and circulated independently of the Chronicler's Work also gives explanation of the repetition of the list of those who returned with Zerubbabel in Ezra 2 (I Esdras 5:7–47) and in Nehemiah 7. The Nehemiah Memoirs quote the Chronicler's Work or draw on a common source at the time when Nehemiah was composed as an independent work. The evidence for the two editions described above appears clear enough; however, there are also good reasons to posit three editions of the Chronicler's Work. We shall label them Chr_1, Chr_2, and Chr_3.

Chr_3 is the final edition, made up of 1 Chronicles 1–9 plus 1 Chronicles 10 through 2 Chronicles 36 plus Hebrew Ezra-Nehemiah. Chr_2 included a shorter version of the genealogical lore in 1 Chronicles 1–9 plus 1 Chronicles 10 through 2 Chronicles 34 (aside from touches of later editing) plus the Hebrew *Vorlage* of Greek First Esdras. Chr_1 included a genealogical introduction plus much of 1 Chronicles 10:1 through 2 Chronicles 36:21 plus the continuing Hebrew material in Ezra 1:1–3:13 (= 1 Esdras 2:1–15; 5:1–62). It ends with its climax in the celebration dedicating the altar and the foundation of the Second Temple—looking ahead to the full reconstitution of Israel's primary institutions centering in the house of David and the house of Yahweh.

The latest member of the high priesthood mentioned within the First Esdras narrative is Yôḥānān I, son of ʾElyāšîb I (1 Esdras 9:1), and the latest member of the Davidic house named is Ḥaṭṭûš (1 Esdras 8:29). On the other hand, in the introductory genealogies of 1 Chronicles 1–9, the list of the Davidids continues for two more generations to ʿAnānî, the contemporary of Yôḥānān II toward the end of the fifth century. Chapters 12 and 13 of Nehemiah refer to these two priests as well; moreover, Nehemiah 12:22 names Darius (II, 423–404 B.C.E.) in its latest references to a Persian king. These data suggest dates for Chr_2 and Chr_3, the former toward 450 B.C.E., the latter toward 400 B.C.E. or slightly later.

Other arguments can be put for dating Chr_3 to ca. 400 B.C.E. No hint of the conquest of Alexander is to be found, and perhaps more important, no reference to the suffering and chaos of the mid-fourth century B.C.E.

when Judah joined in the Phoenician rebellion, harshly put down by Artaxerxes III and his general, Bagoas.[49]

A surprising contrast between Chr_2 and Chr_3 is the treatment of Zerubbabel. Ezra intrudes the list of those who returned with Zerubbabel in chapter 2, making it appear that both Sin-ab-uṣur[50] and Zerubbabel returned more or less together in the reign of Cyrus. 1 Esdras places the list of returnees in chapter five, after the return of Sanabassar in the days of Cyrus and after the narrative recounting Zerubbabel's return to Jerusalem in the second year of Darius I.[51] This appears as a *plus*[52] in 1 Esdras and is almost surely authentic. Since we are told that Sin-ab-uṣur the governor returned and built the foundations of the temple, and since Zerubbabel completed the temple upon Darius's decree,[53] it is quite natural to attribute the return of Zerubbabel to the beginning of the reign of Darius. The chaos that marked the beginning of Darius's reign was the appropriate time for a return to Zion, as it was an appropriate time for prophets to arise anew and proclaim a new David and a new temple, that is, the reestablishment of the Judaean kingdom. Again, the wisdom tale of Zerubbabel's brilliance and reward in 1 Esdras 3:1 through 5:6 is fixed unalterably in the reign of Darius. 1 Esdras 5:55 (ed.) says explicitly that the building of the temple began in the second year after he came to Jerusalem. At the same time, there is a conflict between the account of Zerubbabel's being rewarded with "letters for him and all the treasurers and governors and captains and satraps" by Darius (1 Esdras 4:47), and the Aramaic source in Ezra 5 where Darius before answering Tattenay the "governor of ʿAbar-nahara" and his companions

49. For the extent of the rebellion and evidence of destroyed cities in Palestine in this period, see D. Barag, "The Effects of the Tennes Rebellion in Palestine," *BASOR* 183 (1966): 6–12. The appearance of the Greek loanword *darkĕmōn*[*îm*] in the Chronicler's Work is no reason to assign its final date of editing to the Hellenistic period. Attic *drachmai* were in general use as currency in late-sixth- and fifth-century Syria-Palestine, and Judah's late-fourth-century coins still preserve the owl of Athena. The loanword meaning *drachmai* also appears in a late Phoenician inscription from Greece: *drkmnm* [*KAI* 60:6; cf. 60:3]. Gold darics, introduced by Darius I, were not in general use in Palestine, to judge by the fact that only one coin of Persian mint has turned up in Palestinian tells. See Ephraim Stern, *Material Culture of the Land of the Bible in the Persian Period, 538–332* B.C. (Jerusalem: IES, 1982), 217–228, and especially n. 49. Moreover, we would expect the daric to appear as *dryk, drykwn* in Hebrew; cf. Syriac *darîk, drykwn'*.

50. For a full discussion of the equation Hebrew *ššbṣr* (Ezra 1:8, 11) = *šn'ṣr* (1 Chron. 3:17) = Greek *Sanabassar* = cuneiform *sin-ab-uṣur,* see the long discussion in chapter 9, n. 21.

51. 1 Esdras 5:6, cf. 5:2.

52. 1 Esdras 4:58; 5:7.

53. Ezra 5:16–20; 1 Esdras 6:18–20.

is said to search out his records for the decree of Cyrus. There can be little doubt that the wisdom tale is secondarily attached to Zerubbabel and interpolated at some point into one edition of the Chronicler's Work.[54]

David Noel Freedman has written a persuasive paper sketching the Chronicler's purpose.[55] If he is correct, we must argue for the existence at one time of Chr_1 written to promote the Chronicler's purpose and program. Freedman contends that "the Chronicler establishes through his narrative of the reigns of David and Solomon the proper, legitimate pattern of institutions and their personnel for the people of God; and they are the monarchy represented by David and his house, the priesthood, by Zadok and his descendants, the city and the temple in the promised land. City and ruler, temple and priest—these appear to be the fixed points around which the Chronicler constructs his history and his theology."[56]

The ideology of the Chronicler found in Chr_1, that is, in 1 Chronicles 10:1 through 2 Chronicles 36:23 plus the *Vorlage* of 1 Esdras 1:1–5:62 (=2 Chron. 34:1 through Ezra 3:13), calls upon the old royal ideology of the Judaean kings—chosen David, chosen Zion—as that ideology has been reformulated in Ezekiel 40–48, and especially in the oracles of Haggai and Zechariah. In Haggai and Zechariah, king and priest constitute a diarchy, son of David, son of Zadok. Zerubbabel is called "my servant" by Yahweh and told "[I] will make you as a signet, for I have chosen you."[57] In chapter 3 of Zechariah, Joshua [i.e., Yēšûaʿ] the high priest is crowned and robed for office in the prophet's vision, and the angel of the Lord announces: "Hear now O Joshua the high Priest, you and your fellows who sit before you . . . , for behold I shall bring my servant, the Branch."[58] In Chr_1 "the parallel between the first building of the temple under the direction of David (and Solomon), and the second building under Zerubbabel is too striking to be accidental, and must have formed part of the original structure of the Work."[59] In short, the original Chronicler's Work was designed to support the program for the restoration of the kingdom under Zerubbabel, and the temple and its cultus under Yēšûaʿ. Its extent reached only to Ezra 3:13 (1 Esdras 5:62), with the account of the celebration of the founding of the Second Temple.

54. I am inclined to believe that this happened after Chr_1 and before Chr_2, and that Chr_3 suppressed the tale in accord with his antimonarchic, theocratic views (see below).

55. "The Chronicler's Purpose," *CBQ* 23 (1961): 436–442.

56. Ibid., 437–438.

57. Hag. 2:23.

58. Zech. 3:8; cf. 4:14.

59. Freedman, "The Chronicler's Purpose," 437–438.

The future is open, and the work of restoring the ancient institutions is well begun; all is anticipation.[60] Here the program or propaganda document should end.

In order to supply the full story of the completion of the temple, the editor of Chr_3 added the Aramaic source in Ezra 5:1–6:19 as the preface to the Ezra Narrative which begins at Ezra 7:1. Chr_2 still breathes some of the monarchist fire of Chr_1. Zerubbabel is still called the "servant of the Lord."[61] The story of his wisdom is preserved by Chr_2,[62] and the proper order of the Ezra Narrative is kept (for the most part) only in 1 Esdras. The Nehemiah Memoirs were introduced only by Chr_3, who, following his belief that Ezra and Nehemiah were contemporaries, created confusion by interlarding the Nehemiah Memoirs with part of the Ezra Narrative. Chr_3 apparently suppressed elements exalting Zerubbabel, including his title "servant of the Lord" and the heroic tale of Zerubbabel's wisdom and piety (1 Esdras 3:1–5:2).

The primary argument that may be brought against our view of the original Chronicler's Work is that the Ezra Narrative and the Nehemiah Memoirs reflect the characteristic language and style of the Chronicler.[63] The argument is not compelling; a member of the school of the Chronicler (i.e., Chr_2), imitating the master's style, may easily be responsible for the similarity of style. The two editions of the Deuteronomistic History provide a perfect analogy.[64] Moreover, Sara Japhet has attacked the thesis of the common authorship of the Chronicles and the Ezra Narrative with persuasive evidence of differences in style and linguistic usage.[65] On the other hand there appear to be distinctions to be drawn between the royal ideology of the Chronicler (Chr_1) and the final edition of his work. Chr_3 appears to have omitted some material which tends to exalt Zerubbabel, the anointed son of David, presumably because his movement was snuffed out and his end ignominious or pathetic.[66]

60. Here I cannot agree with Freedman that the original story of Zerubbabel is suppressed in favor of the Aramaic source (Ezra 4:6 through 6:18).

61. 1 Esdras 6:27; the parallel passage in Ezra 6:7 suppresses the exalted title.

62. See above, esp. n. 56.

63. The strongest statement of this view is perhaps that of Torrey, *Ezra Studies*, 238–248.

64. See *CMHE*, 274–289.

65. Japhet, "The Supposed Common Authorship of Chronicles and Ezra-Nehemiah Investigated Anew." Some of her arguments are based on the distinctions between different orthographic practice and the use of archaic or pseudoarchaic forms; these arguments do not hold, I believe, as can be shown by an examination of the two Isaiah scrolls of Qumrân Cave 1, or a comparison of 4QSam[a] and 4QSam[b], where common authorship is certain.

66. In "The Chronicler's Purpose" (440) Freedman argues that in the final edition

In summary, we may list three editions of the Chronicler's Work: Chr_1, composed in support of Zerubbabel shortly after 520 B.C.E., Chr_2, written after Ezra's mission in 458 B.C.E., and Chr_3, edited about 400 B.C.E. or shortly thereafter.[67]

A Sketch of the Era of the Restoration

In the first year of his reign, 538 B.C.E., Cyrus the Great published an edict directing the temple in Jerusalem to be rebuilt, returning the sacred vessels taken as loot by Nebuchadnezzar to their place, thereby initiating the restoration of the Jewish community in Judaea.[68] The leader of the first return was Sheshbazzar, heir to the house of David, son of Jehoiachin. He is given the title *nāśîʾ*, which Ezekiel and his circle preferred to *melek,* 'king,' in designating the new David's office. Beyond the fact that Sheshbazzar led a group of captive Jews to Jerusalem bearing the temple treasures, we know very little. Evidently it was a token return, for we know that a large number of Jews were flourishing in the Babylonian community under the tolerant Persian regime. Sheshbazzar is credited with laying the foundations of the temple in the Aramaic source,[69] as well as named governor.[70] Since the Persian administration

---

of the Chronicler's Work (he reckons with only two editions), there is a positively antimonarchical, clericalist tendency.

67. The fact that all genealogies in Chr_3 end shortly before 400 B.C.E. virtually eliminates the popular view that Ezra followed Nehemiah to Jerusalem in the seventh year of Artaxerxes II, 398 B.C.E. Of the many arguments brought forward to support the position, most are without weight. The most plausible of them, perhaps, is the notice in Ezra 9:9 that God has given "to us a *gādēr* in Judah and in Jerusalem." The term *gādēr* has been taken sometimes as a reference to the city wall of Jerusalem. It must be said that there may have been attempts to build the wall of Jerusalem before Nehemiah succeeded. This would explain his surprise at his brother Ḥănānî's report that "the wall of Jerusalem (*ḥwmt yrwšlm*) is shattered. On the other hand, it is by no means clear that the term *gādēr* here refers to a city wall. Ordinarily it refers to an 'enclosure wall' (of fields or vineyards) or 'fortifications.' Thus it refers to the enclosure wall which fortified the temple (Ezek. 42:7 and *gdrt* 42:12). In Micah 7:11 the expression is in the plural (*gdryk*) and evidently refers to the defenses and fortifications of a city. Specifically in Ezra 9:9, however, the context is quite clear. In rhetorical parallelism Ezra speaks of "raising the house of our God," "making its ruins stand up," and "giving us a *gādēr* in Jerusalem and Judah." As Ezekiel uses *gādēr* of temple fortification, so does Ezra speak of the *gādēr* of the temple. Each parallel refers to the Zerubbabel temple and enclosure wall. The temple was, of course, a bastion as well as a sanctuary.

68. The Aramaic text is found in Ezra 6:3–5; cf. the ornamented version in Ezra 1: 1–14.

69. Ezra 5:6.

70. Ezra 5:14.

frequently appointed a member of the native royal house governor of a local state, and indeed made the governorship hereditary, there is no reason to doubt the notice. In any case, his nephew Zerubbabel succeeded to the governorship of Judaea.

Zerubbabel the governor and Yēšûaʿ the Zadokite high priest, according to 1 Esdras, returned at the beginning of the reign of Darius.[71] This was a time of widespread rebellion in the Persian empire, and in Judaea a nationalist spirit stirred up the populace. The prophets Haggai and Zechariah arose and gave oracles reviving the old royal ideology of king and temple. Zerubbabel and Yēšûaʿ were named the new David and the new Zadok, the "sons of oil," and a program was promulgated to reestablish Israel's legitimate institutions. Above all, the prophets urged the building of the temple and envisioned the return of Yahweh's "Glory"—his refulgent manifestation of this presence—to Jerusalem, there to "tabernacle" as in ancient days.[72] Haggai prophesied the downfall of the Persian empire and blamed the little community's troubles on their failure to build the house of God.

In support of the messianic movement the Chronicler (Chr_1) composed a history which reviewed and reshaped Israel's historical traditions to give urgency and meaning to the tasks at hand: the restoration of Davidic rule, the building of the temple, and the establishment of the divinely appointed cultus with all its kindred institutions and personnel. The restored Davidic kingdom was to be inclusive of north and south, and the temple to be the central sanctuary of all Israel. This first edition of the Chronicler's Work is to be dated to the five-year interval between the founding of the temple and the completion of the temple (520–515 B.C.E.). The mood and progam of Chr_1 is quite different from the narrowing vision and exclusivistic or defensive tendencies in the subsequent activities of Ezra and in the mission of Nehemiah. The Chronicler's program is not to be considered an ideal, much less an apocalyptic, vision. It is a practical program, more or less identical with the propagandistic purpose of Haggai and Zechariah. In short, Chr_1 must be set in particular time, with a concrete political end in view. A dating later than the fifth century turns this first edition into an irrelevant exercise in antiquarianism.

In the face of harassment by Persian officials, including the satrap of Syria, and the jealousy and hostility of peoples who surrounded Judah, Zerubbabel and his party completed the temple on March 12, 515 B.C.E.

71. The floating piece in 1 Esdras 5:63–70 (= Ezra 4:1–5) appears contradictory; cf. 1 Esdras 5:1–6.

72. For this technical language found in the Priestly source of the Tetrateuch, in Ezekiel and in Zechariah, see *CMHE*, 323–324 and references.

The service of God "as it is written in the book of Moses" was thus restored.

We hear no more of Zerubbabel. The prophecies of glory and wealth and peace faded away into silence. We have no hint of Zerubbabel's fate. More than half a century passes before the story of the Restoration is taken up again. This gap in the record is most significant in reconstructing the history of the Chronicler's Work. When the narrative resumes with the account of the mission of Ezra, the royal themes of the earlier narrative are no longer to be heard. Hierocracy supplants the diarchy of king and high priest. We hear nothing of the Davidic prince either in the Ezra Narrative or in the Memoirs of Nehemiah.

In 458 B.C.E., "Ezra the priest, the scribe of the law of the God of Heaven," set out with his company of Zionists armed only with Artaxerxes' commission, some offerings sent to the temple in Jerusalem, and the Book of the Law of Moses. Ezra's first main effort on his arrival in Jerusalem was to undertake stern action against intermarriage with foreigners, especially marriage to foreign wives. He proposed that all enter into a covenant to put away foreign wives, and the issue of such marriages, in fulfillment of the Law. Armed with royal authority to appoint magistrates and judges, he vigorously pressed his reform against all opposition. Two months after he arrived in Jerusalem, in the seventh year, on New Year's Day, he gathered all the people in an assembly before the Water Gate, and standing on a wooden pulpit read from the "Book of the Law of Moses." We judge this book to have been the Pentateuch in penultimate form.[73] On the second day, he read from the Law and then dismissed the congregation in order that they might prepare for the Festival of Succoth.[74]

Here ended the second edition of the Chronicler's Work, the recension reflected in 1 Esdras, combining the Ezra Narrative with the older Book of Chronicles. The date of Chr_2 must fall about 450 B.C.E.

In 445, Nehemiah, the cup bearer to king Artaxerxes I, learned of the troubles of the restored community in Jerusalem and its defenselessness. With the king's commission as governor of Judaea, he set out with a contingent of the king's cavalry for Jerusalem.[75] Spying out the city by night, he kept his own counsel as to his plans, knowing full well that his mission would be hindered by the hatred and schemes of his fel-

73. The arguments of S. Mowinckel are compelling; see *Studien zu dem Buches Ezra-Nehemia,* 3:124–141.

74. Mowinckel is surely right in assuming that the Day of Atonement was fully known and celebrated despite the omission of reference to it in Nehemiah 8.

75. Josephus (*Antiq.* 11:168) gives 440 as the date of Nehemiah's arrival in Jerusalem. The wall was completed in December, 437 B.C.E. according to Josephus (*Antiq.* 11:179), two years and four months after he began.

low governors round about, viz. Sanballaṭ, governor of Samaria, Ṭobiah, governor of ʿAmmon, Gašmu, the king of the Qedarite Arabs, and perhaps ʿAbd, the governor of Dedan. Upon his announcement of plans to rebuild the walls of Jerusalem, supported by ʾElyāšîb II, the high priest, he was accused by the neighboring governors of rebellion against the king of Persia. When work began the governors took action and conspired to send troops to harry them. Nehemiah countered these devices by arming his workers, so that a worker "with one of his hands worked, and with the other grasped his weapon." Ultimately the walls were finished in fifty-two days of labor (Nehemiah 6:15), though work must have continued longer to complete the details of the fortifications, and a service of dedication was held with processions and singing to the sound of harps and cymbals. With his primary task completed, Nehemiah returned to the Persian king in 433 B.C.E., leaving his brother behind to rule in his stead. On his return he appears to have carried out a number of reform measures: enforcing the payment of tithes for the benefit of Levite and singer and preventing the violation of the Sabbath, including the hawking of merchandise by Phoenicians on the Sabbath. Like Ezra, he attempted to put an end to foreign marriages, a perennial problem, it appears. The final words of his Memoirs are these: "Thus I cleansed them from all that was foreign. . . . Remember me O my God, for good."[76]

The Memoirs of Nehemiah here briefly summarized must have been composed and circulated in the late fifth century. Toward 400 B.C.E. a final editor combined the Nehemiah Memoirs with the Chronicler's Work (Chr_2), and otherwise edited the whole. Again darkness falls so far as the Bible is concerned, and the history of the fourth century remains a virtual blank until the advent of Alexander III (the Great) of Macedon.

76. Neh. 13:30–31. It is often said that it is unlikely that great Ezra so failed in his reform that Nehemiah was required to institute a similar reform. But in the Bible the great leaders, Moses and the prophets, regularly fail, or to take a closer analogy, the Deuteronomistic reforms of Hezekiah and Josiah certainly were short lived. Moreover, laws against intermarriage are notoriously difficult to enforce in any age.

9

Samaria and Jerusalem in the Era of the Restoration

I

IN 722 B.C.E. THE CITY OF SAMARIA FELL AFTER A PROLONGED SIEGE to the forces of Shalmaneser V of Assyria, effectively bringing an end to the northern kingdom of Israel.[1] Earlier, in the course of his western campaign of 734–732 B.C.E. Tiglath-pileser III had dismembered the kingdom of Israel, creating three Assyrian provinces from portions of its territory: Gilead, Megiddo (including Galilee), and Dor, leaving a reduced district of Samaria as a subject kingdom under native vassal king Hoshea. Hoshea, shortly after the death of Tiglath-pileser, rose in revolt against the new king of Assyria, Shalmaneser V. Hoshea was taken captive, probably in 724, shortly before or after Shalmaneser invested the city of Samaria. The fall of the city in the late summer or early fall of 722 is described by the Deuteronomistic historian (2 Kings 17:6–23) as the occasion for the deportation of her citizens to Assyria and Media, the final punishment for Israel's apostasy and violations of the law of God. To judge from the records of Sargon II, Israel's last days were somewhat drawn out. Shalmaneser V lived only a few months after the fall of the city, dying in the winter of 722 B.C.E., and the task of taking Israel captive fell largely to his son Sargon II. In 720, Sargon delivered the *coup de grâce* to the rebellious city and took captive, according to his claim, 27,280 people (or 27,290 according to a variant reading). It was Sargon II, too, who organized Samaria as an Assyrian province beginning in 720, and began the settlement of foreign peoples in Samaria and her daughter cities.[2]

The official name of the province was *Šōmĕrōn* (Hebrew), *Šāmĕrayn* in Aramaic (bibl. *Šāmĕrayin*, Ezra 4:10), in Assyrian *sa-me-re-na*/*šāmĕrên*/ (cf. Babylonian *ša-ma!-ra-ʾi-in*/*šāmĕrayn*/).[3] The Aramaic form is a typi-

1. 2 Kings 17:29 and the Babylonian Chronicle 1:27–28 (reading *ša-ma-ra-ʾi-in*). On the fall of Samaria to Shalmaneser, see the discussion of H. Tadmor, "The Campaigns of Sargon II of Assur," *JCS* 12 (1958): 22–40, 77–100, esp. 33–40.

2. This reconstruction of the events follows the definitive study of Tadmor, ibid.

3. From fourth-century B.C.E. Samaria come papyri and coins bearing the Aramaic name *šmryn*. Hebrew *šmrn* is found written in Palaeo-Hebrew on a bulla. See F. M.

cal back formation from the Hebrew *šōmĕrōn,* involving alternations of the locative suffix, Hebrew *-ōn,* Aramaic *-ayn* < *-ān.*[4] This designation is derived, of course, from the name of the city, the capital city of (northern) Israel founded by ʿOmri in the ninth century B.C.E. The gentilic, *šōmĕrōnîm,* found already in 2 Kings 17:29 referring to the inhabitants of Samaria, is found in the Greek Bible in the form *ΣΑΜΑΡΕΙΤΑΙ,* whence our term *Samaritans.* Later the term *Samaritan* came to be used of the religious community with its center at Shechem and Mount Gerizim, which, though Yahwistic—indeed fairly described as a Jewish sect—was separated from the Jews with their religious center in Jerusalem. This shift of meaning, from "inhabitants of the city or province of Samaria" to the denotation of a discrete religious community living in the district of Samaria, has led to confusion. To avoid the confusion of the term *Samaritan,* certain scholars have chosen to use the designation *Samarian* in the former sense, *Samaritan* in the latter, developed sense. However, historical usage dies hard; this distinction in terms is not generally observed, and is eschewed here.

II

The history of the province of Samaria after 722 B.C.E. was strongly shaped by the characteristic Assyrian policy of exchanging populations of defeated states. The account of the deportation of Israelites in 2 Kings 17 appears to assert that the entire population of the northern kingdom was sent into captivity. It is more than likely, however, that only the upper classes were deported, to judge from the analogy of the later captivity of Judah, and in view of the Chronicler's clear statement that a "remnant of Israel" existed in Samaria in the time of Josiah.[5] As noted above, Sargon himself claimed in his extant annals only to have taken captive 27,280 Israelite souls, a number to be compared with the calculations presumed in 2 Kings 15:19–20, where the nobility alone in the northern kingdom are reckoned at 60,000. The account in 2 Kings also telescopes into one event the series of importations of foreign peoples

---

Cross in *Discoveries in the Wâdī ed-Dâliyeh,* ed. Paul W. Lapp and Nancy L. Lapp, *AASOR* 41 (Cambridge: ASOR, 1974), 17–29 and pl. 61; and Y. Meshorer and S. Qedar, *The Coinage of Samaria in the Fourth Century B.C.E.* (Jerusalem: Numismatic Fine Arts International, 1991), 13–14, 45–48, 83 and nos. 1–22, pls. 1–3. In the papyri, there is a regular formula, *bšmryn qryt*ʾ *zy bšmryn mdynt*ʾ, 'in Samaria the city which is in Samaria the province.'

4. The use of the designation *šmrn/m,* 'keepers (of the law),' by Samaritan sectarians is late and secondary, a folk etymology derived through the (secondary) Aramaic gentilic *šāmĕrāʾin.*

5. 2 Chron. 34:9; cf. 2 Chron. 30:1–12.

into the province of Samaria. The biblical account mentions peoples of the cities of Babylon and Kutah (Cuthah) in southern Babylon, and of ʿAvvah, Ḥammat, and Sepharvaim in central Syria.[6] Sargon records the settlement of Arabian tribes in Samaria in 715 B.C.E.[7] The Book of Ezra also furnishes evidence that later Assyrian kings, Esarhaddon and Assurbanipal, introduced foreign peoples into the province of Samaria.[8] At all events the account of exchanges of population in 2 Kings has given rise to the later Jewish polemic which reckoned all Samaritans as foreigners and pagan in origin, and at best syncretistic in their worship of the god of Israel. Accordingly, later Jewish tradition comes to call the Samaritans *en bloc* Kutians (*kwtym*), or sardonically, "lion-proselytes" in light of the anecdote in 2 Kings 17:25–28.[9] For their part, the Samaritans of later times claimed to be the remnant of Ephraim and Manasseh, authentic Israelites who alone preserve the ancient faith and service of the god of Israel unsullied by Judaean innovations.

In fact, neither of these polemical positions can stand close critical scrutiny. On the one hand, there are very strong arguments to support the conclusion that the bulk of the men of Ephraim and Manasseh remained in the land; on the other hand, there is equally strong evidence (to be addressed below) that Samaritanism in the form that we find it in the Roman Age and later is not a survival of old Israelite religion, pure or syncretistic, but rather is essentially a sectarian form of Judaism.[10]

III

In the interval between the fall of Samaria and the destruction of Jerusalem in 587 B.C.E. there is little data concerning life in the Assyrian provinces.[11] The Chronicler preserves a record of Hezekiah's religious

6. 2 Kings 17:24, 30–31. Sepharvaim (*sprwym*, var. *sprym*), perhaps identical with *sbrym* of Ezek. 47:16, cannot be certainly identified.

7. *AR* 2:17 (p. 7). See Tadmor, "The Campaigns of Sargon II of Assur," 78 and 95. Further testimony to the importation of Arabs into Syria, notably into Hamath, is found in the two inscriptions of Taymāʾ that list the gods of Taymāʾ, including the god ʾAšîmaʾ. ʾAšîmaʾ is named in 2 Kings 17:30 as a god made by the people of Hamath. Evidently Arab tribesmen, transplanted to Hamath in accord with Assyrian practice, brought their god ʾAšîmaʾ with them. See F. M. Cross, "A New Aramaic Stele from Taymāʾ," *CBQ* 48 (1986): 387–394.

8. Esarhaddon is mentioned in a Hebrew fragment, Ezra 4:2; Assurbanipal is named in an Aramaic document, Ezra 4:10.

9. The Hebrew expression is *gry ʾrywt*.

10. Note that the overwhelming majority of names in the Samaria Papyri of the fourth century B.C.E. are Yahwistic or names used in common with Jews.

11. From Assyrian eponyms we know the names of Nabû-kēna-uṣur, governor of Samaria in 690 B.C.E., Nabû-šar-aḫḫēšu, governor of Samaria in 646, and Issi-adad-

reforms (and rebellion against Assyria) which describes an attempt to rally the Israelites of the entire North and to bring them to Jerusalem to celebrate the Passover.[12] Until recently, many scholars have been inclined to dismiss the Chronicler's account of the reform of Hezekiah as unhistorical, at least in large part, in view of its absence in the Deuteronomistic record of Hezekiah's reign, suggesting that it is a fabrication of the Chronicler, a reflex of the reform of Josiah. A gradual accumulation of archaeological and literary-historical evidence pertaining to the reigns of Hezekiah and Josiah and our sources for them is now shifting our perspective.[13] It seems increasingly likely that the Chronicler's report is based on a historical source, and that the Deuteronomistic historian's laconic report of Hezekiah's reform is motivated by his desire to magnify the importance of Josiah's reform, the climax of his history.[14] Certainly Hezekiah, like Josiah after him, was involved in an open revolt against Assyria, and like Josiah after him had pretensions of reestablishing the Davidic empire. The religious dimension of such a political revival and program quite naturally would have been expressed in the celebration of the chief covenant festival of old, united Israel.

According to the Chronicler's account, the invitation to the covenant festival of Passover in Jerusalem was proclaimed throughout the North, in "Ephraim and Manasseh even unto Zebulon." Many scorned the call, but "men from Asher and Manasseh and Zebulon" rallied in Jerusalem (2 Chronicles 30:11). Noteworthy is the omission of Ephraim, the heartland of Samaria; however, later we are told of "many of Ephraim,

---

anēnu, governor of Megiddo in 679. See *RLA* 2:449, 451, 455. For reviews of the history of this period, see R. J. Coggins, *Samaritans and Jews: The Origins of Samaritanism Reconsidered* (Atlanta: John Knox, 1975), 13–37; F. Dexinger, "Der Ursprung der Samaritaner im Spiegel der Frühen Quellen," in *Die Samaritaner,* ed. F. Dexinger and R. Pummer (Darmstadt: Wissenschaftliche Buchgesellschaft, 1992), 67–140; and especially M. Cogan, *Imperialism and Religion: Assyria, Judah, and Israel in the Eighth and Seventh Centuries* B.C.E. (Missoula, Mont.: Scholars Press, 1974), 100–110. Note that the provinces were ruled by Assyrian governors.

12. 2 Chron. 30:1–11, 18.

13. See, for example, the paper of J. Rosenbaum, "Hezekiah's Reform and the Deuteronomistic Tradition," *HTR* 72 (1979): 232–243 and references. S. Japhet has traced the history of the scholarly discussion of the reliability of the Chronicler in "The Historical Reliability of Chronicles: The History of the Problem and Its Place in Biblical Research," *JSOT* 33 (1985): 83–107 and bibliography (unhappily she has missed Rosenbaum's article). See also her discussion of the reform of Hezekiah in Japhet, *The Ideology of the Book of Chronicles and Its Place in Biblical Thought,* trans. Anna Springer (Frankfurt am Main: Peter Lang, 1989), 934–936.

14. Our reference is to the historian of the seventh century (Dtr_1). See *CMHE,* 274–289.

Manasseh, Issachar, and Zebulon" who though ritually unclean ate the Passover in Jerusalem (2 Chronicles 30:18). In short, the response of the North was mixed at best. The account presumes the presence in the northern provinces, including Samaria, of a large Israelite population. The reasons for their refusal to join Hezekiah in the Passover and, we should add, in repudiation of their Assyrian overlords, is left unclear in Chronicles. The Chronicler himself may have attributed their refusal to impiety; the actual historical circumstances may have been more complex.[15] After all, the Yahwistic shrines of the North persisted, and fears of Assyria would have been justified as Hezekiah's later, catastrophic defeat by the Assyrians proves. What is remarkable is the invitation and the partial response.

Josiah in the seventh century B.C.E. proved much more successful—if we are to believe the Deuteronomist—in rallying the North to his banner. To be sure, Assyrian power swiftly waned in the last days of Assurbanipal and in the chaotic years that followed his reign.[16] In 2 Chronicles 34:3–7 there is an account of Josiah's first reform activities in the northern provinces, dated to his twelfth regnal year, 628 B.C.E. The date follows hard on the abdication of Assurbanipal and the collapse of Assyrian authority in the west.[17] Inasmuch as these early efforts of Josiah presume the exercise of political power in the northern provinces including at least Samaria and Galilee (Megiddo), it seems that the king and his party were engaged in annexing the North. The major thrust of Josiah's politico-religious program came in 622 B.C.E., the eighteenth year of his reign. 2 Kings 23:15–20 describes measures of control taken in the province of Samaria, notably the defilement and destruction of the sanctuary of Bethel, which until this time had continued to function as a Yahwistic sanctuary. Discoveries at Yabneh-yam, notably a letter to the Judean military commander, tend to confirm the Chronicler's picture of the early date and extensiveness of Josiah's expansionist moves. The letter dates palaeographically to ca. 625 B.C.E., and the site itself must be reckoned a military outpost, protecting Josiah's flank against Assyria's sometime

15. The passage cannot be read in light of later materials in Ezra-Nehemiah, I believe, since the latter belong in a later edition of the Chronicler's history. See below.

16. The precise chronology of the end of Assurbanipal's reign continues to be debated.

17. See F. M. Cross and D. N. Freedman, "Josiah's Revolt against Assyria," *JNES* 12 (1953): 56–58. While our chronology of the last days of Assyria must be updated, we still hold to the general argument of the paper. For a contrary view, see most recently, Nadav Na'aman, "The Kingdom of Judah under Josiah," *TA* 18 (1991): 3–71. Na'aman gives no real explanation for the *threefold* character of the Chronicler's chronological notices (2 Chron. 34:3–8) marking the putative shifts in Judean political policy.

vassal and ally to the south, Saite Egypt.[18] Despite recent arguments to the contrary, I believe that the weight of the evidence is still on the side of scholars who follow the notice in 2 Chronicles 35:20–24 that Josiah died in battle at Megiddo against Necho II. The Israelite city was in Josiah's hands, and it was the strategic site at which to block the Egyptian march north to succor Assyria. In all this we must perceive Josiah's grand aims to reassert the ancient claim of the house of David to the territories of northern Israel, and to establish Jerusalem as the national cultic center of all Israel.

Whereas Josiah's attempts to restore the glory of David and Zion fell short of success, later events give some reason to believe that his religious program found response in Samaria and the North. A fragmentary notice found in Jeremiah 41:3–6 may provide one such testimony. Here we read of "men from Shechem, from Shiloh, and from Samaria, eighty in number," bearing offerings "to the house of the Lord," that is, to the destroyed sanctuary in Jerusalem. Most of these men fell into a trap set by the Davidid Ishmael and were foully murdered, presumably in connection with the overthrow of Gedaliah, the governor of the new Babylonian province of Judah. The motivation of the murders is obscure, but it is apparently unrelated to the intention of the northerners to worship

18. See F. M. Cross, "The Murabbaʿât Papyrus and the Letter Found Near Yabneh-yam," *BASOR* 165 (1962): 34–46, esp. 42 and bibliography. A revised version of this paper will appear shortly in my collected papers in epigraphy and palaeography. It should be stressed that on palaeographical grounds the letter cannot be dated later than the mid-reign of Josiah. It does not date—as Naʾaman seems to believe—to the close of the reign of Josiah or the reigns of his successors Jehoahaz and Jehoiakim at the end of the century. It belongs to the period when Assyrian authority over Judah and the west was collapsing and the Saites, now freed from vassalage to Assyria, were consolidating their sole rule in Egypt, before Necho II's ambitious military campaigns into Syria-Palestine. It is the time when Josiah and his nationalistic party, in the interval when they were independent of dominance by a foreign power, first began to pursue their ambitions to restore the glory of United Israel. This calls into question Naʾaman's contention ("The Kingdom of Judah under Josiah") that the fort at Yabneh-yam was an Egyptian bastion—though manned primarily by Judahite soldiers and corvée workers.

Similarly, I believe that the most parsimonious reading of the notices of Josiah's death in Kings and Chronicles is that Josiah was killed in an action hostile to Necho. Naʾaman posits here (and elsewhere) that the Chronicler invented a story to illustrate his doctrine of retribution. Is it not sufficient that Josiah was killed? While it is true that the Chronicler frequently distorts history to serve his ideological purposes, he does it with some subtlety. He had sources not used by the Deuteronomist and only rarely makes up his history out of whole cloth. For example, his description of the reform of Hezekiah, despite its problems, is certainly superior historically to the laconic description of the reform of Hezekiah written by the Deuteronomist.

in Jerusalem. The account is revealing, however, of the attachment of Israelites of Ephraim and Manasseh to the sanctuary in Jerusalem. Some have seen in this episode merely the response of faithful Israelites who continued to maintain a loyalty to Jerusalem, nourished in certain circles in the North throughout the centuries of the Divided Kingdom. Alternatively, the episode can be taken to reflect the Davidic ideology freshly espoused and promulgated by Hezekiah and in the reform movement of Josiah. One should remember too that in the prophetic literature of the seventh and sixth centuries, the prophets frequently express hopes of the reunion of the North and South in a future Israel. There is no suggestion that the Israelites of the North had ceased to exist or had become irredeemable owing to alien blood.[19]

IV

The return of the Jews to Jerusalem under the decree of Cyrus (538 B.C.E.) set the stage for a new era in the relations of Judah and Samaria.[20] The first period of the Restoration to Zion is little known. Cyrus, in a decree of his first year, ordered the rebuilding of the Temple in Jerusalem and the return of the sacred vessels of the First Temple taken by Nebuchadrezzar. With Sheshbazzar (Sin-ab-uṣur[21]), very prob-

19. See the detailed discussion of Coggins, *Samaritans and Jews,* 28–57.

20. See Ezra 1:1 and 6:3; 2 Chron. 36:22–23.

21. The *ššbṣr* of the Massoretic Text (Ezra 1:8, 11 and 5:14, 16) must be compared with the spelling of the Greek versions. The development of controls on the Old Greek translations stemming from the evidence of the Qumrân scrolls requires that we make careful use of their witness. 1 Esdras's reading in A and its congeners appears to be the least corrupt form of the name (so far as the significant consonants go): Sanabassar; Josephus, *Antiquities* 11:93 also has Sanabasar alongside other variants; in 2 Esdras the B family reads Sabanasar, with metathesis of *beta* and *nu.* These readings point to a Hebrew *Vorlage šnbṣr* reflecting Akk. *Sin-ab-uṣur.* The name Sin-ab-uṣur follows a familiar pattern, a prayer for protection of the father: "O Sin, protect the father." It should be noted that the divine name is syntactically a vocative. As pointed out to me by John Huehnergard, the name Sin-ab-uṣur, written [1d] 30-AD-PAB appears in Assyrian; see T. Kwasman and Simo Parpola, *State Archives of Assyria* 6 (Helsinki: Helsinki University Press, 1991), 334.

In recent years it has been suggested that the original name was Šašš-ab-uṣur or the like. Cf. P. R. Berger, "Zu den Namen שנאצר und ששבצר," *ZAW* 83 (1971): 98–100; P. E. Dion, "*ššbṣr* and *ssnwry,*" *ZAW* 95 (1983): 111–112; J. Blenkinsopp, *Ezra-Nehemiah: A Commentary* (Philadelphia: Westminster, 1988), 79; Baruch Halpern, "A Historiographic Commentary on Ezra 1–6: Chronological Narrative and Dual Chronology in Israelite Historiography," in *The Hebrew Bible and Its Interpreters,* ed. W. H. Propp, B. Halpern, and D. N. Freedman (Winona Lake, Ind.: Eisenbrauns, 1990), 91–92. The element *Šamaš* in the name, however, would normally not appear in the assimilated form (*šaššu* < *šamšu*), since it is a vocative (or a frozen form) in a name of this type.

ably a prince of the Davidic house, at their head, a group of Jews from the Babylonian captivity made their way back to Jerusalem. Sheshbazzar in Ezra 1:8 is called "the prince of Judah" (*han-nāśîʾ lîhûdāh*), a title pointing at once to his Davidic lineage and to his headship of the Jewish community.[22] In Ezra 5:14, in a later Aramaic document, he is said to be governor (*pēḥāh*) appointed by Cyrus. The latter title, "governor" or "governor of Judah" (*paḥat Yĕhūdāh*)[23] is also given to Zerubbabel his nephew, if our argument above is correct, and, in any case, his successor.[24] There has been a tendency for historians to question the reliability of the biblical notices that imply that Judah (*Yĕhūd*) in the time of Sheshbazzar and Zerubbabel was an independent province under local Jewish administration. Albrecht Alt in his influential paper[25] argued that Jerusalem (and what remained of Judah) actually belonged to the province

---

The assimilation of *m* or *w* before *š* in late Babylonian takes place when it is at syllable end (*GAG* § 31f). In fact, from the Greek transcription of such names, we know that the form was pronounced *šawaš* (Gr. Σαϝας), Aram. *šwš*. Cf. the seal of *Šawaš-šar-uṣur* published by N. Avigad, "Seals of Exiles," *IEJ* 15 (1965): 228 ff. Thus the comparison with Tell Faḫariyeh *ssnwry*, "Sass(u) is my light," Assyrian ¹UTU-ZÁLAG, is not persuasive.

In 1 Chron. 3:18, we find the name of the Davidid, uncle of Zerubbabel, spelled *šnʾṣr*. Already Eduard Meyer proposed the identity of *ššbṣr* and *šnʾṣr*. Both easily arise from the corruption of the name *Šin-(ʾ)ab(ʾ)uṣur*. Alternatively, we may take it as an abbreviated form of a three-element name: *Šin-uṣur* for *Šin-ab-uṣur*. Compare the examples of such abbreviation of three-element names to two (of the same person) listed by J. J. Stamm, *Die akkadischen Namengebung* (Leipzig: J. C. Hinrichs, 1959), § 13b.

The practice of the Persian administration to appoint governors from local royal or noble houses is well known. Sheshbazzar should be a Davidid, and Shinazar falls at precisely the proper place in the Davidic genealogy. The corruption of Babylonian names in the biblical text is not unusual; for example, Assurbanipal (Aššur-bān-apli) survives as *ʾsnpr* (Ezra 4:10). Note also that the spelling *šin* for the first letter of the divine name Sin, normal in West Semitic transcriptions of Assyrian, is found also in Babylonian names. Compare *šin-ʾab-uṣur* (RÉS 1791.2), *šnsrṣr*, *šnzrbn* (Sin-zer-ibni), etc. See R. Zadok, *On the West Semites in Babylonia during the Chaldean and Achaemenian Periods* (Jerusalem: Tel Aviv University, 1977), 43, 277 (§ 1111.262, n. 7).

22. In premonarchical times, *nāśîʾ* refers chiefly to tribal heads; it is used of the Davidic prince especially in Ezekiel. In fact, Ezekiel uses the term as equivalent to *melek*, and in Ezek. 40–48 it is the (theologically) preferred designation of the future Davidic ruler. See J. D. Levenson, *Theology of the Program of Restoration of Ezekiel 40–48*, *HSM* 10 (Missoula, Mont.: Scholars Press, 1976), 55–107. "The prince of Judah" must be read in light of these developments in the Exilic and post-Exilic community.

23. Hag. 1:1, 14 and 2:2, 21; Ezra 6:7 (*pḥt yhwdyʾ*).

24. It is, of course, also applied later to Nehemiah, and in the Elephantine papyri (*AP* 30:1, 32:1) to Bagoas. For its use on stamps, see below.

25. "Die Rolle Samarias bei der Entstehung des Judenthums," *Kleine Schriften* 2 (Munich: Beck, 1953), 316–337.

of Samaria and was administered by the governor of Samaria.[26] In such circumstances, he claimed, much of the opposition which harassed the Jews of the Return, which delayed their attempts to rebuild temple and city, and which stood implacably against the full refortification of Jerusalem could be explained as the legitimate interference of the Samaritan authorities determined to prevent Jewish envoys or commissioners with limited mandates from exceeding their authority. A series of discoveries of official stamps, seals, and bullae has now provided evidence against such a reconstruction. Most decisive are seals and stamps belonging to the sixth century B.C.E. which bear the name of a governor, his title, "the governor," with or without the name of the province, *Yĕhūd*. Most important are a bulla and seal, the former with the inscription "Elnatan the governor" and the latter with the legend "Shelomit, handmaid of Elnatan the governor," published by N. Avigad.[27] This belongs to a homogeneous hoard of sixth-century bullae and seals which include other official sealings of the province of Judah. Earlier finds include other official sealings of the province of Judah: "Yĕhōʿezer the governor" and "ʾAḥzay the governor." Avigad, in an exemplary discussion of these and related finds, places these governors of Judah in the interval immediately following Zerubbabel, before the appointment of Nehemiah in 445 B.C.E. Certainly they cannot be later. The seals of Elnatan and Shelomith his handmaid could on palaeographical grounds be placed in the early sixth century; however, historical considerations suggest that Elnatan is best fitted into the sequence of governors—he is not a Davidid—shortly or immediately following Zerubbabel,[28] probably the last of the Persian governors of Judah to be drawn from the house of David.[29]

There is little reason to doubt, in view of the present evidence, that Sheshbazzar returned to Zion as governor of Judah intending to rebuild the temple and reorganize the province. Nor is there reason to doubt that

26. Morton Smith was among the few who protested, justly if somewhat intemperately, that Alt's reconstruction was a skein of surmises and logic with no data to give substance. See his *Palestinian Parties and Politics That Shaped the Old Testament* (New York: Columbia University Press, 1971), 193–201.

27. N. Avigad, *Bullae and Seals from a Post-Exilic Archive, Qedem* 4 (Jerusalem: Hebrew University, 1976). See also E. M. Meyers, "The Shelomith Seal and the Judean Restoration: Some Additional Considerations," *EI* 18 (1985): 33*–38*.

28. As Avigad has observed, the title of Shelomit, "handmaid of Elnatan the governor," suggests that she is an official in the provincial administration. If she is an official and presumably, therefore, highborn, it is tempting to identify her with Zerubbabel's sister (1 Chron. 3:19). While the name is not common in this period, the identification is only a possibility.

29. I do not find the argument for Nehemiah's Davidic origins persuasive. See Ulrich Kellerman, *Nehemiah: Quellen, Überlieferung, und Geschichte, BZAW* 102 (Berlin, 1967).

he failed in his primary mission. It is clearly recorded that opponents blocked efforts to build the temple "until the second year of Darius."[30] The adversaries of the Jews in the era of Nehemiah when the walls of Jerusalem were finally built are precisely specified: Sanballat, governor of Samaria; Tobiah, the Jewish governor of Ammon; Geshem (*Gašmu*), king of the Arab league of Qedar; and probably the governor of the province of Ashdod.[31] That is to say, the rulers of all the surrounding provinces and their allies opposed the initiatives of Nehemiah, no doubt feeling threatened by the possibility of a resurgent Judah with a powerfully fortified Jerusalem at its center. Our records suggest that Sanballat the Samaritan governor took the lead in rallying these adversaries;[32] however, Tobiah played a considerable role, and Gashmu was active in the conspiracy. Sanballat is reported as having sent a letter stating that it is "common talk"—and Gashmu subscribes to it—that Nehemiah and the Jews think to rebel, and that Nehemiah plans to be proclaimed king.[33] The threat was perceived by the allied governors as a political threat to their own regimes. There is no hint of a religious quarrel with the Samaritans in these particular encounters recorded in the Nehemiah memoirs.

In the Aramaic document found in Ezra 4:7–24 and in 1 Esdras 2:15–25,[34] we read of a letter from the Samaritan administration of Mithredat and Ṭab'el, composed by Reḥum the "drafter of the document," *bĕʿēl ṭĕʿēm*,[35] and written by the scribe Shimshay to the king of Persia. An interesting and significant feature of the document, as recognized by Hayim Tadmor, is the claim of the officials of Samaria to be descendants of deportees from Babylon, Erech, and Susa [that is, Elamites], and accordingly, proper "Persians."[36] The placement of the document in 1 Esdras

30. Ezra 4:5 says, "all the days of Cyrus king of Persia until the reign of Darius the King." Cf. 1 Esdras 5:70 (1 Esdras is cited after the Göttingen edition of R. Hanhart here and elsewhere). See also Ezra 4:24; 1 Esdras 2:25.

31. In Neh. 43:1 the adversaries are listed as Sanballat and Tobiah, and the Arabians, the Ammonites, and Ashdodites. Elsewhere Gashmu (Geshem) is named. Votive inscriptions from Tell el-Masḫuṭah give his son's title as "king of Qedar," the Arab league which has displaced the Edomites and encroached well into the southern bounds of Judah. See above in chapter 8.

32. See esp. Neh. 2:10; 3:33–38; 4:1–2; 6:1–9.

33. Neh. 6:1–7.

34. Ezra 4:6, missing in 1 Esdras, has regularly been taken as evidence of a protest written to Xerxes by the opponents of the Jews of the Restoration. I am inclined to the view that Ezra 4:6 is a heading in Hebrew to the Aramaic document which follows, preserving a variant dating (to Xerxes rather than Artaxerxes).

35. This sense of *bʿl ṭʿm* was called to my attention by Jonas Greenfield. Mithredat and Ṭab'el are presumably the governor (*paḥat šmryn*) and prefect (*sgn'*), to judge by the analogy of the Samaria Papyri.

36. H. Tadmor, "qwwym ltwldwt šwmrwn lmn yyswdh wʿd hmqdwny," in *Eretz*

suggests that the editor[37] believed the document to belong to the time of Sheshbazzar—at least it follows immediately upon the Sheshbazzar account. The postscript in 1 Esdras 2:25, "and the building of the temple in Jerusalem ceased until the second year of Darius king of the Persians," suggests the same. The text of the document in 1 Esdras in addition refers to the activities of the Jews in these words: "They are building the rebellious and evil city, are repairing its markets and walls, and are laying the foundations of [its] temple."[38] On the basis of this reading one would be inclined to ascribe the document to the time of Sheshbazzar. There is every reason to believe that he did in fact engage in some building in the city until such time as his efforts were frustrated.[39] Against this placement of this document in the reign of Cyrus, Cambyses, or the beginning of Darius's reign, is the assignment of it in both Ezra and 1 Esdras to the reign of Artaxerxes. Usually scholars have assumed merely that it has been displaced in both 1 Esdras and Ezra, arguing that documents concerning adversaries have been grouped together by "subject matter," not by chronology. This argument does not account for the different orders in the two later editions of the Chronicler's Work, nor for the subscript, nor for the reference to the foundation of the temple in 1 Esdras. Alternately we can hold that the name of the Persian king—Artaxerxes or Xerxes—is a mistake. Josephus thought it a mistake and introduced his conjecture: Cambyses.[40] Josephus, much aware of the confusion of the Persian chronology in the biblical record here and elsewhere, reconstructs his own chronology. His ascription of the document to the time of Cambyses is thus based not on a reading in a document before him in all likelihood, but on his own guess. He then calculates that the building

Shomron, Thirtieth Archaeological Convention, September 1972, ed. J Aviram (Jerusalem: IES, 1973), 67–74, esp. 73.

37. The editor is Chr_2 in my analysis of the editions of Chronicles-Ezra-Nehemiah. See above, chapter 8, for details. See also the studies of H. G. M. Williamson, "The Composition of Ezra i–vi," *JTS* n.s. 34 (1983): 1–30, and Halpern, "A Historiographic Commentary on Ezra 1–6," 81–142.

38. 1 Esdras 2:17. The parallel text, Ezra 4:12 is certainly corrupt. Compare the reconstructed *Vorlage* of 1 Esdras with the text of Ezra 4:12:

bnyn šwqyh	*wšwry'*	*mšklln*	*w'šy hykl'*	*yhbn*	(1 Esdras)
bnyn	*šwry'*	*škllw*	*w'šyh*	*yḥyṭw*	(Ezra)

Note that we have reconstructed an early orthography. Perfects are to be avoided in view of the contexts (1 Esdras 2:18, Ezra 4:13); clearly *šwqyh* has been lost by haplography, and probably *hykl'* as well (note the sequence of letters *y h*[*ḥ*] *y* repeated). Josephus also reads *hykl'* and has generally the text of 1 Esdras (*Antiq.* 11:22).

39. See Ezra 5:16 and 1 Esdras 6:19. Compare Hag. 1:4; 2:15–18; Zech. 1:16; 4:8; 8:9. Also see above, chapter 8.

40. *Antiq.* 11:21–30.

of the city and temple were stopped nine years before the resumption in the second year of Darius. Josephus's notion that the Rehum document is early, however, may be superior to most scholarly reconstructions. Elsewhere there is clear evidence both of the superiority of the text of 1 Esdras in certain readings and of the ordering of the Ezra narrative.[41]

Much ink has been spilled in discussing the relations between Jews and Samaritans in the era of Zerubbabel. Two passages in Ezra record attempts to block the program of Zerubbabel, Joshua the high priest, and the community returned from captivity—especially the plan to rebuild the Temple. In Ezra 5:1–6:15 an independent unit of tradition composed in Aramaic[42] tells the story of an investigation by Tattenai, "the governor of ʿAbar-Nahara," and Shethar-bozenai into the authority by which the Jews undertake rebuilding of the Temple. In a letter to Darius, the officials of the satrapy recount the claim of the Jews that authority was granted by Cyrus to Sheshbazzar, who first laid the foundations of their Temple. Darius, we are told, directed a search and found a record of Cyrus's decree. Accordingly he wrote back requiring the Persian officials to support actively the Jewish community in their enterprise. No doubt the inquiry of the Persian governor was requested by the opponents of Zerubbabel and his government closer to home, presumably officials of a neighboring province or provinces. We may suspect that the officials of Samaria were party, but there is no such statement in the document.

A second obscure passage describes "adversaries of Judah and Benjamin." It is found in Ezra 4:1–5 prefacing the section dealing with adversaries (Ezra 4:1–6:15); in 1 Esdras it is found immediately before the Aramaic document described above (1 Esdras 5:63–70). These adversaries, who are said to describe themselves as descendants of an importation of Esarhaddon, who have long sacrificed to the god of the Jews, request permission to join Zerubbabel in building the Temple. Such permission is denied. There follows the comment that the "people of the land" took various measures to hinder and frustrate the returned exiles in their attempt to build the House of God in Jerusalem. These "adversaries of Judah and Benjamin" and "people of the land" have been identified in tradition and by many scholars with the Samaritans. Josephus is very explicit in this identification.[43] A recent writer has remarked that "if this section is intended to be anti-Samaritan, it is remarkably allusive."[44] Others have taken "the people of the land" to be residents of

41. See below.

42. Note the envelope construction: the passage opens and closes with the prophesying of Haggai and Zechariah.

43. *Antiq.* 11:84–86.

44. Coggins, *Samaritans and Jews,* 66.

Judah of foreign, mixed, or doubtful lineage; still others—regarding the reference to Esarhaddon's importation as a secondary intrusion—have identified the rivals with Jewish residents of the land in contrast with the Jewish community returned from captivity.[45] The problems of the passage are complex, and firm conclusions as to the precise identity of the adversaries cannot be drawn. There is to be found in the passage in any case a reluctance to mix foreigners with sacred things, comparable to the polemic in Ezra against the "holy seed" mingling with foreigners.

The original Chronicler's Work (Chr_1),[46] together with the books of Haggai and First Zechariah, furnish our best evidence for the character of Jewish-Samaritan relations in the era of Zerubbabel and Joshua. The ideology of the early Chronicler takes up anew the old royal ideology of the Judaean kings—chosen David, chosen Zion—as that ideology was expressed in the seventh-century edition of the Deuteronomistic history,[47] reformulated in Ezekiel 40–48 and especially in the oracles of Haggai and Zechariah. In Haggai and Zechariah, king and high priest constitute a diarchy: son of David, son of Zadok. Zerubbabel is called "my servant" by Yahweh and told "[I] will make thee as a signet; for

45. The parallel passage in 1 Esdras reads τὰ δὲ ἔθνη τῆς γῆς (*ʿmy hʾrṣ*), a frequent usage in Ezra and Nehemiah. This reading clearly points to foreign peoples resident in the land.

46. The first edition of the Chronicler's Work (Chr_1), in my present view, included the nucleus of the genealogies of chapters 1–9. The original genealogies evidently ended at the Exile—so did the salient genealogy of the high priestly house (contrast Neh. 12). Certainly the Davidic genealogy in chapter 3 has secondarily been brought up to date (to about 400) by Chr_3 with the addition of vv. 17–24. Chr_1 included also 1 Chron. 10:1 through 2 Chron. 36:21 (aside from touches of later editing) plus the continuing Hebrew material reflected in Ezra 1:1–3:13 (1 Esdras 2:1–15 and 5:11–6:2). It ends with the climax in the celebration of the dedication of the altar and the foundation of the Second Temple—looking ahead to the full restitution of Israel's primary institutions centering in the house of David and the house of Yahweh. For a detailed discussion of the editions of the Chronicler, see above, chapter 8.

47. There is every evidence that the Chronicler used only the Josianic edition of the Deuteronomistic Work. See my comments already in "Samaria and Jerusalem: The Early History of the Samaritans and Their Relations with the Jews (722–64 B.C.E.)" [šwmrwn wyrwšlym: twldwt hšwmrwnym wyḥsyhm ʿm hyhwdym], in *The World History of the People of Israel: The Restoration—The Persian Period* [*hhysṭwryh šl ʿm yśrʾl: šybt ṣywn ymy šlṭwn prs*], ed. Hayim Tadmor (Jerusalem: Alexander Peli, 1983), 272, n. 30; and more recently S. L. McKenzie, *The Chronicler's Use of the Deuteronomistic History, HSM* 33 (Atlanta: Scholars Press, 1984); B. Halpern and D. Vanderhooft, "The Editions of Kings in the 7th–6th Centuries B.C.E.," *HUCA* 62 (1991): 179–244. A number of scholars have recognized the Chronicler's departure from the themes of the Exilic Deuteronomist but have attributed this departure to the doctrinal bias of the Chronicler; this analysis may be true in part, but it is also based on his use of Dtr_1, which lent itself perfectly to his purpose.

I have chosen thee."[48] In chapter 3 of Zechariah, Joshua the priest is crowned and robed for office in the prophet's vision. The angel of the Lord announces: "Hear now, O Joshua the high priest, you and your fellows who sit before you . . . for behold I shall bring my servant the Branch."[49] In Chr_1 "the parallel between the first building of the temple under the direction of David (and Solomon), and the second building under Zerubbabel is too striking to be accidental, and must have formed part of the original structure of the work."[50] In short the original Chronicler's Work was designed to support the program for the restoration of the kingdom under Zerubbabel, the rebuilding of the Temple, and the reestablishment of its cultus under Joshua. Chr_1 in my view reached only to Ezra 3:13 (1 Esdras 5:62), with the celebration of the founding of the Second Temple. The future is open, and the work of restoring the ancient institutions is well begun; all is anticipation. Here the Chronicler's Work, properly a programmatic or propagandistic work, finds its social context and logical close.[51]

The Chronicler's presentation of the northern kingdom is crucial for our understanding of the status of relations between the Israelites surviving in the provinces of Samaria and the North, and the Jewish community in Jerusalem led by recently returned Jews of the captivity. Scholars have observed that the Chronicler omits systematic treatment of the northern dynasties to concentrate on the glories of the house of David.

48. Hag. 2:23.

49. Zech. 3:8; cf. 4:14.

50. D. N. Freedman, "The Chronicler's Purpose," *CBQ* 23 (1961): 439 f.

51. Several recent studies of the Chronicler have attempted to cut off the Chronicler's Work at 2 Chron. 36:21, before the announcement of the Cyrus decree (2 Chron. 36:22–23; Ezra 1:1–3aα). See the important volumes of H. G. M. Williamson, *Israel in the Books of Chronicles* (Cambridge: Cambridge University Press, 1977), and Sara Japhet, *The Ideology of the Book of Chronicles and Its Place in Biblical Thought,* and her commentary, *I & II Chronicles,* Old Testament Library (Louisville: Westminster–John Knox, 1993). Contrast the arguments of Freedman in "The Chronicler's Purpose" and my paper "A Reconstruction of the Judaean Restoration," *Interpretation* 29 (1975): 187–203, elaborated above in chapter 8, and the recent discussion of Blenkinsopp, *Ezra-Nehemiah,* 48–54.

I find nothing in the argumentation of Japhet and Williamson that inclines me to suppose that the Chronicler ended his history at the close of the Exile, but wrote his history more than a century later. To my mind, the Chronicler's Work promulgates a program—a characteristic of most if not all ancient Near Eastern historiography. Further, it would be decidedly strange, if not absurd, if the author wrote long after the Exile, not to bring the review of history up to date. Later the Work was indeed brought up to date, in my opinion, by a second edition (Chr_2), which appended the Ezra Narrative, a stage reflected in the *Vorlage* of 1 Esdras, and finally in an edition (Chr_3) which reworked the whole corpus and inserted the Nehemiah Memoirs. For detail, see above, chapter 8, and the classical studies of S. Mowinckel, *Studien zu dem Buche Ezra-Nehemiah,* 3 vols. (Oslo: Universitets forlaget, 1964).

This has been taken to mean that the Chronicler views Israel as essentially the tribes of Judah and Benjamin, a view clearly reflected in the Ezra and Nehemiah histories incorporated in later editions of his work. Closer inspection of the Chronicler's treatment of northern Israel renders this judgment false.[52] By omitting much of the Deuteronomistic historian's material on the northern monarchy, he also omits its main thrust, the sustained polemic against northern apostasy and idolatry.[53] The peroration of 2 Kings 17:7–11 on the occasion of the fall of Samaria, which rings the changes on the sins of Jeroboam and the North, is omitted in Chronicles; the account of the importation of foreign peoples in 2 Kings 17:24–41 is also passed over by the Chronicler. Surely if the Chronicler sought material for an anti-Samaritan polemic, or rationale for an exclusionist ideology, he could have found them here. Evidently he did not choose to dwell on such matters. His end was to lure the North back to Jerusalem and David, not to exclude them. The speech of Ahijah in 2 Chronicles 13:4–12 has been reckoned by some as an anti-Samaritan addition of the Chronicler. In the speech the sins of Jeroboam are denounced: his rebellion, his cultus, and his rejection of the Aaronid priesthood and Levites. On the other hand, the speech argues that the rule of all Israel was given forever to David and his sons by a covenant of salt, and ends with the cry, "O children of Israel, fight not against Yahweh the god of your fathers; for you will not prosper." The speech is more easily read, not as anti-Samaritan polemic, but as a call to Israel to return to their legitimate king and legitimate cultus of Jerusalem and its priesthood.

The Chronicler's presentation of the activities of Hezekiah and Josiah positively supports the view that he looked to the reestablishment of the united kingdom of Israel and Judah ruled from Zion, a hope framed not in terms of apocalyptic consummation but in terms of an immediate political reality. The description of Hezekiah's overtures to all Israel (from Beersheba to Dan) in 2 Chronicles 30:5–11, 18 presumes that the North was populated by Israelites, some of whom responded, including men of Asher, Manasseh, Zebulon (vv. 11, 18), and Ephraim (v. 18). In the description of Josiah's winning back of the northern provinces in 2 Chronicles 34, the Chronicler adds to the notices of 2 Kings that the contributions for refurbishing the house of the Lord were gathered from

52. See esp. Williamson, *Israel in the Books of Chronicles*, pt. 2.

53. Allusions to sins of the North are, of course, not wholly omitted in the Chronicler's account, including in his special materials. In addition to Ahijah's speech in 2 Chron. 13:4–12, to be discussed below, see 2 Chron. 20:35–37, 25:7, 20, etc. 2 Chron. 28:9–15 is a remarkable passage which presents a most evenhanded account of the hostile act of Israel against Judean "brethren," and at the same time singles out certain heads of the Ephraimites for praise.

"the land of Manasseh and Ephraim, and of all the remnant of Israel" as well as all Judah and Benjamin.

If we are correct in seeing in the Chronicler's Work, and in the prophecies of Haggai and Zechariah, support for the restoration of all Israel, north and south, under the kingship of Zerubbabel, scion of David, we must suppose that the provincial authorities of Samaria and the other surrounding provinces must have responded with fear, and initiated moves to quell any such revival before it gained momentum. However weak Zerubbabel and his support in Judah and the North may have been, the governor of Samaria and his fellows in the neighboring capitals would have had clear memories of Jerusalem's earlier hegemony. Less than a century earlier, Josiah ruled over the territories of the provinces of Samaria and Megiddo and, at least, portions of the territory of Ashdod and the domain of the Arabs. Above we have examined evidence that Sheshbazzar's earlier attempts to rebuild were frustrated, and the documents in Ezra reflecting opposition to Zerubbabel. The full story of Zerubbabel's end is unfortunately not known. He disappears from history to be replaced—so far as our documentation goes—with non-Davidic governors of Judah. Official seals and sealings (labeled *Yĕhūd*) of the period between Zerubbabel and Nehemiah, that is, in the period from the late sixth century to 445 B.C.E., record the names of ʾElnatan, Yehoʿezer, and ʾAḥzay, each called *paḥwaʾ*, 'governor.'[54] But none of these names are found in the Davidic genealogy of this period in 1 Chronicles 3:17–24.

There is a lacuna in the history of the province of Judah—from about 515 B.C.E., the date of the completion of the Temple, until 458 B.C.E., the date of Ezra's return.[55] When the record resumes, the messianic themes of the earlier narrative are no longer heard. Hierocracy supplants the diarchy of king and high priest. We hear nothing of the Davidic prince either in the Ezra narrative or in the memoirs of Nehemiah. All this hints of decisive action on the part of Persian authorities—whether Zerubbabel came to a natural end or was removed by legal or violent means. The initiatives of Jerusalem were aborted. The repercussion of these events in Samaria outside the circles of its chancellery among "the remnant of Israel" can only be guessed at. Some apparently supported the

54. See N. Avigad, *Bullae and Seals from a Post-Exilic Judean Archive.* Note that other names appear on official (*Yĕhūd*) seals or sealings, *ʾwryw, ḥnnh, zbdyw,* and *yʾz⌜n⌝*. Presumably these are fiscal or priestly officers below the rank of governor. The last-mentioned name is on a stamp impression published by Alan Millard, "Belmont Castle 1987: Second Preliminary Report of Excavations," *Levant* 21 (1989): 61 (appendix). Millard reads *yʾl / br yšʿ(?) / yhwd.* The third letter of the first line is certainly an Aramaic lapidary *zayin,* and the whole is to be read: *yʾz⌜n⌝ / br ydʿ*. Millard's paper was called to my attention by David Vanderhooft.

55. On the date of Ezra's return, see the discussion above in chapter 8.

moves of the Persian authorities against Judah. Others, if they had been favorable to the restoration of an Israelite kingdom, would have suffered disillusionment. Such a picture of the dark era would explain the new attitudes toward the North met with by the missions of Ezra and Nehemiah. In any case, we must postulate official repression of Jewish aspirations to expand the power of Jerusalem. Only with the coming of Nehemiah, a favorite of the Persian crown, was Judah finally enabled to fortify the city of Jerusalem, and this relatively modest restoration of the city brought violent opposition of the Samaritan nobility and the ruling classes of the surrounding provinces.

Nehemiah came to Jerusalem in 445 B.C.E.[56] Despite his official commission to refortify the city, he was opposed, as we have seen, by Sanballat of Samaria in league with officials of Ammon, northern Arabia, and Ashdod. Sanballat (*Sin-'uballiṭ*),[57] called the Horonite, i.e., of *Bêt Ḥôrōn*, evidently founded the dynasty of Sanballatids, who ruled Samaria until Hellenistic times. To judge from the names of his progeny, he was of the Yahwistic faith[58] and most likely of Ephraimite extraction.[59] Sanbal-

56. R. J. Saley has resurrected the hypothesis best defended by C. C. Torrey, that Nehemiah came to Jerusalem in the twentieth year of Artaxerxes II, 384 B.C.E.: "The Date of Nehemiah Reconsidered," in *Biblical and Near Eastern Studies*, ed. G. A. Tuttle (Grand Rapids, Mich.: Eerdmans, 1978), 151–165. Saley argues that the early date, while possible, cannot be proved, and he attempts to demonstrate that the later date can be conformed to all hard evidence available. I do not find his arguments compelling. It is very difficult, for example, to suppose that Sanballaṭ II of Samaria, at least the third of his line to rule in Samaria, would bear the biblical sobriquet "Sanballaṭ the Horonite." "Horonite," the gentilic referring to Beth Horon, suggests rather that Sanballaṭ was a newcomer to Samaria, and probably was the founder of the dynasty. On the gentilic form, compare *byt plṭ* > *hplṭy*, *byt hʿrbh* > *hʿrbty*, *byt gdr* > *hgdry*, etc. Again the evidence of the Tell el-Mashuṭah Bowl, an *ex voto* of the son of Gashmu dating minimally to ca. 400 B.C.E. is strong. Josephus, of course, assigns Nehemiah to the reign of Xerxes in his revised chronology. It should be noted, however, that Josephus knows the actual sequence of the Persian dynasts, and places Nehemiah early, despite the telescoping of the genealogy of the high priests. Moreover, in *Contra Apionem* 1:40, citing the canonical doctrine of the Pharisees, he places the close of the canon, which includes Ezra-Nehemiah, in the time of Artaxerxes, son of Xerxes. Saley's reconstruction of the priestly line is also faulty, stretching the length of priestly reigns in the fifth century to incredibly long lengths. These illustrate a number of the more obvious arguments which can be leveled against the late date.

57. This writing of the name is found in an Elephantine Papyrus, *AP* 30:29, on a bulla attached to one of the Samaria Papyri, as well as in the text of a Samaria Papyrus (SP 12:13).

58. His sons' names were Delaiah and Shelemiah (*AP* 30:29), his great grandsons Hananiah and Isaiah (?), as we know from the Samaria Papyri. His own Babylonian name (which persisted in the dynasty) is no more significant in establishing his religion or origin than those of Sheshbazzar and Zerubbabel.

59. See n. 56. It should be added that Persian policy (in contrast with the Assyrian)

lat is described in the Nehemiah memoirs as a devious and malicious enemy. He obviously resented Nehemiah's protection by a contingent of Persian troops and no doubt was held back from open attack by their presence.[60] He openly accused Nehemiah of plotting to become king and revolt against his Persian overlords.[61] Also Nehemiah describes a conspiracy of Sanballat, Tobiah, and their allies, the Arabians (Qederites) and Ashdodites, to resort to military action against Jerusalem.[62] Furthermore, if Nehemiah's suspicions were correct, Sanballat also plotted his assassination.[63] Sanballat's actions and words as reported indicate that he was motivated basically by the fear of a new national revival in Jerusalem, a fear shared by the other provincial governors who were his allies. Evidently Sanballat was deterred from frontal attack, not only by Nehemiah's adroit organization of his supporters in Jerusalem (about which Nehemiah speaks with pride), but also because of Nehemiah's close connections with the Persian court, symbolized by its assignment of Persian troops to protect him. The strife, so far described, was rooted in a political struggle for power; there is no overt allusion, in any case, to an underlying religious quarrel. Nehemiah's pleas that he is innocent of disloyalty to the Persian crown and without designs on the royal office in Judah are, no doubt, to be accepted at face value. Sanballat's fears, resting on the experience of his predecessors, were nevertheless understandable if not justified.

Nehemiah prevailed, of course, proving as wily as he was devout. He fortified the city, increased its population, and completed his first tour of duty as governor in 433 B.C.E. After a sojourn in the royal court of indeterminate length, he returned to the Holy City. At the close of his memoirs, recounting the details of his reforms and good works, he relates a last episode in which Sanballat played a role. Nehemiah discovered that the grandson of the ruling high priest, Eliashib, an unnamed son of Joiada, and the daughter of Sanballat had been joined in a diplomatic marriage uniting the two great families of Judah and Samaria.[64] Nehemiah in righteous indignation chased the young man out of Jerusalem, with the pious comment, "Remember them, O my God, for [their] defiling the priesthood and the covenant of the priesthood and the Levites." Obviously Nehemiah had grounds for being furious over the marriage of the high priest's grandson, a possible heir to the high sacral office, to a

---

ordinarily favored persons or families of native stock for appointment to local, provincial governorships. Cf. Tobiah of Ammon and Gashmu of Arabia, among others.

60. Neh. 2:9–10.

61. Neh. 6:1–14; cf. 2:19.

62. Neh. 4:1–2.

63. Neh. 6:1–14.

64. Neh. 13:28 f.

daughter of his archenemy Sanballat. However, Nehemiah says that his wrath was caused by the priest's defilement of the priestly office. Apparently the crime goes beyond "fraternizing with the enemy." The description of the episode points to a new ideological element in the Judean community. Earlier Ezra conducted his campaign against foreigners. His memoirs report these words: "The people of Israel and the priests and Levites have not separated themselves from the peoples of the lands (*ʿmy hʾrṣwt*) . . . for they have taken of their daughters for themselves and for their sons so that the holy seed has mixed with the peoples of the lands, and the hand of princes and officials has been first in this faithlessness."[65]

Who precisely is meant is not specified beyond the traditional list of peoples: Canaanites, Hittites, Perizzites, Ammonites, Moabites, Egyptians, and Amorites (or Edomites). In Ezra's reform, "foreign wives" (*nšym nkrywt*) were extirpated. In Nehemiah's reforms, he too strikes out at those who marry foreign women, making mention of the women of Ashdod, Ammon, and Moab.[66] Notable is the nonmention of nations imported into the land, above all the peoples of Babylon (e.g., the *kwtym*). Nothing is said of the inhabitants of Samaria and the North. It has been suggested that Ezra's reform at any rate was not directed against Israelite Yahwists of the North.[67] The episode of the priest's marriage into the family of Sanballat makes clear, however, that Nehemiah, at least, extended the marriage ban to a Samaritan who was a Yahwist, and who may have been of Ephraimite extraction.[68] To be sure, one can argue that Nehemiah had personal knowledge that Sanballat was of foreign or mixed blood—or perhaps better, that he assumed that so implacable an enemy with a foreign name must be of doubtful or mixed origin. Whatever the case, there is evidence here that a spirit of separation, quite absent in our sixth-century sources, pervades at least a significant segment of the Jewish community, and we may speak of a "separatist" or "exclusionist" party in fifth-century Jerusalem. Ezra and his legal teaching may have first inspired its development. Nehemiah may have merely continued in Ezra's tradition or he may have developed the separatist tendency to the point that marriage even to an Israelite of the North was questioned or even condemned.

The episode of the marriage of Joiada's son to Sanballat's daughter has sometimes been linked to events recorded by Josephus.[69] Josephus relates that after Joḥanan, son of Joiada, became high priest, Joḥanan killed his brother Jeshua in the Temple. So dreadful was the event that

65. Ezra 9:1–2, 11–15.
66. Neh. 12:23–27, 30.
67. So K. Koch, "Ezra and the Origins of Judaism," *JSS* 19 (1974): 173–197.
68. Compare the Tobiah episode in Neh. 13:4–9.
69. *Antiq.* 11:297–301.

Bagoas, the general (*stratēgos*) of Artaxerxes, entered the Temple by force, defiling it, and imposed a heavy tribute on the Jews for seven years. Taking the Joḥanan of Josephus's text to be the Joḥanan who was high priest at the end of the fifth century, and supposing that the Bagoas is the Judean governor known from Elephantine documents[70]—despite Josephus's explicit identification with the infamous commander-in-chief of Artaxerxes III (Ochus, 358–338 B.C.E.)—it was possible to speculate that this Jeshua may have been the son of Joiada married to Sanballat's daughter.[71] The new data stemming from the Samaria Papyri (see below) confirming Josephus's attribution of Sanballat (III) and Jaddua (II) to the end of the Persian era make the proposal quite unlikely. Rather we must affirm Josephus as correct in placing the episode in the reign of Ochus, when the general Bagoas was engaged in his expeditions to Phoenicia, Palestine, and Egypt during the western insurrections.[72] Indeed, the bad blood between Joḥanan and Jeshua may reflect party strife between factions supporting the Persian crown (presumably Jeshua) and the revolt (Joḥanan the high priest).

V

Jewish and Samaritan history in the fourth century B.C.E. has received welcome illumination from the Samaria Papyri. The papyri and other artifacts were found by Bedouin in a desolate canyon north of Jericho on the rim of the Jordan rift. They were inscribed according to their preambles in "Samaria the city which is in Samaria the province," in the half century before the conquest of Alexander. The papyri are without exception legal documents, not a few executed before the governor and prefect of Samaria. Among the surprises to be found in the documents is the appearance twice of the name Sanballat, or more properly *Sin'uballiṭ*. In each instance Sanballat is listed as the father of the governor of Samaria, one on an official sealing inscribed in Paleo-Hebrew script ([*yšʿ?*]*yhw bn* [*sn'*]*blṭ pḥt šmrn*), once in Aramaic in the context of a document of about the mid-fourth century ([*yšʿ?*]*wʿ br sn'blṭ wḥnn sgn'*).[73] With the existence of two Sanballats firmly established, paradoxically it becomes

70. *AP* 30:1, 32:1.

71. I followed this view in "Aspects of Samaritan and Jewish History in Late Persian and Hellenistic Times," *HTR* 59 (1966): 202 and n. 5.

72. This interpretation of the new data was first made in my paper "A Reconstruction of the Judaean Restoration," 188 f. The same or similar views arrived at independently appear in the papers of H. G. M. Williamson, "The Historical Value of Josephus' *Jewish Antiquities* XI. 297–301," *JTS* 28 (1977): 49–66; and Saley, "The Date of Nehemiah Reconsidered," 156–158.

73. See F. M. Cross in *Discoveries in the Wâdī ed-Dâliyeh*, ed. Paul W. Lapp and Nancy L. Lapp, *AASOR* 41 (Cambridge: ASOR, 1974): 18 f. and pl. 61.

easier to accept Josephus's testimony concerning a third Sanballat in the age of Alexander. We know well that it was the regular practice in the Achaemenid empire for high offices, that of satrap or governor, to become hereditary. It is evident that the Sanballatids held the governorship of Samaria for several generations, as did the Tobiads the governorship of Ammon. Moreover, we know that the practice of papponymy (naming a child for his grandfather)[74] was much in vogue among the Jews and surrounding nations in precisely this period. One may refer to the Tobiads, where papponymy is documented for about nine generations.[75] The high priests of Judah in the Persian and Hellenistic era illustrate the practice in even more impressive fashion.[76] In the Ammonite inscription from Tell Sīrān, the royal name ʿAmminadab alternates over four, and perhaps six, generations.[77]

We can reconstruct with some plausibility, therefore, the sequence of governors of Samaria in the late fifth and fourth centuries, a sequence we can correlate with the high priests in Jerusalem:

JEWISH HIGH PRIESTS	SANBALLATIDS
Yoyadaʿ(I)	Sanballaṭ (I)
Yoḥanan (II)	Delayah
Yadduaʿ (Yoyadaʿ II)	Sanballaṭ (II)
Yoḥanan (III)	Yešuaʿ / Yešaʿyahu (?)
	Ḥananyah
Yadduaʿ (Yoyadaʿ III)	Sanballaṭ (III)

The lists above, it should be observed, are constructs based on what evidence we have, from the Bible (Nehemiah 12:10), from the Samaria Papyri, and indeed from two recently found coins of the fourth century B.C.E. There may be missing names in the lists.[78] The biblical list

74. More complex patterns of naming children, including naming after grand uncles or (dead) uncles, as well as papponymy may be observed in the Hasmonaean line.

75. This reckoning follows the reconstruction of B. Mazar, "The Tobiads," *IEJ* 7 (1957): 137–145, 229–238.

76. See above, chapter 8 and chart.

77. See F. M. Cross, "Note on the Ammonite Inscription from Tell Sīrān," *BASOR* 212 (1973): 12–15. A revised version of the paper will appear shortly in my collected papers in epigraphy and pelaeography.

78. We note that coins minted in Samaria bear the names of a number of persons, fiscal officers and priests, presumably, and possibly undocumented governors of Samaria. The following names occur on Samaritan coins: *yrbʿm* (Jeroboam), *ḥym, ḥnnyh* (possibly the governor of the same name), *bdyḥbl, yhwʿnh, ʿbdʾl, bdyh,* and some abbreviations, including *sn,* which possibly could be the abbreviation of Sanballaṭ. See Meshorer and Qedar, *The Coinage of Samaria in the Fourth Century B.C.E.,* 13–18 and passim.

has a gaping lacuna omitting Yoḥanan III and Yaddua' II. In my paper "A Reconstruction of the Jewish Restoration," I proposed that we restore a missing Yoḥanan and Yaddua', basing my reconstruction both on papponymy and on the improbably long reigns of the priests. While a number of scholars remained unpersuaded—sticking with the Masoretic Text—my reconstruction is now proved correct by the discovery of fourth-century coins of Judah (Yĕhūd) bearing the names of "Yoḥanan the (High)Priest" (in Palaeo-Hebrew script), and "Yaddua'" in cursive Aramaic characters.[79] Sanballat the Horonite, we believe, was the founder of the dynasty. One of his sons, Delaiah or Shelemiah, evidently succeeded him.[80] Sanballat I must have received the governorship at a mature age, and in 445, when Nehemiah arrived in Jerusalem, was probably in his middle years. His son Delaiah acted for his aged father as early as 410 B.C.E.[81] The grandson of Sanballat the Horonite, Sanballat II, named in the finds at Dâliyeh, evidently inherited the governorship early in the fourth century, to be succeeded by an elder son (Yešu' / Yeša'yahu?),[82] and later by his son Hananiah. Hananiah was governor by 354 B.C.E., and his son or brother's son Sanballat III succeeded to the governorship in the time of Darius III, as reported by Josephus.[83]

Josephus furnishes us with the sequence of names of the high priests Joiada-Joḥanan-Jaddua (Yoyada'-Yoḥanan-Yaddu'), placing Joḥanan in the time of Artaxerxes (III, 359–338 B.C.E.) and his general Bagoas, Jaddua in the time of Darius III and Alexander the Great. It is clear, however, that Josephus identified Sanballat III and biblical Sanballat, Sanballat I, and further that he identified Joiada II, son of Joḥanan II, with biblical Joiada I son of Eliashib, thus telescoping the genealogies of the fifth and fourth centuries.[84] Quite likely a haplography occurred in Jose-

79. For references to the coins and discussion of the high-priestly genealogy, together with the contemporary Davidic genealogy, see Cross, "Samaria and Jerusalem," esp. n. 50; D. Barag, "A Silver Coin of Yoḥanan the High Priest [Hebrew]," *Qadmoniot* 17 (1984): 59–61; D. Barag, "A Silver Coin of Yoḥanan the High Priest and the Coinage of Judea in the Fourth Century B.C.," *INJ* 9 (1986–87): 4–21 and pl. 1; A. Spaer, "Jaddua the High Priest," *INJ* 9 (1986–87): 1–3 and pl. 2; and Peter Machinist, "The First Coins of Judah and Samaria: Numismatics and History in the Achaemenid and Early Hellenistic Periods," *Achaemenid History* VIII: *Continuity and Change,* Proceedings of the Last Achaemenid History Workshop, April 6–8, 1990, ed. H. Sancisi-Weerdenburg, Amélie Kuhrt, and Margaret Cool Root (Leiden: Nederlands Institut voor het Nabije Oosten, 1994), 365–380. See also above in chapter 8, nn. 15–17.

80. Delaiah and Shelemiah are mentioned in *AP* 30:29.

81. *AP* 32:1.

82. Yešua' is, of course, the hypocoristicon or caritative of Yeša'yahu. The latter name is reconstructed from a bulla, the former from a papyrus, both names damaged. They probably apply to the same person.

83. *Antiq.* 11:203.

84. *Antiq.* 11:297.

phus's sources, or his sources were fragmentary. Joḥanan II was still in office in 410, as we know from the Elephantine letters.[85] His son Jaddua (Joiada II) is mentioned in Nehemiah 12:10, 22 together with the name of "Darius the Persian." Unless the name Darius was added by a later editor, Darius II (423–404 B.C.E.) is meant, and we must conclude that Jaddua took the high priestly office before 400 B.C.E. It is not at all likely, therefore, that he exercised the priestly office until 332, much less had a brother of marriageable age in 332, as is necessary if biblical Jaddua is identified with Jaddua the high priest whose brother married Nikaso, daughter of Sanballat III. Furthermore, the association of Jaddua's (Joiada II) successor with Artaxerxes III, if correctly identified, settles the matter. We then must insert at least two names into Josephus's list of high priests: Joḥanan II and Jaddua (Joiada III).[86]

In the *Antiquities,* Josephus recounts an episode relating to intermarriage between the high-priestly family of Judah and the ruling family of Samaria.[87] Sanballat III arranged a marriage between his daughter Nikaso and the brother of the high priest Jaddua (Joiada III), a young man named Manasseh. Josephus tells us that the "elders of Jerusalem" intervened and required of Manasseh that he divorce his wife or desist from approaching the altar. Manasseh elected to keep his bride and retired to his father-in-law's realm in Samaria. This was the occasion, if we are to believe Josephus, for the building of the Samaritan temple on Mount Gerizim. Sanballat set up his unemployed, Zadokite son-in-law in business, so to speak, providing him with a temple and the Yahwists of Samaria with a national sanctuary, rival to the temple in Jerusalem. Josephus also relates a tradition that Alexander the Great himself commissioned the construction of the sanctuary on Gerizim shortly after his arrival in Palestine in 332 B.C.E.

These accounts have been the subject of much debate. The resemblance of Josephus's narrative to Nehemiah's expulsion of a son of Joiada for the same crime of marrying into the Sanballatid family is evident. In the past scholars viewing these similar accounts were incredulous. Cowley's reaction was typical: "The view that there were two Sanballats, each a governor of Samaria, and each with a daughter who married a brother of a High Priest at Jerusalem, is a solution too desperate to be entertained."[88] Of course, Cowley's comment has lost some of its force

85. *AP* 30:18, 31:17.

86. See Cross, "Aspects of Samaritan and Jewish History," 205; and Williamson, "The Historical Value of Josephus' *Jewish Antiquities* XI.297–301," 60–65. The discovery of the fourth-century coins of Yoḥanan and Yaddûaʿ add welcome confirmation.

87. *Antiq.* 11:302–312, 321–325.

88. Cowley, *AP,* 110.

now. There were not only two Sanballats but three who were governors of Samaria, and it would not be surprising if all three had marriageable daughters. As for the priests concerned, their names and relationships are different.[89] A few scholars gave credence to an Alexandrine date for the construction of the Samaritan Temple. In an extraordinary reconstruction, C. C. Torrey moved Nehemiah down into the fourth century, claiming that Sanballat, mentioned in the Elephantine Papyri, was the grandfather of Sanballat the Horonite, enemy of Nehemiah and father of two marriageable daughters.[90] Some scholars even moved the building of the Temple on Gerizim back into the fifth century in order to merge the accounts of intermarriage, despite the silence of Ezra-Nehemiah on the question of a separate Samaritan cultus.

I am inclined to give credence to both accounts, each correctly reporting instances of marriages between the aristocracy of Samaria and the theocratic family of Jerusalem. Mixed marriages are well attested among priests and laity in the eras of Ezra and Nehemiah; hence their reforms. The failure of Ezra's reform is, of course, evident in the necessity of Nehemiah to institute a similar program of reform. Nor is there any reason to doubt Josephus's testimony when he reports: "But as many priests and Israelites were involved in such marriages, great was the confusion which seized Jerusalem. For all these deserted to Manasseh, and Sanballat supplied them with money and assigned them places wherein to dwell."[91] Josephus, of priestly stock, and sharing the anti-Samaritan bias of his time, had no reason to invent the story. Past reluctance to admit intimate and repeated ties between the Sanballatids and the Zadokite priestly families has rested on the inclination to read back into the Persian period the extreme alienation, indeed the hatred which marked the relationship between Jews and Samaritans in late Hasmonaean and Roman times. There has been mounting evidence, however, that the schism that separated the Samaritans finally and irreversibly from their Jewish coreligionists came much later, well after the end of Persian rule. For one thing, we have been increasingly forced to recognize that the religion of the Samaritans derived from Judaism. Its feasts and law, its conservatism toward the Torah, and its theological lore show few if any survivals from the old (north) Israelite religion as distinct from Judaism, and no real evidence of religious syncretism. The contrast with the

89. Cowley slants his comment in saying that both "married a brother of a High Priest." The biblical notice speaks of the grandson of a reigning high priest, Josephus of the brother of the reigning high priest.

90. See, for example, his discussion in *The Second Isaiah* (New York: Scribner, 1928), 456–460 and references.

91. *Antiq.* 11:302–312, 321–325.

religion of the Jewish community in Elephantine (stemming in no small part from the Northern Kingdom) could not be more striking. Even late Jewish apocalyptic has left its firm imprint on Samaritanism.

For these and other reasons, scholars have in even larger numbers been inclined to lower the date of the so-called Samaritan schism, some into the late Persian period, some to the time of Alexander, some to even later times.[92] Many historians see in the erection of the Samaritan Temple an event that crystallized the breach in relations that led to the development of Samaritan sectarianism. Their date for the schism has determined the date to which they assign its foundation.

VI

Thanks to the discovery of the Samaria Papyri, coupled with historical data culled from the excavations at Shechem, at Tell er-Râs, and in the city on Mount Gerizim, we are in a new position to discuss Samaritan history at the advent of the Hellenistic Age.[93] But with solutions to old problems furnished by new evidence come a number of intractable and complex new problems.

After submitting to Alexander in 332 B.C.E., the nobles of Samaria rose in revolt in 331, going to the extreme of burning to death Andromachus, Alexander's prefect in Syria. An army of Alexander marched north from

92. For a review of the older literature, see the paper of H. H. Rowley, "Sanballat and the Samaritan Temple," *BJRL* 38 (1955): 166–198; for more recent discussion, one may consult Coggins, *Samaritans and Jews;* A. D. Crown, "Redating the Schism between the Judaeans and the Samaritans," *JQR* 82 (1991): 17–50; and M. Mor, "Samaritan History: I. The Persian, Hellenistic, and Hasmonaean Period," in *The Samaritans,* ed. A. D. Crown (Tübingen: J. C. B. Mohr, 1989), 1–18.

93. On the discovery of the papyri and the historical reconstruction of the events that led to the massacre of their owners and their deposit in the Wâdī ed-Dâliyeh, see F. M. Cross, "The Discovery of the Samaria Papyri," *BA* 26 (1963): 110–121, and the discussion in *Discoveries in the Wâdī ed-Dâliyeh,* 1–29. On the excavations at Shechem, see G. Ernest Wright, "The Samaritans at Shechem," *HTR* 55 (1962): 357–366. Wright's treatment of the classical sources needs some correction, for which see my remarks in the works cited above and Ralph Marcus's appendix C in his Loeb edition of Josephus, *Antiq.* 6:513–532. On the Tell er-Râs excavations, see E. F. Campbell, "Jewish Shrines of the Hellenistic and Persian Periods," in *Symposia Celebrating the Seventy-fifth Anniversary of the Founding of the American Schools of Oriental Research,* ed. F. M. Cross (Cambridge: ASOR, 1979), 159–167 and the cited literature, esp. R. J. Bull and E. F. Campbell, "The Sixth Campaign at Balâṭah (Shechem)," *BASOR* 190 (1968): 4–9. For the excavations in the city on Mount Gerizim, see Y. Magen, "A Fortified Town of the Hellenistic Period on Mount Gerizim [Hebrew]," *Qadmoniot* 19 (1986): 91–101; Magen, "Mount Gerizim—A Temple City [Hebrew]," *Qadmoniot* 23 (1990): 70–96; and R. Plummer, "Samaritan Material Remains and Archaeology," in *Samaritans,* ed. A. D. Crown, 136–177, esp. 167–175.

Egypt intent on quenching these first stirrings of rebellion. It is reported that the rebels were delivered up to the Macedonian forces when they reached Samaria. These events are the background into which we must set the occasion for the deposit of the Samaria Papyri in the cave of the Wâdī ed-Dâliyeh. The content of the papyri, the hoards of coins accompanying the deposit, as well as other artifacts, all point to a date in the time of Alexander for the flight of the patricians into their hiding place in the wastelands. Here the Samaritans were massacred, no doubt by Macedonian troops, leaving to us a cache of papyri, jewelry, and coins, as well as more mundane artifacts, strewn among masses of skeletons. Thereafter Alexander, or rather his deputy Perdiccas (our sources are in conflict), resettled the city of Samaria now organized as a Greek colony. The Sanballatid dynasty in Samaria ended with Sanballat III.

The excavations at Shechem (Tell Balaṭah) have given substance to the view that the Samaritans rebuilt the city as their center after the events we have described. Shechem was rebuilt and refortified in the last third of the fourth century.[94]

The American expedition to Shechem uncovered the remains of a Roman temple on Tell er-Râs dedicated to Zeus Hypsistos, and below it a massive platform. The excavator, Robert Bull, took the platform to be the remains of an earlier Samaritan Temple of Hellenistic date.[95] However, this hypothesis must now be abandoned. Y. Magen in his excavations on Mount Gerizim denies the early date of the platform; the second- to third-century sherds found in Bull's excavations, he argues, belong to a fill taken from the Hellenistic city on the main peak nearby.[96]

The excavations of Magen have laid bare a large fortified town on Mount Gerizim. The mass of the remains recovered, including a large number of coins, suggests that the main phase of the Hellenistic town began in the time of Antiochus III (223–187 B.C.E.), roughly a century after the refounding of Shechem in the valley. According to recent reports, remains of a temple on Gerizim, dating to the late fourth century B.C.E., have been found by Magen in new excavations under the ruins of the Church of Mary Theotokos. We must wait for details to the publication. In any case, I am not inclined to doubt the testimony of Josephus as to the general time of the founding of the Samaritan temple, at the beginning of the Hellenistic period, nor his testimony as to its destruction.[97]

94. Stratum IV B at Shechem. See Wright, "The Samaritans at Shechem," 357–366 and references; G. Ernest Wright, *Shechem: The Biography of a Biblical City* (New York: McGraw-Hill, 1965), 170–184.

95. See above n. 93.

96. See Magen, "Mount Gerizim—A Temple City," 92–94.

97. See Menachem Mor's balanced treatment of the history of this period, "Samaritan History: I. The Persian, Hellenistic, and Hasmonaean Period," 6–9.

Josephus reports that Shechem, Gerizim (presumably the town on the mount), and the Samaritan temple were destroyed by John Hyrcanus in 128 B.C.E.[98] The excavations at Shechem and in the town on Mount Gerizim give eloquent witness to a destruction at precisely this time.

There can be little doubt that the erection of the sanctuary on Gerizim—a rival to the Temple in Jerusalem—further aggravated the tensions between Samaritan and Jew which we have traced through earlier times. At the same time the creation of the new Samaritan shrine need not be regarded as the final or even crucial event leading to total estrangement. Curious to say, the Hellenistic Age would witness the establishment of at least three rival cults to that of Jerusalem. In the second century B.C.E., Onias IV, pretender to the Zadokite high priesthood, built the temple at Leontopolis in Egypt.[99] At the beginning of the second century, Hyrcanus of the Tobiad family may have built a temple in ʿArâq el-ʾEmîr in Transjordan.[100] If Josephus is correct, the Essenes conducted a sacrificial cultus at Qumrân by the Dead Sea.[101]

VII

In addressing the debated question of the date of the Samaritan schism, scholars have not been in agreement on the criteria that constitute "schism." If the term is taken to refer to the emergence of a fully separated sect, then the date of the schism cannot be set in a time earlier than the cessation of direct and profound Jewish influence upon the development of their scripture, doctrine, and praxis.

Thanks to the discovery and study of the Qumrân scrolls, we are enabled to place the Samaritan Pentateuch in the history of the Hebrew biblical text.[102] It proves to be a late form of an old Palestinian tradi-

98. See Josephus, *Antiq.* 13:254–256; *War* 1:63.

99. See M. Delcor, "Le temple d'Onias en Égypte," *RB* 75 (1968): 188–205, and the discussion of Campbell, "Jewish Shrines of the Hellenistic and Persian Periods," 159–167, esp. 164–165 and references.

100. See J. B. Brett, "The Qaṣr el-ʿAbd: A Proposed Reconstruction," *BASOR* 171 (1963): 39–45, and Campbell, "Jewish Shrines of the Hellenistic and Persian Periods," 162–164. However, Brett's results have been called into question by E. Will, "Recherches au Qaṣr el ʿAbd à ʿIraq al-Amir," *ADAJ* 23 (1979): 139–149, and his "Chronique archéologique," *RB* 86 (1979): 117–119.

101. See *ALQ*^{3}, 84–86 (*ALQ*^{2}, 100–102), where the text of Josephus is discussed along with the evidence from the excavations at Qumrân. At Qumrân, however, there was no temple. S. H. Steckoll's paper "The Qumran Sect in Relation to the Temple of Leontopolis," *RQ* 6 (1967): 55–69, is not useful, adding only confusion to the picture as observed by Roland de Vaux in a postscript to Delcor's paper cited in n. 99 (pp. 204 f.).

102. See *ALQ*^{3}, 126–128, 141–142; P. W. Skehan, "Exodus in the Samaritan Recension from Qumrân," *JBL* 74 (1955): 182–187; B. K. Waltke, "Prolegomena to the Samari-

tion which began to develop distinctive traits as early as the time of the Chronicler's Work, and which can be traced in Jewish works and in the manuscripts of Qumrân as early as the mid second century (4QExod-Lev^{f}) and as late as the first century C.E., when an old textual tradition of distinctly different character became regnant, providing the base of the Rabbinic Recension.[103] The Samaritan Pentateuchal text broke off very late in the development of the Palestinian (Proto-Samaritan) text. Early exemplars of this textual family lack most of the long additions from synoptic passages and exhibit stronger affinities with the text underlying the Septuagint translation, which broke away and began its separate development much earlier than did the Samaritan text. The Samaritan text-type thus is a late and full exemplar of a common Palestinian tradition in use both in Jerusalem and Samaria in Hasmonaean times.

The Palestinian textual tradition of the Pentateuch sometimes comes in special dress. At Qumrân it may be inscribed in Palaeo-Hebrew script. The Palaeo-Hebrew script is well known now from seals and seal impressions of the late fourth century from Judah and Samaria, and from Samaritan and Jewish coins of the late fourth century.[104] From the third to second centuries B.C.E. come Palaeo-Hebrew inscriptions recovered from the excavations on Mount Gerizim,[105] as well as official jar stamps of Judah (*Yĕhūd* plus symbol) and Jerusalem (*yršlm* stamps). In the second and first centuries B.C.E., this old national script is well known from manuscripts from Qumrân, as well as from Hasmonaean coins. From the

---

tan Pentateuch" (Ph.D. diss., Harvard University, 1965); the précis in "The Samaritan Pentateuch and the Text of the Old Testament," in J. B. Payne, ed., *New Perspectives on the Old Testament* (Waco, Tex.: Word Books, 1970), 212–239; Judith E. Sanderson, *An Exodus Scroll from Qumran: 4QpaleoExod^{m} and the Samaritan Tradition, HSS* 30 (Atlanta: Scholars Press, 1986); and especially the monograph of James D. Purvis, *The Samaritan Pentateuch and the Origins of the Samaritan Sect, HSM* 2 (Cambridge: Harvard University Press, 1968).

A number of the Qumrân manuscripts allied to the tradition surviving in the Samaritan Pentateuch have recently been given their principal publication: 4QpalaeoExod^{m} in *Qumrân Cave 4 IV, DJD* 9, by Patrick W. Skehan, Eugene Ulrich, and Judith E. Sanderson (Oxford: Clarendon Press, 1992), 51–130; 4QExod-Lev^{f} and 4QNum^{b} in *Qumrân Cave 4 VII, DJD* 12, by Eugene Ulrich and Frank Moore Cross with James R. Davila, Nathan Jastram, Judith E. Sanderson, Emanuel Tov, and John Strugnell (Oxford: Clarendon Press, 1994), 133–144, 205–267.

103. See below, chapters 10 and 11, on the fixation of the text and canon of the Hebrew Bible.

104. See Y. Meshorer and S. Qedar, *Ancient Jewish Coinage* (New York: Numismatic Fine Arts International, 1982); Meshorer and Qedar, *The Coinage of Samaria in the Fourth Century* B.C.E.; and E. Stern, *Material Culture of the Land of the Bible in the Persian Period* (Jerusalem: IES, 1982), 196–214.

105. See Magen, "Mount Gerizim—a Temple City," 78–79.

Herodian Age (37 B.C.E. to 70 C.E.) come monumental inscriptions from Givʿat Mivtar and the Temple area in Jerusalem excavated by Binyamin Mazar, as well as from coins of the First Revolt against Rome. It is now possible to date roughly the periods in the typological development of the Palaeo-Hebrew script. In the typological series, it is evident that the ancestral Samaritan character branches off from the Palaeo-Hebrew character no earlier than the first century B.C.E.

A similar typology can be drawn in the development of spelling practices. The earliest Palestinian texts follow a highly defective mode of orthography. In the course of the second century B.C.E., a special Maccabaean mode of spelling emerged which expanded the use of vowel letter, *matres lectionis,* sometimes in startling fashion. This full (*plene*) style of orthography, in a relatively restrained mode, well known in the late manuscripts of Qumrân, characterizes the Samaritan Pentateuch.

The language of the Samaritan Pentateuch also includes archaizing and especially notable, pseudoarchaic forms found also at Qumrân which surely point to the post-Maccabaean Age for its date.

From whatever angle we examine the Samaritan Pentateuch, by whatever typological series we measure it, we are forced to the Hasmonaean period at earliest for the origins of the Samaritan recension of the Pentateuch.

This evidence suggests that the definitive breach between Jews and Samaritans must be sought in the special events of the Hasmonaean era, before the Roman in which we know well that they looked upon one another as enemies and corrupters of the faith of Israel. In 128 B.C.E., John Hyrcanus laid waste to the Temple of Mount Gerizim and later destroyed Samaria utterly.[106] In these events we perceive John Hyrcanus's policy to impose "Judaean" Judaism, so to speak, on the Samaritans and indeed on his entire realm. In the same campaigns he went so far as to exclude all Idumaeans living in the south of Judah from his realm unless they submitted to circumcision and became Jews. It is clear that his goal was to establish the ideology of Zion in the realm which once made up the land of Israel, the same goal pursued by his predecessors Hezekiah, Josiah, and Zerubbabel. Hyrcanus's attempt to extirpate the Samaritan cultus failed, and when Pompey freed Samaria from vassalage to Hasmonaean priest-kings in 64 B.C.E., we may be sure that the Samaritans severed most, if not all, their relations with the representatives of Judaism in Jerusalem to traverse their own isolated and involuted path.

This reconstruction of the early history of the Samaritans solves many problems that have perplexed us in the past. As suggested above, it dissolves the mystery of the specifically Jewish character of Samaritan-

106. *Antiq.* 13:256, 275–281.

ism; it explains the close ties of Samaritanism to Zadokite tradition; and it provides the background of Essene or apocalyptic Zadokite strains in Samaritan law and doctrine. The historian is no longer required to contend with separate, but convergent evolution between two religious communities over a period of many centuries.

PART V

QUMRÂN AND THE HISTORY OF THE BIBLICAL TEXT

10

The Fixation of the Text of the Hebrew Bible

I

THE HEBREW BIBLE SURVIVES IN MANY MANUSCRIPTS AND IN SEVERAL old versions translated from the Hebrew. In consequence there is a richness of resources for the textual critic unusual in the study of documents surviving from antiquity: the early textual families and editions of given biblical works, as well as recensions of the Hebrew scriptures and of the Greek Bible, including the fixing of the traditional or received text. At the same time the history of the text of the Hebrew Bible has been obscured by an assumption or dogma on the part of the ancients, rabbis and church fathers alike, that the Hebrew text was unchanged and unchanging, unaltered by the usual scribal realities that produce families and recensions over long periods of transmission.

This dogma of the *Hebraica veritas* already found expression in Josephus's apologetic work, *Contra Apionem,* penned between 94 and 100 C.E.: "We have given practical proof of our reverence for our Scriptures. For although such long ages have now passed, no one has ventured to add, or to remove, or to alter a syllable; and it is an instinct with every Jew, from the day of his birth, to regard them as decrees of God, to abide by them, and if need be, cheerfully to die for them."[1] Even when it is recognized that Josephus not infrequently overstated his case in propagandizing a Greek-speaking audience, one must still affirm that he regarded the Hebrew Bible as having, in theory at least, an immutable text.

Origen, too, apparently assumed that his Greek Bible was translated from a Hebrew textual base that was the same as the Rabbinical Hebrew text in current use in his day. Hence in his monumental Hexapla he carefully corrected his Greek manuscripts to the *Hebraica veritas,* with catastrophic results for the subsequent transmission of the Greek Bible.

A popular version of this chapter may be found under the title "New Directions in Dead Sea Scroll Research: I. The Text behind the Text of the Hebrew Bible," in *BR* 1 (1985): 12–25.

1. *Contra Apionem* 1:42 (ed. Loeb).

Already in pre-Christian times in Palestine this tendency to correct the old Greek translation to contemporary Hebrew texts can be documented.

Jerome, writing in the fourth century C.E., extended the principle "correct to the Hebrew" even more radically to the Latin Bible, displacing the old Latin translations (based on the Old Greek Bible) with what has come to be called the Vulgate, a Latin version translated from the standard Rabbinic recension of the Hebrew Bible in use in his time.

Search for the early stages in the history of the text of the Hebrew Bible began in a scientific mode in the late eighteenth century. Extant manuscripts, all of medieval date, were collected and studied, culminating in the monumental collations of Kennicott and De Rossi.[2] The results were disappointing for those who hoped to find traces of archaic forms of the text.[3] Put differently, the sifting of the medieval manuscripts yielded in its mass of variant readings no evidence of alternate textual families or text types. The variants were secondary and late, the slips and errors in overwhelming measure, if not totally, of medieval scribes, who knew only one type of text, one textual tradition. Indeed it could be argued that the theory of a fixed and unchanging Hebrew text was given added support by the evidence from the collections of medieval manuscripts. However, some of the more astute textual scholars came shortly to recognize that all medieval manuscripts derived from a single recension fixed early in the Christian era and that this recension alone survived in the Jewish communities. Direct access to the early development of the text of the Hebrew Bible was thus effectively blocked. J. G. Rosenmueller was the first to enunciate a coherent "one-recension" theory and to express the conclusion that the sea of variants in the great collections of manuscripts were of "little or no help" in the endeavor to recover ancient readings standing behind corruptions in the *textus receptus.*[4] Subsequently, Olshausen and de Lagarde in the early nineteenth

2. B. Kennicott, *Vetus Testamentum hebraicum, cum variis lectionibus,* 1776–80; J. B. De Rossi, *Variae lectiones Veteris Testamenti,* 1784–88.

3. For a contemporary evaluation of medieval variants in manuscripts of the Hebrew Bible and Rabbinic literature, see M. H. Goshen-Gottstein, "Hebrew Biblical Manuscripts, Their History and Their Place in the *HUBP* Edition," *Biblica* 48 (1967): 243–290, and F. M. Cross, "The History of the Biblical Text in the Light of Discoveries in the Judaean Desert," *HTR* 57 (1964): 281–299, esp. 287–292. Both papers are republished in F. M. Cross and S. Talmon, *Qumrân and the History of the Biblical Text* (Cambridge: Harvard University Press, 1975), 42–89 (Goshen-Gottstein) and 177–195 (Cross).

4. The history of the textual scholarship of this era, the emergence of the "one-recension" theory, the "archetype" theory, and the confusion of the two in subsequent

century went beyond Rosenmueller in elaborating the view that not only could one speak of a single Rabbinic recension standing behind the medieval textual tradition, but that one could argue more precisely that the medieval text stemmed from a single archetype (Lagarde), or from single manuscripts of each biblical work, which already possessed the pattern of errors held in common by the medieval text and hence established their filiation. In truth there was little hard evidence available in the nineteenth century to determine precisely the procedure by which the Rabbinic recension came into being and was promulgated. The vigorous discussion subsided, and, it is fair to say, no major advances were made until the mid-twentieth century, when the sequence of discoveries in the Wilderness of Judah began to supply biblical manuscripts in Hebrew and Greek dating back to the centuries immediately before and after the turn of the common era.

The one Hebrew textual tradition generally conceded to stem from pre-Christian antiquity and to have been transmitted in isolation, uninfluenced by the rise of the Rabbinic recension of the Hebrew Bible, was the Samaritan Pentateuch. Strangely, its study has done little to illuminate the early history of the development and fixation of the text of the Hebrew Bible. In fact, gross misconceptions of the origins and recension of the Samaritan Pentateuch may even have strengthened traditional claims for the unchanging purity of the Masoretic text. It has been assumed that the separate development of the Samaritan Bible (containing only the Pentateuch) began in a rift between the Samaritans and the Jews that occurred in the fifth century B.C.E., or at latest in the fourth century B.C.E., and escaped further influences from the Jewish Bible. Its witness thus was seen to be very much older—older, in some instances, than the date given by certain critics for the composition of the latest strands of the Pentateuch. Furthermore, the first studies of the Samaritan text, notably those of Wilhelm Gesenius (1815), confirmed by the later work of moderns, especially that of Paul Kahle and Bruce Waltke, found the Samaritan Pentateuch to be a text strikingly inferior to the Jewish Pentateuch.[5] Comparison showed the Samaritan text to be con-

scholarly discussion is given impressive treatment by Goshen-Gottstein in his article "Hebrew Biblical Manuscripts."

5. See P. Kahle, *Untersuchungen zur Geschichte des Pentateuchtextes, TSK* 88 (1915): 399–439, reprinted in *Opera minora* (Leiden: E. J. Brill, 1956), 3–37; and especially B. K. Waltke, "Prolegomena to the Samaritan Pentateuch" (Ph.D. diss., Harvard University, 1965); and the précis in "The Samaritan Pentateuch and the Text of the Old Testament," *New Perspectives on the Old Testament,* ed. J. B. Payne (Waco, Tex.: Word Books, 1970), 212–239.

flate, expansionist, secondary. That is, it was marked by double readings, explicating additions or glosses, reworking, corruptions, late or modernizing grammatical and orthographic peculiarities, secondary sectarian alterations, all pointing to the relatively pristine and short character of our Masoretic Text of the Pentateuch.

The conclusions drawn from the study of the Samaritan witness to the text of the Hebrew Pentateuch appeared unavoidable: if the inferior Samaritan Pentateuch was an independent witness to the Hebrew text of the fifth century, the received text was an archaic text type which had survived virtually intact and unchanged from Persian times, and deviant witnesses of later date, notably the Old Greek translation of the third century B.C.E., must be based on it or on "vulgar" derivative texts like that of the Samaritans.

As has become evident in the light of recent discoveries, these conclusions rested on a basic blunder. The Samaritan Pentateuch did not have its independent origin in the Persian period. It separated from the common Palestinian Hebrew text following the Samaritan-Jewish crisis in Hasmonaean times when John Hyrcanus, at the end of the second century B.C.E., attempted to extirpate the Samaritan cultus and forcibly Judaize the Samaritans. In fact, the Samaritan recension is a product of the Roman period (from the era after Pompey freed the Samaritans), roughly contemporary with Rabbinic efforts to fix the biblical text. That this was so was anticipated by W. F. Albright as early as 1940 and now is supported with new, overwhelming evidence from finds in the Wilderness of Judah. Indeed the text ancestral to the Samaritan recension, its characteristic secondary readings, in script, orthography, and language, is well represented by manuscripts from Qumrân.[6]

The Septuagint, or more properly the Old Greek translation of the Bible, begun in the third century B.C.E., is a crucial witness to an older stage in the history of the biblical text. To be sure, the fact that it is a translation complicates its testimony since retroversion of its translated text to reconstruct its Hebrew *Vorlage* is a difficult and often precarious enterprise, especially in the absence of Hebrew texts of the type used by the Greek translators. We now know that the Hebrew text underlying the Old Greek translation in major parts of the Bible derived from a stream of textual tradition represented by a family of Hebrew manu-

6. See *ALQ* 2, 172 ff., 192 f.; Cross, "The Papyri and Their Historical Implications," in *Discoveries in the Wâdī ed-Dâliyeh*, ed. Paul W. Lapp and Nancy L. Lapp, *AASOR* 41 (Cambridge: ASOR, 1974), 17–29; and James Purvis, *The Samaritan Pentateuch and the Origin of the Samaritan Sect, HSM* 2 (Cambridge: Harvard University Press, 1968). Cf. P. W. Skehan, "Exodus in the Samaritan Recension from Qumrân," *JBL* 74 (1955): 182–187; and Judith E. Sanderson, *An Exodus Scroll from Qumrân: 4QPaleo-Exodus^{m} and the Samaritan Tradition, HSS* 30 (Atlanta: Scholars Press, 1986).

scripts strongly divergent from our received Hebrew text. Unfortunately, early studies of the text of the Greek Bible were pursued without such controls.

In the last century biblical textual critics attacked the maze of recensions of the Greek Bible with great vigor. These efforts reached their zenith in the program of Paul de Lagarde and in the initiation of the Göttingen Septuaginta, a monumental, eclectic edition of the Greek Bible, as well as in the collations of the Cambridge Septuagint. The presumption underlying the work of Lagarde and his disciples was that there existed behind the tangle of recensions a Proto-Septuagint or Old Greek translation and that, by reconstructing the "hyparchetypes" of the recensions, ultimately one could proceed to the establishment of their archetype, the Old Greek translation. Jerome speaks of three recensions of the Greek Bible current in his day, that of Hesychius in Egypt, Origen in Palestine, and the *koinē* (or recension of Lucian) in Antioch. The task of assorting manuscripts or manuscript readings under these headings advanced swiftly at first, but the establishment of the text of the recensions and the reconstruction of the Old Greek text by eclectic, critical procedures has proved far more difficult and problematic than anticipated. The wealth of manuscripts and the frequency of copying—recensions mixing and crossing—posed very complex problems. Progress was made also in piecing together fragments of the revisions of the Greek Bible, especially the revisions attributed to the "three"—Theodotion, Symmachus, and Aquila—figures of the second century C.E. (but on the Theodotionic revision, which had earlier origins, see below), and to Origen.

In the course of the first half of the twentieth century, as progress in Septuagintal studies slowed and unexpected difficulties emerged, confidence in the program faltered. New voices were raised questioning or repudiating the theoretical framework. One line of argument, attractive to many, sought to show that a number of the so-called recensions or revisions were merely the survivals of a welter of Greek translations, and that the Greek Bible arose, not in an original translation or proto-Septuagint, but in the slow standardization of diverse Greek *targumim*, translations of various date, scope, and fidelity. Indeed Paul Kahle came to argue that the Greek Bible was a product of a process of stabilization undertaken by the Greek church. The ultimate goal of the Lagarde school, to refine the Greek text for use as a tool in the textual criticism of the Hebrew Bible, also receded. Text-critical scholars turned increasingly to studies of the translators. By examining what was assumed to be their errors, their alterations of the *Hebraica veritas*, suppressions, glosses, abbreviations, and blunders, one could discover the theology and bias of the translator, as well as his ignorance or sloppiness. Obviously the study of the idiosyncrasies of translators is a necessary preliminary task of Septuagint research. However, throughout this reactionary era one perceives the specter of a prejudice never laid to rest: that there was one, fixed Hebrew text, and all Greek deviations are suspect. One might freely emend the Hebrew text but hardly on the basis of a Greek reading.

II

The discovery of ancient manuscripts in the eleven caves of Qumrân in the Wilderness of Judah provided the first unambiguous witness to an ancient stage of the Hebrew text of the Bible.[7] The caves in the vicinity of Khirbet Qumrân, found between 1947 and 1956, have yielded some 170 manuscripts of biblical books, most of them in a highly fragmentary state, and their publication is still in progress.[8] The earliest of these biblical manuscripts are mid third century B.C.E. in date, the latest from shortly before the fall of Jerusalem in 70 C.E.[9]

The manuscripts from Qumrân exhibit variants of a type which differ *toto caelo* from the character of variant readings found in later biblical scrolls. Further, the textual variation is not inchoate, the result of indiscriminate mixing of manuscript readings. There exist at Qumrân discrete and, indeed, recognizable families of textual tradition, text types that are different from the Rabbinic Recension ancestral to the Masoretic Text. These variant streams of textual tradition have been called "recensions" or "families" or "local texts."[10] The textual types in question appear to be the product of natural growth or development in isolation in the process of scribal transmission, not of a controlled or systematic *recensio,* revision or collation, at a given place or time. At the same time, in the differing textual families we know from Qumrân, from the text types standing behind the Rabbinic Recension, the Samaritan Recension, and the *Vorlage* of the Old Greek translation, we can discern traits, some more or less sys-

7. In fact the Nash Papyrus had already given a glimpse of an earlier stage of the Pentateuchal text before the fixing of the Rabbinic recension, but its witness was largely ignored. See W. F. Albright, "A Biblical Fragment from the Maccabaean Age: The Nash Papyrus," *JBL* 56 (1937): 145–146.

8. A review of the biblical texts from Qumrân and publication data on those that have been edited may be found in P. W. Skehan, "Qumrân. Littérature," *Supplément du Dictionnaire de la Bible,* 9, cols. 805–828.

9. See F. M. Cross, "The Development of the Jewish Scripts," in *BANE,* 133–202; see also Cross, "The Scripts of the Dâliyeh Papyri," in *Dâliyeh,* 25–27 (the chronology of the earliest scripts from Qumrân).

10. See F. M. Cross, "The Contribution of the Qumrân Discoveries to the Study of the Biblical Text," *IEJ* 16 (1966): 81–95, esp. 85, n. 21, and Cross, "Problems of Method in the Textual Criticism of the Hebrew Bible," in *The Critical Study of Sacred Texts,* ed. Wendy D. O'Flaherty (Berkeley: Graduate Theological Union, 1979), 31–54.

tematic, of each of the textual families. These traits held in common by a given family, include, of course, their "bad genes," an inherited group of mistakes or secondary readings. But they include also such features as orthographic style, reworked chronologies, script, and "modernized" grammar and lexicon. In one instance, the Book of Jeremiah, we possess from Cave 4, Qumrân, text-types that develop from different editions of Jeremiah, a short, older edition (4QJer[b]) known hitherto only in the Old Greek translation, and a longer edition ancestral to (or a collateral witness to) the text chosen by the Rabbis for their recension (4QJer[a]).[11]

At least three textual types or families are now known from pre-Christian Hebrew and Greek witnesses to the books of the Pentateuch and Samuel, two in other books, notably Jeremiah and Job, and in many books, including Isaiah and Ezekiel, only one. In no case, however, do the Hebrew manuscripts from Qumrân exhibit the developed and fixed form of the text that emerged in the Rabbinic Recension, nor can we detect any clear drift toward or narrowing down to, that recension.

Any reconstruction of the history of the biblical text before the establishment of the traditional text must comprehend this evidence: the plurality of text-types or families, the limited number of distinct textual families, and the relative homogeneity of each of these textual families over several centuries of time. A theory of local texts has been proposed to satisfy the requirements of these data.[12] As applied to the Pentateuch

11. Cf. J. G. Janzen, *Studies in the Text of Jeremiah, HSM* 6 (Cambridge: Harvard University Press, 1973); E. Tov, "L'Incidence de la critique textuelle sur la critique littéraire dans le livre de Jeremie," *RB* 79 (1972): 189–199.

12. See the papers of F. M. Cross, "The History of the Biblical Text in the Light of Discoveries in the Judaean Desert," "The Contribution of the Qumrân Discoveries to Study of the Biblical Text," and "The Evolution of a Theory of Local Texts," reprinted in *Qumrân and the History of the Biblical Text,* 177–195, 278–292, and 306–320; and "Problems of Method in the Textual Criticism of the Hebrew Bible." Cf. D. Barthélemy, *Études d'histoire du texte de l'Ancien Testament* (Fribourg: Éditions Universitaires, 1978), 218–254, 289–303, 341–350; P. W. Skehan, "The Biblical Scrolls from Qumrân and the Text of the Old Testament," *BA* 28 (1965): 95–100; and Skehan, "Qumrân. Littérature." Emanuel Tov has attacked my views in recent papers. See his studies, "The Relationship between the Textual Witnesses of the Old Testament in the Light of the Scrolls from the Judaean Desert," *Beth Miqra'* 77 (1979): 161–70 [Hebrew]; *The Text Critical Use of the Septuagint in Biblical Research* (Jerusalem: Sinor, 1981), esp. 253–272; and "A Modern Textual Outlook Based on the Qumrân Scrolls," *HUCA* 53 (1982): 11–27. See my reply, "Some Notes on a Generation of Qumran Studies," in *The Madrid Qumran Congress: Proceedings of the International Congress on the Dead Sea Scrolls,* ed. J. Trebolle Barrera and L. Vegas Montaner (Leiden: Brill, 1992), 1–14. Cf. Eugene Ulrich, "The Biblical Scrolls of Qumrân Cave 4: An Overview and a Progress Report on Their Publication," *RB* 54 (1989): 207–228; and Ulrich, "Horizons of Old Testament Textual Research at the Thirtieth Anniversary of Qumrân, Cave 4," *CBQ* 46 (1984): 613–636.

and Samuel, it may be sketched as follows. Three forms of the text appear to have developed slowly between the fifth and first centuries B.C.E. in Palestine, in Egypt, and in Babylon. The Palestinian text, found as early as the Chronicler's citations of the Pentateuch and Samuel, is frequently the text found at Qumrân and evolved late in Palestine into the text-type utilized in the Samaritan Pentateuch. In its late form this family is characterized by conflation, glosses, synoptic additions, and other evidence of intense scribal activity and can be defined as "expansionistic." Pentateuchal exemplars are sometimes inscribed in the Palaeo-Hebrew hand. The Egyptian text is found in the Old Greek of the Pentateuch and Samuel. The Egyptian is often, but not always, a full text. In the Pentateuch, for example, it has not suffered the extensive synoptic additions that mark the late Palestinian text, but is not so short as the third or Babylonian family. The Egyptian and Palestinian families are closely related. Early exemplars of the Palestinian text in Samuel and Pentateuchal texts, which reflect an early stage of the Palestinian tradition, so nearly merge with the Egyptian that we are warranted in describing the Egyptian text-type as a branch of the Old Palestinian family.[13] The third text-type, probably Babylonian in origin, is known thus far only in the Pentateuch and Samuel. It is the text-type that forms the base of the Rabbinic Recension of these books. In the Pentateuch it is a conservative text which shows relatively little expansion and relatively few traces of revision and modernizing. In the books of Samuel, on the contrary, it is a poor text, marked by extensive haplography and corruption. While it is not especially expansionistic, it is normally inferior to the Old Palestinian tradition preserved in 4QSam^b (mid–third century B.C.E.) and often to the Egyptian.

13. D. Barthélemy has objected to the use of "Egyptian" in describing the form of text underlying the Greek Pentateuch and Reigns. He argues that the evidence is satisfactorily explained by supposing Palestinian manuscripts were brought to Egypt (in the early second century in the case of Reigns) and translated. The difficulty is that the early copies of the "Proto-Samaritan" text of the Pentateuch at Qumrân (notably Palaeo-Hebrew manuscripts) already exhibit the full development of synoptic readings and other secondary traits which require a long period to evolve. The Egyptian text is evidently an early branch of the Palestinian. If Barthélemy wished to argue that fourth- or early-third-century Palestinian manuscripts were used in the later Greek translations, our positions would tend to merge. I am inclined to think, however, that (contrary to Barthélemy and the Letter of Aristeas) the Hebrew text used in the translation of the Pentateuch and of Reigns had been at home in the Jewish community in Egypt for some time.

III

In 1961 publication began of another series of discoveries in the Judaean Wilderness, from Murabbaʿât, the Naḥal Ḥever, and from the fortress of Masada. The biblical documents from the Wâdī Murabbaʿât, Genesis, Exodus, Numbers, and Isaiah, and above all, the great Hebrew Minor Prophets scroll, reveal a text which shows no significant deviation from the archetypal Rabbinic Recension.[14] The Minor Prophets scroll can be dated palaeographically to the second half of the first century C.E., and the fragments from Masada no later than 73 C.E. Thus there can no longer be any reason to doubt that before the end of the first century a recension of the text of the Hebrew Bible had been promulgated which had massive authority, at least in Pharisaic circles, and which came to dominate the Jewish community in the interval between the fall of Jerusalem in 70 C.E. and the suppression of the revolt of Bar Kokeba (Koseba) in 135 C.E. Indeed we can speak for the first time of evidence of external controls which extend even to orthographic detail in the manuscripts carried into the Wilderness by remnants of the host of Bar Kokeba.

Thanks to the discoveries in the Judaean Wilderness of a variety of textual traditions, as well as to the evidence of the Greek recensions, we are able to sketch in part the process by which the Pharisaic Recension—destined to be the official text—came into existence, and, with less precision, we can describe its character. The fixation of the text followed a pattern unusual in the textual history of ancient documents. Unlike the recensional activity in Alexandria which produced a short if artificial and eclectic text of Homer, and quite unlike the recensional activity which produced the Hexaplaric recension of the Septuagint and of the conflate *textus receptus* of the New Testament, the Pharisaic scholars and scribes proceeded neither by wholesale revision and emendation nor by eclectic or conflating recensional procedures. They selected a single textual tradition, which may be called the Proto-Rabbinic text,[15] a text which had been in existence in individual manuscripts for some time. Our evidence now suggests that the recension had a very narrow base. This does not prove that Paul de Lagarde was correct in his speculation that the medieval text stemmed from a single archetype, a single manuscript. However, in a given book of the Hebrew Bible the Rabbis chose exemplars of one textual family or even a single manuscript as a

14. P. Benoit, J. T. Milik, and R. de Vaux, *Les grottes de Murabbaʿât, DJD* 2 (Oxford: Clarendon Press, 1961), 75–85 (pls. 19–24), and 181–205 (pls. 56–73).

15. This text-type has also been called "Proto-Masoretic," a designation which perhaps should be reserved for early exemplars of the Rabbinic Recension.

base. They did not collate the wide variety of text-types available; on the contrary they firmly rejected in some instances a prevailing late Palestinian text.

It should be noted that they did not select, in the case of every book, traditions having a common origin or local background. In the Major Prophets, for example, they chose the relatively late and conflate Palestinian text of Isaiah, Jeremiah, and Ezekiel. In the Pentateuch they chose a short, relatively unconflated text—a superb text from the point of view of the modern critic. It shows none of the secondary traits of the Palestinian textual family found in the Chronicler's text, in many of the Qumrân manuscripts (both in the Jewish and Palaeo-Hebrew scripts), in Jubilees, in the archetype of the Samaritan Recension, in the Genesis Apocryphon, and indeed as late as in the Palestinian text underlying Pseudo-Philo's *Liber antiquitatum biblicarum* (composed shortly before 70 C.E.).[16] In the book of Samuel, where our differing textual families are most clearly marked, the Rabbinic Recension is again based on a short text but, unlike the Pentateuchal text, marked by extensive corruption and haplography. Its textual traits differ sharply from those of the text underlying both the Old Greek sections of Reigns and the Greek text of Josephus; nor is it the Hebrew text-type found in the Chronicler's quotations of Samuel, or in the several manuscripts from Qumrân (which are closely allied to the Chronicler's text and the text of Josephus and Pseudo-Philo). Evidently the text of the Pentateuch and Samuel utilized in the Rabbinic Recension was not taken from the prevailing Palestinian family chosen elsewhere in much of the Bible as the basis of the Recension. According to the theory of local texts, its origin may be sought for in Babylon.

On the basis of the orthography of the Rabbinic Recension we may determine that the Rabbis used relatively late manuscripts as their base, or at any rate as the basis of the orthographic style of the Recension. There is no evidence of the practice of the late Persian period (save in a rare word or corruption), and no biblical book reflects a style as archaic as 4QSam^{b}, a manuscript of the mid third century B.C.E.[17] On the other hand, the Rabbis repudiated the "baroque" orthography that began to develop in the Maccabaean Age and was popular at Qumrân (but never

16. See F. M. Cross, "The Evolution of a Theory of Local Texts," 309–315; D. Harrington, "The Biblical Text of Pseudo-Philo's *Liber Antiquitatum Biblicarum*," *CBQ* 33 (1971): 1–17; J. C. VanderKam, *Textual and Historical Studies in the Book of Jubilees, HSM* 14 (Missoula, Mont.: Scholars Press, 1977); "The Textual Affinities of the Biblical Citations in the Genesis Apocrypha," *JBL* 97 (1978): 45–55.

17. Cf. D. N. Freedman, "The Massoretic Text and the Qumrân Scrolls: A Study in Orthography," *Textus* 2 (1962): 87–102; reprinted in Cross and Talmon, *Qumrân and the History of the Biblical Text*, 196–211.

became regnant in Palestine), or, in any case chose manuscripts that were not inscribed in this new "learned" style.

Particularly interesting and significant is the rejection of the traditional Palaeo-Hebrew script by Pharisaic rabbis and scribes in favor of the common Jewish script, which, as they were well aware, derived from the Aramaic script. The old script, surviving from pre-Exilic times, was conserved largely as a biblical hand for the Pentateuch (and sporadically, at least, Job) and after ca. 350 B.C.E. was used on official seals and coins until its revival in the Maccabaean period with the achievement of Jewish independence. Its national and sacral character is well documented now in the Hellenistic and Roman periods in Judaea and Samaria (including Gerizim), by its use at Qumrân, especially for Pentateuchal manuscripts, and for inscribing the name of God in manuscripts in the Jewish hand, in its use in a monumental inscription from the area of the Temple, as well as its use on the coinage of the First and Second Jewish Revolts. It was, of course, also chosen by Zadokite priests of Samaria for the script of their Pentateuch. The rejection of this script, and, it follows, the late Palestinian textual family recorded in it, has a reflex in the Mishnah: Scriptures written in the (old) Hebrew script do not defile the hands, that is, are not sacred; only those written in the Assyrian (Aramaic) script on leather, in ink, defile the hands.[18]

In the case of a number of biblical books, alternate editions or recensions (as opposed to text-types) were circulating in the several Jewish communities into the Roman period and, as in the case of variant textual traditions, created a textual crisis when found side by side in Palestine in the era before the fall of Jerusalem. We have noted the case of Jeremiah, where two editions were kept in the same library. In this case the long (later) edition was selected for the Rabbinic Recension.[19] Longer editions of Job (vs. the edition underlying the Old Greek) and, most notably, of the Chronicler also were selected.[20] On the other hand, a brief edition of a much wider Danielic literature found its way into the Pharisaic recension.[21] Here the fixation of the text and the stabilization of the canon appear to be interlocked processes.

18. Yadayim 4:5.

19. The short (Egyptian) recension was rejected, and with it Baruch, which was sufficiently part of one edition of Jeremiah to have shared Greek revisers, including, *mirabile dictu,* the Pharisaic revisers we label *kaige*-proto-Theodotion or the Theodotionic school. See E. Tov, *The Septuagint Translation of Jeremiah and Baruch, HSM* 8 (Missoula, Mont.: Scholars Press, 1976), 168–170.

20. On the editions of Chronicles-Ezra, of which a torso survives in 1 Esdras, as well as Chronicles-Ezra-Nehemiah, see above, chapter 8.

21. Possible long and short editions of the Psalter will be treated below in the discussion of the fixation of the canon.

The time in which the recensional activities of the Rabbis took place and the date of the promulgation of an authoritative Pharisaic Text can now be fixed within fairly narrow limits. The evidence of late biblical finds in the Wilderness of Judah point to its existence in Pharisaic circles by 70 C.E., although Hellenistic Jewish works of the first century, including even Pseudo-Philo and Josephus, largely escaped its influence. Certainly the Rabbinic Recension became regnant only in the interval between the two Jewish revolts when the Pharisaic party came wholly to dominate the surviving Jewish community and rival parties diminished and disappeared, save as they survived in sectarian isolation, especially in the continuing Christian and Samaritan sects. Rabbinic Judaism survived and with it the Rabbinic Recension.

The forces at work giving rise to the recensional activity in Pharisaic circles can be reconstructed with some probability. Beginning in Maccabaean times a Zionist revival and Parthian expulsions brought a flood of Jews from Babylon, Syria, and Egypt back to Jerusalem.[22] By the first centuries B.C.E. and C.E., competing local texts and editions of biblical works had found their way to Judaea, causing such confusion as we find reflected in the library at Qumrân. Moreover, the uncontrolled development of the text of individual families was sufficient to give rise to a textual crisis once the urgent need for precise theological and halakhic exegesis was felt. Concurrent with these events was the rise of party strife beginning in earnest in the polarization of the Sadducean, Pharisaic, and Essene parties in the mid second century B.C.E. and in the doctrinal and legal disputes between the parties. By the beginning of the first century C.E. further sectarian splinters appear, and there is evidence of intense intraparty dispute as well as interparty and sectarian argument and contention. In the time of Hillel and the schools of Hillel and Shammai in the first century C.E. we witness the fixing of hermeneutical rules, as well as reported discussions which reflect a more or less fixed text.

The history of the Greek recensions, which more or less recapitulates the history of the developing Hebrew Text, also sheds light on the date of the fixing of the Rabbinical Recension.[23] The earliest Palestinian revisions of the Old Greek Samuel-Kings (Reigns), the so-called Proto-Lucianic recension of the late second or more likely the first century B.C.E., presume not the Proto-Rabbinic text of Samuel but the common Palestinian

22. 2 Macc. 2:14 contains an interesting reference to massive destruction of books in the Antiochan conflict and the replacement of the books by Judah the Maccabee.

23. On the history of Greek recensions, and above all on the Proto-Theodotionic or *kaige* Recension, see D. Barthélemy, *Les Devanciers d'Aquila, SVT* 10 (Leiden: Brill, 1963); and Cross, "Problems of Method in the Textual Criticism of the Hebrew Bible."

text-type described below. The first evidence of the Proto-Rabbinic text in Samuel is found in the recension of the Theodotionic school (*kaige*). This systematic recension from the end of the first century B.C.E., or the very beginning of the first century C.E., is inspired by principles similar to those that emerged in the Hillelite era and, no doubt, may be assigned to scholars of the same party that published the Rabbinic Recension. To be sure, the Hebrew text used is Proto-Rabbinic, not identical with the fully fixed Pharisaic Bible at all points. Only the revision of the Theodotionic-*kaige* recension by Aquila brings the Greek text fully in line with the Rabbinic Recension.

Taken together these data suggest that we should look to the era of Hillel and his disciples in the early first century C.E. for the initiation if not the completion of the recensional labor which fixed the Hebrew text of the Bible, the text we may fairly call the Pharisaic-Hillelite Recension, of which the Masoretic Text is a direct descendant. That Hillel (and his circle) were responsible for the selection of the Proto-Rabbinic manuscripts which stood behind the recension would also explain certain of its peculiarities: the rejection of the prevailing late Palestinian text of the Pentateuch and Samuel, the rejection of the Palaeo-Hebrew script (in the Pentateuch), and the "baroque" orthographic style, in favor of what appears to be a text-type of Babylonian origin in these books.[24] Hillel came up from Babylon and became the dominant and most creative spirit of his day; he was a giant whose impress on Pharisaism cannot be exaggerated and whose descendants were the principal leaders in the normative Jewish community for many generations. It would not be surprising if the conservative Torah scrolls which he knew, and to which he was accustomed, became under his urging the basis of the new Recension. It is not impossible too that an old saying embedded in the Babylonian Talmud preserved a memory of the role of Hillel in the events leading to the fixation of the Hebrew text and canon: "When the Torah was forgotten in Israel, Ezra came up from Babylon and established it [*wysdh*]; and when it was once again forgotten, Hillel the Babylonian came up and reestablished it [*wysdh*]."[25]

24. See already Cross, "The History of the Biblical Text in the Light of Discoveries in the Judaean Desert," 291; D. Barthélemy notes Josephus's reference to increased contacts between the Palestinian Jewish community and the Babylonian Jewish community during the reign of Herod (*Antiq.* 17:24–27); see his *Études d'histoire du texte de l'Ancien Testament,* 241 f.

25. Sukkah 20a. E. E. Urbach, *The Sages, Their Concepts and Beliefs* (Jerusalem: Magnes, 1975), 588 and n. 91 (p. 955), comments on this statement attributed to R. Šimʿon bin Laqiš: "It appears that he added the reference to R. Ḥiyya and his sons to a much older dictum." This reference to Sukkah 20a was first called to my attention

This much seems certain. The vigorous religious community in Babylon repeatedly in Jewish history developed spiritual and intellectual leaders who reshaped the direction of Palestinian Judaism and defined its norms. Such was the case in the Restoration of the Persian period, in the person of Hillel, and in the rise of the Babylonian Talmud.[26]

---

by Dr. Lee Levine of the Hebrew University. Hillel's "reestablishment of the Torah" has, of course, been taken heretofore more generally to apply to his role in the interpretation of oral and written law, or even figuratively to his exemplary "living of the Torah."

26. This study does not extend beyond the appearance of the so-called consonantal text—actually a text with incomplete vocalic notation based on a system of *matres lectionis.* The development of the fully vocalized or "pointed" Masoretic Text has recently been treated by Moshe Goshen-Gottstein in an important paper, "The Rise of the Tiberian Bible Text," in *Biblical and Other Studies,* ed. A. Altmann (Cambridge: Harvard University Press, 1963), 79–122; see also Barthélemy, *Études d'histoire du texte de l'Ancien Testament,* 355–364.

11

The Stabilization of the Canon of the Hebrew Bible

I

THE TERM *CANON* HAS ACQUIRED MANY MEANINGS. IN ORIGIN IT MEANT a rule, and concretely in the usage of the church fathers, a closed list of books deemed authoritative for religious faith and practice. The notion of a fixed list of books of scripture, invariable in that it was not to be added to or subtracted from, appears in the ancient sources first in Flavius Josephus writing in the last decade of the first century C.E.[1] The term *canonical* also has been used loosely—and anachronistically—to specify a level of authority acquired by a literary work (oral or written) which may be expressed in a variety of ways: "mythological" or "theological" or "sociological." Josephus uses the terms "decrees of God" and "inspiration." Earlier, the Chronicler uses the designation "Torah of Yahweh by the hand of Moses" or simply *Torat Yahweh.* The Rabbis used the terms "Holy Scripture" (*ktby qwdš*) and "books that contaminate the hands" (*hsprym hwṭm'ym 't hydym*). The claim of inspiration, or of being the "word of God," of course, asserts the authority of a book; at the same time, even when such claims were broadly accepted, the canonicity of the book, *sensu stricto,* was not guaranteed, and indeed the attempt has been made to define "canonical" writings which were not inspired, a category, for example, into which authoritative Rabbinical treatises might be placed.[2] Contemporary study of the Hebrew canon has devised also definitions of a level of authority which may warrant the general designation "canonical" based on the social function of a given traditional complex, or crystallized literary work. The study of the evolving levels of authority of biblical works and their emerging canonicity is of the first importance; in the present study, however, it belongs to the prehistory of the fixation of the canon.[3]

1. *Contra Apionem* 1: 37–43 (ed. Loeb).

2. See the elaborate categorization of "canonical works" in Sid Z. Leiman, *The Canonization of Hebrew Scripture: The Talmudic and Midrashic Evidence,* Transactions of the Connecticut Academy of Arts and Sciences (Hamden, Conn.: Archon Books, 1976).

3. On the prehistory of the canon, i.e., the early stages in the formation of authoritative Holy Writ, see especially D. N. Freedman, "The Law and the Prophets,"

II

The "canon" of Josephus[4] merits closer examination:

> It therefore naturally, or rather necessarily follows (seeing that with us it is not open to everybody to write the records, and that there is no discrepancy in what is written; seeing that, on the contrary, the prophets alone had this privilege, obtaining their knowledge of the most remote and ancient history through the inspiration which they owed to God, and committing to writing a clear account of the events of their time just as they occurred)—it follows, I say, that we do not possess myriads of inconsistent books, conflicting with each other. Our books, those which are justly accredited, are but two and twenty, and contain the record of all time. Of these, five are the books of Moses, comprising the laws and the traditional history from the birth of man down to the death of the lawgiver. From the death of Moses until Artaxerxes, who succeeded Xerxes as king of Persia, the prophets subsequent to Moses wrote the history of the events of their own times in thirteen books. The remaining four books contain hymns to God and precepts for the conduct of human life.
>
> From Artaxerxes to our time the complete history has been written, but has not been deemed worthy of equal credit with the earlier records, because of the failure of the exact succession of prophets.[5]

Josephus, writing in Rome in the last decade of the first century C.E., asserted that there was a fixed and immutable number of "justly accred-

---

SVT 9 (1962): 250–265; J. A. Sanders, "Adaptable for Life: The Nature and Function of Canon," in *Magnalia Dei: Essays on the Bible and Archaeology in Memory of G. Ernest Wright,* ed. F. M. Cross, W. E. Lemke, and P. D. Miller Jr. (New York: Doubleday, 1976), 531–560; and his more popular study, *Torah and Canon* (Philadelphia: Fortress, 1977); E. Jacob, "Principe canonique et la formation de l'Ancien Testament," *SVT* 28 (1974): 101–122; Jacob, *Canon and Authority,* ed. G. W. Coats and B. O. Long (Philadelphia: Fortress, 1977); and J. Blenkinsopp, *Prophecy and Canon* (Notre Dame: University of Notre Dame Press, 1977). A review of the discussion of the theological significance of the canon may be found conveniently in P. D. Miller Jr., "Der Kanon in der gegenwärtigen amerikanischen Diskussion," *Jahrbuch für biblische Theologie* 3 (1988): 217–223; see also Thomas A. Hoffman, S. J., "Inspiration, Normativeness, Canonicity, and the Unique Sacred Character of the Bible," *CBQ* 44 (1982): 447–469; and James A. Sanders, "Canon, Hebrew Bible," in *The Anchor Bible Dictionary,* 1:837–852.

4. See G. W. Anderson, "Canonical and Non-Canonical," *Cambridge History of the Bible,* vol. I, ed. P. R. Ackroyd and C. F. Evans (Cambridge: At the University Press, 1970), 113–159, and R. Meyer, "Bemerkungen zum literargeschichte Hintergrund des Kanonstheorie des Josephus," in *Josephus Studien, Otto Michel Festschrift,* ed. O. Betz, K. Haaker, and M. Hengel (Göttingen: Vandenhoek und Ruprecht, 1974), 285–289.

5. *Contra Apionem* 1: 37–41.

ited" (*ta dikaios pepisteumēna*) books, twenty-two in number. The logic of their authority rests in their derivation from a period of uncontested prophetic inspiration beginning with Moses and ending in the era of Nehemiah. Excluded specifically are works of Hellenistic date and, implicitly, works attributed to pre-Mosaic patriarchs. Josephus in the subsequent paragraph adds that the precise text of these works is fixed to the syllable.

Where are we to seek the origin of Josephus's assertions concerning the closed canon of Hebrew Scriptures? As we shall see, there is no evidence in non-Pharisaic Jewish circles before 70 C.E. (the Essenes of Qumrân, the Hellenistic Jewish community of Alexandria and Palestine, the Jewish-Christian and Samaritan sects) for either a fixed canon or text. Until very recently there has been a scholarly consensus that the acts of inclusion and exclusion which limited the canon were complete only at the "Council of Jamnia" (Yabneh), meeting about the end of the first century C.E. However, recent sifting of the Rabbinic evidence makes clear that, in the proceedings of the academy of Yabneh, at most the Rabbis discussed marginal books of the canon, specifically Qohelet and Song of Songs, and asserted that they "defiled the hands."[6] The passage in *Mišnah Yadayim* 3.5 records traditions about a dispute concerning Qohelet between the schools of Hillel and Shammai, with the Hillelites insisting (against the Shammaites) that Qohelet defiled the hands. The academy of Yabneh in the days of Rabbi ʾElʿazar ben ʿAzaryah and Yoḥanan ben Zakkay apparently upheld the Hillelite dictum on Qohelet or on both Qohelet and the Song of Songs. It must be insisted, moreover, that the proceedings at Yabneh were not a "council," certainly not in the late ecclesiastical sense.[7] Whatever decisions were taken at Yabneh, they were based on earlier opinions, and they failed to halt continued disputes concerning marginal books: Song of Songs, Qohelet, and Esther of the "included" books, Ben Sira among the "withdrawn" or apocryphal. In any case, it is clear that Josephus in Rome did not take his cue from contemporary or later proceedings at Yabneh, nor did he manufacture a theory of canon from whole cloth.

Thinly concealed behind Josephus's Greek apologetics is a clear and coherent theological doctrine of canon. There can be little doubt that he echoes his own Pharisaic tradition and specifically the canonical doctrine of Hillel and his school. Josephus is not alone in his testimony. We are now able to reconstruct an old canonical list, the common source of the so-called Bryennios List and the Canon of Epiphanius, which must be dated to the end of the first or the beginning of the second cen-

6. See Leiman, *The Canonization of Hebrew Scripture*, esp. 72–120.

7. See J. P. Lewis, "What Do We Mean by Jabneh?" *JBR* 32 (1964): 125–132, and more recently D. E. Aune, "On the Origins of the 'Council of Javneh' Myth," *JBL* 110 (1991): 491–493.

tury C.E.[8] It is a list of biblical works "according to the Hebrews" and reflects the same twenty-two-book canon we find in Josephus, echoed in the independent canonical lists of Origen and Jerome. The twenty-four-book canon mentioned in Fourth Ezra (ca. 100 C.E.)[9] and in the Rabbinic sources (most elaborately set out in *Baba Batra* 14b–15a) almost certainly is identical in content but reckons Ruth and Lamentations separately. The writing of Ruth with Judges, Lamentations with Jeremiah is quite old, to judge from its survival in the Septuagint and the explicit testimony of Origen to the Hebrew ordering. The Rabbinic tradition that Samuel wrote Judges and Ruth (in addition to Samuel) and Jeremiah the Book of Lamentations may be an indirect witness. The association of Ruth and Lamentations with Qohelet, Song of Songs, and Esther in the *Five Megillot* evidently reflects a secondary development, growing out of their liturgical usage in the festivals. One notes also that Josephus and the early list place Job among the Prophets; the old list places Job in close association to the Pentateuch. The use of Palaeo-Hebrew for Job alone outside the Pentateuch as a biblical hand suggests that this is an early feature, as does the Rabbinic tradition attributing the authorship of Job to Moses.

A *terminus post quem* for the fixation of the Pharisaic canon is suggested by evidence derived from the *Kaige* Recension. We have noted above that these revisers used as their base a Proto-Rabbinic text-type, not the fixed Rabbinic Recension. Similarly their revision extended to Baruch and a longer edition of Daniel, an effort difficult to explain if the Book of Baruch and the additions to Daniel had already been excluded from the Pharisaic canon. Since their recensional labors can be dated to the late first century B.C.E. and their Pharisaic bias is clear, it follows that, as late as the end of the first century B.C.E., an authoritative canonical list had not emerged, at least in its final form, even in Pharisaic circles.[10] On the other hand the pressures and needs leading to the final form of the text and canon of the Rabbinic Recension are well under way.

There are also bits of evidence not hitherto used which tend to support an early-first-century C.E. date for the Recension. There is the bizarre

8. See the study of J.-P. Audet, "A Hebrew-Aramaic List of Books of the Old Testament in Greek Transcription," *JTS* n.s. 1 (1950): 135–171. Not all of Audet's arguments for the early date of the list are convincing, but his conclusion appears sound and even overly cautious.

9. 4 Ezra 14:44–46.

10. See the discussion of E. Tov, *The Septuagint Translation of Jeremiah and Baruch, HSM* 8 (Missoula, Mont.: Scholars Press, 1976), esp. 168 ff.; E. Tov, *The Greek Minor Prophets Scroll from Naḥal Ḥever (8ḤevXIIgr), DJD* 8 (Oxford: Clarendon Press, 1990). On the date of this manuscript, see Peter J. Parsons' contribution to Tov's volume, pp. 19–26. Parsons and Skeat date the manuscript to the late first century B.C.E. It need not be added that 8ḤevXIIgr is not the autograph.

phenomenon of the *qĕrê' perpetuum* in the Pentateuch where the feminine pronoun *hî'* is spelled *hw'* in the *kĕtîb.* The most plausible explanation of this is that the manuscript or manuscripts copied for the Pentateuchal Recension was a manuscript in which *waw* and *yod* were not distinguished in the Jewish script. This occurs at only one time in the development of the Jewish scripts: in the Early Herodian Period (30–1 B.C.E.).[11] Note also the rejection by the Rabbis of the Palaeo-Hebrew script used at Qumrân for copying Pentateuchal manuscripts and Job, in formal inscriptions from the temple area in Jerusalem and in Samaria, in the Samaritan Pentateuch, and on coinage of the Hasmonaean and Roman periods. This also involves a rejection of the common Palestinian text of the Pentateuch in use at Qumrân, and in the Sadducean priesthood of Samaria, and of course in the later Samaritan Recension of the Pentateuch. This rejection is remarkable given the nationalism of the time and is explained only by the assumption that Proto-Rabbinic manuscripts inscribed in Palaeo-Hebrew script were not available.

In view of the evidence, I am inclined to posit the thesis that the same circumstances that brought about the textual crisis which led to the fixation of the Hebrew text—varied texts and editions, party strife, calendar disputes, sectarianism, the systematization of hermeneutic principles and halakhic dialectic—were the occasion for a "canonical crisis" and the fixation of a Pharisaic canon, and further that Hillel was a central figure in sharpening the crisis and responding to it. The fixation of the text and the fixation of the canon were thus two aspects of a single if complex endeavor. Both were essential to erect "Hillelite" protection against rival doctrines of purity, cult and calendar, alternate legal dicta and theological doctrines and, indeed, against the speculative systems and mythological excesses of certain Apocalyptic schools and proto-Gnostic sects.[12]

The principles guiding exclusion of works from the Pharisaic canon, reflected in Josephus's notices, no doubt operated well in eliminating works offensive to Hillel and the house of Hillel. The host of pseudepigraphic works in the name of Enoch, Melchizedek, the sons of Jacob, Amram, and the like, which became popular in Hellenistic times and which fill the Qumrân library, were eliminated: the Prophetic sequence

11. See "The Development of the Jewish Scripts," in *The Bible and the Ancient Near East: Essays in Honor of William Foxwell Albright,* ed. G. Ernest Wright (New York: Doubleday, 1961), fig. 2, line 9.

12. The Halakhic Epistle—so-called MMT—is an excellent example of halakhic debate and polemics in this era. See E. Qimron and J. Strugnell, *Qumran Cave 4 • V Miqṣat Ma'aśe ha-torah* (Oxford: Clarendon Press, 1994); appendix 1, written by Y. Sussman, is of particular interest.

began with Moses. There can be little doubt, moreover, that the Rabbis recognized their recent date since such cycles as Enoch and the Testament of the Twelve Patriarchs were in their creative, fluid phase of composition, unfixed as literary works, into the Roman period. This is not to say that the earliest works in this genre were late and without authority. The astrological work embedded in First Enoch began its development no later than the mid-third century B.C.E. and may even go back to the end of the fourth century. The principle of excluding works of "post-Prophetic" authorship permitted the suppression of the propagandistic book of Maccabees, certain of the Hellenistic novellae, and Ben Sira, although the case of pseudepigrapha written in the name of "prophets," especially the Jeremianic apocrypha, Baruch, and the Letter of Jeremiah, must have caused difficulty and dispute, as well as the partitioning of the "Solomonic" literature. In the latter case, it is not without interest that Qohelet has proven to be much earlier than scholars have generally thought—a copy of the work from the beginning of the second century is known from Qumrân—and a Persian date (first half of the fourth century B.C.E.?) is not excluded. Qohelet, Song of Songs, and Ezekiel were controversial works, in probability, because of their content, but were sufficiently old and recognized not to be passed over. Most mysterious is the selection for inclusion of an edition of Daniel—a work not earlier than the Maccabaean Age, though it contains earlier material—and the selection of Esther. It must be said, however, that, in general, the Rabbis chose for inclusion in their canon works or editions which in fact reached literary fixation by the end of the Persian period. Thus the late Persian date for the final edition of the Chronicler's Work (Chronicles-Ezra-Nehemiah), and the edition of the Psalter containing 150 psalms is strongly supported by recent studies.[13] To be sure, the canonical theory of the Pharisees, while confirming the canonicity of Israel's oldest religious literature, much of which had reached an immutable level of authority, also was shaped to exclude the vast Hellenistic literature which contained the doctrines and halakhic lore of the Jewish parties and sects alien to Pharisaism in its later Hillelite form. At the same time the Hillelite canon was not radically conservative. One contrasts with it the truncated canon of the Samaritans, which included only the Pentateuch. Some scholars have suggested too that the Sadducees held to a shorter canonical list. Unfortunately we do not have sufficient evidence to determine the nature of the canon of the Sadducees, if indeed they defined a canon; if we take the Qumrân community—the Essenes—to be an apocalyptic branch of the Sadducees (for they called themselves "Sons of Zadok" and have halakhic doctrines akin to Sadducean as opposed to

13. On the Psalter, see below; on the Chronicler, see above, chapter 8.

Pharisaic doctrine) we can say that at least one branch of the Sadducees had no fixed canon. One finds it hard to believe, however, that the conservative wing of the Sadducees who returned to high-priestly power in the Herodian era would have held the late apocalyptic book of Daniel, with its explicit doctrine of resurrection, to be authoritative.

If we are correct in perceiving the hand of Hillel in the promulgation of a Pharisaic text and canon, we must nevertheless add that this canon and text did not immediately supplant other traditions or receive uniform acceptance even in Pharisaic circles. The ascendancy of the Hillelite text and canon came with the victory of the Pharisaic party and the Hillelite House in the interval between the two Jewish revolts against Rome.

III

The discovery of the ancient library of the Essene community at Qumrân provides us insight into the nature and variety of religious works, their text and editions, at home in a non-Pharisaic religious community, and presumably given reverence by it. The library contains specimens of all the works of the Hebrew canon with the exception of the book of Esther. Its absence, however, may be owing only to chance. The Book of Chronicles has survived at Qumrân only in a single small fragment despite its larger size; an additional hungry worm, and Chronicles, too, would have been missing. Many of the manuscripts represent the Palestinian text-type as we have seen. Similarly a large pseudepigraphic literature, largely of Palestinian provenience, both of pre-Essene and of sectarian character, is present, as well as certain books of the so-called Apocrypha: Tobit and Ben Sira.[14] At Qumrân we see the apocalyptic movement in Judaism in all its chaotic vigor.

There is no clear evidence at Qumrân of a fixed Essene canon or of the influence of the Pharisaic canon. Variant editions and texts of biblical works were copied and in use until the end of the community in 68 C.E. The suggestion has been made that criteria of style in the copying of manuscripts (writing material, format, and script) may supply a clue to the canonical or noncanonical category of a given document. Thus canonical works were written on leather, in columns of a length double their width (in accordance with later practice), in a formal—but not cursive—script. Unhappily the criteria do not always hold even for works of unquestioned authority which found their way into all later canons. And even if they had held true invariably for, say, the earliest books to gain immutable authority, the Pentateuch and Prophets, this circum-

14. For a review of this literature with bibliography, see P. W. Skehan, "Qumrân. Littérature," *Supplément du Dictionnaire de la Bible*, 9, cols. 805–828.

stance would not have established the existence of a fixed canon at Qumrân. On the other hand, it is true that such a work as Daniel receives unusually free treatment in copying: there is a manuscript on papyrus, a manuscript on leather, but in cursive script, and manuscripts in atypical format. This may indicate that it had not yet reached the stage of authority necessary to be regarded as "Holy Scripture." Complicating this analysis, however, is a unique factor. The earliest manuscript of Daniel, the text written in a cursive hand, dates within fifty years of the completion of the final edition of Daniel, when it is unlikely to have had time to gain a place of authority broadly in the Jewish community, even if later it came to be regarded as canonical in the Pharisaic and Essene parties.

The Psalter at Qumrân has been the subject of controversy. The great majority of manuscripts of the Psalter appears to reflect roughly the order (with minor variations) and content that stands behind the Rabbinic Psalter so far as they are preserved (mostly in the first four books of the Psalter, Psalms 1–106). Included in this group is 4QPs[a], which dates from the early second century B.C.E. and preserves portions of the Psalter from Psalm 5 to Psalm 71. The five-book, one-hundred-fifty-psalm collection is reflected also in the Greek Psalter (again with minor variations), suggesting that it received literary fixation at a fairly early date. From Qumrân, Cave 11, however, comes a collection of psalms in two copies, which has in the preserved portions radically different ordering, and the introduction of compositions not found in the traditional Psalter. The larger of the two manuscripts, published by J. A. Sanders in 1965,[15] preserves psalms beginning with Psalm 101. From the end of Book IV of the Psalter and from Book V, eleven psalms are missing from the collection (Psalms 106–108 and 110–117). The order is bizarre except for Psalms 121–132 (most of the "Songs of Ascents"). In the last ten columns of the collection, there are no fewer than ten insertions and additions: a hymn known also from Ben Sira 51, the "Last Words of David" from 2 Samuel 23, seven noncanonical hymns, and a prose insert, "David's Compositions."[16] The question is, what is this collection of psalms? My initial reaction was expressed as follows: "If the so-called 11QPs is indeed a Psalter, despite its bizarre order and non-canonical compositions, mostly of the Hellenistic era, we must argue that one psalms collection closed at the end of the Persian period (the canonical collection), and that another remained open well into the Greek period (11Q), but was rejected by the Rabbis."[17]

15. *The Psalms Scroll of Qumran Cave 11, DJD* 4 (Oxford: Clarendon Press, 1965).

16. This is to ignore the insertion of Ps. 93:1–3 (from Book IV of the traditional Psalter).

17. F. M. Cross, "The History of the Biblical Text in the Light of the Discoveries in the Judean Desert," *HTR* 57 (1964): 281–299; reprinted in F. M. Cross and S. Talmon,

The editor of the 11QPs[a] manuscript took the document to be the Essene Psalter and concluded that the Psalter, at least in its final third, was fluid and "open," revealing the state of the Psalter before final canonical fixation.[18] The late Patrick W. Skehan has argued convincingly that the traditional Psalter of 150 psalms was known at Qumrân, and indeed that the aberrant collection of 11QPs[a] shows dependence on it.[19] We are left then with the alternatives that the 11QPs[a] collection is either a "long edition" of the Psalter which stood alongside an older short edition or that 11QPs[a] is an independent work, a liturgical collection of Davidic hymns, presumably of Essene or proto-Essene composition, whose precise design is not yet wholly clear. There is a parallel composition (or compositions) from Qumrân, Cave 4, using Pentateuchal materials. Breaking up extended sections of familiar Pentateuchal text are (rare) intrusions of extracanonical lore, as well as omissions of sections of text.[20] Yet in the case of the Pentateuch, the early literary fixation of the fundamental text is certain, and (contrary to the case of the Psalter) the Pentateuchal materials at Qumrân are extensive enough to prove that the primary form of the Pentateuch at Qumrân does not differ in edition or in compositional elements from the received text; its variation is not literary but for the most part textual in origin, wrought by the mundane changes arising in scribal transmission.

The state of the scriptures at Qumrân—innocent of the imprint of canonical fixation—is not unlike the state of the Greek Bible in the pre-Christian Alexandrian Jewish community. Older views postulating the existence of an "Alexandrian canon" have dissolved under closer scholarly scrutiny.[21] The longer canon of the Old Testament, derived from the Alexandrian Greek Bible, is a creation of the Church.[22]

---

eds., *Qumrân and the History of the Biblical Text* (Cambridge: Harvard University Press, 1975), 177–195.

18. See J. A. Sanders, "The Qumrân Psalms Scroll (11QPs[a]) Reviewed," *On Language, Culture, and Religion: In Honor of Eugene A. Nida,* ed. M. Black and W. A. Smalley (The Hague: Mouton, 1974), 77–99.

19. P. W. Skehan, "Qumrân and Old Testament Criticism," in *Qumran: Sa piété, sa théologie, et son milieu, BEThL* 46 (Leuven: University Press, 1978), 163–182. See also M. H. Goshen-Gottstein, "The Psalm Scroll (11QPs[a]): A Problem of Canon and Text," *Textus* 5 (1966): 22–33.

20. See E. Tov and Sidnie White, *Qumran Cave 4 • VIII Parabiblical Texts, Part I, DJD* 13 (Oxford: Clarendon Press, 1994), 187–352.

21. See esp. A. C. Sundberg Jr., *The Old Testament of the Early Church* (Cambridge: Harvard University Press, 1964); and Peter Katz, "The Old Testament Canon in Palestine and Alexandria," *Zeitschrift für die neutestamentliche Wissenschaft* 47 (1956): 191–217.

22. On the Christian canon, see H. von Campenhausen, *The Formation of the Christian Bible* (Philadelphia: Fortress Press, 1972).

IV

The order of books of the Bible was not fixed with the closure of the canon. The received Hebrew and Christian orders are both late, stabilized only after a long period of vacillation. Josephus lists a tripartite division corresponding to the Law, Prophets, and Writings, referred to already in the Prologue of Ben Sira ("the Law, the Prophets, and the rest of the books"). Luke 24:44 mentions "the law of Moses, and the prophets and psalms." If a tripartite division of the canon was relatively early, however, the books assigned to the latter two divisions were in flux. In Josephus's list only Psalms, Proverbs, Qohelet, and Song of Songs belong to the Writings; the remainder of the later traditional Hagiographa was reckoned among the Prophets. His number, twenty-two books, presumes the writing of Ruth with Judges, and Lamentations with Jeremiah, a reckoning and practice certainly antecedent to the later Rabbinic reckoning of twenty-four when Ruth and Lamentations were removed from the Prophetic section to join Qohelet, Song of Songs, and Esther in the *Five Megillot.* The placement of Job in the earliest canonical lists is early in the Prophets. On the other hand, Job became firmly attached to the "Davidic" and "Solomonic" group (Psalms, Proverbs, Qohelet, and Song of Songs) in some early lists. Jerome, whose familiarity with the Palestinian Jewish order was intimate, actually lists Job immediately following the Pentateuch in one of his works, the first of the Hagiographa followed by the "Davidic" and "Solomonic" books in another.[23] It may be that the explanation for the basic difference between two major orders, the placement of the Latter Prophets before or after the Hagiographa, stems from this vacillation in the placement of Job and the attraction of other works of the hymnic and wisdom genres to Job, or Job to them. An older division into Law and Prophets, simply, may be postulated, for in the canonical theory of the Pharisees all books were written under prophetic inspiration by an unbroken sequence of prophets. The expression "Law and Prophets" used of the Hebrew Scriptures is found at Qumrân, in the New Testament, and in the Talmud.

If we look into the prehistory of the canon, it is clear that none of the orders extant follow a consistent historical principle. None follows the sequence of the dates when the works were actually written, or reached literary stability, or the dates when they gained permanent authority as scripture, or the dates to which later tradition assigned them. Particularly baffling in the Hebrew order is the breakup of the Chronicler's

23. See the study of P. W. Skehan, "St. Jerome and the Canon of Holy Scriptures," in *A Monument to Saint Jerome,* ed. F. X. Murphy (New York: Sheed and Ward, 1952), 259–287.

Work (Chronicles-Ezra-Nehemiah) and the placement of the early part of the work (Chronicles) after the later part (Ezra-Nehemiah). In the biblical period, and indeed at Qumrân, for the most part single books or small collections (such as the Twelve Minor Prophets) were inscribed on individual scrolls, and a firm traditional order—except for gigantic continuous works like the Pentateuch or the Deuteronomistic History (which were secondarily broken down into scroll-size units)—did not fully develop until medieval times.[24]

24. At Qumrân we have Pentateuchal books written on single scrolls, in three instances two Pentateuchal books on a single scroll (Genesis-Exodus, Exodus-Leviticus, and Leviticus-Numbers), but in no case more than two on a single scroll. The Twelve are inscribed usually on one scroll and in all but one instance in their traditional order. In the case of the *Five Megillot,* extant Qumrân manuscripts contain but a single book on each scroll extant.

PART VI

TYPOLOGY AND HISTORICAL METHOD

12

Alphabets and Pots: Reflections on Typological Method in the Dating of Artifacts

IN WRITING A MEMORIAL ON THE OCCASION OF THE DEATH OF WILLIAM Foxwell Albright, I sought to identify a central element which characterized and gave special distinction to his scholarship. I wrote then as follows:

> Albright was a master of typological method. In his programmatic studies and in his large syntheses of historical data, he is to be found normally to be imposing the discipline of typological analysis on unclassified and chaotic bits of evidence. This is most evident in his three volumes of *The Excavation of Tell Beit Mirsim.* In this work Albright established the fundamental chronology of Palestinian archaeology. He accomplished this by removing sequence dating of ceramic forms from the realm of intuition and guess, placing it upon a systematic footing. Sir Flinders Petrie first recognized the importance of the evaluation of pottery forms for archaeological dating. But Albright became the father of Palestinian archaeology with his minute and precise observation of the typological features of pottery, and with his grand synthesis of ceramic chronology in the Bronze and Iron Ages.
>
> In 1937 Albright published an essay entitled "A Biblical Fragment from the Maccabaean Age: The Nash Papyrus."[1] In it he established the framework of Aramaic and Jewish palaeography in the Hellenistic and Roman ages. All subsequent palaeographical studies, including those of the Qumrân (Dead Sea) scrolls, build on this foundation. And it must be said more than [five] decades after his study, during which fabulous new materials have been found [not to mention carbon-14 dates], his date for the Nash Papyrus has re-

The W. F. Albright Lecture delivered at the Johns Hopkins University, April 14, 1980.

1. W. F. Albright, "A Biblical Fragment from the Maccabaean Age: The Nash Papyrus," *JBL* 56 (1937): 145–176.

> quired no adjustment. In other studies he fixed early Phoenician palaeographical dates. These data permitted him to write his programmatic work, "New Light on the Early History of Phoenician Colonization" and his papers on the early history of the alphabet.[2] He applied the discipline of typology with equal rigor to problems of linguistic change and orthographic development. In his essay "The Oracles of Balaam" (1944)[3] he began his analysis of the typology of Canaanite and early Hebrew prosodic forms and styles. In his last major volume, *Yahweh and the Gods of Canaan* (1968), this work was carried to maturity.[4]

These studies are but illustrations of Albright's labors as a typologist of archaeological artifact, of scripts and orthography, of literary and artistic forms and themes, and ultimately of ideas, especially the development of religious ideas.

It has seemed appropriate to me, in the light of Albright's contributions to the typological sciences, to take up the subject of typological method and to present some of my own reflections on typology in the dating of artifacts, especially pots and scripts.

Much energy has been expended in recent years on the philosophical analysis of scientific method and of historical method, and the relationship between the two.[5] The shock of the revolution in physics, symbolized by the names of Einstein and Niels Bohr, has been the occasion for new interest in and sharp debate upon theoretical questions of scientific method, its nature and its postulates.[6] On the other hand, typologists generally have not been particularly self-conscious about their method and its postulates. They have tended to be specialists, lost in the details of Grey-Burnished Ware or in the definition of emergent national scripts. Typology, one of the principal historical and archaeological disciplines,

2. See especially, "The Phoenician Inscriptions of the Tenth Century B.C. from Byblus," *JAOS* 67 (1947): 153–160; "The Early Alphabetic Inscriptions from Sinai and Their Decipherment," *BASOR* 110 (1948): 6–22; and *The Proto-Sinaitic Inscriptions and Their Decipherment, HTS* 22 (Cambridge: Harvard University Press, 1966).

3. W. F. Albright, "The Oracles of Balaam," *JBL* 63 (1944): 107–233.

4. "William Foxwell Albright (1891–1971)," *Yearbook of the American Philosophical Society* (Philadelphia: American Philosophical Society, 1972), 114.

5. See, for example, A. C. Danto, *Analytical Philosophy of History* (Cambridge: Cambridge University Press, 1965), and Morton White, *Foundations of Historical Knowledge* (New York: Harper and Row, 1965; Harper Torchbook edition, 1969).

6. See the provocative essays of Gerald Holten, *Thematic Origins of Scientific Thought: Kepler to Einstein* (Cambridge: Harvard University Press, 1973; rev. ed., 1988); cf. Thomas E. Kuhn, *The Structure of Scientific Revolutions* (Chicago: University of Chicago Press, 1962; rev. ed., 1970), and Peter Medawar, *The Limits of Science* (Oxford: Oxford University Press, 1984).

has thus escaped serious theoretical analysis. It is curious that Petrie, who was the first to develop sequence dating of pottery—in the present century—had to defend the validity of his typological method of dating pottery. After all, sequence dating—called by whatever name—had developed in many fields. Greek and Latin palaeography had been studied systematically. Historical linguistics had come of age as a developed science. And so on. But curious walls were erected between these disciplines, and abstract thinking about the nature of typological judgments rarely informed the minds of specialist practitioners. Each typologist, palaeographer, historical linguist, art historian observed typological features and clusters of typological characters in complex change. Each dated them, arranged them in sequences, and applied his own technical jargon to them. Each field or community of specialists developed its own language and esoteric lore; and rarely was there discussion of typological method as such, or what we may call the typological sciences.

Perhaps it will prove worthwhile to examine what we do when we make typological judgments, construct typological series, and proceed to the description and dating of artifacts. All of us instinctively make typological judgments. My first endeavors in this field came when as a boy I became fascinated with automobiles. I learned to date models of cars: Packards, Fords, Studebakers, Cords, almost at a glance, to the year. Most of us can date buildings within a decade or two, or styles in dress even more precisely.

All artifacts are amenable to typological study—including creations of the hand: pots and scripts, armor and architecture; and products of the mind which we ordinarily do not call artifacts: linguistic forms, prosodic canons, religious ideas, musical styles.

What are the assumptions, presuppositions, postulates, and procedures of typological analysis and dating?

I

The fundamental assumption of all the typological sciences is that artifacts of a given category or class change in the course of time. An alphabet or a cooking pot develops, evolves or devolves, over centuries of time. The shapes of letters in a living script do not remain static. The shape, decoration, and paste of a given ceramic form, to name only a few typological characters, never remain the same over extended periods of time. This notion of universal and inevitable change in artifacts is posited as a methodological assumption. All sequences of artifacts we examine exhibit such change. But we cannot prove our assumption. We cannot examine all human artifacts of the past—much less of the future. Our methodological stance is not unlike that of the physical scientist who assumes that there are regularities in nature—laws—which, once validly described, may be assumed to have operated in the past and will operate in the future. Anomalies or singularities, of course, do persist stubbornly in our descriptions of nature, but the scientist has faith that they are merely problems awaiting solution by new measurements or new insights or theories, as the case may be, transforming anomaly into a part of a grander regularity and symmetry. This "faith" was expressed drolly by Einstein in his remark that God doesn't play dice. I remember once hearing a lecture by an archaeologist who asserted that in a site he had dug—belonging to a little-known culture—the repertoire of pottery showed no significant change for nearly half a millennium. The archaeologists present who possessed some methodological sophistication all reached one conclusion: that the lecturer was a bad typologist or a bad stratigrapher or, more likely, both. And this, in fact, proved to be the case.

There are two kinds or two levels of typological change. One we may describe as inadvertent, unconscious or spontaneous change. Such change resembles the changes in biological evolution. For example, scribes in writing have slightly different hands—idiosyncrasies in penning letters. Indeed, it may be said that no two scribes' hands are identical, though each essentially tries to write with standard letter forms. The idiosyncrasies of one scribe or one scribal school may become the standard letter forms of the next generation. In effect, substandard forms become standard. Sound changes in language ordinarily represent the same kind of unconscious change. One is reminded of the old joke of a Texan talking about President Johnson: "He may not be of much account as a president, but at least he ain't got no accent."

Often in a typological series, a useful or functional element will devolve. A famous case is the storage jar with wavy ledge handles used by Sir Flinders Petrie in developing sequence dating in Palestine and Egypt. The classic jar had a ledge attached to either side by which the jar could be held. The ledges were "wavy," molded to fit the fingers that grasped them. In later jars these handles became vestigial, the ledge too small to be functional—but the wavy molded form persisted. In the latest jars one often finds on either side of the jar just a wavy line—as an incised decoration—the old function and form long forgotten.

Another famous example of devolution or degeneration is to be found in the decoration of Byzantine lamps. On many, in elegant Greek letters, was inscribed the motto: *ΦΩΣ ΧΥ ΦΗΝΙ ΠΑΣΙΝ* (*sic!*). Later lamps have a sequence of Greek-like letters with no sense, and finally the inscription became conventional decoration, its origin in letter forms unrecognizable.

The second kind of change in typological sequences we may designate "creative innovation." An element of human freedom or intelligence may be discerned. A most dramatic example is the invention of the alphabet, a change which involved radical simplification. Older writing systems were logographic—signs representing words—or syllabic, signs or graphemes representing syllables. Such writing systems often required a repertoire of signs numbering three hundred or more. Scribes necessarily were scholars, a small elite, who held a monopoly on higher culture. Actually in the system of Egyptian hieroglyphic writing there existed signs for single consonants, for two consonants, for three consonants, and for words (so-called determinatives). The canons of writing called for use of this complex set of signs. Yet this system, which evidently gave inspiration to the inventor of the alphabet, actually possessed a set of simple alphabetic signs—what has been called a pseudo-alphabet. The Old Canaanite alphabet came into being when the notion was grasped that one could write using a single sign for a single consonant; vowels were not given notation in this early alphabetic system. The result was a simplification in which twenty-seven or twenty-eight signs—pictographs—represented the consonantal phonemes in Canaanite speech. This writing system, wholly phonetic, could be learned by a native speaker of Canaanite in a matter of weeks if not days. The upshot was a revolution comparable only to the invention of writing itself or to the invention of the printing press. For the first time in human history there was a possibility of the democratization of culture, and with it the surge of a new dynamic for cultural change. And yet, all the materials for the invention of the alphabet were available for centuries, awaiting a creative moment.[7] Another example of creative simplification may be found in the history of warfare. Subsequent to the domestication of the horse, chariot warfare soon developed. Only much later (with the invention of the stirrup) there came the simple insight that cavalry, men on horses, was a more maneuverable and efficient weapon than a man on a chariot drawn by horses.

Many innovations involve a feature of improved function: slips, burnishing, and finally glazes on ceramic ware improved pottery, preventing evaporation of liquids. Other changes reflect aesthetic innovation

7. See F. M. Cross, "Early Alphabetic Scripts," in *Symposia Celebrating the Seventy-fifth Anniversary of the Founding of the American Schools of Oriental Research,* ed. F. M. Cross (Cambridge: ASOR, 1979), 97–111; "Newly-Found Inscriptions in Old Canaanite and Early Phoenician Scripts," *BASOR* 238 (1981): 1–20; and "The Invention and Development of the Alphabet," in *The Origins of Writing,* ed. Wayne M. Senner (Lincoln: University of Nebraska Press, 1989), 77–90; see also J. Naveh, *Early History of the Alphabet* (Leiden: Brill, 1982), and more recently, B. Sass, *The Genesis of the Alphabet and Its Development in the Second Millennium* B.C. (Wiesbaden: Harrassowitz, 1988). More generally on the impact of new writing systems on human culture, see J. Goody, *The Domestication of the Savage Mind* (Cambridge: Cambridge University Press, 1977).

FIGURE 2

Development of *Dalet* and *Reš* in the Eighth and Seventh Centuries B.C.E.

or simply desire for novelty. Beautiful pots or scripts or architectural forms replaced less beautiful. Still another category of innovations reflects adjustment of forms—ceramic, alphabetic, glyptic and so on—to new techniques of manufacture or to new materials. The invention of the potter's wheel stimulated change. The development of papyrus as the material on which to write with ink and reed pens brought with it new cursive writing styles.

Conscious or directed changes in typological development may be illustrated by yet another example taken from the history of scripts. In the course of development, often letters evolved toward each other, causing confusion or ambiguity. *Reš* and *dalet* are examples (see figure 2). In the late ninth century and early eighth century B.C.E., the leg of *dalet* (see first pair of signs) began to lengthen in cursive scripts, and *reš* and *dalet* became much alike and were often mistaken for each other. Later in the eighth century, and especially in the seventh century, distinguishing features were developed (see second pair of signs), the head of *dalet* remained angular, the upper line broke through to the right, and the stance of the letter shifted further counterclockwise. *Reš,* on the other hand, developed a more rounded and proportionally smaller head.

There is here a principle of polarity operating; converging in evolution, the letter forms then spring apart, developing new characters which distinguish them—which give increased clarity. In this typological change we perceive the operation of human reason.

II

Creations of the human hand or human spirit change in time: the change may be propelled by inadvertent or conscious factors; it may be spontaneous or free. However, the discipline of typological analysis does not operate merely on the assumption of change or innovation in time. Equally important is a paired postulate: that a typological sequence always reveals a continuity of types. Each emergent type is related to and continuous with its antecedent type.

If man is the most creative and innovative of creatures, he is at the same time the most imitative of creatures, whether he is devising languages or scripts, constructing houses or philosophies, designing automobiles or flints. I can think of nothing so imitative as an adolescent daughter in the selection of wearing apparel—unless it is an Ivy League professor choosing a wardrobe. In the case of languages or scripts one recognizes that continuity is inevitable and necessary. A letter (grapheme) must be recognizable in the community in order to communicate. A sign or phoneme must contrast with other significant signs or phonemes. Hence, radical innovation or change, if attempted, is rejected. A sufficient continuity within change must be maintained to insure intelligibility. Thus change is controlled, freedom sharply limited.

The case is not different with cooking pots or literary forms or even ideas. An attempt at radical innovation, in discontinuity with the past, if it could take place, would produce the unrecognizable or unintelligible or unacceptable—and drop out of the typological sequence. In discoursing on the history of ideas Hegel best develops his notion of the dialectic or logic which he regards as belonging to the nature of the human mind: ternary sequences—thesis, antithesis, synthesis, the synthesis becoming the new thesis. In Hegel's system this dialectic movement ultimately reflects the logic of the Absolute Spirit, a metaphysical construct which interests me, if at all, only as a philosophical artifact. Yet the Hegelian dialectic is rooted in a valid observation of historical sequence. Each new emergence in a typological sequence in some sense takes up the past into itself. Novelty appears only in an orderly set of relationships with past antecedents. There is continuity. At least the typologist postulates continuity in constructing his typological series.

Here there may be an objection: do we not in fact observe what may be termed an occasional radical discontinuity in historical sequences? Certainly historians and typologists have made such claims. However, these must be disallowed on methodological grounds. What happens when a typologist comes upon an apparent discontinuity in a pottery sequence or in the development of letter forms in a Hebrew script?

Let us say one is peacefully digging in a Syrian tell and, amid the expected assemblage of typical ninth-century Syrian pottery, comes upon a sophisticated, apparently unique pot decorated in elaborate geometric designs unlike any extant Syrian motifs: the form of the pot, its decoration, and its paste, all fall outside the known ninth-century repertoire. It does not occur to the archaeologist to suggest that a highly inventive or imaginative potter created an utterly new pottery type without ancestry or progeny. He rather assumes that the pot has been imported from another cultural milieu and presently identifies it as Attic Geometric ware belonging precisely in a sequence of ninth-century Attic ceramic types.

Another example. In 1953, while examining a lot of Cave Four Qumrân manuscripts bought from Bedouin, I came on some fragments of a Samuel manuscript which appeared surprisingly archaic. In fact the elegant bookhand of the manuscript exhibited letter forms characteristic of

FIGURE 3

Development of *ʿAyin* from the Fourth to the Second Century B.C.E.

the mid–third century B.C.E. If my preliminary analysis were correct, the manuscript would be the oldest biblical scroll in existence. There was, however, one problem. All the letters of the Aramaic hand conformed to mid-third-century forms except one: the letter *ʿayin.* The *ʿayin* has some peculiarities, but similar *ʿayins* were second century.[8]

The "break-through" below the bowl of the *ʿayin* appeared to be a development in early-second-century scripts. How did I propose to handle the problem? There were several possibilities. I could date the manuscript to the second century, claiming that the scribe was attempting to archaize, slipping up on *ʿayin,* which he wrote inadvertently in contemporary fashion. Or to say much the same thing, I could declare the manuscript a forgery. Rather I made—with some fear and trembling—an alternative proposal. I proposed that the manuscript was third century and belonged to a formal script tradition hitherto not extant from the third century. As it happened, all extant third-century scripts were highly cursive in tradition: graffiti and ostraca. My notion was that parallel series, one formal, one cursive, were in simultaneous use. My advanced *ʿayin,* I argued, was presumably an innovation in the formal series no later than the third century and possibly earlier—invading the cursive series only later in the second century. It was a rather bold theory in view of the fact that innovation occurs more frequently in a cursive series, later infecting formal traditions. But this is by no means invariably the direction of influence. At all events, new data later came to light. In 1962 papyri were found in the Wâdī ed-Dâliyeh written in an elegant formal hand of the late fourth century B.C.E. On a dated papyrus of 335 B.C.E. the scribe regularly used the narrow "broken-through" *ʿayin.* It was in fact a late-fourth-century innovation in a formal script style. The Samuel manuscript was in fact mid–third century in date.[9]

Another kind of objection may be raised. This postulate of continuity may very well be methodologically sound in dealing with such matters as pots and alphabets and spelling practices. But what of higher elements of culture, of the human spirit? Does not here the individual,

8. The *ʿayin* was small and high, an archaic feature, but the right stroke broke through deeply below the junction with the left. See figure 3.

9. See F. M. Cross, "The Oldest Manuscripts from Qumrân," *JBL* 74 (1955): 158, and *Discoveries in the Wâdī ed-Dâliyeh,* ed. Paul W. Lapp and Nancy L. Lapp, *AASOR* 41 (Cambridge: ASOR, 1974), 26–27.

the imaginative range more freely? Are we not to expect the breaking in of the *sui generis,* the radically new, in poetry, in religious ideas, in philosophical speculation? I do not think so. I believe it is as illegitimate methodologically to resort to the category of the *sui generis* in explaining historical sequences as it is contrary to scientific method to resort to the category of miracles in explaining natural occurrences.

Two examples may be briefly mentioned: the sudden appearance of cosmological speculation in sixth-century Ionia, and the emergence of Israelite religion in the late second millennium B.C.E. Philosophers have often treated Ionian cosmology as if it emerged fully mature like Athena from the head of Zeus. In one of his last and most extraordinary papers, Albright deals precisely with the Oriental origins of early Greek cosmological speculation, tracing continuities and connections that prepared for its flowering.[10]

The religion of Israel has been conceived as a unique, isolated phenomenon, radically or wholly discontinuous with its environment. In extreme form these views are rooted ultimately in dogmatic systems, metaphysical or theological, and often serve an apologetic purpose. I think it is fair to say that the shrillest claims of uniqueness for Israel's religion were made precisely when the burgeoning archaeological enterprise began to produce rich new data linking Israel's religious language and concepts with those of her West Semitic past. The claim that Israelite religion "was absolutely different from anything the pagan world ever knew," to quote the late, great Yehezkel Kaufmann, is now being swept away under an avalanche of archaeological evidence.[11] But his claim should never have been made. It violates fundamental postulates of scientific historical method. The empirical historian must describe novel configurations in Israel's religion as having their origin in an orderly set of relationships which follow the usual typological sequences of historical change. This is not to denigrate the importance or majesty of Israel's religious achievement. It is rather to study it under the discipline of a particular scientific method, a historical method governed by established postulates which, if legitimate, must be applied universally to historical data.[12]

10. "Neglected Factors in the Greek Intellectual Revolution," *Proceedings of the American Philosophical Society* 116 (1972): 225–242.

11. *The Religion of Israel,* trans. M. Greenberg (Chicago: University of Chicago Press, 1960), 2.

12. Much of the first three sections of my volume *CMHE* deals with the continuities and novelties in the emergence of early Israelite religion.

III

There are a number of other principles or postulates of typological method that deserve detailed discussion but can only be touched on here.[13] The speed of change of typologically significant features is not constant. We observe that in a script of twenty-two characters each letter evolves at a different speed. Indeed, the tension between letters retaining old features and those that exhibit new features is crucial to dating. In a pottery corpus the situation is essentially the same. Thus, in a given archaeological stratum we might plot the sequences of pottery types as shown in figure 4.

Typological judgments are precise in direct ratio to the speed of change in a typological sequence. Between 200 B.C.E. and 70 C.E., the Jewish script evolved rapidly, and one can date scripts within fifty-year units—roughly the maximum *floruit* of a scribal generation.[14] There are archaizing scripts, however—Palaeo-Hebrew, Lapidary Aramaic, the medieval biblical hand—which evolve very slowly. In such cases the palaeographer may err by a century or more. I am told that certain Greek vases may be dated to decades, and, of course, older American automobiles may be dated to the year.

The emergence of new styles is often rapid. By style I mean a cluster of typological elements that have mutually influenced one another. The national Hebrew script arose abruptly in the ninth century. Earlier Israel used the Early Linear Phoenician alphabet at home in Syria-Palestine. But we observe a feature, of cursive origin, which spread through appropriate letters: a downward tick made at the end of final horizontal strokes as the scribe moved to the next letter (on the left). See figure 5.[15] This typological trait marks all subsequent Hebrew scripts—though it is always absent from the mother Phoenician script.

The Jewish script we call "Herodian" also emerged suddenly, exhibiting a peculiar style. Aramaic scripts, from which the Jewish script was derived, hung letters from a theoretical or actual ceiling line. Letters varied strikingly in length below this line. In the early Herodian period the notion of a base line appears, and letters quickly assume a uniform length, giving rise to what is traditionally called the "square character," the ancestor of the modern Hebrew bookhand.

13. Detailed discussion of problems of method in palaeography may be found embedded in my long study, "Development of the Jewish Scripts," in *BANE,* 133–203.

14. In fact, skilled scribes, like skilled artists, developed new styles or elements of style during the course of their professional careers.

15. The letters are taken from the Gezer Calendar (line 1), tenth century B.C.E., and the Samaria Ostraca (line 2), eighth century B.C.E.

FIGURE 4

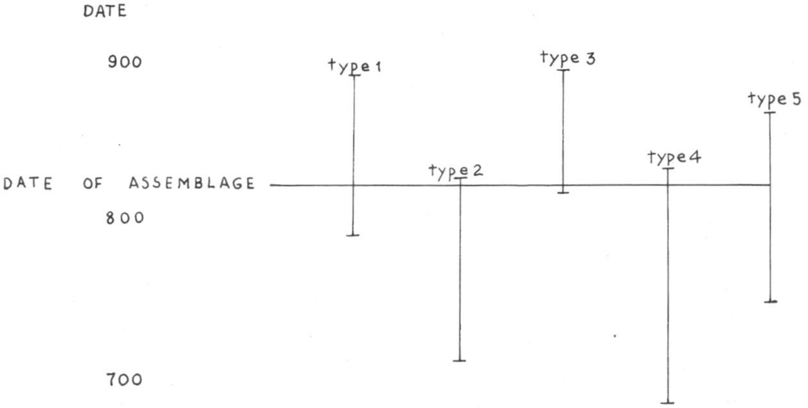

Dating an Assemblage of Artifacts (including Alphabets and Pots) by Typology

This tendency of new styles to appear suddenly does not alter what we have said earlier concerning continuity in type series. One finds analogies in revolutionary changes in political systems or even in shifts of scientific theory in the natural sciences.[16] The new style is "prepared for"; its elements can be perceived as latent in the late stages of the older, more slowly changing sequence. But the new style, like revolutionary upheavals, may evolve with extraordinary rapidity, at such speed indeed that, if our data are sparse or incomplete, the new style may appear to be an overnight introduction.

Let me turn finally to two paired postulates of typological method. The past development of artifacts—pots and alphabets—their sequence of changes, if sufficiently documented, can be understood or explained. On the contrary, the future sequence of typological developments—its speed, direction, and character—cannot be predicted. Let us look at each. The relationship between items in a typological series can be understood and explained. Given a sufficient number of individual elements in a series, we perceive the reasons for continuity and change. Evanescent or idiosyncratic features drop away. The effective innovations become transparent in context. We recognize changes arising from the altering of writing material or pen, changes adapting form to new material or modes of manufacture. We understand a simplification that

16. See, for example, the study of Kuhn (above, n. 6); and in the field of biological evolution, N. Eldredge and S. J. Gould, "Punctuated Equilibria: An Alternate to Phyletic Gradualism," in *Models in Palaeobiology,* ed. T. J. M. Schopf (San Francisco: Freeman, Cooper, 1972), 82–115.

FIGURE 5

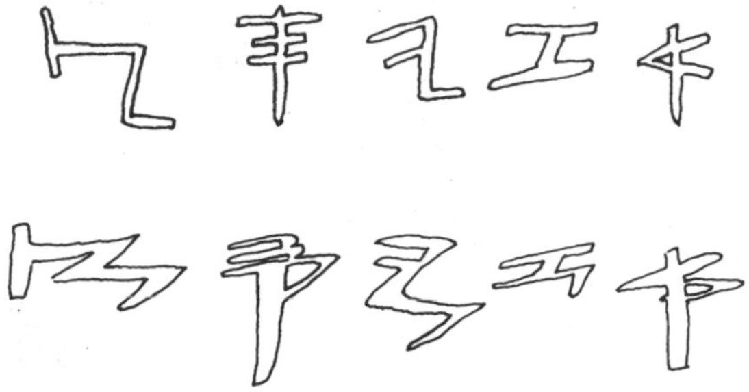

Emergence of a Cluster of Typological Features Characteristic of the Old Hebrew Hand ca. 800 B.C.E.

improves function, or an aesthetic impulse uniting form and function. We also perceive the occasion or reason for unconscious change, cursive simplification owing to speed of hand, or ornamentation owing to shading from pressure on a reed pen. In some cases a gap in a sequence can be bridged or predicted.

An example is the letter *he* in Old Canaanite. In figure 6, the first line of signs gives the typological development of the letter *he* between 1500 B.C.E. and 800 B.C.E. The bracketed form was predicted in 1954 by the writer for the thirteenth-century *he,* not then extant. In 1977 an inscription from ʿIzbet Ṣarṭah was published dating from ca. 1200 B.C.E. It exhibited the form of *he* drawn in line two of the figure, a form not distant from that predicted for the thirteenth century.[17]

There is a close analogy in historical narrative. An isolated event has no meaning. Placed in a historical narrative, an event, one in a series of events, gains meaning. Its antecedents and its impact on subsequent events provide means for understanding the event and its significance. On the other hand, we cannot predict or extrapolate the line along which a typological series will develop. We can predict change. We can affirm that typological lines of development are irreversible. There is no true repetition. The phenomenon of archaism always includes novel as well as traditional elements. But the direction of change, the speed of change, and the shape of the new emergent type cannot be predicted or plotted in mathematical or even probabilistic terms.

Students of palaeography who are experts in a single period of palaeographic development of a given script cannot date scripts accurately at either end of the range of their competence. Unless the earlier series or

17. See Cross, "Newly-Found Inscriptions in Old Canaanite and Early Phoenician Scripts," 10 and references.

FIGURE 6

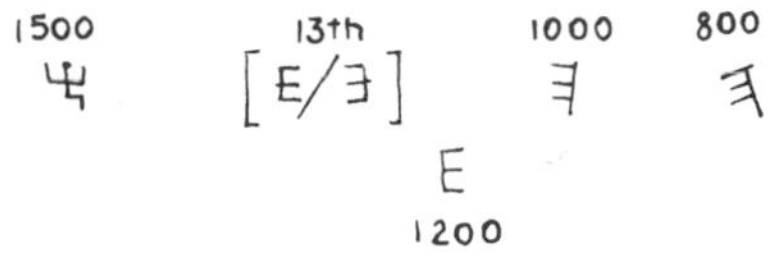

Reconstruction of the Typological Sequence of the Letter *He* from ca. 1500–800 B.C.E.

the later series is known, the palaeographer is helpless to distinguish between the idiosyncratic or transient and those features which are typologically significant: those of earlier scripts that affect the direction of typological change, those innovations that survive and determine the direction of development in the later series.

I believe that this postulate of the typological sciences is not without significance for the philosophy of historical method. Indeed, can the historian *qua* historian deal with the meaning of the present until future events place present events in context? Can the historian within the confines of historical method predict the future? The experience and presuppositions of the typologist suggest not. To be sure, historians and social scientists generally are ever tempted to seek regularities in their data which may be construed as general laws, and hence capable of use in historical prediction. I find myself skeptical of most macro-historical laws on both empirical grounds and out of habits developed in pursuing the typological sciences under the discipline of their methodology.[18] I suspect that such schemes or laws, which provide a basis for the prediction of the future or detect the rhythm of a world-historical logic, are grounded in substantive philosophies of history: Idealist, Marxist, Christian, etc. In their own universe of discourse, within the framework of their own methods and postulates, they are no doubt legitimate humanistic enterprises. At the same time the typologist—and I should say the historian—engaged in typological or historical discourse and analysis must eschew prediction and reject schemes which posit inevitable future development. Sound method requires it.

18. Some will recognize that here I find myself at odds with my teacher W. F. Albright, who would not have accepted our postulate of unpredictability. G. E. Mendenhall's *The Tenth Generation: Origins of the Biblical Tradition* (Baltimore: Johns Hopkins University Press, 1973) in some ways stands closer to Albright in applying fixed, predictable schemata to the evolution of Israelite religion.

Index of Biblical Citations

Index of Technical Terms

Index of Authors

General Index

Aaron, 45, 59, 60, 61, 70
Aaronid priesthood, 59, 60, 70, 187; Aaronid polemic, 63; at Bethel, 60
Abiathar (of the priests of Shiloh), 92
Abishag, 93, 94
Abraham (Abram), 15, 27, 41, 48; Abraham-David typology, 40, 41; Abraham-Moses typology, 40; covenant with, 40
Acrostic sequence (*pe* precedes *ʿayin*), 120, 121
Adê documents, 10, 18n
Adonijah, 92n, 93, 94
Ahab, 17
Ahijah, 187
ʾAḥzay the governor, 181, 188
ʿAkor (Achor), valley of, 55n, 68
Alalu, 76
Alexander III (the Great), 153, 172, 193–194, 197–198; conquest of, 165, 192
Alexandria, 213; Jewish community of, 212n
Alphabet(s), 233; culture and, 237; Old Canaanite, 237; typological development and, 238
ʿAmmînadab of Ammon, 157, 193
Ammon(ites), 49, 54, 69, 182, 182n, 189, 191, 193
Amorite(s), 191; kinship names of, 6
Amphictyony, 47, 49n
Amūn, 77
ʿAnani, the Davidid, 161–162, 165
Anaximander, 81, 81n
Anaximenes, 81
Andromachus, prefect of Syria, 197
Animal names for military officers, 119
Antiochus III, 198
Anu, 75, 76
ʿApiru (ʻclientʼ), 69, 69n
Apocalyptic, Jewish, 197
Apsu, 74, 77, 78
Aquila, 209, 217
Arabia, 64n, 189
Arabians, 188, 190
ʿArâq el ʾEmîr, temple of, 199
Ark of the Covenant, 45, 46, 47, 49, 85, 90–92; at Shiloh, 92
Arnon, 54, 56n, 65
Artaxerxes I, 157, 164, 171, 183, 189n
Artaxerxes III (Ochus), 153, 192, 194–195
Ashdod(ites), 182, 188–191
Asher, 187
Asherah, 128n
ʾAšîmaʾ, god of Taymāʾ, 175n
ʿAštar-Chemosh, 57
Assurbanipal, 175, 177
Astarte (Aštart), 76, 82
ʿAθtar, 49
ʾAyyam el-ʿarab, 32

Babylon, 23, 79; importees from, 175, 191
Bagoas, 153, 153n, 192
Balaam, 61
Baʿl (Baʿl-Haddu), 22, 76, 77n, 86, 91, 101; battles with Sea and Death, 80, 90, 127–128, 128n
Baʿl Ḫamōn (epithet of ʾEl), 88
Baʿl-peʿor, 56–59, 61
Bar Kokeba (Koseba), revolt of, 213
Baruch (Bārûk/Berekyāhû), 157n; book of, 222
Bathsheba, 93, 94
Beersheba, 37n, 47
Benaiah, 92n
Ben Sira, 221, 225
Bethel, 37n, 44, 45, 47, 60; destruction of sanctuary of, 177
Beth Ḥoron, 189

LIBRARY OF CONGRESS CATALOGING-IN-PUBLICATION DATA

Cross, Frank Moore.
From epic to canon : history and literature in ancient Israel / Frank Moore Cross.
p. cm.
Includes bibliographical references and indexes.
ISBN 0-8018-5982-4 (alk. paper)
1. Bible. O.T.—Criticism, interpretation, etc. 2. Judaism—History—To 70 A.D.
I. Title.
BS1171.2.C77 1998
221.6—dc21 98-7322
CIP